FUNCTIONS OF DRESS
Tool of Culture and the Individual

PENNY STORM

Florida International University

Prentice-Hall, Inc., Englewood Cliffs, New Jersey 07632

Library of Congress Cataloging-in-Publication Data

Storm, Penny. (date)
  Functions of dress.

  Includes bibliographies and index.
  1. Costume. 2. Clothing and dress. I. Title.
GT511.S86 1987   391   86-3191
ISBN   0-13-331943-1

Editorial/production supervision and
   interior design: **Marjorie Borden**
Cover design: **Diane Saxe**
Manufacturing buyer: **Harry P. Baisley**
Page layout: **Peggy Finnerty**

© 1987 by Prentice-Hall
A Division of Simon & Schuster, Inc.
Englewood Cliffs, New Jersey 07632

Printed in the United States of America

10   9   8   7   6   5   4   3   2   1

ISBN 0-13-331943-1   01

Prentice-Hall International (UK) Limited, *London*
Prentice-Hall of Australia Pty. Limited, *Sydney*
Prentice-Hall Canada Inc., *Toronto*
Prentice-Hall Hispanoamericana, S.A., *Mexico*
Prentice-Hall of India Private Limited, *New Delhi*
Prentice-Hall of Japan, Inc., *Tokyo*
Prentice-Hall of Southeast Asia Pte. Ltd., *Singapore*
Editora Prentice-Hall do Brasil, Ltda., *Rio de Janeiro*
Whitehall Books Limited, *Wellington, New Zealand*

In memory of my parents

Contents

chapter 3   Modesty   *83*

PART II COMMUNICATIVE FUNCTIONS OF DRESS

chapter 4   Communication   *102*

chapter 5   Roles   *123*

chapter 6   Status   *145*

Preface

Dress is unique to humans. However, it is not merely a personal idiosyncrasy. It is a social as well as a personal behavior, and therefore reflects the society and culture in which it has evolved and is used.

Dress is any body covering, attachment, or treatment;[1] it is essentially our appearance. It is found in or is common to every culture and therefore is a *cultural universal.* Murdock listed 73 cultural universals, including: family unit, language, cooperative labor, age status differences, supernatural beliefs and rituals, tool making, housing, law, funeral rites, and dress.[2]

Why should dress be a cultural universal? It is one of the most powerful mediums of expression ever devised by humans. It serves as a frontier to the human body and as a determinant of the individual's inner consciousness. It is also one of the primary links among people. Our dress affects not only us, the wearers, but also our audience, the observers. It sends messages to every other sighted human being with whom we come into contact. Those messages cause others to form an idea about us and to hold certain expectations that can influence the course of our relationship with them. In this regard dress is as powerful as verbal language.

---

[1]In this text, we shall use the words *clothing, attire, garb,* and *apparel* as synonyms for *dress.*
[2]Murdock, G. P., The Common Denominator of Cultures. In *The Science of Man in the World Crisis* (R. Linton, ed.). (New York: Columbia University Press, 1945), p. 124.

Dress provides a great deal of information about the culture in which it has evolved. It has an interdependent relationship with social institutions like religious, stratifying, political, and economic structures. It is a factor in the organization of a society, in its roles and their status. A society's organization determines what social institutions it will have and how those institutions will be used; thus dress can change and be changed by society. Dress is a powerful social force, especially in unstable societies where the existing order is frequently challenged. In such societies, dress provides an instantaneous and universal means of recognition of those in power, those in rebellion against that power, and those who have no interest in the conflict.

All dress is functional with one or many purposes. This text is organized into four parts based on the functions of dress. In the first, we shall examine three intrinsic functions of dress: 1) adornment, 2) utility, convenience, and protection, and 3) modesty. The second section will look at the communicative function of dress, including its use as an indicator of social roles and status. In the third part, we shall focus on the sociological function of dress by examining the relationship between dress and four major social institutions: social class, economic system, government, and religion. Lastly, we shall investigate the psychological functions of dress, including an exploration of chosen theories of individual development and of group functioning, and attempt to relate them to the uses of dress. We shall also examine the relationship of clothing to behavior. Finally, these concepts are applied to two major issues: 1) values, and 2) integration vs. differentiation.

Before beginning our exploration of this fascinating subject, I wish to offer this codicil: although the data are often presented as truths, they are in fact merely the most currently accurate or best supported generalizations. These generalizations are not totally appropriate to all eras, all cultures, all individuals. Their value is not as absolutes, but as important tools to help us organize and illuminate our understandings of humans, culture, and dress. Thus, let us enter the world of dress with respect for its power; humility at our inability to completely fathom it; and excitement in our effort to increase our understanding of it, ourselves, and our universe.

Acknowledgments

Many people have contributed to this text. Especially important to me have been the authors of the many books and journals—cited or not—who were my primary and constant source of information and stimulation.

My special thanks to:

Addie, a super proofreader.

My professional colleagues, especially Betty and Bob, who read parts of the manuscript and provided me with their insightful reviews, and Trudy, who has given so many inspirational thoughts.

My friends, especially Patty, who diligently and quickly read the text to see if it communicated well enough.

My students (especially those who argued and discussed the points), for letting me try out the ideas and the words.

Dee Dee, whose encouragement and presence has meant so much in so many special ways.

My sister, Mary, who read the manuscript, checked boring details like commas, and typed, typed, typed.

Most of all, I thank my husband, Allan Briggs Pell, who gave me time, encouragement, support, and lots of love and laughter through the six years of my "distraction."

1

Adornment

Of the major theories of the first function of dress, adornment is the most widely accepted today since it is commonly assumed that humans first donned dress to enhance their appearance. Adornment is a universal function of, and motive for, dress, and most modern dress is worn, at least in part, for adornment. Thus, in the United States alone, $27 billion was spent in 1983 on beauty products and services; food has been the only product to sell more units per year than beauty (McLaughen 1983).

But adornment is not just a modern motive. Neanderthal man appears to have used dress for this purpose, and most primitive cultures continue to do so. In fact, it has even been suggested that the simpler a culture is, "the greater its love of adornment" (Webb 1912, p. 7). However, much ornamental dress is multipurpose, and adornment may be its least important function and perhaps not even its original purpose. Amulets, for example, are protective as well as decorative. Protection, however, was their original motive and is still the more important function. There is even dress that was first worn to frighten other people but eventually became ornamental after it had become the norm. Because of the power of habit, that which we become accustomed to and perceive as good we will ultimately perceive as attractive.

Any behavior that makes an individual feel more positive about himself or herself and/or more secure in his or her society will present an inherent motive for being repeated. Thus, an article of dress worn for some purpose other than adornment may continue to be worn, and it will be worn at least partially for adornment if the wearer is openly complimented on it. If, on the other hand, others communicate a negative reaction to the dress, the wearer is unlikely to continue wearing it. Adornment or beauty, therefore, is a social concept. For example, the Mount Hageners are one of the most ornamented peoples in the world. They adorn themselves to enhance their sexual attractiveness, indicate their social competence, and/or denote their role in the particular event for which they have dressed. However, the social nature of their ornaments is reflected in their belief that "it is not worthwhile decorating too well for an event that occurs at night, when people cannot see properly" (Strathern and Strathern 1971, p. 40).

Obviously, self-display depends on being seen by others. It is also a narcissistic behavior, most evident in egocentric individuals such as children and adolescents and, perhaps, primitive people. Self-display is uncommon when the individual has an inferior social position. However, research has found that it is a strong motive for a woman to purchase a specific dress. Garments are purchased that cover up the woman's physical defects and bring out her best qualities (Barr 1934). This does not appear to be just a modern phenomenon. There is much historical evidence of the use of clothing to camouflage a perceived deficit. For example, Queen Elizabeth I wore neck ruffs to hide her thin neck, and her mother, Anne Boleyn, wore long sleeves to hide her sixth finger. Short men sometimes wear shoes with lifts to hide their shortness.

There are two types of ornamental dress—corporal adornments that alter the body itself and external adornments that are put on or hung from the body. The latter is a temporary ornament, which can be put on or taken off at will. The former is permanent and thus involves an element of commitment. In our fast-moving, ever-changing modern society, temporary adornment is the more common, although a few corporal adornments such as pierced ears, tattoos, and cosmetic surgery are still used. But since the nature of fashion is change, permanent adornments are generally unfashionable.

In this chapter we shall examine both types of adornment as well as hair dressing, which combines elements of each. We shall analyze the relationship between natural resources, climate, and adornment. The purpose of adornment will also be explored. Since adornments are worn because they meet psychological or sociological needs that have been "shaped and directed by a long series of culturally established associations and interests," it is vital for understanding an adornment's use(s) that we understand "what these associations are and, to a lesser degree, why they [the culture] have become attached to it" (Linton 1964, pp. 301–302). Thus, we must understand a culture in order to truly comprehend its use(s) of dress. Unfortunately, such understanding is too complex for us to pursue here. The assumption of this chapter is that adornment is usually a positive behavior that is highly social in nature. What is beautiful is determined by the culture in question. Therefore, adornments are described without pejorative labels or descriptions. We will not examine mutila-

Figure 1.1 The dress of this couple from Oceania reflects the principle that men are more amply dressed in cultures where the primary motive for dress is adornment. Yet precisely what each item is used for is impossible to know without a thorough understanding of the Oceanic culture. (Library of Congress)

tions. The negative association of this term makes it inaccurate; piercing the septum, for example, is no more self-mutilating in New Guinea than ear piercing is in the United States. Both are positive behaviors—efforts to belong to or conform with the cultural ideal.

All of the body parts have been decorated by some people at some time, most frequently the hands, feet, mouth, ears, and head hair. The body's natural form has not limited the method or placement of adornments. In fact, the body has often been altered to fit a cultural or individual ideal or concept. Such distortions tend to become less common as a society advances.

NATURAL RESOURCES AND CLIMATE

There have been as many materials used in adornment as have been available. Every kind of metal, leather, bone, tooth, tusk, horn, shell, seed, feather, and vegetation has had at least a trial run as an article of adornment. Most manufactured materials, from plastics to glass, have been used as well. Even manmade articles that would not normally be associated with dress, such as beer cans, jelly jars, fish lures, brass keyhole plates, and automobile light rims, have been worn to adorn, even when they have been inconvenient or painful to wear. Resource use has primarily reflected resource availability. Eskimos, for

Figure 1.2 The wig worn by this Komblo tribesman uses bamboo and vine for a framework, bark cloth as a frame cover, adhesive burrs to hold human hair trim, golden tree-gum and ocher for color, yellow fibers for a braided border, and green scarab beetles for a border. His outfit also uses shells and feathers from at least 5 kinds of birds. (Courtesy of Malcolm Kirk)

example, had an abundance of sea animals and some mammal species, but birds and vegetation were limited in their availability. Thus, they relied on bones, teeth, tusks, skins, and other body parts of mammals and fish for clothing materials. The Cherokee Indians, on the other hand, used more vegetation and bird materials, since they were abundant. Their dress utilized bark, shells, feathers, porcupine quills, seeds and nuts, and deerskin and other pelts. But adornment has also reflected climatic needs. In the case of the Eskimos, the climate necessitated waterproof clothing, so they could not embroider or use any other adornment that required puncturing the hide. However, for the Cherokees, waterproof clothing was not a necessity, and they embroidered their deerskins with porcupine quills and, later, trade beads. Thus, the differences between the clothing of the Cherokee and of the Eskimo reflect differences both in resource availability and climate.

People have been quite ingenious in utilizing their resources. For example, the Zulu man's head ring was made from a cocoon by a special craftsman. After extracting the larva, he would chew the cocoon to make an elastic latex, which was crushed to an even texture and melted by boiling. Then the doughlike material was kneaded and elongated into a long, fat snake shape. While it was still warm and pliable, the craftsman would wind it around the outer and upper sides of an oval framework, which consisted "of a 'rope', half an inch thick, made of palm-fibres, [that] had been . . . placed in position on the client's head, and been firmly sewn to the underlying hair with tendon or string." As it cooled, the material hardened into a stiff black latex. When it was firmly attached, it

> was rubbed with grease, and polished with a small pebble or with the stone-like root of the *isiDwa* gladiolus, till it attained the gloss and appearance of polished jet. Inside the oval framework and around it outside, the hair was shaven away, so that the ring sat cleanly and alone upon the head. As the hair to which it was attached, grew longer, the ring rose higher, and sometimes reached a height above the skull of four or five inches. . . . (Bryant 1970, pp. 141–43)

Such utilization of resources is really no more inventive than the process of creating fabric from cotton, wool, or silk.

The kinds of resources available continue to influence dress. For example, the cotton cloth of India, Mexico, and Egypt is best suited to a draped garment, such as the sari and toga. This type of garment, usually one piece, is draped over the body and gets its form from the pull of gravity on the fabric. Developed in southern latitudes where dress was needed not for warmth but to promote evaporation and water absorption, this form of dress is also known as southern or gravitational. The flax of Eastern Europe suits a more flared or tailored style. Tailored dress began in northern latitudes, where dress needed to fit the body more closely, to provide greater warmth. Tailored dress is usually sewn from cut material and uses curvilinear pieces to get a better fit and flatter seams. It is also known as northern or anatomical dress. The United States, with its great variety of fiber resources, could be expected to have more diversified styles and use a combination of tailored and draped techniques. These expectations are accurate when one controls for the importation of clothing and clothing resources.

Figure 1.3 Zulu male with head-ring. (Library of Congress)

PURPOSE

Why should we be interested in dressing to enhance our appearance? The most likely reason is a combination of two factors: by making ourselves more socially attractive to others we will (1) be more acceptable to them and (2) increase our self-confidence. Laver's (1957) hypothesis that "women's clothes are functional in that their purpose is to attract men. They are certainly functional in no other sense" (p. 22) seems an oversimplified and superficial view. Dress is fundamentally a social behavior, and he failed to recognize the social situation in which it occurs. Wax (1957) suggested that the modern American woman "grooms (dresses) herself to appear as a desirable object, not necessarily as an attainable one. . . . she is preparing to play the part of the *beauty*, not the part of the erotically passionate woman" (p. 407). She is, therefore, dressing for a social rather than a sexual purpose. However, Wax limits the social nature of female dress to the sexual role. A prostitute's dress may be most in accord with Laver's theory, but Wax has incorporated the dress of a single woman who is on the prowl for a man. Obviously, most women do not fit into either of these categories. That young adults tend to spend more on clothing than any other age group has been cited as support for both Wax's and Laver's hypotheses. However, young adults are expanding their social roles in a variety of areas and altering their social status as well as seeking mates. They are also still involved with experimentation in their self-image and their dress. All of these factors contribute to their high clothing expenditures, and their attempt to be fashionable is motivated more by self-image needs and the need to belong than by the desire to get a mate.

When Gill (1931) asked whether women had begun to expose their legs because they so outnumbered men that they needed a mating advantage or because contraception was enabling them to be less afraid of sex or because they were sexually indifferent (p. 12), he was overreacting to the fashion change of the 1920s. The flapper with bad legs still showed her knees. However, this exposure did not guarantee that she was sexually active any more than it indicated sexual indifference. What it did guarantee was her level of social awareness. She was knowledgeable enough about the current fashion to want to fit in even though the style was not the most flattering to her. It was better looking than a more flattering style might have been because it did fit in; it was her badge of belonging to her society and her era. Of course, some fashions can camouflage a physical deficit and could therefore be considered sexual attractants. However, what of the woman who has attracted a mate because of her large, but padded, bust? What happens to her, to him, and to their relationship after he removes the padding and suddenly finds a flat chest? If he was attracted to her bust size, the relationship will be over. However, if their involvement is not so superficially based on appearance, it will continue even though he may have a pang of disappointment when he finds out about the padding. He may even offer a prayer of thanks because it sparked the initial attraction.

We want to look into the mirror and see someone who is attractive according to our cultural ideal; someone who will be considered, therefore, attractive to all the members of our culture. We don't want to be left on the sidelines or outside looking in. We want to be considered as an integral member of the social group.

We adorn ourselves in ways meant to enhance our appearance. This does not mean we accentuate our assets and deemphasize our liabilities since assets and liabilities are relevant to the aesthetic ideal of our culture. It means rather that we dress so as to more closely approximate the cultural ideal. We thus meet four important psychological needs: (1) we enhance our sense of self-esteem, (2) we increase our sense of belonging to the group, (3) we become more confident, and (4) we improve our self-concept. Our adornments can be categorized into two types, corporal and external.

CORPORAL ADORNMENT

Corporal adornment is the decorating of the physical body itself. Such an adornment is a permanent alteration as opposed to a temporary decoration since it actually changes the body's surface or shape. It is most common in those tropical societies where more of the body surface is exposed. Societies with a rigid and stable social organization also favor corporal adornments as their group belongings tend to be more permanent and the adornments

> are badges that can never be taken off, and that set their owners apart from all other groups until the day they die. Frequently the application of the decoration is performed at a special ceremony, a tribal initiation, with the initiate suffering great pain in the process. This pain is an important part of the bonding—a physical horror that binds him even tighter to those who share it with him. Acquiring the status of belonging to the group is made such an ordeal, so difficult to endure, that forever afterwards it will be felt as something vitally important in his life. The very intensity of the experience helps to widen the gulf between him and those who have not shared it. (Morris 1977, p. 222)

Most corporal adornments involve an element, often the major element, of some other motivating factor, such as the indication of social status or group membership. Thus, even though these adornments are thought to enhance the individual's appearance, their designation of one's social and psychological identification is usually more important.

All corporal adornments can be categorized into several types according to the procedure used and/or the body part(s) involved. Each category has been used, at various levels of frequency, throughout the world and the ages. However, no nomadic or hunting peoples have used a form that impaired their use of their bodies. Only more "advanced" societies have been able to afford adornments that cause physical dysfunction.

Cicatrisation

Cicatrisation, or scarification, is the embellishment of the human body with scars. It is particularly prevalent among dark-skinned peoples on whom tattooing is not easily visible. It is not common among cultures with a strong Judeo-Christian background since Mosaic law prohibited such cutting of one's flesh. Thus most modern Western cultures have had little exposure to the practice, which they find unaesthetic or even noxious. We have even considered such "self-mutilation" symptomatic of some kinds of psychopathology. However, in cultures where it is the custom, it is appropriate, even psychologically healthful, behavior. It is also beautiful. Early explorers to Africa wrote of the women with skins like "flowered damask," "Flowers on Silk"; or "a fine black, flowered Sattin, which has a pretty Look" (Sieber 1972).

Scarification is a fairly safe procedure with risk of infection or disease the only health danger inherent in the process. The scars are made by cutting the skin with a sharp object such as a shell, stone, or piece of glass; by branding the skin with a hot object such as a stick; or by puncturing the skin with a sharp object such as a thorn or wood splinter. Each of these variations creates a unique type of scar; some scars will be flat, others depressed, and others pimplelike elevations. A caustic substance, which may be a mixture from a variety of sources—sand, animal fat, bird's down, ash, cow dung—is usually rubbed into

Figure 1.4 Oceania woman with body scarification. (National Anthropological Archives, Smithsonian Institution)

the wound to retard the healing process and thus enhance the formation of scars. The length of time for healing varies with the kind of scar(s) being made. The entire process is often quite painful. Cutting the front of the body, especially from the breasts to the genitals, is much more painful than cutting the back (Junod 1966). In spite of this, the back is less frequently used, perhaps because the individual would be unable to appreciate any design on his or her back. While children are sometimes forced to submit to scarification, most older individuals will willingly, and often stoically, submit when the results have sufficient promise—for instance, to give high status or make one sexually desirable.

The pattern of scars is usually predetermined when they have a specific purpose or provide particular information. For example, among the Nubas of Sudan three rows of about fifteen to twenty "pimples" made on the left side of the upper back are believed to be a kind of love charm. In these cases cicatrisation is a language, with each scar's shape, placement, technology, and ritual combining to form symbols not limited to the sensual or aesthetic. However, not all scars are so purposeful; some appear merely to reflect the individual's personal taste. In some cultures both types appear to be used. In any case, cultures that practice scarification generally view the scars as beautiful.

However, many scars have a purpose beyond mere adornment. For example, scarring has been done to cure or prevent diseases. A unique modern medical application of scars was practiced by a doctor in Afghanistan. Finding it difficult to persuade the people to have a smallpox vaccination, he began to scratch "the person's name in Arabic script on the arm . . . applying the vaccine directly on the marks. After taking effect the scar is left in the shape of the patient's name." Soon such vaccinations were in great demand (Field 1958, p. 85). A few peoples have attempted to scar themselves in order to appear grotesque and frightening to their enemies. In parts of Africa the natives trace cicatrisation to "the days of the Arab slavers, when beautiful girls" scarred themselves in order to be less desirable to the slavers (Tyrrell 1968, p. 148). Others have used the process as a means of strengthening their devotion to some belief or cause. Some, such as the Pondo, have used scarification as a way to placate their ancestors by fulfilling an old custom (ibid.). Obviously, they recognize the power of habit.

Just as ranchers scar their cattle with a brand to mark the animals as their property, slaves and serfs have been marked with a brand of their owners. Scars have been used to indicate an individual's social identity; both his status within a group and his group belongings have been shown in this way. Many African tribal marks are scars. The Bornouese, for example, make twenty linear scars on each side of the face extending "from the corners of the mouth towards the angles of the lower jaw and cheekbone. They also have one cut in the centre of the forehead, six on each arm, six on each leg, four on each breast, and nine on each side, just above the hips" (Avebury 1972, p. 47). These marks are even subject to styles of fashion. Around 1916 a Tiv boy tried to make his facial scars with a flattened iron nail, producing a flat scar that soon became the rage among the young Tivs, although their elders found this flatness unnatural (Vlahos 1979). Fashion changes have also reflected cross-cultural contact rather than technological changes. Since scars did serve as a tribal mark, the governments of some African countries have discouraged continuation of the practice because it promotes tribal rather than national loyalty.

The only modern Western example of scarification to show group membership comes from Germany in the 1930s. Some of the German students belonged to dueling fraternities. They would pour wine into their dueling wounds in order to heighten the scarring, which indicated their virility and fortitude. This was an attempt to create "battle wounds" and thus gain the status attributed in a militaristic society to those who have successfully engaged in battle. In the same way, primitive people have often attempted to deepen scarring that came from battle wounds, and one's "battle scars" are deserving of respect and even honor. Scars on the back traditionally have been considered dishonorable since they suggest that the individual was injured while retreating (Flugel 1930). Marital and age status have both been indicated by scars. Initiation rites of passage at puberty have often involved scarification as have other ritualistic rites, such as mourning, in which scars are generally self-inflicted. Nuba girls, for example, "begin a series of body scarifications at the age of nine or ten" (Faris 1972, p. 32) when their breasts begin to enlarge. The second set is made after the onset of the girl's first menstrual period. The final set is made after her first child is weaned. This set covers her entire back and the backs of her neck, arms, and thighs.

Cicatrisation may have begun when a particular scar was given some magical or religious significance that the individual tried to extend or that other individuals attempted to duplicate. It may have been the serendipitous result of rituals involving bleeding. However, it is unlikely that it was first done in an effort to beautify the body. Adornment would have become a motivation only after a people were so accustomed to the scars that they viewed those without them as different and, therefore, less good and less attractive.

Tattooing

Tattooing is the making of an indelible mark with dye on the skin surface or just under it. It may have begun for the same reasons that scarification did, although it is less likely that tattooing resulted from rituals involving bleeding since tattooists have generally attempted to minimize any associated bleeding. It has a wide geographic distribution but, like cicatrisation, is especially prevalent in warm climates where less clothing is worn. It has been practiced since at least as early as the second millennium B.C. (Field 1958, p. 4) in both primitive and advanced societies. It is a universal adornment, probably tried by all peoples at some time in their dress history. However, tattooing is less common in cultures with strong Judeo-Christian or Moslem traditions as it was prohibited by Mosaic law, in the Koran, and in the eighth century by the emperor Constantine. The disapproval of the three largest monotheistic religions in the world has decreased the incidence and acceptability of tattooing in the modern Western

Figure 1.5 Mbaya woman with facial tattoos. (National Anthropological Archives, Smithsonian Institution)

and Middle Eastern worlds. However, tattooing is one of the most acceptable forms of corporal adornment to the modern Western sensibility.

Polhemus (1975) suggested that in modern Western society, tattoos are

> aggressively conservative, and *un*fashionable, for typically they are the bodily expression of small social enclaves which are being swallowed up in the overall wave of social change and in what seems to be a general trend towards social impermanence. (p. 32)

There is evidence that supports this hypothesis. Cuban tuffs, for example, frequently have tattoos on the inside of their lip or between their thumb and forefinger. Purportedly, these were made while the men were in prison. There has been some speculation within the law-enforcement community that these tattoos indicate the kind(s) of crime(s) in which the individual has been involved. However, while this may be true for some, it is more likely that most tattoos were either efforts to gain status, part of Santeria ritual, or the more typical love affirmations which were just symbols of belonging. In the late nineteenth century, Italian and French criminals frequently had boastful, antisocial tattoos of a similar nature. They wanted to scare others and to express their own lack of fear of death. In this sense their tattoos were protectively both *Reizschmuck* and *Schreckschmuck*. (See pp. 74–75 for an explanation of these terms.)

Only about 10 percent of the population of the United States are tattooed. Most of these are men, and most of them were tattooed during a period of emotional crisis when they were teenagers or young adults. Tattoos have been associated with sailors, merchant or navy; truckers; and to a lesser extent, the army and marines. Belonging, conformity, or fitting in have been the primary motives for most modern Western tattoos. While tattooing is a social act for subgroups such as the Hell's Angels, it is "antisocial with reference to the larger social group" (Polhemus 1975, p. 32). Military men have frequently used tattoos for status, an association inconsistent with nonmilitary attitudes. Thus, they sometimes regret their tattoos after they have left the military.

Tattooing may have a risk of infection, although this risk has been largely undocumented. It is possible that an unsterilized needle could transmit diseases such as syphilis, viral hepatitis, or yellow fever (Renbourn 1972). An adverse reaction to the dyes introduced is another health danger inherent in the process, with swelling and fever as common side effects. (Field 1958)

Most tattoos today use a standard technique, but there have been four basic methods under which all the techniques can be classified: burning, sewing, cutting, or pricking either followed by rubbing in a dye or done with an instrument dipped in a dye (Scutt and Gotch 1974). In burning, either the pigment was put on the skin with an extremely hot instrument, or the design was burned into the skin and dyes then rubbed into the wound. Soot or charcoal could be introduced on a thread sewn with a needle through the skin. This technique was employed only by Eskimos in Greenland and by certain northern North American Indians. Pricking or cutting the skin before rubbing in the dye, a more common method, could be done freehand or over a previously drawn design. The Mohave Indians used this method in tattooing the chins of their young adults. A sliver of stone (later a steel needle) was pricked over the charcoal-drawn design until bleeding resulted. Ground mesquite or willow charcoal was then rubbed into the wounds. The painful process took several hours to complete and several days of quiet healing during which time fresh charcoal applications were rubbed in after frequent bathings (Taylor and Wallace 1947). As early as the mideighteenth century some American Indians used a group of sharp objects, such as thorns, in a clump attached to a flat piece of wood or tied together with their points close together and of equal length. This method allowed a series of multiple pricks. When a knife is used to cut the designs, linear designs with a slight curvature can be produced. Modern tattooing with an electric needle is a refinement of the method of inserting the dye with a sharp-pointed instrument and is less painful than the other methods.

Tattoos may be either representational or nonrepresentational. In some cultures the designs are limited to one or a few parts of the body, while in others they may cover the entire skin surface. In certain instances this appears to be related to the kinds of other body coverings worn. For example, in Siberia, where a man's body is completely "under wraps," tattoos are made just on the wrist, which is the body part most frequently, though fleetingly, exposed. The body parts adorned may also be related to gender. The Marquesans, for example, tattooed their girls around the lips, behind the ears, on the arms and hands, and from the waist down; but the boys were tattooed over their entire body, even including the eyelids and tongue (Linton 1974).

While some cultures, such as the Ainu, have tattooed their young children, most have begun the tattooing at adolescence or during young adulthood. Designs on young children who are still growing will become distorted;

Figure 1.6 Marquesan man with body tattoos. (National Anthropological Archives, Smithsonian Institution)

thus, they would have to be redone in order to appear as desired. While the Ainu willingly renew their tattoos, most peoples seem to have adopted a "once is enough" attitude. Once may also be too much since the removal of tattoos is a difficult and usually unsatisfactory procedure. Lasers have been used to remove them, but the laser method results in a scar. Dermabrasion and excision produce better results *if* the tattoo was done by a professional who did not insert the tattoo needles too far into the skin. The cost of removal is also a negative since it is generally a great deal more than the cost of the original tattoo.

In some cultures, such as Japan, tattoos are primarily ornamental. However, one might question whether the tattooed man in our circus side show and the tattooed Japanese are really so different. If we conclude that they are not, then we must attribute an additional and more important motive to the tattooed Japanese—exhibitionism. The tattooed side-show man has this motive as well as the motive for material profit. In fact, most peoples use tattoos for reasons other than, or in addition to, adornment. For example, in India tattooing is related both to religion and to magic. Thus, it is a common practice among both sexes. Whenever tattoos have been popular in Western cultures, the primary motives have been other than adornment. For instance, in the early 1930s tattoos were used for identification, and they are sometimes used to provide medical information, such as blood type. Tattoos have been used to express personal beliefs and values; loyalty to a loved one; and belonging, especially family and tribal membership. They have often been used to indicate status. For instance, prisoners have been tattooed, as was done in the early nineteenth century when Massachusetts enacted legislation to require the tattooing of all second-term convicts. Although a lower status has generally been attributed to tattoos in our society, this has not always or even usually been the case in other cultures. In primitive societies, in fact, more tattoos have usually been associated with higher status. Tattoos have been used as battle trophies, as marital marks, to avoid the evil eye, to appease the spirits of the dead, to physically shield the wearer from weapons, to cure such ailments as rheumatism and poor vision, and to preserve youth. They have been used by pilgrims as talismans to assure safe passage on their pilgrimage. Such an association with passage has frequently been extended to passages or transitions from various life stages—childhood to adulthood or life to death. However, as primitive cultures have become more exposed to Western ideas, the practice of tattooing has tended to lessen and the meanings of the tattoos have often been lost.

There has also been a common association of tattoos with sexuality or sexual attraction. In fact, Parry (1933) even hypothesized that the tattooing process itself is sexual. "There are the long, sharp needles. There is the liquid poured into the pricked skin. There are the two participants of the act, one active, the other passive. There is the curious marriage of pleasure and pain" (p. 2). Some tattoos may have had a sexual relationship, such as the Polynesian practice of tattooing women on their buttocks and/or their mons veneris. Numerous theorists have observed the involvement of tattoos with homosexuality, latent or overt. Sailors and prisoners have traditionally tattooed each other under circumstances in which heterosexual sex was unavailable for an extended period of time. Some theorists have even posited that the process of tattooing is a symbolic castration or circumcision. Scutt and Gotch (1974), for example, suggested that tattooing became a symbol of such rituals since it even caused similar, although less intense, pain.

Contortion

Contortion, or plastic body, is the alteration of the form of the body through a molding process. It may not be permanent if the molding period is too brief or occurs at a point too late in the individual's physical development. In the West plastic body has often been considered deforming. However, unlike deformation, it is not necessarily physically harmful. Still, some contortions are also deformations. For example, the wasp waist, which has been a consistent fashion theme since 1500 B.C., can cause physical dysfunction that can even result in death. Efficient function of organs in the chest and upper abdomen is reduced when the ribs are pushed into the chest cavity so that the lungs are pushed out of place and into other organs. Tight corsets have been the suspected cause of a variety of physiological ailments and problems, including reproductive and menstrual difficulties, weakened abdominal and back muscles, malformation and displacement of the liver, respiratory insufficiencies and discomforts, spinal deformities, constipation, indigestion, headaches, circulatory difficulties, apoplexy, and consumption. Nervous disorders, insomnia, apathy, and hysteria have also been reported (Davies 1982). It would be interesting to correlate the decline in the frequency of hysteria, a syndrome common among Freud's patients but rare today, with corsetry. Corsets have been worn by both sexes. In some eras corseting was so constant and extreme that the removal of the corset was actually painful. For this reason nineteenth-century women wore night stays and even continued to wear corsets during pregnancy. The modern corset was originally a laced bodice worn as an exterior garment, introduced by the Spanish in the sixteenth century. As the corset began to be worn as an undergarment, it got stiffer. However, people who were physically active—peasants, for instance—did not use such stiff corsets. Children from fine families did, though, as children were believed to be miniature adults. Because of the emphasis put on a small waist as a desirable physical feature, children were often forced to sleep in their corsets, reducing the need for, and the incidence of, rib removal as a means to achieve a tiny waist. Infants have usually but not invariably been immune from such rigorous encasement.

The corset forced the middle torso in so that the excess flesh was pushed upward to the bust or downward to the hips, both of which were exaggerated. In the early twentieth century the corset was replaced by the girdle, which did not

Figure 1.7 The importance of a small waist is evident in this 1885 photograph of a young woman whose already tiny waist was touched up so that it would seem even smaller. (Library of Congress)

Figure 1.8 *A Dainty Toilet,* ca. 1901, demonstrates one way to achieve a smaller waist. (Library of Congress)

cause a permanent alteration but was simply a temporary way to smooth out and firm up the torso, hips, and buttocks. The girdle allowed women's abdominal muscles to strengthen, and freed from the constricting corset, women had more energy and became more physically active. Ultimately, by the mid-1960s, even the girdle was being rejected as too cumbersome and inhibiting.

Breast binding to constrict or flatten the breasts was practiced in ancient Greece, medieval Europe, and the Western world in the 1920s. But when the small-breasted or flat-chested look returned to popularity in the 1970s, women rejected such binding. Instead, many of them removed their brassieres, garments that in the 1940s and 1950s had been designed to make the bust appear as large as possible. While breast binding can cause atresia of the breasts and damage to some supporting breast tissue, it is not really a health hazard.

Steatopygia, or the bustle bottom, was developed through diet and exercise by the Hottentots and other African tribes. It was not a health hazard any more than breast binding was, but the Hottentots also practiced waist binding, one of the only African peoples to do so. The women constricted their waists in order to exaggerate their hips and buttocks, and that was a secondary health hazard. Morris (1977) hypothesized that a big, round behind is an ancient "gender signal," which simply exaggerates a natural difference in the distribution of body fat between men and women. The rounded parts of the female body, primarily the breasts and buttocks, may even be "the key female Gender Signal for the human species . . . [and] the male response to this basic shape has become an inborn reaction" (p. 235).

Elongation of body parts, particularly the neck and the limbs, is another example of a common contortion. The Padaung women of Burma are the most famous practitioners of neck elongation. Their chins often rest on small pillows above their graceful and long brass-ringed necks. Starting at about five years of age a Padaung girl has a brass rod one-third of an inch wide wrapped into a ring around her neck. More rings are added to this as the girl grows until the entire set may weigh as much as eighty pounds for a woman of high status. More typically they weigh about twenty pounds and are approximately one foot high. The neck is not stretched by the rings; instead the rings push down the collar bones, which push down the ribs. The neck muscles are no longer used and atrophy so that the rings become necessary to hold up the head. Since the head is in a rigid position from which it cannot be tipped forward or backward, a woman must lean her whole body forward in order to sip a drink from a straw. Should the rings be removed, as they are when a woman has committed adultery, a neck brace will be needed until the muscles have sufficient time to regain enough strength to hold the head up. Without the brace, the head would incessantly wobble and could even, in the case of a woman of the highest status and, thus, the longest neck, fall over and cause asphyxiation (Keshishian 1979). Other peoples have achieved similar, though less dramatic, results with grass or cord rings and with collars. The Padaung women also have rings on their legs and arms so that they present a long-limbed, giraffelike appearance. However, in some tribes leg bindings have been designed to enlarge the calves

Figure 1.9 An African Bushwoman with steato-pygia. (National Anthropological Archives, Smithsonian Institution)

Figure 1.10 Padaung girls of Burma with neck elongation. (Library of Congress)

Figure 1.11 African woman with an arm bracelet resulting in contortion. (Library of Congress)

rather than elongate the limbs. Another form of elongation was the Hottentot apron, created by constantly pulling on the vulva until the labia hung downward. Junod (1966) represented the modern Western view of this adornment when he called it an "immoral" and "very ugly habit" which fixed "the imagination of the girl on sexual relations" (p. 182). However, whether that is in fact the case is certainly not known from the available data. We are not even certain whether the practice was sexually motivated.

Head binding has a wide geographical distribution: Melanesia, Europe, parts of Asia, North and South America from Alaska to Peru, and the Caribbean. Skull deformations were mentioned in ancient Greek writings describing other nations and tribes, and the practice dates from at least as far back as ancient Egypt. In the 1940s many German parents tried to make their children's skulls more like the valued delichocephalic "Aryan" head (Broby-Johansen 1968), and to this day some African tribes continue to bind their babies' heads. While this custom might appear particularly dangerous and painful, most of the evidence suggests that it is neither. In fact, the infant seems to be in pain only when the bindings are released. However, French children whose heads were bound in the nineteenth century did show some negative effects, such as headaches and deafness, that were attributed to the bindings. The process is always begun immediately after birth when the skull is still soft and—because the skull bones are not yet fused—quite malleable. It is usually continued for eight months to one year. Some head deformations may have been unintentional, a serendipitous result of tying infants to cradleboards, thus causing a flattening of the back of the head. Most such deformations, however, were probably the result of intentional efforts to alter the shape of the skull. In some cases a flat brow and even a flat nose were achieved by putting a board or pad across the infant's forehead while he or she was on a cradleboard. Because there was no lateral pressure the head bulged out wider at the sides. Elongation of the head was achieved by binding the head with strips of cloth, leather, raffia, or some similar material. The Choktah Indian strapped a bag of sand onto the brow of his children to produce an indentation in the brow that foreshortened it. The motives behind skull deformations were probably quite varied. Many practices were probably accidental results of methods of infant care. For example, children habitually carried on one arm seem to develop an obliquity in the shape of the skull. As this shape becomes the norm, it also becomes a thing of beauty, an adornment. It is thought that head binding has been variously motivated by a desire to enhance vision, to frighten enemies, or to indicate status. The latter appears to have been the most common and has been found among peoples throughout the world. Most European binding has been done for status. In twentieth-century Germany, the purpose was to show membership in the "supreme race"; in France until the nineteenth century, head binding was done to denote high intelligence. Most of these practices would ipso facto have had an element of conformity, of belonging to one's cultural group.

Other contortions of the head have focused on the facial features. Mayan children, for example, were made to be cross-eyed by hanging a ball directly between their eyes from their forehead-flattening board. Both ear lobes and lips have been weighted down or stretched over some object to elongate them. Enlightened, concerned, and affluent parents in the modern West would feel guilty were they to ignore any imperfection in the straightness of their child's teeth. Even when the bite is perfect, the well-cared-for child will be forced to undergo the pain and discomfort, both physical and psychological, of braces. In the same way, Senegalese parents use a method to make their child's teeth buck since buck teeth are the aesthetic ideal in their culture.

Contortions of the feet are less common than most other forms of plastic body perhaps because few societies can afford to reduce the mobility of part of their population. The Chinese Lily Foot, the best-known example, began about one thousand years ago and lasted, in spite of having been outlawed, well into the 1930s. To produce this tiny foot—the ideal was just three inches long and two inches wide—a young girl's four small toes were bent back under the sole of the foot. The foot was wrapped, starting at the instep and then over the toes and around the heel, so that the toes were kept bent under the sole. This pushed the arch up so that the heel and toes would nearly meet. After a month, the foot was unwrapped; along with the bandages, skin and even a toe or two might come off. After a soaking and a massage to maintain some flexibility, the binding was redone even more tightly.

Figure 1.12 Kwakiutl woman whose head has been bound. (National Anthropological Archives, Smithsonian Institution)

Figure 1.13 The bound Lily foot. (Peabody Museum)

Since the foot was a strong erogenous zone, it was used in sexual foreplay. Not only was the woman excited when her foot was rubbed, licked, kissed, or sucked but the man was aroused by the smell of 'the foot. The big toe could simulate fellatio, and the chasm formed between the heel and toes formed soft and fleshy pseudo-labia (Rossi 1976). Bergler (1953) suggested that the process of foot binding was actually a symbolic castration of the penisless female. Whether it was done for sexual, sociological, or psychological purposes, it did immobilize the woman, who could take only small, mincing steps for short distances since she had to balance herself and carry her weight on her two big toes and the backs of her heels. Unable to walk unaided, she required a cane or the support of another person. The process also prevented five-to-seven-year-old girls from physically exploring their environments because they were in constant pain from the binding for about two years. In fact, the pain was so intense during the first year that the girl could do "nothing but lie and cry and moan" (Flower 1882, p. 17). Fortunately, the pain eventually ceased when the nerves as well as the muscles were destroyed and the foot atrophied. Instances of foot binding have been primarily localized to Asian cultures (Rossi 1976).

While we enlightened moderns may wince at the barbarism of such a custom, we practice foot contortions that are as unhealthy as the Lily Foot. High-heeled shoes worn by many women cause anatomical changes; tight shoes impede circulation and cause misalignments of the foot and toes; and most modern shoes impede the proper functioning of the foot in walking. High heels have been worn for centuries and by both sexes. Pedestal and platform shoes, which date at least from ancient Greece, cause problems similar to those caused by high heels. High heels reduce the degree of elasticity of the Achilles tendon and cause such poor posture that "no single organ retains its natural position" (Broby-Johansen 1968, p. 13). Since the heels force the feet to meet the ground on an angle, the body must compensate for balance by bending the knees and curving the spine forward while the buttocks are thrown backward. Most modern shoes encase the foot without any semblance to the foot itself. The human foot goes from its narrowest point at the heel to its widest point at the toes. However, modern shoes narrow at the toes; they can even be narrower at the toes than at the heels. As a result, the foot becomes misshapen. One of the first distortions involves the big toe, which starts to lean in toward the next toe rather than standing apart, pointing straight ahead. Examine an infant's foot and note its strength and flexibility and the mobility of its big toe. Compare it with an adult foot to see the effects of "civilized" shoes. Much of the back, hip, foot, and knee pain experienced by adults may be a result of these distortions just as corns, ingrown toenails, and bunions are.

Removal of Body Parts

Removing body parts may result in an almost infinitesimal change or in a radical change. Many Westerners practice such removal in clipping or filing their toenails and fingernails or cutting their cuticles. Less common in the

West, although hardly rare, is the removal or filing down of the teeth. In most instances tooth filing is done in order to cap the tooth and teeth that have been removed are replaced by a bridge, full plate, or implants. However, most cultures remove or file their teeth with no intention of making a replacement. Alterations of the teeth usually involve the front teeth, generally the upper ones, and are most common in the South Pacific, Malaysia, and Africa. The Australian aborigines and many tribes in west Africa commonly knock out one or more teeth, often as part of initiation ceremonies at puberty or as a mourning ritual. Hypotheses regarding the motivation for this custom have ranged from the practical—the Masai knock out teeth in order to feed the individual should he develop lockjaw—to the symbolic—one Australian aborigine group knocks the teeth out to make a hole symbolic of a rain cloud, the group's totem (Abbie 1970). Sometimes teeth are also chipped or filed into patterns. If that is done to most of the teeth, it will be a health hazard because it interferes with chewing. Often several or even all the teeth are filed to a point, filed short and even, or filed on the surface to remove the enamel. This latter is usually done in order to get a surface that is more amenable to dyeing or, in modern dentistry, bonding. Other reasons for filing are less obvious, although in some cultures it is believed that the custom distinguishes humans from the baser animals and thereby assures that their souls will go to heaven. Teeth that are not filed, chipped, or removed can still be cosmetically enhanced by dyeing them or inlaying them. Inlays are usually of some shiny, reflecting material such as brass, gold, silver, or gemstones. While inlaying has been a practice

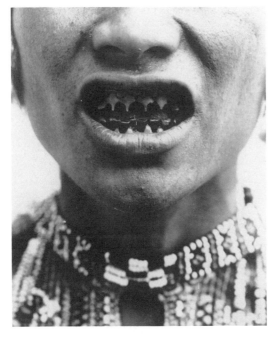

Figure 1.14 A Bagobo man of the Philippines whose upper teeth have been filed and lower teeth have been blackened. (National Anthropological Archives, Smithsonian Institution)

primarily of more "primitive" cultures, it has periodically found favor in Western fashion. Adornment appears to be a prime motivation for inlays, dyes, chipping, and filing.

Some tribal marks involve the removal of areas of skin. For example, the African Bunns's tribal mark, which is three bold ridges going from the mouth to the crown of the head, is made by cutting out strips of flesh and rubbing palm oil and wood ashes into the wound (Avebury 1972). Another African tribe marks its nobles by partially detaching the skin from the forehead so that the skin falls "like an awning over the eyebrows and nose." This partial scalping is often fatal, but those who survive are given the highest status (Hiler 1930, p. 100). Equally radical was the practice attributed to the Amazons of removing their right breast so that it did not interfere with their archery. Such radical procedures, however, have been rare; perhaps groups who practiced them were more prone to die out. Rib removal is the only radical procedure to have been practiced in the history of modern, "civilized," fashion.

Finger joints have been removed by numerous peoples of Africa, Australia, and the Americas. However, this was apparently done not for adornment but rather for preventing or curing illness, to placate the spirits of one's dead ancestors, as a pledge, or to fulfill some ritualistic requirement of a role.

One of the most common and universal practices of this type has been circumcision and other genital alterations. These are often part of the puberty rites and, as such, it has been hypothesized that the ritual serves as public proof that a boy has become a man, can withstand the pain, and has made a sacrifice

Figure 1.15 Sudanese woman with deep facial scars resulting from the removal of strips of skin. (Library of Congress)

in order to belong with other men. Pain is the high price that gives the belonging—the social group—a greater importance. The Australian aborigine practices circumcision in his rites of puberty. Traditionally, a male relative performed the operation with a sharp stone. Today doctors may also perform the operation, and a razor or some other more efficient instrument is used. Abbie (1970) hypothesized that the circumcision is a phallic symbolism of the death of the boy and the birth of the man—the removal of the foreskin reveals a "man's" penis. Certainly the sense of manhood that a boy gets from circumcision would be worth the price. It serves as his college degree, as a visual reminder to both boy and group of his membership in, and status within, the group. It changes him from all the "theys" into an "us."

Some cultures, such as our own, inflict the procedure on their infant boys, who grow to believe that the appearance of their circumcised penis is proper. In our culture the earliest medical reason for circumcision, dating from the eighteenth century, was to inhibit masturbation and thus prevent the insanity and other disorders believed at the time to be associated with it. Circumcision was popularly accepted from the 1880s until the 1930s as the best method for avoiding the horrors caused by masturbation. By the 1950s most males born in hospitals in the United States were being routinely circumcised just after their birth. Yet, this belief in the horrors caused by masturbation had been dismissed by most of the medical community during the previous two decades. Another medical theory for circumcision was that circumcised males had a reduced frequency of penile cancer. This theory eventually led to the belief that circumcision was necessary for reasons of cleanliness since some men could not be relied upon to properly clean between their foreskin and the glans. However, evidence today clearly suggests that there is no medical reason for routinely circumcising men. Circumcisions have been discontinued by most cultures except those in which it has a religious significance. The only exception is the United States, where in less than one hundred years circumcision has become so established a tradition that it continues in spite of its being an unnecessary procedure with some inherent health risks (Paige 1978).

Other procedures that alter the male genitals have been much less widespread, limited primarily to some Australian aborigines and South Pacific peoples. The Australian aborigines are the only people known to have practiced subincision or urethrotomy. This slitting of the skin and urethra along the penis was practiced as part of their puberty rites. The purpose is not known. It has been hypothesized that it was done to make the male genitals look more like the female's and thus gain for men the power of women. Another hypothesis was that this procedure made the male's penis resemble the kangaroo's, the tribal totem, which has a small hypospadias. Whatever the original reason, it is likely that the practice was continued so that the sons should be like their fathers and their fathers before them. Superincision, practiced only in the South Pacific, is a puberty ritual in which "the top of the penis [is cut] so the foreskin hangs down in a drape, leaving the glans exposed" (Guthrie 1976, p. 87). Its function is not known.

Females have been subjected to similar procedures. Introcision, the rupturing of the hymen, has been practiced in many cultures as part of either the pubertal or the premarital rites. Women have also had clitoridectomies and/or removal of the clitoral hood or even the labia minora. Removal of the clitoral hood was practiced in Europe from the 1850s to the early 1900s. In the United States, clitoridectomies were also performed, and removal of the clitoral hood has not been uncommon (Paige 1978). But the procedure has been most common among certain African tribes, some of whom still perform it. Reasons for such procedures have been contradictory, ranging from preventing frigidity to reducing sexual pleasure. From clinical reports, it would appear that removal of the clitoris does in fact reduce the intensity of some erotic sensations, but it appears that the nerve endings are still sufficiently intact that there is a diffuse but pleasurable sensation from the area that had surrounded the clitoris.

PLASTIC SURGERY.   Plastic surgery also involves removing body parts such as skin or cartilage, although sometimes parts are added—as with a breast implant. There are two types of plastic surgery today, cosmetic surgery and reconstructive surgery. Cosmetic surgery is performed to improve the patient's appearance. Reconstructive surgery is performed either to correct structural defects such as a cleft palate or to repair damage done to the body, for instance, a face damaged in a car accident. The popularity of cosmetic surgery is evident in the increase of such operations from the late 1940s, when about fifteen thousand a year were performed, to the early 1970s, when there were nearly seven hundred times more operations. The most common cosmetic procedures are breast enlargement (augmentation mammoplasty), breast reduction (reduction mammoplasty), nose jobs (rhinoplasty), eyelid lifts (blepharoplasty), face lifts (rhytidectomy), abdominal lifts (abdominoplasty), and ear jobs (otoplasty). These operations cost between approximately $2,000 and $6,000 plus hospital costs. Except for nose and ear jobs, they are normally done in a hospital with the patient under a general anesthesia. Thus, the dangers of any major surgery are present, including hematoma, infection, and reaction to the anesthesia. Some of these operations, like certain breast reductions, may be medically advisable. However, most are done for the purpose of enhancing the appearance by making it more closely approximate our cultural ideal of beauty.

PIERCING

The nose, lips, and ears have commonly been pierced to create a receptacle for some adornment. Less common, although hardly rare, has been the piercing of cheeks, chin, prepuce, and labia. In fact, the smallest flap of skin can be used so that there have been men and women "whose bodies are pierced in some way or other in . . . a hundred different places" (Flower 1882, p. 163). The initial piercing is usually made with a needlelike object or an awl and enlarged with bigger instruments. In one South American Indian tribe an infant is given beer before his or her lip is cut in order to help lessen its sensibilities. The tribe gathers together for the occasion, and the mother is kept to one side where she can watch yet not interfere. The piercing is done with a special knife. The individual performing the operation firmly grasps the infant's lip and pulls it out. He pushes the knife in and turns it several times before removing it. If the hole seems well formed, a disc is placed in it; if not, the procedure is repeated. Needless to say the infant must be held down, but his or her voice cannot be stilled!

At puberty young girls from many of the Northwest Pacific Indian tribes had their lower lips pierced and began to wear a plug of wood or abalone through the slit, which was about half an inch below the mouth. The plugs were increased from about the size of a nail to four inches wide, six inches long, and one-half inch deep, according to the individual's age and rank. The lowest rank would not have a plug, the next would have one the size of a small button, and so on. By old age the lip would be so extended that it drooped down and exposed teeth and gums, a sign of both mature beauty and high rank.

Typical ornaments hung from such receptacles were of stone, shell, wood, feather, metal, animal's claws and legs (especially birds' and crabs'), tusks and teeth, bamboo, ferns, twigs, and bones. Some of these were probably primarily ornamental while others were protectors or status indicators.

Figure 1.16 Eskimo woman with pierced ears, nose, and chin. (Library of Congress)

Figure 1.17 Makondi woman of Tanzania with a lip disc. (Library of Congress)

Most peoples who wear lip ornaments begin the piercing with their infants. Gradually the hole will be enlarged by adding bigger ornaments. Depending on the size, some of the front teeth may have to be knocked out to create a space in which the disc can fit. Ornaments are usually in the shape of a disc, collar button, or teardrop extending from a flat tail. Labrets or lip ornaments have been found among Eskimos, Indians of North and South America, and some African tribes as well as such groups as punk rockers. One theory hypothesizes that

> lip ornaments everywhere are keyed somehow to an emphasis on the spoken word, on eloquence and song. It is a persuasive theory but hard to demonstrate worldwide, for the use of the labret is sometimes decreed for women, not for men. And while women, it is true, are responsible for developing in their children the power of speech, they are seldom permitted public oration.
>
> The political gathering punctuated by harangues is well known, for example, to Nilotic herdsmen of East Africa. Women may be seen at such an event but are not heard. Yet one finds women's lips more frequently plugged than those of men. To remove the plug and put out one's tongue through the aperture constitutes the ultimate insult [for the Nilotic]. (Vlahos 1979, p. 42)

Other theories have suggested that discs were worn to frighten away enemies or to repulse slave hunters. Pierced lips have denoted interest in marriage as well as the state of being married. In one African tribe women wear a disc up

Figure 1.18 South American Indians with various lip and ear discs. (National Anthropological Archives, Smithsonian Institution)

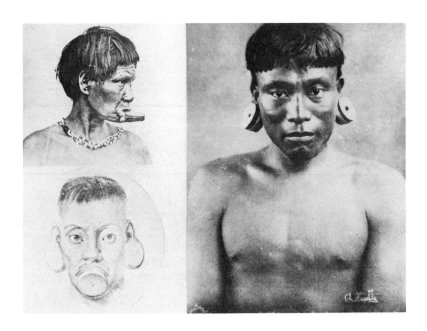

Figure 1.19 Nubian woman of Sudan with a nose ring through her pierced nose and attached to her hair. The ring partly covers her facial scars. (Library of Congress)

to nine and one-half inches in size, which seems to be a mark of ownership made by their fiancés during the betrothal ritual.

Cheek ornaments have been much rarer. The Aleuts cut their cheeks and wore a stud or the muzzle hairs of a seal in the slits. Some South American Indian tribes have worn feathers through their cheeks.

Nose ornaments have had a wider distribution than lip and have been worn by Eskimos, North and South American Indians, Africans, Asians, Arabs, and the aborigines of Australia and New Zealand. Rings and sticks have been especially popular adornments, but a variety of items have been worn through the septum. If the shape was inappropriate, the object could be tied to a piece of cord that was passed through the hole. Nostril holes have usually been decorated with a stud. Just as with lip piercing, the nose has generally been pierced with a small needle or thorn. To enlarge the opening, thicker items would be gradually introduced. The objects could be wide enough and long enough to force people to breath through their mouths and also to affect their speech. Septum piercing has been used for purposes other than adornment, for instance, to prevent the individual from smelling "bad" smells or to indicate marital status. After some American Indians were exposed to white culture, they stopped wearing nose ornaments. However, they continued to pierce the nose. What was the motivation? Adornment does not seem to be the answer, although it may have been a primary motivation earlier. Habit or conformity may have been the final cause.

The most universally pierced body part is the ear; the lobes are most commonly pierced, but the cartilage has also been used. In fact, the only peoples known to have never pierced their ears are the Bushmen, Fuegians,

Figure 1.20 Moi women of Indonesia whose ears have been pierced and the lobes weighted down so that they extend below the shoulders. Note also their nipple treatment. (Library of Congress)

Andaman Islanders, and some Sumatran tribes (Hiler 1930). Since at least Neolithic times, ear studs have been worn. Items that appear to have been worn primarily for adornment range from live snakes to dead rats, inflated fish bladders to strings of beads. Ear ornaments do not interfere with eating or speaking. Except for the possibility of infection, there is no inherent danger in the process. Holes may be quite tiny or so large that the rim of the lobe touches the shoulder. In one African tribe newborns can even be passed, for luck, through the loop of the medicine man's earlobe. A few peoples have extended the lobes until they split.

Ear piercing has been part of protective ritual, such as the ceremonial "christening" piercing of infants among some North American Indians and some aborigines of the South Pacific. It may also be done to enhance development, to indicate status, and as a means of portage.

The development of the clip-on and screw-on earrings led to a decrease in ear piercing in the United States. Having one's ears pierced even became a sign of lower status in some communities. However, in the 1960s piercing began to regain popularity. Fashion was striving for a more natural look with less make-up and more natural hair styles. Somehow pierced ears became associated with this look.

While both sexes have pierced their ears, men have been more likely to pierce just one or to pierce one ear differently from the other. In the West, for a male to wear a single earring has sometimes indicated certain role af-filiations—sailor, pirate, motorcyclist, homosexual. However, some men, such as in certain Indian tribes on the Pacific Northwest coast of North America, used the number of ear holes to indicate rank, so that a high-ranking man might have his lobes pierced and six more holes along the rim of each ear.

EXTERNAL ADORNMENT

External or temporary adornment can be worn or removed whenever the wearer chooses. Except for body paint, it is most common in clothed societies. There are five kinds of external adornment: paint, which is applied directly on the skin surface; proprioceptive, which is adornment that relates to the body in space; sartorial, which is applied onto an article of dress; intrinsic, which is adornment having some special value; and local, which is dress designed to focus on some part of the body.

Paint and Make-Up

The use of paint and make-up to decorate the body stems from prehistoric times and was probably one of the first forms of adornment. Paint may be localized or may cover the entire body. The latter is more common for ceremonial or special occasions, where it is a way to "dress up," to dress differently from the ordinary. "Dressing up" can also be done by using special paints, such as a special color paint or a paint gathered at a special place. Daily facial and body painting has been practiced among many primitive peoples, among them, some American Indians, various South Pacific aborigines, and a few African tribes. Many have used paint in conjunction with washing or with greasing the skin.

Figure 1.21   Body painting is often an interpersonal activity—as it is for these South American Indians. (National Anthropological Archives, Smithsonian Institution)

Figure 1.22 Last Horse, a Sioux, wears body paint that was probably designed both to protect him in battle and make him more war-like. (Library of Congress)

Paint has often been used to designate transient roles or status or to provide protection. Among many peoples each color has had a specific meaning; for others, such as the Nuba, the colors have been chosen only for their beauty. Most African cultures as well as many other societies have used red, white, and black more than other colors (Zahan 1975). Red has probably been the most commonly used, perhaps reflecting the ease in finding red powders such as ocher or camwood or else the fact that of the primary colors red has the longest wavelength perceived by humans. While red has been used for protection from the sun or from military enemies, it is most often a facial highlight or some other form of beautification. Red has usually symbolized (1) blood or life, (2) health or wealth, or (3) protection from the "evil eye." Both black and white have frequently been used for protection from evil.

Unfortunately, paint usually lasts only a short time relative to the time needed to put it on, and unless mixed with oil or grease, it may even dry and become uncomfortable. Dye has therefore been a more satisfactory form of temporary adornment.

Henna has been the dye with the widest distribution and the most frequent use. It was popular at least as early as ancient Egypt. Depending on where and how it is applied, henna can last up to three weeks. It has been used to dye fingernails and tint head hair as well as to adorn the skin. Even today "at least a dozen different preparations of henna are sold for producing different shades of color" (Field 1958, p. 97). Arab women, for example, use a black henna on their soles and hands and a red for their toes and fingertips. While the henna appears to be used primarily for adornment, it does help to harden the skin, a result that could be an asset on the soles and hands.

Lime juice and peroxide are two of the ways humans have found to bleach hair. The golden-red hair of the Venetian women we see in Titian's paintings "was usually achieved by sponging the hair with a solution of soda, alum, and black sulfur, and then allowing it to dry in the sun. . . ." (Cooper 1971, p. 75). Hair dyes have long come in all the natural hair colors. Red has been particularly popular. Gaelic women used goat grease mixed with the ash from a beech tree to dye their hair red. But hair has also been dyed more unusual colors. For example, "Anglo-Saxon men dyed their hair and beards blue, . . . green or orange" (ibid. p. 101) just as their punk descendants did in the early 1980s. Hair dyes, bleaches, and rinses such as henna remain common external adornments.

Dyeing or staining the teeth is not a practice in the modern West. But it has been common throughout much of the world. Black and red have been popular tooth colors in parts of Asia, the South Pacific, and the Indian subcontinent, and among some of the Gulf Coast and South American Indians. Betel nuts, mangrove roots, and a mix of tobacco and wood ashes have been used to achieve these marks of beauty. Some peoples have even stained alternate teeth with different colors to achieve a patterned effect.

The major form of body paint used in the modern West is make-up. Cosmetics date from at least the Mesolithic period (10,000–5,000 B.C.) in the Nile Valley. The ancient Egyptians taught cosmetology to the ancient Hebrews, and both helped to further spread the art. Make-up has been used as a charm against evil by some primitive men and, according to Angeloglou (1970), it is still used for this purpose by the modern Western woman. Cosmetics have been associated with witchcraft (Shalleck 1973) as well as trickery. They have also been a badge of belonging for primitive man and in the modern West, where women "equip themselves with Identikit faces" (Angeloglou 1970). Every new fashion season beauty magazines provide step-by-step instructions on exactly how to apply make-up to achieve the "in" look.

Figure 1.23 The ritualistic application of henna to the soles of a Middle Eastern bridegroom's feet. (Library of Congress)

The early Christian church condemned the use of cosmetics; only "loose" women or women of power could use them. However, in the fifteenth century both the French and English kings and other male members of the court did use cosmetics. France's Henry III, for example, wore a flour-and-egg-white mask to bed. His face was painted red and white; he plucked his eyebrows; and he wore his hair up in a false chignon, which allowed his pierced ears to be more easily seen. Other men in the court wore beauty patches, rouge, and perfume and used a variety of skin lotions (ibid.). Women did not begin to use cosmetics commonly until the Elizabethan age, when ladies of elegance

> dyed their hair, plucked their eyebrows, covered their exposed breasts with white plaster and painted their faces. The revolution was in the foundation of their beauty rather than the addition of colour, although that was startling enough. Lotions, potions, ointments and creams were churned out by alchemical confidence tricksters or in the still rooms and bedchambers of country houses. . . . Two "brandname" lotions appeared in the sixteenth century which were to survive for the next two hundred years. One was Soliman, or Soliman's Water, obviously a derivation from Solomon, who was still a magical name in necromancy. It was supposed to eliminate all spots, freckles and warts, and its chief ingredient was sublimate of mercury which polished off the outer layer of skin and corroded the flesh beneath. The girl's teeth fell out even more rapidly than was usual at this date, her gums receded, and by the age of thirty the devotee of miracle lotions would be a rotting wreck. (ibid., p. 48)

The white lead paint used to whiten the skin was an irritant to skin and eyes and could even be fatal (Shalleck 1973). Some modern cosmetics also have adverse effects on health if they contain allergens or carcinogens. However, women still persist in taking the risk just as they did in past centuries. Why do they? It may be, as Hoebel (1958) suggested, that cosmetics are

> universal cultural responses to the basic human need for favorable response. They are designed to heighten the stimulus intensity of the physical presence of one person upon the touch, smell, sight, and perhaps taste of others. The others are usually of the opposite sex, but not exclusively so. If personality is the social stimulus value of an individual, then cosmetics intensify personality. (p. 283)

Body lotions, oils, and cleansing creams have had a universal distribution, from the Bushwoman who made her cleansing cream from the chewed pips of a plant to the modern woman who shops for her jar of cleansing cream at a department store, pharmacy, or supermarket. A silky, shiny skin appears to be a universal desire. The oil used probably reflects the most accessible source so that animal fats such as hippopotamus grease have been typical in Africa, while in the South Pacific coconut oil has been the favorite. Red ocher lipstick and rouge date at least from ancient Egypt and have been used by primitive people throughout most of the world. Rubbing red flannel or red paper across the cheeks, rubbing beet juice into them, or just pinching them have also been ways of giving the cheeks a rosy glow. The glow was particularly evident in a face whitened by such things as chalky ceruse mixed with vinegar, sulphur, or borax. Nails have been tinted with henna or other products, such as a concoction of pink balsam leaves and alum.

The eyes have perhaps had the most universal attention. Eyebrows have been plucked, shaved, shaved and redrawn, dyed, bleached, and darkened with a pencil or some other substance. Kohl has been a popular eye liner. Its primary function has been to protect, strengthen, cool, or adorn the eye, depending on the ingredients used to make it. Eye shadow has been primarily a feminine adornment. Guthrie (1976) hypothesized that eye shadow is intended to make the female seem more vulnerable since it mimics a physiological reaction to emotional stress. "In the midst of deep emotional trauma, the lower lids of human eyes droop and the area around the lids turn a purple-brown pastel, which exposes the sclera to its highest degree" (p. 123).

Perfume is also universal. It is generally made from plants or from the "musk" glands of animals such as the civet or from the ambergris secreted by sperm whales. Flowers and/or seeds from flowers or herbs have been mixed with oil(s) to make perfumes by peoples as widely divergent as the ancient Egyptians and natives of the South Pacific islands. However, some peoples have simply worn a plant or have pulverized it and rubbed the powder over their skin. While perfume has been used by both sexes, it has most frequently been worn by women. This suggests that at least some perfumes have been intended as masks of the body odor coming from the apocrine glands since there are more of these emotion-activated glands in women than in men.

One of the uniquely modern uses of perfume has been the development of scented genital deodorizers for women. It is an oddity since the perfume is intended to be sexually enticing yet it masks the genital aroma of a healthy female, which is itself a sexual stimulant. But as we have reduced our awareness of natural scents and bombarded our senses with unnatural ones, we may have altered our perception so that it is the unnatural that appears to us natural. Scent may also be used to mark out one's personal space. At puberty the body produces more scent, and the teenager's ability to differentiate the scent increases. Combined with the egocentricity of the adolescent, this would be sufficient to explain the teenager's love affair with genital deodorants and scents. The young child's less developed sense of smell may be the reason children so often give their mothers such strong perfumes.

In one study the majority of the American men surveyed were turned on by perfume worn by a woman in a casual outfit, such as jeans and a sweatshirt. However, when the perfume was worn in conjunction with a somewhat dressier outfit, such as a blouse, skirt, and hose, it received a negative response from men (Baron 1981).

Proprioceptive

Proprioception is the awareness of one's body and its movements in space. Proprioceptive adornments fall into two categories: (1) power extenders, which increase the amount of space taken up by the body and (2) stimulators, which focus the senses on the movement(s) of the body in space.

POWER EXTENDERS. Power extenders enlarge the individual's sense of power and control over all the space within his or her touch. Their incidence has been correlated with social power; the highest-powered individuals usually have the most power-extending adornments. However, this relationship does not appear accurate for modern America, where the young adult female wears the most power extenders. Leisure has also been related to the wearing of power extenders, and this relationship continues to be evident in the differences between work dress and leisure wear. Flugel (1930) suggested that

> the "extensive" function of garments should be such as to be in harmony with our conations rather than that they should be under our direct control. A plume or scarf or skirt blowing in the wind, or emphasising our movements through their inertia, may be very satisfying so long as they do not interfere with the carrying out of our desires. We then, quietly, as it were, annex the effects of wind and inertia, treat them as if they were produced by ourselves, and feel that our own bodily power is increased thereby.... But if these effects of wind and inertia interfere with our movements (as when a skirt or coat impedes the free use of legs or arms), they at once begin to diminish rather than enhance our feeling of power and extension.
>
> The determination of the conditions which produce the optimum extension is clearly a somewhat difficult and delicate matter, since these conditions obviously vary with circumstances and with individual tastes and habits. It is perhaps most often true, as Flaccus suggests, that "the less the attention is distracted by irritating features in the surface of actual contact, the more perfect will be the illusion" (of extension). In this way unyielding materials, which make a series of rough contacts with the skin, may resist the necessary incorporation into the self. Nevertheless, there can be little doubt that, under certain circumstances and if used with due precautions, stiff fabrics are also capable of adding very considerably to this illusory extension of our personality. (p. 38)

One of the most effective ways to increase one's sense of personal space has been to wear large, full skirts. Stiff hoops, which have relatively less give, have been more effective than crinolines. But both act as physical barriers, keeping others at a distance and thus expanding one's own personal space. Trains are less effective since they are usually barriers only to the rear or sides. However, Catherine the Great's coronation robe had a train seventy-five yards long, which required many bearers and certainly acted as a rear guard just as Lady Diana's long wedding train did.

While most shoulder pads and epaulettes are examples of local adornment, unusually large ones that are so big as to be ill-proportioned to the natural body no longer focus on the shoulder but act to extend the width of the body itself.

Figure 1.24 This full, stiff crinoline expanded a woman's personal space and kept others necessarily at a distance. (*Punch*, Sept. 1, 1864)

Figure 1.25 The Indian's feather bonnet was a power extendor. (Library of Congress)

Wide-legged pants and large sleeves can also be control adornments, although when the material is soft enough, they may be more for stimulation than control. The use of shoes as power extenders is rather unusual since most shoes that increase height tend to reduce ease of mobility. Thus, additional height has tended to be achieved in less inhibiting ways, such as the bearskin military hat worn by the guards at Buckingham Palace, the full-feathered Indian bonnet, the top hat, and the tricorn. Hair styles can accomplish the same thing; for example, the rococo hair style of the eighteenth-century female aristocrat could easily add thirty inches to her height.

STIMULATORS. Adornments that focus on the movement of the body in space are universal. While they may be related to an individual's sense of power, this relationship tends to be less one of controlling space than one of controlling one's body in space. Therefore these adornments emphasize or deemphasize body movement. Movements of the body actually change the appearance of most dress, especially looser-fitting garments since they most effectively incorporate wind, body, and inertia. Thus, dress that is light, loose, and/or not firmly attached is most effective as a stimulator adornment. Time lag, which is

> the tendency of the dress material, in movement, to lag behind the movements of the body itself, so that momentary folds and creases are produced, capable of distorting the form of the design . . . is inherent in costume; there is necessarily some delay between the movement of the body and that of the dress over it as it

adapts itself to the new position. It is a defect which is evaded by the loose-fitting garment or equally by the stiff one which preserves its own shape. It is exaggerated in the "skin-tight" materials, because of course no dress material is—or can be—absolutely as mobile as the skin itself. (Cunnington 1941, p. 80)

Gowns of chiffon or some similar material are excellent examples of this phenomenon as are dangling earrings; long, loose hair; and dress made from or adorned with feathers, fringe, or ribbons. The gentleman whom the seventeenth-century writer Evelyn (1661) spied walking through Westminster Hall was bedecked like a May pole in enough ribbon to have come from six shops and to set up twenty peddlers. A newly rigged frigate in a storm could not have shown more movement than

> this Puppets streamers did when the Wind was in his Shroud's; the Motion was Wonderful to behold, and the Colours were Red, Orange, and Blew, of well gum'd Sattin, which argu'd a happy fancy: but so was our Gallant over charg'd . . . that whether he were clad with this Garment, or (as a Porter) only carried it, was not to be resolv'd. [p. 12]

In either case his awareness of his body's movement in space must have been excitingly heightened so that he would have felt a propensity to move still faster to increase his natural exhilaration.

The sensations we perceive from our dress as we move in space are

Figure 1.26   This chiffon shawl simply demands movement. (Saint Laurent Rive Gauche)

primarily tactile and auditory; visual sensations are far less important. Thus, the noise made by the movement of an article of dress is also an important consideration. The Haida chief's eelskin coat, decorated with dried berries and bird beaks that rattled when he moved, used auditory stimulation. While stimulators remain a factor in leisure wear, they are unusual in work dress since stimulation could distract the worker's attention from an assigned task.

Intrinsic

An intrinsic adornment is an ornament that has a special, positive value. Primitive men have often attributed higher value to objects with a high sheen or an unusual color. In more advanced civilizations rarity has been an important factor as has difficulty in attainment. For example, jewelry other than costume jewelry has an instrinsic value because of its metal, its designer, and any stones set into it.

Flowers have had a universal role as intrinsic ornaments, both fresh flowers and flowers that have been dipped in gold or laminated. Seeds, berries, and other fruits have been used for longer-lasting ornaments.

Teeth, horns, and bones have also been popular ornaments with an intrinsic value. Siberian graves from over thirty thousand years ago have revealed mammoth ivory bracelets and necklaces of Arctic fox teeth. The teeth of a variety of animals, from men to dogs to kangaroos, have also been popular. Their value may have been totemic or trophic in nature or symbolic of the animal's value. Ivory and other horn has been popular in many eras and civilizations. The coolness and smoothness of the medium may have been a factor in its popularity as they were for jade and similar stones.

Shells with a high gloss or unusual coloring have had universal popularity as have feathers with high sheen, unusual color, or fine texture. Beads, an early and universal adornment, have often had an intrinsic value perhaps because they could be both tedious and time consuming to make. The earliest were probably just objects with a natural hole or that were easily pierced, such as berries or seeds. Later bead-making techniques were more complex: fire sticks burning holes into an object; actually producing the bead itself from clay or a similar substance; drilling a hole into an object like the quahog clam shell, which was used as wampum by many of the North American Indians. Beads have also often had a protective value which may increase with age, so that in many cultures beads are passed down from generation to generation as the most valuable of heirlooms.

Precious metals and gemstones have been popular because of their rarity, difficulty to obtain, and/or sheen or sparkle. As with any adornment, when they have been given economic value, their worth has always increased. In Africa, for example,

> slave hunters found brass collars more prized than human beings and traded these for slaves. The Africans, in turn, used these collars to buy wives.

Figure 1.27 Tamil woman of Ceylon with jewelry having intrinsic value. (National Anthropological Archives, Smithsonian Institution)

> Brass and copper were introduced by Portuguese traders and prized for ornaments and implements alike. In ring form they were used as currency and said by the Bantu to be "white" and "red" of the same metal. Their indigenous metal was iron. (Tyrrell 1968, p. 110)

Gold, silver, pewter, and bronze have been popular metals in jewelry, which continues to be a major area of intrinsic adornment.

Sartorial

Sartorial adornment is the decoration of an already existing garment. A wooden bead, for example, can be carved into the form of an animal or a face. Ivory, shells, and precious stones have frequently been carved or cut to add to their decorative appeal. But sartorial embellishments can be much less elaborate than these; the practice of one New Zealand people is to decorate the hemline or some other area of a garment by rubbing it with clay to produce a dark border. Sartorial adornment is used more for "dress-up" clothing. European folk costumes were prized possessions because of the time and effort put into their embroidered splendor, and those who wore them considered them their best outfits.

Some garments are beautiful only because of their sartorial treatment. For example, in West Africa, where cotton-and-raffia fabric continues to be woven by techniques that have not changed substantially since ancient times, they use a single heddle loom that can weave complex designs. Yet many of the tribes weave a plain cloth as a background for embroidery or appliqué. The women embroider with raffia fibers that have been dyed and softened by rubbing (Mack 1980). They use a variety of embroidery techniques, including openwork, oversewing, and cut pile. The cloth done in cut pile has relatively varied

a   b

Figure 1.28 Each of these costumes employs sartorial adornment. (a) During the 1920s, beadwork was frequently used to make elaborate the simply cut garments. (Library of Congress) (b) Golden clovers highlight this 1980's chiffon dress. (Pauline Trigère)

and complex designs, each with a symbolic meaning. "These velvets are worn as high-prestige costume, and their richness and variety are a clear indication of the great value traditionally placed on them" (Sieber 1972, p. 163). Patterns frequently use a variety of embroidery techniques so that the fabric is covered with different textures.

Bark cloth has been painted, block printed, stenciled, oiled, and even perfumed. Animal skin—for instance, a deerskin dress—has been adorned with feathers; teeth and bills; bones; bark; embroidery of moose, dog, rat, or rabbit hair; dyed porcupine quills; metals; beads; animals claws; shells, including turtle; reeds, and raffia; brass tacks; ribbons; tassels; buttons; coins; fringe; fur; and dyes and paints. Ornaments were often transferred from an old garment to a new. Designs made on the leather itself by puncturing it were similar to designs carved on bark belts or wooden buttons.

The designs themselves may or may not be representational. Often geometric shapes were combined in different ways to create a wide variety of patterns. The Seminole's patchwork designs were always geometric because of the sewing techniques that they used. The designs were stylizations of natural elements such as plants, fire, or lightning, "as well as various forms of the cross, arrow, diamond, and swastika" (Downs 1979, p. 34). Popular motifs in representational designs have been animal heads and/or forms and vegetation forms.

It has been common to adorn fabrics and skins with paints and dyes even though the process for making the dyes has often been time and energy consuming. The color could be achieved by dyeing or painting the garment or material or dyeing the thread used in weaving a piece of cloth. The weave of a fabric can also result in a design. The Navahos, for example, had six types of weaves including a plain one, a twill, a pile, and one with a different design on each side.

Much sartorial adornment, particularly among primitive peoples, is also proprioceptive because it makes a noise. Belts and sashes, anklets, collars, and even entire shirts and jackets have often been adorned with bells, shell beads, tubes of metal, or some similar items that twinkle, clang, or ring when the individual moves. In the noisy environment of modern industrial society, such adornments serve more as irritants than as sensory stimulators or amusements.

The importance of sartorial adornment can be seen perhaps most effectively in footwear. Shoes are subjected to more abrasion and pulls than probably any other garment. Ornaments would therefore be more apt to fall off or be damaged on a shoe than on any other garment. In spite of this, the sartorial adornment of footwear has been a universal theme throughout the ages. Shoes have been embroidered with metal strips or braids or silk yarns. Some have been "densely worked with patterns as compact as those on a Kashmir shawl or a Persian miniature" (Davis 1980, p. 48). Shoes have been made of silk and satin in every imaginable color variant. It seems obvious that such shoes were not worn for any practical purpose. Instead, they were worn as a way to cover the feet in sartorial splendor.

Local

Local adornment emphasizes or even symbolizes a body part. Western women's fashion can actually be analyzed just in terms of which body parts it has emphasized. Attention has been focused primarily on padding, tight covering, display, and sartorial decoration. Cunnington (1941) hypothesized that local adornments are often circular in order to focus attention on the round or curved body contours. He suggested that convex curves like the bosom or hips are more important fashion themes than concave curves like the waist. However, the best fashions should have "an ingenious blending of the two in the form of a series alternating and in proportion to each other" (p. 91). Cinched-in waists emphasize the hips and the bust, and the latter is also emphasized by its movement when a woman takes shallow breaths from the top part of her lungs (Crawley 1931). Crinolines, panniers, and bustles focused attention on the hips and also caused the eye to be drawn to the bust. False bottoms or padded derrieres have been popular throughout the ages, from primitive to advanced cultures. The modern padded derriere is not so different from the nekbwe, which was a woven "seat" some African women wore over their derrieres. When the tribal women peformed their rather sedate dance, their "nekbwe twitched and shifted slightly at every movement, with a most alluring

Figure 1.29 The bustle focused attention on the derriere. (Library of Congress)

effect" that was enhanced by the beauty of the nekbwes, which were "made of woven colored fibers in geometric or other designs" (Cotlow 1966, p. 99). Tight pants also stress the hips, and their very tightness may make the wearer more aware of this region of his or her anatomy. The primitive cousin of tight pants would be the Dyak woman's brass or rattan rings, which tightly encased her from her thighs to her breasts.

Brassieres, while covering the breasts, actually make "the bosom more conspicuous, so that, even beneath several layers of clothing, the onlooker can appreciate the feminine form." This form, as shaped by the bra, will coincide with an aesthetic ideal all too often not akin to nature's reality (Wax 1957, p. 403). Women have used a variety of items from inflatable rubber bags to rolls

Figure 1.30 The hip and waist rings worn by the Dyak women of Borneo focus attention on the hips, waist, and buttocks. (National Anthropological Archives, Smithsonian Institution)

of cloth to increase their apparent bust size. They have also worn necklaces, particularly pendants, and pins or brooches to focus attention on their bosoms.

Men's fashions have focused on the male chest primarily with vests, medals, pocket handerchiefs, ties, chest plates, boutonnieres, and corsets. Epaulettes and shoulder pads have stressed the shoulders. But the local adornment most worn by men has focused on the male genitals. The penis case, cod piece, jock strap, and padded jock strap are all examples of such local adornment. Females have focused attention on their genitals with beaded, fringed, or tasseled hip girdles; grass skirts; see-through and/or lace-trimmed panties, and G strings. They have bleached their pubic hairs, trimmed them into designs, shaved the pubic region, and even wore pubic-hair wigs (Cooper 1971).

The head has been focused on with any number of head-coverings of the type categorized under hats or caps. But forehead bands and pendants as well as hair styles have also been used. Earrings stress the neck as do collars, chokers, and multistrings of beads. In one African tribe the chief's wife wore over eighty pounds of beads around her neck! Her counterpart in the Congo traditionally wore a brass neck collar weighing between sixteen and twenty pounds. Since this could get quite hot, attendants would dump water over her neck to cool her collar.

Some leg and ankle treatments have been equally uncomfortable. Ibo women, for example, had plates over eight inches in diameter riveted on at their ankles. In parts of India women have worn even wider leg rings of heavy brass with serrated edges. High heels and hose and socks have been other ways of focusing attention on the legs.

Figure 1.31 Indian boy with local adornment. (Library of Congress)

Figure 1.32 This outfit focuses attention on the head, neck, and shoulders. (Library of Congress)

Figure 1.33 Tamil woman of Ceylon with adornment of the head and feet. (National Anthropological Archives, Smithsonian Institution)

Both the upper and lower arms and the fingers have been adorned since prehistoric times. Straps worn on the wrists and elbows (as well as the knees) have needed to be somewhat flexible, unless the intent was to reduce mobility. Thus, skin has been a popular local adornment for the arm. The Aleut's use of sealskin and the Australian aborigine's use of opossum are examples. Bracelets and rings have been made from a wide variety of materials, including ivory, metals, ribbons, vegetation, hair, string, plastics, and strung-together beads.

Hair Dressing

Hair dressing is unique because it involves principles and elements of both corporal and external adornment. It also may include the actual removal of body parts—the hair or part of it—yet it is a temporary adornment. Thus, hair has readily lent itself to experimentation so that there is an incredible variety of treatments and styles of hair.

Head hair is the most important hair from an adornment perspective. Its styles have generally been created not just for, or even primarily for, adornment. They have frequently been used for self-expression, social identification, portage, and ritual. In many cultures hair styles differ according to role so that an individual may change hair style as he or she changes role. Head hair has often been related to growth and/or strength. The Hopis, for example, cut their children's hair to enhance their physical growth. Samson was not so unusual; similar stories and beliefs have been found throughout much of the Mediterranean, South America, the South Pacific, and the Indian subcontinent. Head hair has also been associated with sexuality. It has even been suggested that the head is the symbol of the phallus; the hair, of semen; and hair cutting, of castration. In this theory long hair is equated with sexual freedom, whereas short hair has symbolized restricted sexuality, and shaving has shown celibacy (Hallpike 1969). However, this Freudian interpretation, while perhaps accurate for some cultures in some eras, does not seem to have universal relevance. Hallpike theorized that long hair symbolizes an individual's being outside or less involved with society, and cutting indicates social reentry. The long-haired intellectuals, teenagers, and women are, he suggested, the individuals most resistant to social control. Again, this theory appears to have only a limited validity. As with most theories, both of these seem to have some merit for the culture and during the era in which they were devised. But attempts to apply them to a variety of cultures and eras fail. It is possible that a hair style that differs from the cultural norm may reflect an antisocial stance. And when that hair style is changed for a more conforming one, it probably would indicate some abatement of that antisocial position. Likewise, there are societies in which hair has been or still is associated with sexuality. But this is by no means a universal symbolism. Thus, hair style, like any adornment, can be understood only in the context of its own era and society.

The kinds of head hair styles men have worn are innumerable. However, certain techniques have been more commonly used, such as shaving; plaiting or braiding; knotting; crimping, pleating, or curling; adding support structures within the hair style; adding hair by means of a wig or hair piece; and adding sartorial adornments to a hair style. It is not uncommon for a curly-haired people to straighten their hair and a straight-haired people to curl theirs. Quite different styles may even be used on the same head at the same time. A few North American Indian tribes combined hairdressing with body painting. For example, men of one tribe shaved all of their head hair except for a crest on top and then painted the scalp with undulating lines of red (Berlandier 1969). Today's man does not want a bald spot to paint; transplants and hair weavings are available as methods of hiding such a spot. Some men have even resorted to drug experimentation in an effort to keep or get back their head hair!

Hair has been decorated by tying objects to it. For example, some American Indians have tied silver conchos, beads, scalps, clumps of other hair, or beads to their hair. Flowers, feathers, and bull or other animal tails have been worn in or on the hair.

The most unusual hair styles in the history of Western fashion are probably those of the rococo period in the eighteenth century, particularly in France. One woman, for example, wore on the top of her already built-up hair "modeled ducks swimming in a stormy sea, scenes of hunting and shooting, a mill with a miller's wife flirting with a priest, and the miller leading an ass by its halter" (Cooper 1971, p. 95). Such styles took hours to fashion and were therefore kept as intact as possible for as long as possible, even for a week or more.

a

b

c

Figure 1.34 (a, b, c) Hair can be a unique adornment in itself, as these three photos demonstrate.
(Library of Congress)

This necessitated sleeping in a sitting-up position. The hair was built up over a support structure or padding of a combination of wool with tow, hemp, or horsehair. False hair was used to increase the height. A pomatum was used to plaster the hair down; this pomatum had a beef-marrow base, so that "the smell gradually became anything but alluring. . . ." (ibid.). Since hair during that period was washed only once or twice a year (Woodforde 1971), these styles proved veritable "boarding houses" for a variety of vermin, from lice to mice. Obviously, itching had to be a problem, so long ivory or silver sticks were carried as scratchers. Along with this discomfort was the need to walk carefully lest one knock one's hair askew in a doorway. Carriage riding was especially difficult, and even when the coach seats had been lowered, women had to bend forward while riding. Women, however, have not been the only sex to wear such enormous styles. The Macaroni wigs, worn by men of the Macaroni Club in eighteenth-century England, were as high as eighteen inches.

Body hair is less variable in styling; it is usually left natural. Most alterations have been limited to oiling, bleaching, or removing. This last has been the most common alteration, and the hair has been removed by shaving, cutting, plucking, depilatories, or electrolysis. Sharp stones were early razors; split twigs and bivalve shells were early tweezers. Depilatories were made from hot water mixed with shell ashes, wax, and secret pastes, which after drying were torn off, bringing any hairs with them. Plucking was a common method when only a small portion of hair was to be removed. Eyebrows are still trimmed and shaped by plucking, as is, though less frequently and for more erotic reasons, pubic hair.

The motives for body and head hair removal are varied. For example, some African and South American tribes removed their body hair to distinguish themselves from other animals, while the ancient Egyptians removed theirs for reasons of aesthetics and hygiene. In the modern West most women shave off their axillary body hair in order to conform to the aesthetic ideal. However, some do so to give their bodies a more childlike or youthful appearance, which reinforces a concept that to be feminine is to be childlike and dependent. Among some American Indians, ancient Chinese, and various modern societies, criminal status has been demonstrated by shaving off the head hair of a convicted criminal. Adultery, religious devotion, mourning, and life transitions have also been so denoted. Hair has been cut for utilitarian purposes—to make cloth, adorn dress, prevent it from becoming a source of danger in times of war. Primarily, however, it has tended to be involved with ritual or aesthetics; conformity to an aesthetic ideal seems the most likely explanation for the plucking of eyebrows, for example.

Beards and mustaches have enjoyed periods of popularity even though we now know that they collect dirt and toxic substances that affect the wearer and anyone who kisses him. A smoker's whiskers, for example, will cause him to receive "six to ten times more toxic substances into his lungs than a nonsmoker's" (Warning 1984).

In modern Western culture hair dressing seems to be motivated primarily by either adornment or belonging, although there are numerous instances when other factors assume greater importance. The same thing is true of the Western use of dress in general.

SUMMARY

Adornment, the most widely accepted theory of the origins of dress, is a universal motive for, and function of, dress. Most modern dress involves at least an element of adornment, although it may not be the primary function. Adornment or beautifying dress is a social concept based on its receiving a positive reaction from others and being worn often enough to be perceived as the norm.

There are two types of ornamental dress, corporal adornment and external. Corporal adornment actually alters the body; it is permanent and therefore involves an element of commitment. It is most common in tropical societies, where more of the body surface is exposed, and in societies with a rigid and stable social organization. Cicatrisation, tattooing, contortion, removal of body parts, and piercing are the major categories under which the types of corporal adornment fall. External adornment is temporary and can be put on or taken off at will; it is most common in clothed societies. Paint and make-up, proprioceptive, sartorial, intrinsic, and local are the categories under which the kinds of external adornments can be placed. Because hair dressing involves elements both of external and of corporal adornments, it represents a unique category of ornamental dress. In modern Western culture, adornment or belonging appear to be the primary motives for hair dressing, both of which are also the most common motives evident in most Western dress today.

2 | Utility, Convenience, and Protection

Most of the early theories of the functions of dress focused on utility, particularly protection. And protection is the first response when the average person is asked why we use dress. Actually, physical protection is unlikely to have been the first function of dress, although psychological protection could easily have been the original motivation. In most cultures utility has been and continues to be a function of dress, and in certain instances it is the primary one. Certainly most dress does have an inherent element of protection or utility.

In this chapter we shall explore some of the uses of dress for utility, convenience, and protection and analyze the efforts of human beings to order or gain greater control over their environment through dress, specifically amulets and totems. The use of dress as fertility charms, developmental aids, repellents of evil, and controlling devices in death or an afterlife will be investigated, as will dress that physically enables people to perform or to enhance their performance of specific tasks or in a nonviable environment. We shall also examine dress designed for physical protection from weather and climate, other animals, vegetation, and disease.

CONVENIENCE

It is likely that convenience as a factor in dress was less a cause than a result. Most items of dress were probably first worn for some reason other than convenience. For example, the copper-plate ornaments used by some American

Indians as sweat wipers (Swanton 1969) were probably already being worn when some practical Indian decided to wipe his sweat off with his neck piece. The modern corollary to this example is the use of a sleeve as a means of removing sweat from one's face. Certainly it is unlikely that sleeves evolved for this purpose. Rather, it is more probable that the sleeve had already been developed for some other reason. However, this use has been an asset in certain situations so that the continued use of sleeves has been reinforced.

Cowboy attire is an excellent example of this principle in dress. The Stetson—the ten-gallon hat—evolved because its many and varied uses made it more appropriate than other hat styles. Its broad brim provided protection from both sun and rain; its deep crown allowed it to be pushed well down over the head to afford extra security, especially in windy conditions. (The crown was also a water trough for man and horse.) Would a beret, baseball cap, or other hat form be quite so versatile in a cowboy's environment? Levi's were especially suitable because of the heavy, sturdy denim and because they were made with reinforced seams. A cowboy could be riding the range, taking cattle to market, or doing some other task that required him to be gone for weeks at a time. During these periods he had to rely on the clothes on his back, and he did not carry a sewing kit in his saddle bag. Thus, denim's sturdiness and durability and the strength of the Levi's reinforced seams were important assets as was the ability of denim to hide dirt. The cowboy's boots were suitable for riding and for such tasks as roping livestock: The pointed toe and wide high

Figure 2.1 Cowboys of 1904. (Library of Congress)

heel let the boot fit easily into a stirrup without easily and dangerously sliding all the way through, and the heel gave better traction on the ground; the height of the boot top afforded the cowboy increased protection from abrasions caused by stirrups, vegetation, or animals. The tight cuffs of his shirt helped to keep dust out, its reinforced seams and back yoke gave more durability, and its loose collar allowed for greater mobility and for increased protection from the elements. His bandana could be a dust mask, a protector from neck chafing or sunburn, a sweat wiper, a handkerchief, and an emergency bandage. In short, the cowboy's dress was the safest, most protective, and most appropriate form he could conveniently wear, and as a result, it has undergone almost no changes in over one hundred years!

Although convenience has generally been more a secondary than a primary motivation for clothing, utilitarian applications have almost certainly been the sole motivation for some dress. For example, the earliest pins were pieces of bone or thorns developed out of the need to have more secure closures. Staffs or canes developed as a way of providing support for an individual walking over rough terrain.

ORDERING THE ENVIRONMENT

Some dress may have evolved out of attempts by humans to bring more order to their environment and/or to control it. One primitive example of such dress is the calendar necklet worn in Micronesia. This neck string was knotted to record data about the passage of time. The watch is a modern effort to gain more order and control. For primitive people a more significant order was achieved by establishing an understanding, whether correct or not, of how the universe operates. The primitive human's conceptual ability was not as developed as ours. In fact, it more closely resembles the earliest stage of reasoning in current theories of the development of cognitive skills. Primitive understanding of cause and effect and generalizations about it would have been amusing by our standards. Since they viewed themselves as helpless creatures acted upon by superior, supernatural forces, they did not perceive that they were causative agents. Thus, rather than alter their behavior in order to change its result(s), they were concerned with changing their behavior to make it more pleasing to some superior power(s). Therefore, many early uses of dress were probably efforts to gain protection or assistance from these powerful forces. In fact, many theorists believe that the motivation for the first paint, adornment, and rudimentary clothing was

> to attract good animistic powers and to ward off evil. Costume originated in the service of magic and although this motive no longer survives among us on a conscious level, it might still reign supreme.
>
> Once magic formed a precedent for man to hang strange odds and ends around his body, other reasons for wearing costume emerged and remain very much with us. (Kemper 1977, p. 9)

This premise, which we will call the superstitious factor, can be supported by the findings of investigations into primitive art that have shown that all decorative designs have some symbolic significance (Boas 1922). This superstitious factor is universal. It is also not limited to primitive cultures. Most modern, urbane Americans, whose conceptual powers should be considerably more developed than their primitive counterparts', generally have some item(s) of dress involved in or with superstition. This dress is usually something that is always worn and without which the individual would feel "naked"—vulnerable to some element or force, such as luck, that is beyond the individual's control. For many modern adults, their wedding and/or engagement rings become associated with this factor. Thus, when they misplace or forget to wear or are forced to remove their ring(s), they experience a strong sense of foreboding. Just as with the more "primitive" lucky tattoo or scar, it is not necessarily the making of the mark or the wearing of the ring that gives one luck. Rather, having the tattoo or wearing the ring prevents the sense of foreboding we would have were we not following our own or our society's custom or habit. These modern "lucky" clothes are essentially no different from the primitive amulets, talismans, or charms, although the beliefs of primitive and modern people in the power of these articles have been at different levels of intensity. Still, both have responded to the element of hope for control that amulets offer.

Amulets

People have developed thousands of ways to use dress to avoid danger and/or to get good fortune. Such a vast number, spread throughout the world and across the ages, forces one to wonder if superstitious dress works. In fact, it does *because* it increases the individual's sense of confidence, and that confidence will enhance his or her performance. But we can only speculate about whether it works in more supernatural or magical ways. For our purposes we shall examine amulets, talismans, and charms as one category—amulets—which we define as being an object believed to be able to give the wearer good luck and/or provide protection from some danger. This power may be inherent in the object itself or may be the result of some special treatment it has received.

The alliance between the amulet and the wearer uses one of two principles of magic: (1) homeopathic magic and (2) contagious magic. In the latter some power of the amulet can enter into the wearer. Thus the Surinamese wear iron to be strong. In homeopathic magic, an attempt is made to imitate or symbolize the esteemed object in order for the wearer to become more like it or like one of its traits (Crawley 1931). Thus the Eskimo wears a rabbit's ear to enhance his hearing (*Inuit Amautik* 1980).

If the whole object cannot be worn, either a part of it or a symbol of it can be used as the amulet. When, for example, an Australian aborigine male dies, his hair is cut off and made into a girdle, which is given to his closest paternal male relative, who wears it for special occasions. Through it he gains "all the

Figure 2.2 War dress from Ghana that is covered with amulets. (Museum of Cultural History, UCLA)

warlike attributes of the dead man" (Spencer and Gillen 1969, p. 538). Small pieces of the corpse's hair may be worn as an amulet by other relatives. His fur-string girdle and head band also have his attributes and these go to a maternal male relative and to a member of another local group—which helps to maintain positive relationships between groups (ibid.).

Primitive men tend to wear amulets at or near their body orifices since openings seem more vulnerable to the entrance of evil. Placing the amulet near the area to be influenced is also a common theme. Amautik Eskimo women, for example, sew a hare's udder over their breast in order to ensure production of ample milk (*Inuit Amautik* 1980). The modern American will most likely wear amulets as jewelry.

An innumerable number and kind of objects have been worn as amulets. Many have some religious association. For instance, texts from the Bible or the Koran have been printed on paper or cloth and worn, and there are many religious symbols, such as the cross or a St. Christopher's medal, that are commonly worn even today. But most amulets have no known association with organized religions. The Nuba's leather bag containing Arabic writing to ensure his success, give him power, or protect him from the evil eye (Faris 1972) has no apparent religious significance, nor does the Aru islander's amuletic pouch holding such tabooed objects as "curiously shaped and coloured pebbles, pearls, animals' gallstones, pubic hair from women" (*CIBA Review* 1965, p. 375).

Many gemstones have been used as amulets. Pearls, for example, have been thought to ensure a long life. Among peoples who use gems in this way, beads often have the same powers, so the poor can be protected. Are modern men and women more sophisticated in their amuletic choices? To enhance their luck they wear items such as four-leaf clovers, horseshoes, shamrocks, black cats, and mustard seeds.

The wearing of amulets tends to increase in frequency and importance during times of increased vulnerability, either physical or psychological, such as pregnancy, infancy, competition, war. Thus, many a "modern" soldier has carried a special coin, photo, or letter for protection while back home a special person wore a yellow ribbon to ensure his safe return. During World War II jewelers reported numerous sales of gold and diamond lucky charms in the form of elephants with their trunks in the air in a symbolic effort to "uphold" the luck (Binder 1953). Eskimo women cover their parkas with a large number of amulets designed to protect both themselves and their children. Because they believe that an amulet's power increases with its age, they begin as children to wear amulets for their future sons (*Inuit Amautik* 1980). Competitions have a component of psychological stress. Thus, competitors often try to replicate those conditions under which they have previously won or performed well. Some tennis players, for instance, have worn the same clothes throughout an entire *series* of tournaments as long as the winning streak continues. In the same way, many football or other coaches can be spotted wearing the same outfit or part of that outfit time and time again.

Tattoos have been used as amulets. In some cultures all tattoos are permanently fixed charms to protect from a variety of dangers and to provide such attributes as strength. Sailors and fishing peoples of coastal or island areas especially have used tattoos to protect themselves from sharks and sea monsters. Since the tattoos could neither be washed away nor lost in the water, they provided the only "sure-to-stay-on" protective amulets. Body paint has also been used; the Thompson Indians used red paint over scars, fresh wounds, or sores since these areas were deemed vulnerable and needed extra protection (Teit 1928).

Totems

A totem is a material object which represents all like objects, having a special, symbiotic relationship with an individual and/or his family, clan, tribe. The totem offers protection if it is respected "by not killing it if it be an animal, and not cutting or gathering it if it be a plant" (Frazer 1935, p. 4). Interestingly, Eskimos with the same totem cannot intermarry (Birket-Smith 1971), a taboo perhaps similar to the modern proscription against the intermarriage of cousins and other close relatives. The influence of totemism on primitive dress has been significant, perhaps because the totem may be the clan's emblem. The decorative design of the totem may be so impressionistic that we would need an explanation of just what the totem is, or it may be realistic. However, not all representational art is totemic. The Nuba's representational body painting, for instance, is just for decoration (Faris 1972).

The totem has not been a significant factor in modern Western dress. However, in societies where the general population feels alienated from the greater group and identifies only with small groups such as the family or school unit, totems could gain more importance.

Magic

Clothing has often been used in magic practices, although this is no longer common in most modern societies. In many cultures it is believed that by destroying a person's clothing or by using it in black magic, an individual's physical and/or psychological self can be destroyed, injured, or controlled. Because of such dangerous potential uses of clothing, some peoples, such as the Papuans, try to keep everything that they have ever worn.

Some cultures have even buried a corpse's clothes to represent its body or counted an absent mourner as actually present if his clothing was in attendance.

FERTILITY CHARMS AND DEVELOPMENTAL AIDS

Humans have had a universal concern with finding ways to ensure their reproduction, and fertility charms are a common theme throughout the world. In fact, it seems more likely that the motivation for genital adornment has been to gain protection from infertility for women and protection from castration for men, rather than for beautification or support. The hip girdle, or loin cloth, for example, would have been an excellent way to protect the genital or anal openings from supernatural dangers as well as to attach a fertility charm near the body area associated with pregnancy. The cowrie shell has been used as a fertility charm throughout the world, and cowries or other fertility charms were—and still are—often suspended from the girdle so they might be "as near as possible to the organ their magic was supposed to stimulate" (Smith 1919, p. 153). Pregnancy symbols have also been used, like the necklaces of large, round, blue beads worn by Yuchi American Indian women (Swanton 1969), which could have been symbolic of a pregnant belly. In many cultures knots have been taboo on the dress of pregnant women since they believed the knot could cause the baby to be strangled by its umbilical cord. But other fertility charms have no obvious or apparent relationship to pregnancy. Some tattoos have been fertility charms, although precisely what they meant has not always been known even to the wearer. Some, however, are known to have an impact because of their timing. For instance, in parts of the Middle East a woman is tattooed during her menstrual period in order to induce pregnancy.

In some primitive cultures that understand the role of the male in reproduction, fertility charms are used even by men. Men of one South American people, for example, tie herbs near their genitals for potency. Hair has often been associated with virility in which case it has become a fertility charm for men. Thus, some cultures have developed laws or rules forbidding a man from shaving his beard or cutting his hair.

After conception, amulets have been used to ensure a safe pregnancy and/or delivery. In parts of Africa, pregnant and menstruating women wear veils to help keep evil spirits out (or keep in any that lurk inside them). There are few modern examples of amulets related to fertility, pregnancy, and childbirth. However, one tradition among some American ethnic groups is to prevent stretch marks in pregnancy by braiding three strands of black yarn that have been soaked in turpentine and wearing them on each wrist.

After birth, amulets are sometimes used to enhance development. For example, in one South American Indian tribe, the medicine man slashes a child's skin with a piece of fish. After a ritual blood letting, the wound is cleaned and then rubbed with pepper juice. The pain is a small price to pay for the expected benefits of being able to see and hear better and therefore be a more successful hunter (Schultz 1961). The Chinese even had a longevity robe, which was believed to lengthen the life of its wearer (Frazer 1959).

REPELLING EVIL

A more frequent theme than the positive one of enhancing development has been the negative one of repelling evil. Every evil that could befall them was attributed by most primitives to an evil spirit rather than to natural causes. Thus, attempts to prevent or cure illness or injury were generally attempts to get the evil out or appease the evil force causing the problem. Veiled peoples, such as the Tuareg, may use the veil to prevent illness-causing evil spirits from entering them through their mouths (Keenan 1977). Among American Indians scarifications were often used to prevent illness through the ritual letting of blood. In India brands and tattoos have been used to cure or relieve illness by appealing to the evil spirit causing it. Some African tribes, like the Fengu and Zulu, cut off a child's first joint on the little finger of the left hand to appease ancestral spirits and prevent sickness by giving the spirits this healthy part of the child. The Venda African tribe uses beads to represent and appease their ancestors who are the evil forces behind illnesses and other woes.

> The witchdoctors divine which of the ancestors is disquieted, point out the associated bead on its wearer and name the cure, part of which is to be propitiated by blowing upon the bead with water to "cool" it, in ritual kneeling position, with suitable incantations. (Tyrrell 1968, p. 45).

Among the Zulu and the Swazis white beads, called bones, symbolize the bones of one's ancestors. White is therefore used to appease the spirits of those ancestors (Twala 1951). Even in modern life there are some similar associations. The medical doctor and hospital staff wear white, symbolic of purity, and are thus exempted from the normal taboos pertaining to the parts of another person's body a relative stranger may see or touch (*The Pure Physician*, 1979).

Some peoples have made imperfections in their realistic designs, such as the wrong color bead in a necklace pattern, so that evil spirits can escape. That may not have been so different from the Australian aborigine who pierced his septum to protect himself from evil odors (Abbie 1970). Nose ornaments, eye make-up, earrings, and mouth tattooing have often been attempts to protect the body orifices from evil spirits just as decorated borders do for the clothing itself.

Circles and knots have often been used to bar the entrance of evil. Both have been themes in the dress associated with marriage ceremonies. Dress repellent to evil is especially prevalent during life-transition periods, such as marriage, when the individual seems more vulnerable. The Malays smear a "neutralizing" paste on the bride and groom to avert bad fortune (Hiler 1930). Many peoples try to confuse the evil spirits by having the bride and groom wear the dress of the opposite sex or of someone else. Such a procedure is also common for pregnant women and children, who are particularly vulnerable, and in times of severe natural conditions like a drought. In many eastern European cultures children wore the clothing of their parents for protection from evil. The Chinese father traditionally hung his trousers in the room where his children were sleeping so that any evil that entered the room would go into his trousers rather than into the children.

It is also thought that evil influences will pay less attention to individuals of the inferior sex, so men and boys have often been dressed in the clothing of women (Crawley 1960). In Asia some boys have also been

> hung about with demon-scaring amulets and mirrors; lucky locks would be fastened about their necks to lock them into life; and a belled anklet would be fastened round one foot to frighten away devils. Their survival was supplicated by longevity necklaces of peachwood and peachstones, and sewn into their dress were magic-protective spells, auspiciously printed on lucky red or yellow paper and auspiciously folded into lucky triangles. Their horoscopes, engraved on metal plates, were fastened on to their breasts for further security. (Binder 1953, p. 74)

Such precautions may have reflected the higher mortality rate for male than female infants.

The evil eye has been a recurrent force from which people have sought protection by two principal means: (1) covering the face to prevent the evil eye from seeing the wearer and (2) wearing things to divert its attention away from the wearer and toward the item. Wearing eye beads or something to resemble an eye was a primary way to accomplish the latter. Red, symbolic of life, has been used to protect from the evil eye; white can stop and divert it; and black neutralizes its evil power (Field 1958). Since demons cannot look at themselves, glass can also be an effective deterrent; thus many peoples of the Indian sub-continent wear mirrored dresses. (Perhaps the people of Transylvania needed to adopt such attire, although mirrored nightclothes might have had their own "bloody" dangers!)

Many peoples have used masks and headdresses to cover their faces and keep the evil eye from reaching them. This is a possible explanation of the modern custom of covering the face of the dead.

AFTERLIFE AND THE DEAD

Of course, the most vulnerable and traumatic transition period in life is death. One major afterlife consideration is identification. How, for example, will your ancestors know you if they have never seen you? One common remedy for this problem has been tattoos and ear and nose piercing. Especially in the Far East, South Pacific, and Indian subcontinent, these are believed to survive death and ease, or even enable, the journey from this life to the next. The marks can serve as easy identification for ancestors and/or deceased in-laws or for proof that the decedent truly did live on earth. While many people, including modern man, tend to attempt to deny death (we want the corpse to look as lifelike as possible), others focus their attention on ensuring a safe journey to an afterlife or in providing themselves protection from the anger of the deceased. The Ovambi tribesmen in Africa have their top two front teeth filed to create a hole by which their souls can escape should they die with their teeth clenched (Tyrrell 1968). The ancient Egyptians put scarabs on their corpses to ensure eternal life. This tradition seems unusual since the living wore scarabs to prevent their death (Binder 1953), and in the case of the deceased, the scarabs could not have lived up to their billing. Again we see an example of the power of hope.

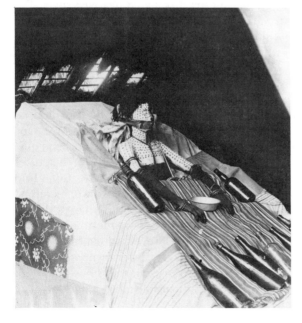

Figure 2.3 A corpse of the Congo. (Library of Congress)

But, perhaps unsurprisingly, the more universal concern of human beings has been to protect themselves from the spirit or ghost of the dead. Even more than the afterlife concerns, this very issue reinforces the hope of an afterlife. Thus, attempts—nearly always successful—are made to prevent the ghost or spirit of the deceased from returning. The Hindu corpse, after being washed, dressed, and adorned with jewels, has its big toes and its thumbs tied together to prevent his or her ghost from returning (Binder 1953). The Chinese attempt to keep the ghost away by placing jade at the corpse's orifices; the Malays plug the corpse's mouth with glass beads. Appeasing the dead by giving them a living part of oneself such as a finger joint or a tooth has been an all too common theme. While some peoples wear something of the deceased's, such as a bone or an item of dress, to serve as a reminder and/or as a protector from the dead, others give away their clothing and destroy or hide their bones.

PHYSICALLY ENABLING DRESS

Physically enabling dress refers to dress that allows the wearer to perform or enhance his or her performance of a task. The number and kinds of enabling gear developed for specific activities is nearly overwhelming. The reader will be able to think of many more than can be mentioned here. Sports-related dress often has this function. Ice skates, for example, are necessary in order to ice skate just as roller skates are for street skating. While baseball gloves are not required in order to catch a ball, they do enhance an individual's ability to catch one. Today, polarized gloves are available, so a fielder has a sun shield right in the glove to further enhance the ability to catch under certain conditions.

Much of this type of enabling dress has a protective aspect. For example, padding and helmets of various types have been developed for many contact sports. The boater wears specially soled shoes to prevent slipping and a life vest to prevent drowning, while the mountaineer wears specially soled shoes to prevent falling.

Many occupations require dress that can protect workers and/or their clothing or the product. Early examples of protective "work clothes" were clothes too worn to be used for daily wear. Other clothes could be added to provide further protection. Aprons, overalls, or coveralls protect clothing from dirt, and are sometimes useful for carrying tools or wood. Garments could also protect from other things. The pioneer's wool apron, for instance, was safer near open flame as it was less flammable than linen or cotton. However, even though such work clothing may have protected the worker's daily wear, it was often nonprotective of the individual (Bettenson 1974). Dress designed to protect the individual has been a more recent phenomenon. This could have been as simple as the aviator's silk scarf, which prevented chafing of the neck from the leather collar of the early flying jackets, or as complicated as the various kinds of breathing apparatus designed to prevent the inhalation of germs, heat, and chemicals. Those have ranged from simple cloth masks covering the nose and mouth to elaborate gas masks. Thimbles, rubber finger shields, barrier creams, and gloves are examples of hand protectors developed to protect workers employed in jobs that might be abrasive or dangerous. Eye protectors, such as goggles, glasses, and shields, and ear plugs and earmuffs have been developed for use in a variety of industries. Many workers in construction and similar work wear hard hats and steel-toed shoes to protect their heads and feet from falling objects. The firefighter wears a variety of gear that must be flame retardant, heat resistant, waterproof, warm for cold weather but not too warm for hot weather, and easy to ventilate.

Methods of Portage

Probably the most common or universal type of physically enabling dress is dress designed to enable the wearer to carry things. In fact, it is possible that the first articles of dress were tools or other utilitarian items that were being carried. Thus, for example, some primitive hunter might have inserted his scraper into his hair in order to free his hands for carrying meat or hides, and the American Indian sometimes rolled his long hair on top of his head, where it served as a quiver for his arrows.

The poncho and the skirt may have evolved from efforts to carry a blanket. The early Scotsman used his kilt as a blanket at night, and there are

Figure 2.4 Carrying baskets. (Library of Congress)

Figure 2.5 The Mexican's serape can serve as a blanket. (Library of Congress)

numerous examples of nomadic people who "wear" their blankets. In the same manner, the back skirt, a cloth worn over the buttocks, may have resulted from attempts to carry a "seat."

Peoples who carry large items on their heads have often developed special hair styles or used carrying pads to assist them in their efforts. Headbands and turbans have been used as carriers as well as a way to keep hair out of one's eyes. The Seminoles used the folds of their turbans as pockets and also carried some items in pouches suspended from their belts. Small items like coins were knotted in the corners of their neckerchiefs. A variation on the headband theme is a net bag made of string and suspended from a headband. These bags hang down the back and can be used to carry up to about fifty pounds of goods. Children can even be toted in them, and a carrying basket can be inserted into the net for small items.

An early method of carrying goods was the girdle, which was probably one of the earliest articles—perhaps even the first—of dress. The waist girdle, the belt's precursor, was not originally used to hold up a garment, although, as cloth apparel evolved, belts were useful ways to help distribute a garment's weight from the shoulders to the hips. Even today the hip or waist girdle is sometimes the only article of clothing worn, especially in hot climates. From the belt a wide assortment of articles can be hung thereby leaving the hands free for other tasks. For example, the Australian aborigine carries his boomerang, weapon, and axe in his. The early Danish wore belt boxes, "a cup or round box attached to the belt by two strap loops" (Briard 1979, p. 127). Probably these were first made of wood, but by the early Bronze Age metal ones had evolved.

Figure 2.6 Clothing for carrying a baby can be found throughout the world. This South American Indian mother carries her baby in a net shoulder bag which keeps him conveniently close to his food. (National Anthropological Archives, Smithsonian Institution)

The addition of a cloth garment such as a tunic set the stage for an exciting new method of portation. When the belt was worn over a tunic it could serve, during periods of physical activity, as an instant method of shortening the length of the tunic. The cloth would then be bunched around the waist, and the folds created in this process became pseudopockets.

The attachment of a pouch to the belt was an advancement in the evolution of the pocket. This pouch could be hung in front, like a sporran, or at the hips or back. Pouches, especially large ones, could also be worn suspended from the shoulder. This method seems to have been more popular among the American Indians, whose pouches were made from entire animal skins, gourds, hide, horn, or woven vegetation. Eventually, pouches were worn under an outer garment that had slits in it so that one could reach in the pouch. The full hips of the rococo period enabled women to have two pouches, one on each hip. The slim Empire fashions precluded such a style (Swan 1979). Both pouches and cloth folds used for carrying finally evolved into the pocket. However, it was not until the late seventeenth century that pockets began to be popular, especially in men's wear. Pockets are, to some degree, dependent on fashion. When clothing fits tightly, pockets are less suitable. Thus, for example, when menswear got tighter in the 1970s, men had to find different ways to carry wallets and other essentials. The shoulder or handbag, a return to the pouch, was one alternative, although it was rarely adopted since it had a strongly feminine association. Unfortunately, since the handbag is easier to snatch than some other carriers, such as pockets, it may become less popular in the future.

Figure 2.7 A Scottish peer with a sporran at the Coronation of King George V. (Library of Congress)

Life Maintenance

Some clothing is uniquely protective in function and origin. It is designed to enable people to perform in an environment that is incapable of supporting human life. The space suit is a good example of this. Space is a nonviable environment for human life because it lacks oxygen for respiration, an atmosphere to filter out solar rays and heat, and atmospheric pressure to prevent the gases in human blood from forming bubbles (*NASA Facts,* 1975). All space suits must address each of these deficits. However, since the various space programs have required the astronauts to perform different tasks, the space suit has had to change to fit the unique demands of each mission.

Each of the six layers of the first suit, designed for the Mercury missions, had a specific role. The cotton underwear provided ventilation by circulating cooled water; the nylon liner gave comfort; Neoprene, a coated nylon, was inflated to maintain an air pressure of five pounds per square inch; the layer of link-net nylon prevented the other layers from ballooning in vacuum conditions; the aluminized nylon layer reflected solar radiation and withstood heat (in 1970 a poncho made of this material was manufactured and marketed for the general public); and the sixth and last layer to be developed provided protection from fire. The suit was a microenvironment with systems to support all of the necessary functions of its wearer. The helmet allowed visibility while keeping radiation out; its mikes and headsets provided a means of communication. A bioinstrumentation system kept a check on blood pressure, heart action, temperature, and rate of respiration. The waste-removal systems removed metabolic heat, carbon dioxide, water vapor, and urine and fecal matter. The life-support systems provided oxygen and external pressure. Refinements in this last have increased the oxygen supply in the current system to allow a full working day and included a fan to circulate air throughout the suit and a microprocessor to monitor the condition of the suit itself. Current space suits are more durable and complex and no longer have to be custom fitted. They allow the astronaut to bend at the waist and have finger-joint flexibility.

Because of enabling dress, humans can perform tasks underwater as well as in outer space. Scuba gear provides a breathing system. The outer layer and the skin-tight inner layer of the diving suit provide warmth and keep the body dry, both of which are essential for long periods of scuba diving. New innovations in diving gear let divers go to depths as low as two thousand feet. The Wasp, for example, is a fiber-glass capsule with aluminum arms and a clear plastic helmet and a system for normal breathing and sea-level air pressure. The diver can maneuver laterally with external motorized propellers that are controlled with the toes (O'Reilly 1982). There is a wide variety of less sophisticated diving gear like that used by the Japanese women who dive for pearls and abalone. They weight themselves with stones and wear special goggles with rubber balls that force air into the eyecups so that the pressure cannot squeeze the cups into their eye sockets (Marden 1971). The snorkel is a more limited breathing system, which allows the swimmer to breathe through a tube that is held in the mouth with the other end extending above the water. Gas masks and ventilated suits enable humans to work in environments polluted with gas, chemicals, or radiation. But one hopes that we humans will not so pollute the earth with any of these that we are all forced to adopt enabling dress just to survive on our own once viable planet.

PHYSICAL PROTECTION

The use of dress for physical protection has always been universal, although the relative importance of this factor has varied. Among some peoples the protective factor has been so minimal that it could be overlooked by the casual observer. Yet at the other extreme dress has been a prerequisite to life maintenance. The ancient Greeks and Chinese believed clothing originated as protection (Hiler 1930), and many theorists have hypothesized that protection was the primary function of early clothing attempts but that this function has now become, at best, secondary. Whether protection was of primary or secondary importance in clothing's beginnings is a moot point since it continues to be an important function of some dress and is an inherent factor in most.

Probably the first circumstances one thinks of as requiring the protection of clothing are dangers from weather or climate, vegetation, or humans or other animals. These dangers, while perhaps the most obvious, may be of less importance than one might expect in both historic origins of dress and current motivations for it. However, they have been factors in its evolution and diversification.

Climate and Weather

Apparel has often been used for protection from the elements. Evidently, peoples living in cold climates have used clothing as protection more frequently than have those living in warm climates, for whom adornment seems to have been the more powerful motivator. Clothing makes relatively little difference to thermal comfort in moderate temperatures from 55 to 75°F. Thus, since human beings evolved in warm climates, where clothing was not vital to survival, it is unlikely that the earliest dress had the primary function of physical protection. Some theorists have posited that it was only when humans migrated into colder climates that the function of clothing as protection from weather assumed any significant importance; indeed, it may even have enabled such migration. But even then, this protective function may have been secondary to some other factor(s) such as adornment. The presence of the natural protection offered by the heavy body hair of early humans further reinforces the improbability of protection as the major motive in early dress. Even in the development of Western dress, protection from the elements seems of minor importance when we consider the relatively late invention of seasonal indoor dress and its continuance despite its having been rendered largely unnecessary, or even inappropriate, by modern technology. And men's wear is typically too heavy for summer while women's is too light for winter. However, nontemperate climates did lead to two distinct styles of dress: the draped style for warm climates and the tailored style for cold ones.

The human body produces body heat internally through the process of metabolism, which is the cellular combustion of food. But the body also gets heat and removes it from the body surface through convection, conduction, and radiation. Both convection and conduction involve the transfer of heat from the body to the air around it; convection occurs when the air is moving, and conduction when it is still. Radiation depends on the emission of energy; it cools, as does convection, when the air temperature is lower than the body temperature. The body also controls its internal temperature by dilating or constricting the blood vessels near the skin surface. This can significantly alter the amount of blood circulating. When the vessels are dilated, more blood flows near the surface, and if the air temperature is lower than the body temperature, the body temperature will be lowered. One of the main ways the body has to promote cooling is evaporation, which sweating promotes.

People have varied in their physiological and psychological ability to cope with extreme weather conditions. There are thermostatic differences in people; as a human ages his or her thermostat deteriorates in both effectiveness and efficiency. Women are more resistant to temperature extremes than are men; this may reflect a better functioning thermostat or their greater amount of fatty tissue, which serves as an insulating layer. Thermostatic differences may also result from habituation since research has found that a body accustomed to being well covered is in fact more sensitive to the cold. Thus, the advice of such sages as Plato and Ben Franklin that one go barefooted, bareheaded, or even bareskinned for better health may have been accurate.

Different metabolic rates also influence the body's thermostatic ability. The Eskimos have a high rate of metabolism, which produces a larger amount of heat in their bodies. This increased rate may be a result of their diet, which is high in both fat and protein and/or their caloric intake, which is double that of the average American (Coon, Garn, and Birdsell 1972). The Australian aborigines must withstand extreme temperature fluctuations; they have a low metabolic rate as well as low body temperature, pulse, respiration rate, and blood pressure (Wulsin 1949).

Peoples of the cold Arctic Circle region tend to have a body structure adapted for their climatic conditions, with a thick-set, short trunk and short appendages so that the least amount of skin surface is exposed to external air in proportion to volume and weight (Coon, Garn, and Birdsell 1972). Physical differences may also be involved in the case of the Feugians and other such peoples who have worn little or no clothing while living in extremely harsh climates. However, the grease and paint with which they purportedly covered their bodies would have provided excellent protection from their specific

Figure 2.8 Eskimos. (The estate of Dr. Cook, courtesy of Janet Vetter)

weather problems. Such a possibility seems more likely when one considers the declining health sometimes experienced by such peoples after their acceptance of "civilized" clothing forms.

COLD. Tailored clothing is most effective in cold climates since it provides less space for chilled air to enter, keeps the air next to the skin warm, and almost gives a "tropical microclimate near the skin" (Renbourn 1972, p. 221). However, in warm climates this advantage becomes a drawback. Thus, one might assume that tailored clothing was developed for protection by peoples of cold climates. The evidence supports this assumption.

The United States military clothing recommendations for cold zones notes that in the coldest zone (−30°F or below), clothing is insufficient protection from the cold. Constant physical activity is also needed in order to maintain high body-heat production. Thus, a high-caloric diet is necessary to provide energy for the activity as is a well-insulated shelter to provide a place to rest. Until an artificial heat source can be provided in the clothing, such temperatures prevent the use of clothing as the *sole* protection from the extreme cold (Siple 1949).

However, for climates that are less cold, dress can provide sufficient protection and some clothing and clothing materials have been—and still are—used specifically for protection from conditions of cold. Such dress often employs the insulating qualities of a still layer of air, which can be achieved by using two or more layers of fabric so that air can be trapped between the layers or by trapping air in loosely woven fibers, as in thermal underwear. The body warms the layer of still air, which thereby becomes an insulating layer. Fur, feathers, rough cloth, and clean cloth all work on roughly the same principle. Many peoples have developed winter clothing that uses these principles. The Paiutes, for example, turned strips of rabbit skin fur side in for their warm robes (an adult male's needed about one hundred skins) (Maxwell 1978).

The Eskimo has developed a clothing style uniquely suited to the climate and operating on these same principles of insulation. Two layers of loosely fitting fur are used rather than one thicker layer. This allows a layer of warm air to form between the skin and the first layer of clothing and permits efficient evaporation of perspiration. For maximum warmth the inner layer is worn fur side in while the outer layer is worn fur side out. The winter parka is usually made from three skins—one for the front, one for the back, and one for the two sleeves. Although it fits loosely, it is pulled tight at the waist to keep the cold air out and the warm air in. The parka is usually hooded since a hood can most effectively cover the back of the neck and ears, which is important as up to 50 percent of one's body heat can be lost through the head. Fur trousers, mittens, stockings, and boots are worn; grass may be stuffed into the boots for greater warmth. Caribou skin is used only for the warmest clothing; it is too hot in 0°F or above (Gubser 1965). Since the hollow hairs of the caribou will freeze any moisture or moisture vapor that touches them, it is never worn around the neck (Coon 1971). For midwinter sealing, hunters wear four layers of caribou fur on their feet (Maxwell 1978). In spring, temperatures rise with the sun so there may be considerable fluctuation in temperature during the day. Thus,

> selection of clothing is more difficult, especially footwear. In the early morning of a typical spring day, the temperature may be well below 0°F. If a hunter plans to leave the house long before the sun rises, he usually puts on a pair of all-caribou winter boots. By the early afternoon the sun may have warmed up the air and the snow so much that his boots become wet with sweat and melted snow. Then in the evening the temperature drops and his outer boots freeze. (Gubser 1965, p. 237)

The Eskimos are aware of the dangers of dampness, as is evident in the care they take to ensure that when they put their dress on, it is completely dry. The Eskimo kaiak man must constantly deal both with cold and water. Water, a good conductor of heat, can reduce body heat more than thirty times as fast as air at the same temperature can. Thus, water tightness is a crucial consideration for the kaiaker, who wears an akuilisak, a half jacket of dehaired watertight skin that has been sewn with sinews, has a drawstring bottom, and is held up by suspenders or straps. To his arms he lashes loose skins for sleeves, and he wears water-tight mittens (Nansen 1893). The sea-mammal gut used for waterproofing coats is so effective that should the Eskimo fall in the water and drown, he will probably die dry. The Aleut also was concerned with cold, wet conditions. He wore a wet-weather dress made from the skin of a whale's tongue or a halibut's bladder. For colder weather his dress was of tufted puffin skin (Gunther 1972).

Figure 2.9 Nunivak Eskimos wearing waterproof parkas. (Library of Congress)

For the modern Eskimo the protective aspect of clothing has become a secondary function. Many are exchanging their traditional garb for less protective attire that has the status of being "store bought" and is consistent with typical American fashion.

Snow has been a factor of climate with which the Eskimo has had to contend. Snow goggles made from wood or walrus ivory had narrow slits at the eyes to keep out the glare from the sun's reflection on the snow. In spite of this, snow blindness was not uncommon (Krieger 1928). The snowshoe was used by the Eskimos and other North American Indians who wore moccasins. Although the ski gives greater speed with less effort, it never became popular among the peoples of North America. But when "equipped with the proper type of snowshoe, a hunter could jog along over deep snow for hours, easily keeping pace with a floundering caribou" (Maxwell 1978, p. 340). Moccasins

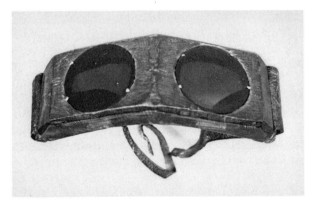

Figure 2.10 The explorer, Dr. Cook, studied Eskimo dress and developed this version of their snow goggles. (Janet Vetter)

Figure 2.11 Snow shoes are still used in sport and hunting. (Library of Congress)

developed in areas with cold climates and uneven terrain. They were rarely worn in hot or rainy areas. These most noted items of Indian attire were quickly adopted for use by the settlers, and the General Court of Massachusetts even ordered five hundred pairs each of snowshoes and moccasins for use in frontier areas. This type of footwear has continued to be used in occupations such as lumbering (Hallowell 1972). In the 1850s, west-bound pioneers commonly bought moccasins from the Indians or traded for them. Shoes were a luxury worn only for special events, and even then they were often carried to the occasion. Barefoot pioneer children carried a piece of heated clapboard so that when

> they could walk no further, they could warm their feet on the board.... Even when shoes were worn, additional protection was often needed. On occasion, to keep the dry snow out of the shoes, boys and girls drew a stocking leg or tubular piece of cloth over the ankle and the top of the shoe. (Feightner 1977, p. 56)

Other peoples, such as the Aymara Indians of the Andes, carry their shoes or sandals when traversing rough or stony terrain that might damage them. This suggests that protection is not their primary reason for wearing shoes.

Mittens were worn by many of the North American Indians, who often attached them to a string around the neck so that they would not be lost if they were briefly removed. In the United States today this practice is continued by the wise parent of the young child. Some hunters carried a muff to keep their hands warm while allowing quick freedom of the hands in order to shoot their bow (Driver 1970). Muffs have been used by men and women in many cultures and eras.

Head coverings have been particularly important in cold areas, especially at night when the body temperature naturally lowers. Thus, nightcaps were an asset in the era before central heating, and men and woman properly wore hats or wigs indoors to keep their heads warm.

MODERATE COLD AND DAMPNESS. The Scotsman had to consider cold and wet as he trudged over the moors covered with wet heather. The kilt gave him better protection than trousers would have since the wet trousers flapping about his ankles would have been unhealthy as well as uncomfortable. In climates with moderate cold combined with fairly constant dampness, it is important to prevent heat loss and keep the body as dry as possible. The Pacific Northwest American Indians wore flared rain capes of tightly woven shredded cedar bark that hung below the elbow and were water repellent. Wool or human hair were sometimes interwoven. A fur neckband helped to prevent chafing. Because of the constant dampness they wore no footwear. The Japanese, in a similar climate, have developed wooden clogs that are flat on the top and sole and rest on two transverse cleats sufficiently high to keep the foot above the mud. The wooden clogs worn in parts of western Europe have also been quite effective at keeping feet warm and dry in rainy 60°F weather.

Feathers have been commonly used in rainwear among diverse groups from the South Pacific to the East Coast American Indians. Fringed buckskin was also effective since the fringes helped to keep the bottom layers dryer and promoted the rapid run-off of the water. Rainwear from abas to waxed cloth, tarred cloth, rubberized cloth, and oilskin has been developed for cold, damp climates as have waterproof umbrellas and galoshes. Rain-resistant fabrics,

Figure 2.12 The Japanese peasant's rain gear. (Library of Congress)

which have an inherent resistance to the penetration of water; rain-repellent cloth, which has a finish that repels water; and waterproof cloth have been other developments in efforts to keep dry and warm. Unfortunately, most of these still allow water to enter through the seams; only the Eskimos have been able to develop a method of stopping this seepage.

The most universal rain gear has been the hat. The only hatless rainy areas are in forests, where the trees provide protection and a hat with a broad protective brim would get in the way of easy mobility. Among American Indians the Pacific Northwest tribes, such as the Utes and the Tlingits, wore basket hats, which they needed for the frequent rain; and the subarctic tribes had hoods (Krieger 1928), which were more effective in cold weather since the back of the neck, which lets out a lot of body heat, was kept warm. Basket hats, broad-brimmed straw hats, conical hats of bamboo and grasses, coonskin caps, Stetsons, and hoods are all types of headgear designed to afford protection from rain. In a real sense, they are wearable umbrellas. Some peoples have converted their normal hats into rain gear; the Koreans did this by adding a waterproof layer over the hat.

HEAT. Human nakedness is natural; "man gets his highest comfort when naturally warm environmental air is freely playing over and on his skin" (Dearborn 1918, p. 5). The human body has been able to make some physiological adaptations to heat. People living in hot climates have been found to sweat more, to have a lower salt content in their sweat and urine, and to have the skin-surface blood vessels dilate so that more blood circulates (Roach and Eicher 1973). All of these factors would enable more effective coping with the heat. Peoples such as the Saharan Tuareg, the Somali of the Horn of Africa, and the Australian aborigines, living in hot, dry climates, tend to be skinny with short bodies and long arms and legs and narrow hands and feet. Thus, they have a larger skin surface area in proportion to their volume and weight. And, since 50 percent of the body's blood is in the legs at any one time, long, thin legs make a good coolant area (Coon, Garn and Birdsell 1972).

Certainly it may be speculated that the ideal clothing in hot, humid, tropical climates may be little or none, as exemplified by the Panare people of Guiana—at most, the Panares may wear a necklace or hair ornament. However, since the evaporation of sweat is a major problem in such a climate, a single layer of thin fabric has sometimes been recommended to help absorb sweat and create air currents that promote evaporation (Bates 1952). In the tropical forests of South America domestic cotton and bark cloth are used for clothing in a manner consistent with this recommendation.

In the desert, where there is an extreme difference between the heat of the day and the cold of the night, layers of clothing, which can be easily reduced or multiplied, may be the best protection. In early desert cultures, clothing was brief; this may have reflected the shortage of textiles, low economic status, or the infrequency of cultural contact with peoples of colder climates (Wulsin 1949). For work, it was common to strip (Bates 1952). Today

Figure 2.13 Panare women. (National Anthropological Archives, Smithsonian Institution)

a robe worn without underwear would appear to be the best answer for desert clothing. Women's dresses and skirts are basically more suited to desert wear than trousers. The next best approach would seem to be the use of a short, loose jacket and loose trousers suspended rather than belted. By being kept loose, these garments should have some of the benefits of the robe. (Siple 1949, p. 401)

North African nomads have found a dress style well suited to their desert environment. The combination of a long, loose, tentlike tunic of wool or cotton and a thick wool robe that covers the arms and legs creates air currents as they move, thus allowing evaporation while maintaining a somewhat moist environ-

Figure 2.14 Bedouin men. (Library of Congress)

ment. No underwear is worn as this would interfere with the process. The thickness acts as an insulator, and the sun's heat is absorbed away from the body; the dark colors allow the radiant heat to be absorbed at the surface. Thick-soled sandals protect the soles of the feet from the extreme heat of the sun and sand. The turban protects the head from solar radiation and heat while being constructed in such a manner that it stays on without worry even in the highest of winds; the more modern pith helmet has these same benefits (Siple 1949). The Bedouins wear a white head cloth, which gives them protection from the sun and wind. "In a sandstorm it can be wrapped around the head and held in the teeth for protection" (Fertile-Bishop and Gilliam 1981, p. 24).

SUN. Headgear has often been used for protection from the sun. The ancients believed in the benefits of sun to all the body parts except the head. Thus, travelers wore wide-brimmed hats, and the theater goers of ancient Rome wore straw hats or took canopies to the amphitheaters. The Roman helmet had a lining of sponge or felt, which could be wet down to cool the head. It has been suggested (Renbourn 1972) that the protection this gave from the sun and the heat might even explain the success of the Roman armies. Hats or other sun-protective headgear have been worn, and still are, by many peoples and can cut the glare from water or snow as well. The sunbonnet of the American pioneer women gave protection from the sun, the dust, and the wind. The ruffle at the back of the neck kept the sun off the neck and the dust out of the back of the clothes; ties kept the bonnet on in the wind. Other examples of the use of headgear for protection from the sun are the umbrella hat, used in much of the Orient; basket or feather sun visors; scarves; and spine cloths, which are coverings for the spine or back of the neck. Among modern developments to aid in keeping a cool head is a safari hat with a solar-powered fan in it. The interior headband is terry cloth, to wet for greater coolness through evaporation.

Parasols have been used for protection from the sun in such divergent geographic areas as the Indian subcontinent and the southern United States. The Japanese have also used the fan to keep cool, and that device has also provided protection from rain, the stimulation of a toy, and a means of communication. Body paint and eye make-up have also been sun protectors. Some modern sportsmen wear dark "paint" around the eyes for protection from solar glare when they cannot use sunglasses to accomplish the same thing. The Tibetans have eyescreens that look like sunglasses but have no lenses and are made of woven yak hair (Shalleck 1962), and some North American Indian tribes developed rawhide eye shields. In some cultures, solar protection has been so complete that rickets has increased. Upper-class women of India and China, who stayed indoors as much as possible to protect themselves from the sun, suffered from a high rate of rickets.

But not all peoples of the world appear to have developed devices to protect them from the sun. For instance, the Marquesan Islanders of the Pacific seem to have none. In fact, in much of the tropics of Africa, the Americas, and the South Pacific, primitives who had to deal with dampness as well as heat wore little or no clothing. Their nudity was an asset, as their skin could dry more quickly in the sun than clothing could. An application of coconut or another oil could easily help to keep the rain off the skin, but only if the skin was bare of fabric. If a bark-cloth outfit was worn, oil was rubbed into it to protect it from rain and water. Clothing worn under such conditions might be of a temporary form designed only for brief protection, such as the palm frond poncho of New Guinea or the ti leaf cape of Hawaii.

Animals

Protection from animals other than humans seems of less importance in dress than protection from other humans. Knight Dunlap (1928) presented the only theory of any significance to the contrary; he suggested that clothing originated as an attempt to protect people from animals, more specifically, insects. He theorized that early attachments to the body moved and thus acted as "fly chasers." But remembering the limited power of reasoning of primitive people, we must assume that such reasoning was too abstract for their cognitive skills. Only after donning clothing, which acted as a fly chaser, would early humans have connected such moving attachments to successful fly chasing.

Certainly the mucous membranes of the perineal region are especially in need of such protection because of their relatively high temperature and sebaceous nature. Thus, intercrural strings of leaves suspended from girdles or hip cords would have been an asset in the battle against insects (Crawley 1931). And any body cover offers an inherent degree of protection from insects. Pompoms and tassels might be as effective a "fly chaser" as a cow's tail, but it is unlikely that either the tail or the pompom first existed for this purpose. However, throughout much of Africa, individuals of high status have adopted the cow's tail to keep insects away. Many peoples have covered their hair with a thick layer of mud to act as an insecticide while others have applied different mixtures of materials such as cattle dung and urucu to kill their head lice. When it was discovered that head lice carried typhus, soldiers had to cut their hair quite short to reduce the incidence of lice infestations (Fisher 1973). The body louse was the most annoying insect for the Eskimo, who developed a back scratcher "louse trap." To their long scratch stick they would attach a tuft of bear hair, which served as a louse lure.

Since many primitive people had weapons suitable only for hand-to-hand combat, they had to be able to get near to any enemy or prey. Thus, they developed camouflage. Paints and tattoos were commonly used, as were natural materials such as a wolf skin. Some American Indians wore a wolf skin when hunting bison since the bison was not afraid of the wolf. Boots and leggings provided hunters some defense from the bites of snakes or other animals.

There are, however, relatively few articles of dress used today for protection from animals. Insect repellents are a refinement of primitive attempts, and

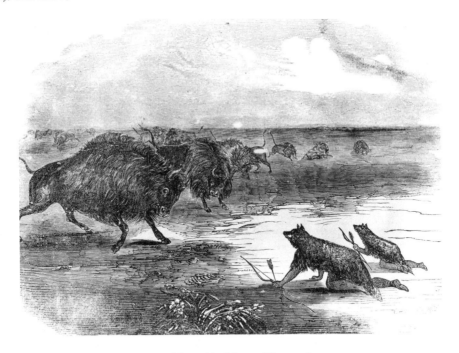

Figure 2.15   Indian buffalo hunters of the prairie. (Library of Congress)

the beekeeper is quite safe behind the gauzelike veil. But the animal from which the human has been and continues to be most in need of protection is the human. The time of greatest danger is that of war, and humans have spent considerable time and effort in devising forms of battle dress that afford some protection from a foe or provide an edge in destroying him. This could be as simple as the Timucua Indians' practice of keeping their nails quite long and sharp to use as weapons to wound and blind their foes; or it can be as complex as armor.

Masks or make-up have been used by many peoples in an effort to terrify their enemies. Hiler (1930) distinguished two types of "war paint": (1) *Reizschmuck*, which serves to excite the wearer, and (2) *Schreckschmuck*, which serves to frighten the observer. Reizschmuck may have been the more important element, but the effect on the wearer had to be on the subconscious level since any awareness would have defeated the purpose. The Nubas appear to have used both types in their body painting; they wore black paint to make themselves look bigger and thus frighten their enemy, and they wore sacred mud, which gave them confidence since it was supposed to ward off their opponent's blows in stick and bracelet fights (Faris 1971). Melanesian tribesmen and tribes of the Mato Grosso outlined their ribs in white clay so they would appear to be death or an army of the dead as they relentlessly approached their enemy. A later adaptation of this custom may have been the

Figure 2.16 African warriors painted to frighten their enemies. (Library of Congress)

Figure 2.17 The Masai warriors' lion mane headdress was both Reizschmuck and Schreckshmuck. (Library of Congress)

braiding on the Hussar's and other military jackets, which could serve as an outline of the ribs.

Some American Indians, including the Blackfoot, Crow, and Omaha, decorated their war dress with weasel skins because they "considered the weasel to be the most aggressive and . . . destructive animal on the plains—for its size" (Ewers 1977, p. 261). Similarly, one African tribe decorated their elephant- or buffalo-hide war helmets "with the jawbones of men, killed by them in battle" (Sieber 1972, p. 61). Both of these practices are examples of Reizschmuck.

Masks, skull deformations, and some kinds of facial painting and tattooing are generally Schreckschmuck, used to inspire terror. For this reason many tribes forbid women to use masks to avoid instilling fear of women in their children. The Matto Grosso and Caraja Indians of Brazil do not allow their women even to know anything about the masks as the tribesmen consider that the women, who are inferior to men, talk too much. Generally, masks are used more to scare spirits than to scare people.

Armor has been designed in a wide variety of forms and materials, from the necklace serving as a breastplate or upper-chest protector to magic armor reminiscent of the emperor's new clothes. The Sioux, for example, believed that a cotton war shirt could be treated with incantations making it invulnerable to bullets. The magic power of a totem or of a blessing has also been used for armor. Because the head is the body part most vulnerable to fatal wounds the most basic piece of armor is the helmet. But a greater variety of armor has been found in body armor. Tough hides from animals such as the moose or elephant, large woolen pads, and bark belts, which could be thrown over the shoulder, are all examples of simple body armor.

Scale armor, made by attaching small plates of metal to a garment, was one of the first forms of body armor and has been one of the most common. The ancient Egyptians sewed buttonlike objects on their soldiers' upper garments to form one of the earliest examples of scale armor. Even "though the materials have changed from bronze and iron to highly sophisticated plastics and alloys, the basic system is still in use in the bulletproof . . . 'flak jackets' . . . of the combat infantryman" of today (Wilkinson 1970, p. 6). However, scale armor is limited because of its relatively heavy weight, its inability to conform to the body enough to cover all the vulnerable body parts, and its limited flexibility.

Mail of metal ring(s) or chains was a better full-body protector for swords, daggers, arrows, bolts, and light lances striking with less than full force. "Indeed, no better testimony is needed as to its merits than the fact that for at least two thousand years it was worn constantly and in large numbers, in spite of . . . its average price of purchase . . . [being] greater than that of any other type of armor" (Dean 1920, p. 30). However, although it was somewhat more flexible than scale armor, it had to be worn over heavy padding to protect the body from the shock of blows. This reduced its flexibility, increased its weight, and made it uncomfortable because its entire weight rested on the shoulders. Mail was also more dangerous if one was wounded since fragments of the broken links could enter the wound adding to the possibility of infection.

The Eskimo sewed ivory sticks together to form a primitive plate armor. The Eskimo's "cousin," the Tlingit, plated hides with Chinese coins and reinforced the whole affair with slats. Another Indian group, the Chukchis, made a hoop armor from strips of baleen tied together with whalebone over the joints. In spite of its awkward appearance, it was somewhat flexible. All of these are examples of plate armor, which was the type of armor used by the knights of the Middle Ages. When armor changed from link to plate in the fourteenth and fifteenth centuries, men's clothing was designed as a padding for the armor. Crawford (1940) noted that this was the first time marked sex differences appeared in European dress. She hypothesized that armor thus forms the basis of the evolution of modern male attire.

Plate armor was more of a hindrance than an asset, as King James I noted when he called it an excellent invention since "it not only saves the life of the wearer but hinders him from doing hurt to anyone else" (Anspach 1969, p. 61). When an armored knight fell, getting up was difficult, if not impossible. His movements, although slowed by the heaviness of his attire (a typical suit weighed about 55 pounds, and tilting armor weighed up to 125 pounds), were a danger to himself since his visibility was severely limited. Many a knight swooned from the heat of his portable oven, and his profuse sweating may well have accelerated the rusting of his suit. The surcoat, introduced as an effort to keep the armor dry, increased the already enormous weight. Fortunately for the common soldier, only the wealthy could afford a suit of armor. By the sixteenth century, armor was becoming more decorated, which made it less effective. At the same time, the use of firearms was increasing. Both of these changes signaled the decline of armor.

Straps and bracelets have provided protection and support, especially for warriors using bows. Skins wrapped around the forearm can create a simple shield, and the Scots, when engaged in battle, wrapped their tartans around their arm for the same purpose. In parts of Africa weapons have dual functions. Sticks and umbrellas, for example, are weapons to those trained in stick fighting.

Uniforms have even been painted on the body to designate rank and faction; these could easily be changed so that an enemy would be unable to copy them and thereby infiltrate the lines. Uniforms may function as Reizschmuck or Schreckschmuck by employing bright colors and tall hats. The Spartans' use of red battle dress hid blood stains, a fact that may have served to bolster the Spartan and frighten his enemy. When Napoleon found that the white trousers of his guards showed blood too easily, he changed the color to blue. In World War I German soldiers were terrified by the soldiers of the Scottish regiments who, preceded by a strange noise (the bagpipes), would suddenly appear as skirted giants (Binder 1953). Humans tend to fear that which is alien.

Early soldiers represented competing tribes or feudal estates and wore their regular dress. Not until one monarch rose to take power over an entire country did uniforms develop. A monarch needed an instrument of force to demonstrate his power since he was a more distant authority figure than a

Figure 2.18 Kikuyu men carrying umbrellas and sticks, which can serve as weapons. (Library of Congress)

feudal lord had been; the uniform became the visual symbol of his force. The more attractive, comfortable, and sturdy the uniform, the more positive an association was made with the military as a profession. As Napoleon noted, soldiers must love soldiering and need to gain a sense of honor from their duties, "which is why handsome uniforms are so useful" (Schick 1978, p. 129). As the armies became larger, order became more difficult to maintain so standardization of military dress became an important asset. During times of war, the cost of the military increased. Uniforms wore out quickly and their colors faded and became muted by layers of soil. Distinguishing the enemy by color was less effective than distinguishing them by some other sign, such as the shape of headgear (ibid.).

It was not until the late nineteenth century in England that uniforms were examined with any scientific intent of creating a better design. This research resulted in the British soldier being, by the start of World War I, "the most sensibly dressed and accoutred fighting man in Europe" (ibid., p. 156).

Modern soldiers receive relatively little protection from their uniforms. Modern warfare's sophisticated weaponry is not easy to defend against. They do get some protection from items such as gas masks, bullet-proof vests, and camouflage, and specialized equipment is sometimes designed for specific missions or tasks. Improvements on traditional gear are constantly being made. In the early 1980s, for example, the United States army traded in its traditional steel helmet for a helmet that looks more like the German helmet of World War I. The new helmet is made of resin and Kevlar, which is more protective than steel, and its shape provides added protection to the neck and temples. Still, many soldiers were unhappy with the change because the new helmet did not seem as versatile as the old, which had been successfully used as a cooking pot, bucket, wash tub, seat, hammer, and chock. But the most important aspect of the modern uniform is probably its impact on morale, its ability to impress the enemy and give pride and courage to its wearer. While modern dress uniforms may satisfactorily address the issue of morale, the day uniforms are less appropriate. The government is currently making an effort to change this situation.

Modern men and women are also developing street-wear fashions to protect themselves from other people. Bullet- and knife-proof garments have been styled to resemble ordinary fashions. Some are bullet proofed with panels of Kevlar 29 that can withstand a large handgun or small rifle shot from as close as fifteen feet. One manufacturer offered a million-dollar insurance policy to each purchaser, payable if the wearer was injured by a weapon under the guaranteed conditions. The Japanese are developing a fabric to protect the human body from radiation after the detonation of nuclear warheads. They hope that the fabric will be capable of absorbing high-speed neutrons if they have already been slowed down by, for example, the walls of a nuclear shelter. Without such a fabric, nuclear shelters would be unable to protect the body from neutron rays. It is discomfortingly conceivable that protection from other humans could become the primary motivation for dress in the future.

Vegetation and Terrain

As early humans foraged through rough terrain, their bodies were subject to scrapes and abrasions from sharp vegetation or rocks. It is likely that some clothing developed out of an effort to gain protection from vegetation or terrain. For example, all of the American Indians who were horsemen had leggings, which were worn primarily for traveling. The Tehuelche Indians of Patagonia made their leggings from the skin of a horse's leg. When a tribe had large animal skins available to it, leg skins were frequently used in this manner. But most early leggings were made by wrapping the leg with leather strips that were suspended from a belt or hip girdle. Leather is one of the few natural materials able to withstand the abrasion and pull of shrubs and bushes. The west-bound American pioneers discovered that their clothing did not hold up well as they walked through terrain thick with sage, prickly pear, and other vegetation. Buckskin leggings and moccasins became items to be treasured. Those unable to obtain them tried to protect their clothes in other ways. Men tucked their trouser legs into their boots; women raised their skirts, even pulling them up as high as their knees. Those whose shoes had worn out and were unable to get moccasin replacements had to bind their feet with cloth

Figure 2.19 The Pueblo Indians protectively wrapped their legs. (Library of Congress)

Figure 2.20 The cowboy's chaps protect his legs from abrasions from vegetation he might brush against as he rides. (Library of Congress)

wrapped to a sufficient thickness to protect the feet from the terrain and the vegetation.

Shoes have been the most obvious clothing used to provide protection from rough vegetation and terrain. Examples of sandals or shoes have been found in Syrian artifacts from about 3000 B.C. and in Egyptian ones from 1450 B.C., although the typical person probably did not wear shoes at that time. Prehistoric hunters probably used animal hides for shoes, and leather has continued to be a popular choice. Remnants of leather shoes dating from the Bronze Age have been found in the bogs of Denmark. But shoe construction has certainly not been limited to leather. In fact, there are very few solid materials that have not been used, including wood, metal, fibers, and synthetics such as plastic. However, leather has been the most universal and common material.

Aside from the wearing of shoes, protection from vegetation and terrain is no longer a significant function of dress to most urban dwellers.

Disease

Clothing has created an environmental hazard to the body, causing problems ranging from body odor to epidemics. That is because it has reduced the surface of skin open to the elements and hindered good ventilation and evaporation. But clothing has also been used to assist humans in their fight against disease. That fight has been going on for a long time. One of the earliest associations between dress and disease was the use of oil, clay, or paint for the prevention or treatment of insect bites. The Australian and Tasmanian aborigines, for example, covered themselves with a mixture of red ocher, earth or clay, and fat or fish grease as protection from biting flies and mosquitoes and to prevent their generation. In Africa the Nubas have used oil to treat assorted insect bites as well as wounds and swellings (Faris 1972). Other tribes used body paint. In the Americas tribes have used various oils, grease, or oil- or grease-based solutions to keep insects away.

There are, in fact, a wide variety of materials that have been worn on or applied to the body for curative purposes. For example, the Indians tied the bone of a bat to their ankles to treat rheumatism, and wounds were healed by wearing a peacock's feather. Wearing eelskin has been a European treatment for rheumatism. During the Renaissance fossilized fish teeth were worn to cure dropsy, and rings made from special gold coins were worn to prevent cramps. The Irish treated sprains by wearing a black wool thread with nine knots tied in it. Carnelians and sapphires have been worn to prevent or cure eye disease, amber to prevent goiters, coral to cure dermatological problems.

Saffron and indigo dyes have been used for centuries to inhibit the "spontaneous generation of vermin" in clothes, where the body louse, for example, is fond of breeding in folds and seams (Renbourn 1972, p. 16). Such inhibition was an important preventive measure against certain diseases, including typhus.

The aqueous infusion of the [henna] leaves applied to the external surfaces of the body was used as a prophylactic against certain skin diseases which are quite prevalent in the eastern tropical and semi-tropical countries. Another property of this infusion was said to be that of producing a cooling sensation to the part applied, acting gently on the sweat-glands, reducing their activity, benefiting both health and comfort. The root of the henna plant was upheld as a specific in leprosy and also in drying up certain ulcers of the mouth and gums. (Field 1958, p. 107).

The possibility of clothing harboring infection has been recognized by many peoples. Among some American Indians, for example, clothing of a critically ill person was burned. If the illness was less severe, the clothes were merely cleaned with clay or soil. Many peoples have practiced burning the clothes of those whose illness has resulted in their death. Modern knowledge of the communication of disease has led us to be more aware of the part clothing plays. But if we have had contact with a specific disease and are uncertain as to how it is spread, we are apt to simply wash the clothes we were wearing at the time. Special efforts are made in certain situations by modern medical person-nel at keeping their clothing as clean (sterile) as possible so that they will not risk adding additional infection to a patient, and masks are worn in the modern medical fight against infection.

While the use of dress to limit conception has a long history, condoms were originally associated with the control of infection when Fallopius in-vented them in the mid-sixteenth century. His condom, a linen sheath that was worn under the prepuce, was used by the wealthy as a protection against venereal diseases. By the end of the eighteenth century, condoms were widely available. The condom continues to have a role in the control of venereal infection and even appears helpful in preventing the spread of AIDS. It is also recommended for any woman who has multiple sex partners as a way to decrease the possibility of her developing an allergic reaction to male semen. Other clothing may play a role in reproduction. For example, when the scro-tum is warmer than normal, sperm production decreases. Therefore, it is possible that wearing tight-fitting garments such as briefs or jock straps could temporarily impair a man's fertility. This possibility has led to the develop-ment of briefs with a pouch to provide a looser fit. There is also evidence that some of the chemicals in polyester may inhibit sperm production. (Benedict 1982)

Undergarments can protect the skin from irritating, coarse outerwear. This is especially important at the openings of the garments, where chafing is most apt to occur. Preventing or reducing abrasions on the skin helps to de-crease infections, especially of the skin.

Splints, slings, casts, support hose, support bandages, braces for limbs, braces for teeth, canes, false teeth, glasses, contact lenses, hearing aids, voice boxes, pacemakers, monitoring devices, hospital gowns, surgical and hospital gowns, health IDs, garlic-clove neck pendants, Kleenex and handkerchiefs, hair nets, and a variety of diapers and rubber pants are all examples of dress currently used for medical reasons. While many of these have a long history of use, current applications and refinements are continually making them more effective or enlarging their scope of usefulness. For instance, plaster casts can now be used to correct most leg or feet nonalignments in infants as well as to immobilize limbs with broken bones or sprains. However, some of these clothes may be used more for reasons of superstition or custom than of science. For example, Roth (1957) found that masks, gowns, rubber gloves, and hair coverings were worn least frequently by the highest tier of hospital personnel (doctors), and the frequency increased with each lower level. Thus, those most aware of the actual protectiveness of these garments were the least likely to wear them.

SUMMARY

Convenience as a factor in dress was probably less a cause for dress than a result of it. But some dress probably evolved out of the attempts by humans to bring more order to their environment and control over it. The earliest efforts to do this were probably attempts to gain protection from, or the assistance of, those forces to which humans attributed control of the universe. Even modern people usually have some item(s) of dress involved with superstition or the supernatural. Such totems, amulets, or charms are used for a variety of things, such as to ensure fertility or to repel evil.

Physically enabling dress allows the wearer to perform or to enhance his or her performance of a task. Much sports-related and occupational dress is enabling. But the most universal kind of physically enabling dress is dress designed for carrying tools, babies, food, and so on. Some enabling dress permits humans to perform in an environment, such as outer space, which is not capable of supporting human life.

The primary motivation for utility of dress is dress designed to physically protect the wearer. While early theorists believed that clothing originated as protection, most current theorists disagree. They think that physical protection is a secondary rather than a primary function of most dress. The major circumstances from which dress protects are weather and climate, animals, vegetation, and disease. While these dangers have been factors in the evolution and diversification of dress, protection from psychological or supernatural dangers was probably a greater factor in the early functions of dress.

3

Modesty

Early theorists considered modesty to be second only to protection as the most likely original function of dress. Their theories reflected the social mores of their time, the Victorian era, including the attitude that the human body was an embarrassment to be hidden. Sexual organs could not be mentioned in polite society. Thus, the hypothesis of the role of modesty in the evolution of dress was consistent with that era's use of dress as a body cover to conceal and draw attention from the sexual and sexually associated body parts. This use of dress has been employed by other societies in other eras in order to help maintain their organizational structure of sexual exclusivity. However, modesty is a rein on self-aggrandisement as well as on sexual allure. Therefore, it can prevent both self-satisfaction and "disgust, shame, or disapproval" (Laver 1969, p. 13).

The role modesty played in early dress was probably minimal at most. There may have been some intent to hide the body orifices but probably to protect the body from pollution rather than to be decorous. Since many cultures have labeled acts of excretion and/or menstruation as nonsocial and have even associated them with shame, there may have been a motive to conceal the related body parts. However, modesty is more likely to have resulted from habitual dress rather than to have been its cause. As a Upoto chief so wisely observed when asked why the tribe's women were habitually naked, "Concealment is food for the inquisitive" (Ellis 1918). Clothing as a means of attracting attention, especially sexual attention, to the body appears to have been—and still is—a much more important function of dress. Thus, many peoples only adopt clothing or cover their sexual organs after marriage, when they are no longer attempting to attract a sexual partner. We know from observing unclothed societies that nudity is not an aphrodisiac or sexual provocateur. In fact, habitual nakedness appears to reduce any sexual excitement caused by the naked human body.

Obviously, modesty is complex. "Put together of any number of ill-fitting parts, it reveals itself in more or less irrational taboos that differ not only with every civilization but often within a civilization itself. Like most taboos, they defy logic" (Rudofsky 1974, pp. 25–26). The unpredictability of such modesty taboos is evident both in the constant changes in our society's ideas of just what is modest dress and in situational nuances of what is modest. For instance, nude female models have been found to have no apparent effect on male artists. But if the nude puts on, say, a hat or stockings, the same artists then exhibit restless behavior (Kefgen and Touchie-Specht 1976). The same degree of exposure may be acceptable in one circumstance while so immodest in another that the individual would be subject to arrest for indecent exposure. For example, two naked men could be running down a street. Male *A* is "im-

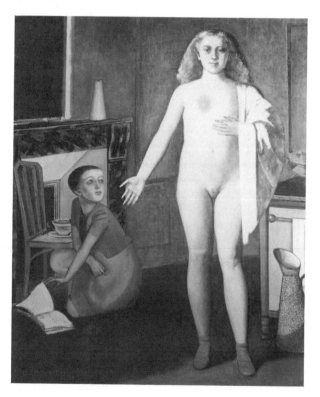

Figure 3.1 The model for Balthus' painting, *The Room,* would have had greater affect on a male artist because of her socks and towel. (Hirshhorn Museum and Sculpture Garden, Smithsonian Institution)

modestly" engaged in an exhibition called streaking. If a policeman sees him, he may be placed under arrest. Male *B,* on the other hand, has just rushed from his house, which is engulfed in flames. If the same policeman sees him, the officer will offer assistance that may include the offer of some kind of body cover. The first instance involves intentional immodesty, which is unacceptable; the second is accidental and is permitted because of the extenuating circumstances.

In this chapter we shall examine how modesty develops, is maintained, and pertains as a motivation for dress. We shall investigate the factors that influence the rules of modesty. A major theory of fashion, the theory of shifting erogenous zones, will be presented, as will be Flugel's theory of the five variables of modesty. We shall also briefly look at nudity, as both modest and immodest behavior.

HABIT

The basis of modesty is habit, which determines what is or is not modest. It does so by maintaining an unconscious psychological equilibrium that when disturbed, will become conscious. The individuals involved will attempt to return to the state of equilibrium in order to reduce the psychological discomfort caused by the change. This power of habit to produce conforming behavior rests in two things: (1) the unconsciousness associated with the behavior and (2) the psychological discomfort, fear, or anxiety experienced when the habit is broken. There may also be some cultural indoctrination through written laws or social mores to further ensure conformity. These laws or mores, by providing a rational basis or explanation for perhaps irrational behavior(s), also reinforce the continuation of the behavior(s) (Sumner 1965). The Eskimos are unique in that they have two quite different habits. They are fully clothed outside of their igloos, yet once inside, they remove all of their clothing except for a waist cord. Such an extreme difference is unimportant because habit has made them unconscious of any anomaly and comfortable with both behaviors. The power of habit is evident in many situations. In the 1930s, for instance, Comanche men continued to wear a G-string under their Western trousers. To omit it was a cause for great embarrassment even though no one but the wearer could know of the omission. After prolonged exposure to a more clothed society, primitive people have traditionally adopted at least some additional clothing item. While such adaptation may reflect motives such as status seeking, it is likely that they also reflect habit. Prolonged exposure to a different form of dress results in the eye's becoming accustomed to the novel style, and perhaps one even comes to appreciate it. Eventually, it can also make the old style seem less modest than the new, "and if they last long enough, such changes can affect the standards of modesty and propriety throughout the society" (Anspach 1969, p. 41).

a   b

Figure 3.2 (a & b) The Eskimo is one of the few peoples who seem equally comfortable dressed or nude. (The estate of Dr. Cook, courtesy of Janet Vetter)

Figure 3.3 Comanche with loin cloth under his trousers. (Library of Congress)

Modesty is not an innate human need but a learned response to certain cultural stimuli. This response is, for the specific culture, universal as well as habitual. However, between cultures the response can be completely reversed so that the wearing of clothing is immodest behavior in some while modest in others such as our own. In the modern West the sense of modesty does not seem to exist before age three but appears to have developed by age five. The sense of modesty probably develops simply through the process of acculturation—getting accustomed to the habit. Chimpanzees have been "taught" modesty in dress simply by rearing them clothed in a clothed society. The effectiveness of this technique is evident in the hysteria of such a chimp when placed naked in a room of clothed humans (Langner 1959). Such hysteria reflects extreme psychological discomfort. Compounding these feelings for most modern Americans is another fear, the fear that their body or body part(s) will be judged as inadequate or inferior. Thus, they have another motive to cover their body or certain parts or it. Modesty seems to be "most often found in people, of either sex, who are embarassed by what they think is their own imperfect body compared to our culture's endless images of ideal nudity or semi-nudity" (Fraser 1981, p. 250). These images of the ideal are the basis for the assessment of one's body in relation to others. The topless look introduced in lounge and swim wear in the mid-1960s never achieved success. Because the fashion look prior to this had stressed big bosoms many women had worn padded bras or falsies—thus the inaccurate concept of the average female body as having big breasts. Women who exposed their breasts with the new fashion tended to be the ones who were confident that their breasts would receive a positive judgment. However, most women did not have such confidence, and the topless look was not accepted. Thus, women chose to conceal their breasts not because they feared that their exposure would attract a man, but because they feared that their breasts would be inadequate and would fail to attract one. When the braless look was introduced, more women adopted it because it coincided with a change from the desirability of a big breast to that of a small one.

Many primitive men, from Africa to Micronesia, wear or have worn a prepuce or penis cover as their main article of dress. While it seems likely that habit played a major role in the continuation of such dress, it sems improbable that it was worn for modest concealment. Although research findings suggest that the adequacy of the male's sexual performance is not related to the size of his penis, male concern for penis size seems to be universal (Guthrie 1976), and it is this concern that may be most related to penis covers. For example, the Danai's sheath is made from a gourd averaging between twelve and twenty inches in length. If his sheath is lost, a man hides until someone can bring him a replacement (Cotlow 1966). A gourd this long cannot be explained as a modest covering, in spite of the embarrassment a man feels without it. It is definitely an attention getter rather than an attention diverter. And it is small wonder that a man without a sheath goes into hiding. Imagine how small his penis would appear to eyes used to seeing a twelve-to-twenty-inch facsimile!

Figure 3.4 Oceania men with penis wrappings. (National Anthropological Archives, Smithsonian Institution)

Figure 3.5 Zulu male with cock-box. (Library of Congress)

The Papuan Pygmy also uses a gourd as his penis sheath. Since the gourd is typically fifteen inches long, one-fourth as tall as he is (Bryant 1970), it seems that again the motive for this covering is the antithesis of modesty. Such examples abound. In Borneo the best gourd penis sheaths are long enough to go over the shoulder and strong enough to stand erect without having to be held up by a waist cord (Bennett-England 1968). The Cuna Indians wore gold penis sheaths, other tribes have used nuts or bamboo sheaths that have been decoratively incised. Men from primitive tribes as well as men of the resplendent Renaissance have wrapped their penises with leaves or cloth. These wrappings can be up to two feet long, are often quite colorful, and may even be decorated.

SHIFTING EROGENOUS ZONES

The ancient Greeks seemed to view the body as a whole. They found and enjoyed beauty in its entirety, and their sexual focus apparently was not limited to the genitals (Taylor 1954). Modern people tend to conceive of the human body "as composed of interesting bits and dull: bits to be exploited and bits to be suppressed" (Cunnington 1941, p. 20). This dichotomizing of the body has been evident throughout the history of modern fashion and is the basis on which one major theory of fashion rests—the theory of the shifting erogenous zones. This theory hypothesizes that fashion is a social method of maintaining and controlling sexual interest. Certain body part(s) are exposed or focused upon while others are concealed, depending on the fashion.

> Stripped to its essentials, fashion is no more than a series of permutations of seven given themes, each . . . a part of the female body: the breasts (neckline), waist (abdomen), hips, buttocks, legs, arms, and length (or circumference) of the body itself. Organs "appear" and "disappear" as the theme of fashion changes, and one and then another part of the body is emphasized by succeeding styles (Bergler 1953, p. 117).

For example, in the 1950s fashion focused on the waist (small) and the bust (large). The hips were stressed less frequently, and the legs were nonexistent beneath skirts reaching to the middle of the calves or even lower. Necklines plunged toward the breasts, which were lifted and thrust forward by specially designed brassieres. Bra cups were pointed to provide extra accentuation. At first glance it would seem that the breast was the sexual feature of the 1950s female body. However, this is only partially accurate. The longer this fashion focus remained, the more exciting the legs became. High school boys eagerly awaited glimpses of girls in physical education classes, where their legs were exposed. By the 1960s, the focus was beginning to shift. In the fall of 1960 kilts reaching to just above the knee were worn over tights by daring young women. But the style did not become popular because it was too drastic a change. Those styles with less radical hemline changes were more successful because they allowed the change to occur in a low-key way. Thus, the *habit* of covering the legs could be altered slowly enough that it did not cause great psychological discomfort. Not until the fall of 1965 were knees commonly exposed, and even then, after a six-year period of slowly rising, the high hemline caused concern to some of the population. When this author arrived at school with her knees just showing from beneath her suit skirt, another faculty member suggested that she be asked to leave until she was wearing more acceptable attire! By 1972 the micromini and hot pants had provided the complete exposure of the leg, and slowly the hemlines reversed themselves. However, when designers suggested the macroskirt with its midcalf length, they moved too quickly, and the suggested style was ignored. Not until the 1978 season did the hemline *commonly* drop to just below the knee. All of these changes exemplify the purpose of shifting erogenous zones: by the habitual concealment of some part of the body, that part is given greater sexual attraction. Thus, its exposure becomes sexually titillating. The longer it is revealed, however, the less exciting it becomes. Therefore, to maintain sexual interest, various body parts should be concealed after brief periods of exposure.

Of course, this theory applies only to postmedieval Western female fashion. In much of Asia and Africa and in modern Western male fashion, fashion changes are more in fabrics and colors than in style. The same body parts are habitually concealed or habitually exposed. What seems to be reflected is the primary use of dress. In the West women's dress is a sexual tool much more than it is in most of the Asian and African cultures or for the Western male. This difference in sexual uses of dress in the West probably reflects differences in the social view of each sex since it is women, not men, who have been considered sexual objects. The entire female body has had sexual meaning attached to it. Thus, there are many examples of excitement provoked by a woman's toe, elbow, derriere, waist, stomach, neck, bust, hips, thighs, calves, ankles, feet, and so on. The sexuality of a female is generalized over her entire body; however, the male's is focused only on his genitals. While there have been periods where another male body part has been considered an aesthetic ideal, such as big calves during the reign of Henry VIII, these have been based on considerations of physical attractiveness rather than sexuality. Further, the male's sexuality has been offensive in most Western philosophies. Thus, the male's genitals are more likely to be hidden under a leaf or inaccurately presented in art since they are not considered sexually attractive. Similarly, the Western male fashions have been, except for the period of the mid-fifteenth to the late sixteenth centuries, as sexless as possible. In that period of exception, men wore a cod-piece, which we today "regard as so indecent that it is hardly ever mentioned . . . in costume books . . . though it was an essential part of male dress . . . [as seen] in all portraits of the period, and . . . [in] armour" (Binder 1953, p. 19). As Gill (1937) noted

> any protuberance by which his sex might be known is carefully and shamefully suppressed. It is an organ of draining and not of sex. It is tucked away and all sideways, dishonoured, neglected, ridiculed and ridiculous—no longer the virile member and man's most precious ornament, but the comic member, a thing for girls to giggle about—comic and, to nursemaids, dirty—"You dirty little boy, put it away!" (pp. 1–2)

This view of the male genitals is not, unfortunately, an anachronism. A male's manliness is wrapped up in his penis, both in its appearance and in its ability to instantly make a "command performance." It is wrapped up because men have perpetuated a belief that they are such sex-responsive creatures that they cannot be held responsible for their sexual actions. Women have had to shoulder such responsibility! And for men the locus of this sexual need is found in one place and one place only—their genitals. Unfortunately, the penis seems, to men, "too unsubstantial to warrant display" (Rudofsky 1974, p.59).

In most Asiatic and African religions dress has not been strongly associated with sexuality. Modesty has more frequently involved posture or behavior rather than dress. But the Judeo-Christian tradition has so related sex and clothing that dress is the major consideration in its concepts of modesty, and we have tended to equate the kind of dress worn with the level of prurient interest. Thus, dress can be an obstacle to, or a stimulant for, sexual desire, and this role has given dress an erotic function. Semitic laws forbade public nudity and post-Exilic Jews could not even wear tight trousers "for fear of an involuntary discharge" (Taylor 1954, p. 246). The Bible implies that dress originated out of an instinctual desire to be modest, and this was taught by the church from the days of ancient Rome until the early twentieth century (Hiler, 1930). Most Christian philosophic writers from the seventeenth to the nineteenth centuries even related sin to body exposure. Innocent XI preached that women's immodesty was "the fatal origin of innumerable sins against purity, and consequently

Figure 3.6 Titian's *Charles V* of Germany and Spain. (Mansell Collection)

Figure 3.7 Andaman Islanders practicing their culture's version of decorous dress and posture. (Royal Anthropological Insitute)

one of the principal occasions of the numerous calamities which also afflict Christianity" (Boone 1853, p.15). Until the Renaissance, Christian women were expected to reduce their physical attractiveness by keeping their heads covered with veils or hoods, and in many parts of the world Moslem women are still expected to be veiled. These customs of veiling may be a reflection of a view that the woman is the property of her husband (Crawley 1931). Yet such complete concealment of the body, as practiced by some Moslems, may actually serve to heighten the sexual allure of the female body. The promise of so much forbidden fruit is a kind of lure to more active fantasizing by the men about the woman's entire body (Lane 1966).

This association of dress with sexual allure and sexual flirtation is heightened by dress that both exposes and conceals, a kind of immediate application of the shifting erogenous-zone principle. Thus, "it is where the dress gapes, where it is tucked up, where it is a potential restriction, defense, obstacle or delay that it best fulfills erotic function, due to its function of modesty" (Perrot 1981, p. 168). Even primitive peoples have been aware of this concept. The grass skirts of Melanesia and Micronesia, for example, offer brief glimpses of the legs. Most, however, have so many layers of grass from the hip to the midthigh that these regions are rarely revealed.

Figure 3.8 This George Samen gown is made sexy by the "hide and seek" nature of its slit skirt and lace midriff. (Mollie Parnis)

MODESTY VARIABLES

Since modesty is culturally taught, the concepts pertaining to it vary between cultures. In some cultures modesty does not even involve dress but relates to issues such as posture or expression (Kefgen and Touchie-Specht, 1976). The Australian aborigines, for example, are perfectly at ease nude and do not mind being watched when defecating. They will, however, experience shame at breaking the rules of modesty by being observed eating!

Rules of modesty can change according to role expectation and status. The variables generally are the types of place, activity, and individuals involved as well as the era. In fact, Goffman (1963) noted that "any state of dress is proper or improper only in terms of what other evidence is available concerning the individual's allocation of involvement and hence his orientation to the social occasion and its gatherings" (p. 213).

Place

The setting is a factor in the kind of behavior that is appropriate. More revealing dress, for example, is generally acceptable in an outdoor, water-oriented setting. Thus, a swimsuit is acceptable on the beach, at a pool, or in certain areas near them, such as an open-air bar or hot dog stand, but a beach cover would be expected were one to leave the beach or pool area to go, say, to a restaurant. But in seaside resorts where many activities involve water, these rules may be somewhat more relaxed so that one could wear swimsuit and

Figure 3.9 Imagine these members of the 1918 Australian Swimming Team wearing so revealing an outfit away from the pool. (Library of Congress)

cover to do grocery shopping or other errands that might reasonably need to be done before or after the day's water activities. It has been suggested (ibid.) that the brevity of much modern swimwear reflects the relaxation of social limits at the beach, where, for instance, one might lie in close proximity to a member of the opposite sex with whom one has had no previous contact. This casualness also extends to the ease with which relationships can be formed. The situation is dependent on a belief that everyone at the beach will be friendly and trustworthy. However,

> as beachwear has become skimpier, sunglasses have been getting darker and . . . [larger, to preserve] modesty of the eye. At present, sunglasses are modesty's last frontier, the masks behind which people protect their thoughts—a more intimate matter than sexual encounters. It's not our bodies we're interested in keeping hidden so much as our reactions to others. . . . Sunglasses are the perfect accessory for that part of the modern sensibility which prides itself on being "cool." . . . If ever women are plump and white again and people all take off their sunglasses, there's a fair chance that old-style modesty will be revived. (Fraser 1981, pp. 53–54)

Activity

The kind of activity is also a factor is determining what is modest dress. Women's formal wear, for example, is often rather exposing, with plunging necklines or slit skirts. This may be acceptable in the formal situation because it is an acknowledgment that the participants are so

> tightly in step with the occasion as a whole, and so trustful of the good conduct of their socially homogeneous circle, that they can withstand this much temptation to undue mutual-involvement without giving in to it. (Goffman 1963, p. 211)

When we are participating in a school or work activity, we are expected to be more modest in our dress.

Japanese strictures against public nudity for display are so stern that the Japanese will not pose nude. However, they will bathe nude in public communal baths unsegregated by sex. In the United States bathing is an intimate activity, and most Americans would experience psychological discomfort at a Japanese bath. Yet posing nude is acceptable behavior for some modern Americans.

Individuals

In general, the closer the social relationship is between individuals, the more social norms for body exposure may be relaxed when they are together. Thus, for example, roommates may wear very little when at home with just each other. This relationship is evident in such comments as "Take off your coat and loosen your tie, make yourself at home" and in the removal of attire such as shoes—suitable in the home of a close friend but not in a casual acquaintance's home.

Social norms for modesty in dress can vary between subcultures or social classes. For example, because ballet dancers exposed their lower extremities, until comparatively recent times their occupation was only for women of the lower social echelons. In fact, when Abigail Adams first saw ballet dancers in Paris in the 1780s, she was horrified at seeing their garters and drawers through their thin skirts. Eventually, she became inured to such exhibition and began, with embarassment, to enjoy the dance (Bernier 1981). However, when Nijinsky forgot to wear a jock strap at a performance attended by Russia's empress mother, he was fired from the Imperial Ballet (Cawthon 1979). In this case the breech involved the offensive exposure of a person before his social superior.

When individuals from different cultures intermingle there can be problems because of differences in their respective norms. For instance, when members of a society where the women's breasts are traditionally uncovered meet members of one that conceals the breasts, both sides will feel an element of discomfort.

What is acceptable as modest attire also differs according to an individual's age. While granddaughter may wear a teeny-weeny string bikini, grandmother would not be considered sufficiently covered. In the same way, elderly Nubas stop decorating their bodies

> because their bodies are no longer considered firm, young and attractive to look at, and in fact they normally begin to wear clothing at this time. This attitude toward exposure of the attractive body pervades the entire society, however, so that men of any age who are sick or injured, or whose bodies are otherwise incapacitated, will wear clothing or some type of cover for the duration of the illness or until the injury heals. (Faris 1972, p. 54)

Era

The differences in social norms in dress have differed radically from era to era. For instance, while today's modest woman may wear a neckline revealing her breasts, her nipples must remain concealed. Yet in other eras both breast and nipple could be exposed, and in still others neither could be. Each era has had its own body areas that could or could not be exposed. For example, not until the reign of Charles I did women expose their forearms, and then the exposure drew a bitter attack from the Puritans (Binder 1953).

Until the twentieth century upper- and middle-class American women did not show their legs; yet by the late 1960s even the upper thigh was acceptably exposed. Swimwear played a role in these different concepts of modern dress. In the seventeenth century women wore stiff canvas swimming dresses so that the wet fabric would not cling to, and thus "expose," the figure. By the eighteenth century the fabrics were softer, and the concern was in keeping the legs covered while in the water. Thus, the skirts had weights sewn into the hem. In neither instance were women able to actually swim. While men fared somewhat better, their swimwear did not permit the development of great prowess. Thus, in 1857 Newport had periods of the day when a red flag was put up, making the beach off limits to women. During these times the men were able to swim nude. By the turn of the century regulations governing swimwear for amateur swimming meets called for the legs of men's suits to extend only eight inches below the crotch, and women's suits could expose the leg up to three inches above the knee (Kidwell 1968). Such exposure helped the eye become accustomed to women's exposed legs, leading the way for the shorter skirts a scant twenty years later.

Flugel's Theory

Flugel (1930 pp. 53–67) presented a theory of the five variables he believed could describe the motivation for any instance of modesty in dress. His theory remains a useful tool for understanding the modern role of modesty in dress. Each variable represents a tendency that modesty is designed to inhibit, and any instance of modesty, while primarily motivated by one, can be related to all five variables. The first variable we shall call the situational factor. There are two kinds of situations against which modesty may be directed—the social and the sexual. In both cases dress is modest when it is appropriate to the specific event. For example, if one woman wore a swimsuit to a poolside party where everyone wore cocktail dresses, her suit would be considered immodest for the social situation. If a female teacher was asked to dinner by the single male parent of one of her students who only wanted to discuss his child, and she dressed in a revealing manner as if for a date, her dress would be considered immodest for the sexual situation.

There is also a variable we shall call the Christian factor because it reflects the traditional Christian viewpoint that the body is an evil lure to lust, sin, and eternal damnation. This factor causes the individual to try to prevent physical exhibition of the naked body, as would be inherent in wearing a see-through dress. It may also provoke a different kind of modesty, the attempt to prevent the psychological exhibition of the clothed body, as would be inherent in cases where the gown is wearing the woman rather than the reverse.

The third variable we shall call the concealment factor since it reflects two different motivations for concealment. In the first the individual wants to be modest out of an inherent desire; in the second, out of someone else's desire (although the desire to please the other is motivated from within himself or herself). Thus, two women might both wear dresses with a high neckline to hide their breast cleavage. The first does so to please herself; the second, to please her husband.

The fourth variable we shall call the discomfort factor. In this case the person dresses modestly to prevent causing uncomfortable psychological feelings in himself or herself or in others. There are two types of feelings to be avoided. The first is lust or desire that could arise, for example, out of admiring one's own legs. Ashamed of this vanity and aware of the lust one's legs might provoke in others, one conceals the legs and thus prevents both arousing others and self-vanity. The second type of feeling is disgust that could arise, for example, out of awareness that one's thighs are fat. To prevent disgust in oneself or others at being exposed to such lumpy areas of cellulite, one conceals the thighs.

The final variable we shall call the anatomical factor because it reflects the fact that modesty varies in its anatomical incidence. In parts of the world it is the fingertips that must be concealed, or the knees or arm or some other body part. To the Botocudo tribe in South America, one is immodestly exposed only if seen bare of ear or lower-lip plugs. Feet have been so immodest a body part that even mentioning them could cause embarrassment in many Western cultures. In fact, for nearly two thousand years the Western view of acceptable dress behavior by "ladies" was that feet must not be seen (peasants and other laboring women have been able, out of necessity, to expose their feet). Carriages in eighteenth-century Spain were equipped with doors that could be lowered to hide any view of a descending lady's feet. When Queen Maria Louisa, who was French, married the king of Spain, she brought to court the French custom of sitting on chairs. Thus, the long overskirt that Spanish women wore to hide their feet when they sat on the ground was no longer needed, and the young Queen ordered that this unfashionable style cease. Her

Figure 3.10 When this Los Angeles shop-girl was asked to model the sheath gown, she modestly wore high boots to hide her ankles and feet from "unseemly" exposure. (Library of Congress)

order met much resistance since it was believed that a peek of a toe, equivalent to being seen in the altogether, could unleash sexual wildness in the observant man (Bernier 1981).

NUDITY

Whether we see beauty or ugliness in the naked human body or feel attracted to it or repulsed by it reflects our own symbolic interpretation of the body. It seems that few of us would agree with Gill (1937) that "the human body, unclothed and even unkempt, though lacking all the panoply of dignity and ornament, is a kind of generalization. The necked [sic] man is simply man, Homo Sapiens, noble or ignoble, that and nothing else" (p. 16). Instead, most of us tend to judge the aesthetic appearance of a body and its parts. It is because of this tendency that some authorities—religious leaders, anthropologists, and the like—have recommended that young couples see each other nude before they marry. They hope that this would strengthen the marriage by reducing any negative judgments or disappointment on the wedding night.

Unconscious Nudity

Complete nudity as the social norm is quite rare. Most societies have some form of dress even if it is as simple as a flower in the hair or red paint on the arm. Unconscious nakedness is not immodest and does not, therefore, cause psycho-

Figure 3.11 Unconscious semi-nudity. (Library of Congress)

logical discomfort. In fact, habitual nakedness may elevate people to a less erotic view of others. Among many habitually naked peoples, eroticism comes from putting on clothing since the clothing merely serves to draw more attention to the body of which they are normally unconscious.

Certainly, Laver's (1969) suggestion that prudery titillates is consistent with the theory of the shifting erogenous zone and with research findings showing a correlation between modesty and repressed exhibitionism (Bergler 1953). Nudity also reduces the possibility of stressing status in human interactions since the nude individual is less likely to visually indicate his or her status. Of course, hair style can be and has been used to show status.

Conscious Nudity

However, when nudity is not the norm it is not motivated by habit or correctness but by other motives, such as a desire to rebel from the norm or a desire to change the norm or a specific situation.

REBELLION.   Rebellion can be either political or psychological. Examples of political nudity have been found in religious sects and leaders as well as in ethnic groups such as the Masai. Laws against nudity have been particularly common among cultures with a Judeo-Christian tradition. Punishments have ranged from social censure to death. A variety of groups have used nudity as a means of nonviolent protest against some aspect of the status quo. It is an interesting method since it implies a certain vulnerability, that is generally attributed in our society to a nude. Nude, defenseless humans must have a strong sense of security since they must be confident in themselves in order to

Figure 3.12 In 1903, members of the Doukhobor sect used nudity to demonstrate for the right to own land communally. (Saskatchewan Archives)

assume so vulnerable a state. It is a method of strength in humility. It is also a method that is difficult to attack. In a clothed society arguments are unlikely to occur between naked individuals. In fact, it would be interesting to see what would happen if, at the start of a battle, one side quietly disrobed and stood exposed before the enemy. Would the other side, like a wolf, refuse to attack their now vulnerable foe, or would they, like a dove, revel in the foolishness of the opposition? It is unlikely that such an experiment will ever occur, but as individuals we can make our own tests when arguing with individuals before whom we have sufficient trust to disrobe. The probability is that the argument will quickly end since the nudity will probably be taken as a sign of trust or security (Goffman 1963).

In clothed societies psychological rebellion also may involve nudity. Thus, teenagers have a greater tendency to make antisocial statements through various degrees of physical exposure. During the protest movement against American military involvement in Vietnam, young people used nudity as an act of both political and psychological rebellion. Even certain forms of emotional illness, such as schizophrenia, may include nude episodes in their symptomatology.

RITUAL.   Ceremonial nudity is often used as "a magic way to negate the world as it is. It may be used as a way of declaring that one wants to see a major change in nature" (Fisher 1973, p. 87). In fact, in a clothed society nudity is "the most violent negation possible" of the normal state (Crawley 1931, p. 111). Nudity has been common in rain rituals; rituals that are humbling, such as food- or attention-seeking ceremonies; and purification and fumigation ceremonies. The removal of clothing has also often been used as a sign of respect, for instance, a man lifting his hat when meeting a woman. In the same way that we take clothing off to indicate respect, nude societies may put some on, so that their ceremonies frequently involve some form of dress.

SUMMARY

Although modesty was prominent in early theories of the origin of clothes, it was probably not a function of early dress. Instead modesty is more likely to have resulted from the adoption of habitual dress. Modesty is determined by habit. Certain behaviors are universally learned as appropriate for one's culture, and these behaviors are habitually performed. Any break in the habit will invariably cause psychological discomfort and, perhaps, social sanctions. Modesty in dress is further reinforced by the fear that one's body will not live up to the aesthetic ideal. Thus, exposure risks negative judgment. Dress, which helps make the body appear closer to that ideal, reduces the risk of such negative judgment.

In the West we hold a dichotomized view of the body because we perceive it as the sum of its parts rather than as a whole entity. This perception has led to the use of fashion as a way of producing sexual excitement by shifting the body focus of a fashion period. When one part of the body is concealed, attention turns to another, more exposed, part. However, as this part will finally become boring, the exposed part will be concealed and another part exposed in order to maintain interest. This theory of the shifting erogenous zones is applicable to modern female fashion because the entire female body has a sexual association. The male's sexuality, focused solely on his genitals, makes this theory invalid for male fashion.

Rules of modesty can change according to the situation, the individuals involved, and the era. Modest dress is dress that is appropriate to an individual's specific role expectation at that moment in that setting during that era. The more casual the situation, the more relaxed are the demands for concealing dress. Restriction occurs as the situation itself becomes more demanding. There are five variables that represent a tendency which modesty inhibits. These are the situational, Christian, concealment, discomfort, and anatomical factors. Any instance of modesty can be understood by analyzing the relative degrees of importance of each of these variables.

Concepts of nudity are based on symbolic interpretations that are both personal and cultural. Complete nudity as the social norm is rare since almost all societies have some form of dress. However, when nudity is unconscious, it is not immodest. Generally, when nudity is conscious as it would be in a clothed society, it is used for political and/or psychological rebellion or for ceremonial purposes, just as clothing is used in nude societies.

Modesty is a complex, unpredictable, and irrational concept. While in some cases it may be or may have been a secondary motive for the adoption of dress, it is probably the least important of the four most commonly accepted motives for dress.

4 | Communication

Communication is the transmission by symbols of information and ideas. It is the most modern theory of the function of dress. However, communication was an unlikely function of our earliest dress since primitive humans' mental capacity was not developed enough for them to think in abstracts and develop symbols for abstractions. But communication is a function of all dress that has evolved in organized societies with roles and statuses. This function may be primary or secondary, intended or serendipitous. It is a universal *result* of dress and, on a subconscious level, it may well be the most common function of, or motivation for, dress. Its power is obvious in that an entire section of this text is needed just to briefly examine aspects of the communication function. The purpose of this chapter is to build a framework for understanding the principles of the language of dress and the variables that influence that language.

In this chapter we shall examine dress as a medium of communication and analyze the perceptual process with a special focus on person perception, including the formation of first impressions. Dress symbols will be investigated, as will dress communicators—aspects of dress with a specific language.

MEDIUM OF COMMUNICATION

Dress is a medium of communication; it communicates social information and personal identity. "Society needs structure, structure needs symbols, and the most obvious place to put symbols is on the human body" (Coon 1971, p. 40).

The more complex a society is, the more necessary such symbols become in ensuring that society's efficient functioning. These symbols form a language that, like speech and the written language, can send many complex and varied messages. However, because it is a nonverbal language that is communicated primarily through the sense of vision, although all of the senses may be involved, it is unavoidable. Thus, the question, "What is being communicated by clothes?" (Gibbins 1969) is perhaps most significant in the study of dress as well as fashion.

Of course, for dress to be a language, it must be conventional enough to allow a mutual understanding of its symbols. Without a common understanding, responses to the symbols would be idiosyncratic. Although precision in language has rarely if ever been achieved even in spoken or written language, accurate communication relies on a core of mutuality in understanding the meanings of each symbol whether it is a word or an item of dress. Unfortunately, communication occurs even when this mutuality of understanding is absent. And unlike spoken or written language, the language of dress, because it is often unconscious, may prevent the participants from being aware of the inaccuracies. While we will be aware of a foreigner speaking the language of another culture, we may not be aware that his language of dress probably is also different. Thus, for example, if we should meet a Society Islander who was wearing three ponchos—a long white one, a medium red one, and a short brown one—we would probably not be wary. We would not understand that this outfit symbolized hostility (Hiler 1930). Meanings within a culture may change from era to era. For instance, many shoe ornaments were originally genital symbols. Large dual buttons or knobs symbolized testicles, a large semi-rigid flapping tassel suggested a penis, and the fur trimming around the shoe's collar represented pubic hair (Rossi 1976, pp. 222–33). Today, these items have lost their phallic symbolism for most people. The Freudian psychiatrist might utter a significant "aha" at the woman with a fur-collared slipper or the man with a tasseled loafer, but few others would make such an association. To further complicate this language, a dress behavior may have several meanings. The Chinese Lily foot, for example, indicated social status, economic status, gender status, aesthetic ideal (Kefgen and Touchie-Specht 1970), social role, and level of social integration.

Fouquier (1981) suggested that the language of dress interprets the items of clothing and the class of the clothing, i.e., "slovenly" dress, "nonconformist" dress. "Each item is . . . the result of a combination of possible forms and shapes . . . , colors and patterns of fabrics" (p. 180). Meaning can be given according to the item or an aspect of it or its class. Fowles (1974) equated the language of dress with verbal communication. Fabrics and colors were the phonemes, dress items the words, wardrobes the vocabulary, outfits the sentence, and the pattern of putting an outfit together the grammar (p. 344). The primary communication of dress, he hypothesized, is one's social place. "Our clothes broadcast our sex (usually), our rank (decreasingly), and our up-todateness (increasingly)" (p. 348). They also indicate the degree of formality associated with an activity, and the same events that require more formal speech also require more formal dress. Unfortunately, both of these systems for a grammar of dress have omitted the body part(s) covered or exposed and the source of the dress material, both of which can have idiomatic repercussions on a message.

Societies with a stable or unvaried fashion have been able to evolve a more precise language of dress. The Chinese used fabrics and decorative motifs for symbolic purposes. The motifs were "a visual vocabulary . . . [which] employed both grammar and syntax to express the ideas and sentiments of Chinese civilization" (Vollmer 1980, p. 42). They formed words or phrases and by combining them in different patterns with other motifs, created sentences and paragraphs. The Chinese evolved an oral language which often lacked precision of meaning since many words were homonyms requiring the context to give the meaning. However, their written and symbolic languages were both quite precise. By using rebuses for abstractions, their symbolic language was also quite versatile (ibid.). The Japanese kimono is also an elaborate, well-defined, and culturally understood symbol, although it is a less complex language. Precise meanings are determined by such variables as the fabric, colors and their use in the design, number and positions of family crests, style of the kimono, and style of tying and width of the obi.

As variety in dress and/or frequency in fashion changes increase, the precision of the language of dress decreases. Western dress is fashionable, thus constantly changing so that its language is always changing, much like slang in the spoken language. Thus, we must make an effort to keep up on new meanings and those who take a Rip Van Winkle-type break may lose their ability to accurately understand the meanings of new fashions. Imagine someone going to sleep in 1957 to awaken just a decade later. She would have found dress that she considered appropriate for only the most casual situation being worn in more formal situations. Not knowing the current fashion rules, the awakened individual would be uncertain as to the appropriate dress for a particular situation, would seem out of step to others, and would feel alienated.

Dress is a visual statement of the individual, about just who we each are and to which groups we have allegiance. In fact, as Twain (1905) noted, we would be nothing without clothes, since

> the clothes do not merely make the man, the clothes *are* the man; . . . without them he is a cipher, a vacancy, a nobody, a nothing. . . .
>
> There is no power without clothes. It is the power that governs the human race. Strip its chiefs to the skin, and no State could be governed; naked officials could exercise no authority; they would look (and be) like everybody else—commonplace, inconsequential. A policeman in plain clothes is one man; in his uniform he is ten. Clothes and title are the most potent thing, the most formidable influence, in the earth. They move the human race to willing and spontaneous respect for the judge,

the general, the admiral, the bishop, the ambassador, the frivolous earl, the idiot duke, the sultan, the king, the emperor. No great title is efficient without clothes to support it. (pp. 321–22)

Dress differentiates us from others while concomitantly asserting our social integration. Thus, it serves to help form us, our own self-image, and our interpersonal relationships. Turner's (1969) observations about the Tchikrins' symbolic use of dress are also applicable to urban man whose dress, like our Tchikrin counterpart's, "expresses a wide range of information about social status, sex, and age. . . . [Not only does it] communicate this information from one individual to another: at a deeper level, it establishes a channel of communication *within* the individual between the social and biological aspects of his personality" (p. 59). Thus, greater understanding of a culture's language of dress gives us more freedom to participate in that society since we will be better able to determine the most appropriate behaviors for each particular social situation.

Correct dress facilitates a social interaction just as incorrect dress will limit it. Because of the physical nature of dress it is one of the only concretes in most social interactions. It is also a stable element since only infrequently would we change our dress during an interaction. Thus, by conforming in our dress to the occasion, we can gain greater control over the situation and thereby increase our self-confidence. However, this requires a command of the language of dress in the specific social group or society involved. It also depends on the audience's having a similar command.

PERCEPTION

Perception is the process of taking in data through our senses and transmitting that data to the brain where it is selected and identified and given significance through organization and interpretation. It is an unconscious process that is almost instantaneous. Perception is an intrinsic part of communication. However, no two people ever perceive anything—whether a word, event, person, or behavior—in precisely the same way. Each person's perception reflects numerous variables that make it unique to that person. Yet even though perception is only a reflection of our own personal reality, it is the cause for all of our behavior. We believe or perceive, and therefore we act or behave. We will distort any incongruous stimuli to make them conform to our expectations.[1] And we behave in ways to make our perceptions more consistent. Thus, we create ourselves and our environments to be consistent with our expectations. We see what we expect and want to see. We do this by selecting certain data to

[1] Many stimuli are never perceived; they are "selected out" in the perceptual process.

perceive and other data to dismiss. This selectivity of perception explains how humans see the people they love as more beautiful than they may have perceived them to be before they loved them.

Variables

Our perception is never accurate in the sense of its being absolute truth or reality. Rather it is a reflection of our own personal reality. Therefore, perception is very much determined by our unique life experience such as our culture, the people significant to us who have formed our frame of reference, and our education. The association of greater clothing awareness with higher socioeconomic level, higher educational level, and higher participation in more social groups (Rosencranz 1972) reflects opportunities for building more command of the language of dress. Culture, for example, provides us with certain information that will restrict our perception by causing us to make erroneous and unconscious assumptions about a situation. The following problem may illustrate this. Connect the nine dots with four lines. The lines may intersect but may not trace over each other, *and* your pencil may not be lifted off the page until all the lines are drawn.

This task is quite simple but most individuals with an American cultural "set" will make certain assumptions that will impede or even prevent their solving this problem. These nine dots are not a square, but most of us probably see a square, and that prevents a solution. If we went to a kindergarten where we were taught to color within the lines or if our first-grade teacher taught us to print and stay within the lines, we probably also assume that these dots are part of lines within which we should stay. Such an assumption could also prevent a solution. (The solution is given at the end of this chapter.)

What would be an example of cultural conditioning in dress interpretation? A clean-shaven man who wore a silk robe was civilized to the ancient Chinese, but to a Turk this manner of dress was an effeminate sign of weakness. The bearded Turk's proper dress was of wool, which to the Chinese was a sign of a barbarian or a bandit. The most masculine Greek male wore a draped chiton, and the Scotsman wears a kilt, both of which most modern American trouser-clad males would consider effeminate (Fairservis 1971, p. 33). Mind sets make it difficult, if not impossible, for the observer to perceive the behavior of an individual from another culture without evaluating or judging it in terms of the observer's own culture. Part of the power of a mind set is its resistance to change. The halo effect noted in psychology in the early twentieth century is an aspect of mind set; it results from our continued evaluation of others on the basis of our past experience with them. All of us have experienced this phenomenon within our own families when our parents or some other family member continued to behave toward us and expected us to behave as we did in our childhood or adolescence. Thus, for example, we find parents believing that their thirty-year-old cannot keep a secret or know the best way to cook a turkey.

Perception also depends on an individual's more immediate past experiences. For example, if an average-looking person is walking down the street behind an extremely attractive person, viewers will perceive the average-looking person as less attractive than they would were he alone on the street or following an unattractive person (Fisher 1973).

The stimulus itself is also a variable. We are more apt to perceive stimuli that are intense or contrast in some other way with other stimuli. If a stimulus has some noxious element, we are more apt to view it in its entirety in a more negative manner. But if the stimulus interests us positively, we will be more apt to attend to it longer and concentrate more on it so that we will increase our awareness of it, and we will tend to perceive the data in its entirety in a more positive light. If the stimulus coincides positively with one of our needs, then this concentration and positive perception will increase even more.

The physical setting is also a factor. For example, when a situation is bombarding an individual with sensory data, she will tune out or not perceive much or even most of the available data. In a sensorially sterile environment the same individual will perceive very minute sensory data. Yet when one sensory mode is bombarded with a steady barrage of the same stimuli, she will not continue to perceive the data. This explains why people living by train tracks may not notice a passing train even though it is extremely loud.

Our physical body also influences our perception. Sensory equipment has an obvious influence; for example, the deaf cannot hear auditory stimuli, and the blind cannot see visual stimuli. Functioning of the nervous system, which influences the transmittal of sensory data to the brain and the treatment of those data by the brain, is also a variable. Drugs can alter this functioning to the point where perception becomes so distorted that the individual lacks any contact with reality. Certain other chemical imbalances, such as those associated with schizophrenia, act in the same way. Brain damage can also interrupt the perceptual process. Thus, a stroke victim may repeat the last word he has heard rather than answer a question correctly. Illnesses causing delirium can temporarily cause similar kinds of perceptual difficulties. Illness may also have an adverse impact on the individual's degree of mobility and/or energy level, both of which, if reduced, may decrease the sensory data he is able to receive. Even body structure and sex will influence perception.

The self-concept is also an important variable influencing perception. For example, it is our self-concept that determines our expectations, and those in turn are a strong determinant of our selective perception.

Person Perception

Humans like to determine something about the people they meet. Person perception refers to the way we learn and think about other individuals, their characteristics, intentions, and inner states (Taguiri and Pettrullo 1958).

FIRST IMPRESSIONS.   The first step in the process of personal perception is forming a first impression. That can be done within the first few seconds, or it may take as long as the first two minutes of one's initial contact with another individual. This impression includes judgments and assessments of the individual, including personality, social roles, and status. First impressions have a significant impact on the future interactions of the individuals. For example, we tend to avoid or limit contacts with those individuals about whom we have a negative impression, whereas we promote such contact when we have a positive impression. We will generally reinforce our initial impression in our future contacts. We tend to behave more formally with those about whom we have a negative impression, while a positive impression will generally lead to warmer and more friendly behavior. These impressions also influence our immediate behavior since we tend to behave as we believe the perceiver expects us to.

Figure 4.1   This 1880 ad visually demonstrates the role of dress in first impressions. (Library of Congress)

Thus, our impression of another individual's first impression of us will influence our immediate behavior (Ryan 1966).

Research has shown that these impressions are primarily based on demeanor, including posture, behavior, and dress. In fact, because dress or appearance is evident from a greater distance than many other characteristics, it will usually be of greatest importance when the initial contact is visual. The importance of dress in first-impression formation is so significant that the "universe of appearance may, in fact, be regarded as the guarantee, foundation, or substrate of the universe of discourse" (Stone 1970, p. 231).

These impressions are made so quickly and subliminally that the perceiver is often unaware of the judgments he has made and upon what he has based them. But perceptual stimuli provide the cues upon which the observer bases his expectations about the other individual(s) and the situation. His interpretation of the cues will reflect his past experiences. Thus, if all moustached men have been villains in our past, we will probably have a negative first impression of any man with a moustache, and we will be wary of him. When data are contradictory, the perceiver will select and/or rearrange it in order to reduce the inconsistency. Obviously, the less one knows about a person, the more important these cues become. In the 1950s a study related clothing to "attractiveness ratings of some college-age men when the pictures were rated by college students unacquainted with the men pictured." Men pictured wearing "appropriate" dress were rated more attractive than they were when pictured wearing less "appropriate" dress (Hoult 1954, p. 328). A high attractiveness rating has been related to a more positive personal evaluation of an individual and of his or her products. This relationship is so powerful that clothing has been found to be a significant factor in the viewer's judgment of credibility in an advertisement and, therefore, in the likelihood of his purchasing the advertised product (Olfers, 1975). Evidence also suggests that when people dress according to their role expectation(s), others are more likely to respond to them as the roles would dictate. Thus, students have been found to work harder for teachers who are more formally attired. This may involve psychological comfort since role-appropriate dress reduces anxiety about the roles and the individuals filling them.

People have been found to be more cooperative with other individuals whose appearance is similar to their own. Thus, they have been found to be more likely to talk with, sign a petition for, or provide information to an individual dressed similarly to themselves (Suedfeld et al. 1971, 1972). In fact, similarity in dress appears to be more important than attractiveness per se, perhaps because greater similarity appears related to a judgment of more attractiveness (Buckley and Roach 1981). We like that which relates to us or is similar to us. This similarity in clothing may be interpreted by the viewer as symbolic of a similarity in values, attitudes, and social identification and belongings. It appears to suggest the adoption of the same reference group, the group to which we give allegiance and from which we develop our lifestyle, including standards of behavior and a code of morality. It is our reference group with whom we "share a 'collective consciousness' (Durkheim), a common 'socio-logic' (Lévi-Strauss), a collective 'ideology' (Marx) . . . [and with whom we] share ideas . . . about what constitutes proper dress . . . ideas . . . [which]set guideline limitations" (Polhemus and Procter 1978, p. 21). We judge the clothing of others from the perspective of our reference group (Noesjirwan and Crawford 1982). Thus, the reference group is an important factor in first-impression information. It may even be that the degree to which dress leads to a perception of reference-group congruity is the most important factor in first-impression formation. Gibbin's (1969) research suggested that

> "fashionability" dominates judgments of clothes to a greater extent than their sheer evaluation. This result does seem, at first sight, somewhat surprising: surely what dominates an individual's judgment of an outfit is far more likely to be whether the individual likes it rather than whether she perceives it to be fashionable? However, . . . if "fashionability" is a reflexion of a group norm to a greater extent than is "liking," and if it makes sense to consider each subject's response to an outfit as including two components, one of liking (evaluation) and one of fashionability, then, in so far as the fashionability component is less variable across persons, . . . correlations . . . will be primarily determined by the fashionability component rather than by the liking one, for, by hypothesis, this is more variable in individuals. (p. 311)

However, another study has found that fashionability was perceived to indicate sociability (Johnson et al. 1977). One of the most important factors in evaluating an individual as a potential friend is his or her friendliness, and friendliness is related to sociability. Thus, Gibbin's findings should be neither surprising nor difficult to understand.

First impressions and dress cues are generally more important in urban than rural or small-town settings. Urban contacts are brief and infrequent or even unrepeated. Rural or small-town contacts are more repetitive and longer, and some things about the other individual have usually already been ascertained. For these reasons it is also easier to use dress to mislead others in an urban than in a rural setting. Dress can be a visual symbol of one's material success, which in our culture we equate with personal ability. An expensive outfit then can suggest that one has acquired financial affluence, implying personal success and talent. In an urban setting an individual could, by donning such an outfit, get others to react to her as if she were successful/wealthy. However, in a rural setting where individuals tend to already have some information about other members of their community, people would be less likely to be fooled by such an outfit. Thus, politicians in local elections do not have to be as concerned with their dress since their constituents will probably already know them or know someone who knows them. As constituencies get larger, and an elected official represents more people, dress becomes a more influential factor.

Men's dress has been found to be a less important cue than women's, although dress seems to be used as a cue by men more than women. Evaluations of others appear to be more extreme when made about individuals of the opposite sex. In fact, it appears "that dress is one of the most salient cues in sex stereotyping . . . [and this] is so marked that sex stereotype origins may be a result of the predominance of dress as a cue in early socialization" (Hamid 1969, pp. 193–94).

STEREOTYPES. Stereotypes are organized biases, which influence our behavior by giving us rigid expectations. They are examples of logical error based on gross generalizations, which are *never* truly accurate because they assume that a group of traits automatically go along with one attribute. Thus, when we see a fat person, too often we might assume that she is also happy, funny, and sociable. Unfortunately, stereotypes that depend primarily on the superficial element of appearance, especially dress (ibid.), are also a factor in first impressions. Stereotypically oriented people tend to perceive different groups according to their dress uniforms—a parka for the Eskimo or a grass skirt for the Hawaiian. In spite of the inaccuracy of such old-fashioned perceptions, these people continue to maintain them (Bush and London 1960, p. 360). Imagine how much more difficult it would be to change a nonvisual stereotype when such obviously inaccurate visual stereotypes are so resistant to change.

Stereotypes are caused and reinforced by selective perception. Everyone nods in agreement at meeting a "dumb blonde" or a "happy fatty." The smart blonde or the depressed fatty is not noticed *even* though those kinds of people might make up the majority! Selective perception was evident in the following situation, which occurred when some students were having a poolside graduation party. One black coed asked not to be thrown in since she could not swim. Another student announced to her neighbor, "You know, blacks can't swim!" Yet several black students had been swimming in the pool while that student was there.

Research has found certain items of dress are associated with specific stereotypes. Some of these associations are glasses with intelligence, religiousness, shyness, naiveté, lack of physical attractiveness, conventionality, and dullness; make-up, bright colors, and high hemlines (which were stylish at the time of the study) with sophistication, immorality, and physical attractiveness. Research (Mathes and Kemper 1976) has also shown that "people do believe that certain kinds and styles of clothing are indicative of liberal sexual attitudes and behavior" (p. 497). These items were, for men, tank tops, bare feet, open shirts, hip-hugger pants, cut-offs, sandals, football shirts, shirtlessness, and net shirts. For women, they were cut-offs, hip-hugger pants, hoop earrings, tops exposing midriffs, work shirts, bralessness, T-shirts, blue jeans, short shorts, halter tops, sun dresses, sandals, sweaters, and bare feet. However, for men such a correlation did not *actually* exist, and for women the correlation was significant only for cut-offs or tops that exposed the midriff (ibid.). A physical-attractiveness stereotype has been found to lead to judging a physically attractive person as happy, fulfilled, poised, sensitive, kind, modest, strong, sociable, outgoing, sensible, of good character, interesting, and exciting.

Unfortunately, personality traits and intelligence have not been found to be indicated by dress. Some occupations, particularly those with uniforms, are indicated by dress, and on a less precise level, so are age, sex, socioeconomic status, and certain group affiliations. But in general dress is a poor cue to nonsuperficial data about individuals. This may reflect the mass-production methods of clothing manufacturers through which fashionable clothing is available to all social levels. It may also "reflect the existence and acceptance of large variations in clothing behaviour" (Nielsen and Kernaleguen 1976, p. 779) since more homogeneous groups have greater agreement as to dress meaning or symbolism.

DRESS SYMBOLS

Dress has so much meaning that it would be far easier to produce a Shakespearean play on a stage without sets than without costumes. The information contained in dress may be quite detailed. The Ethiopian toga, for example, shows economic status, whether the individual lives in a city or a rural area, occupation, mood, level of interest in social interaction, role desires, and the function for which he is dressed. All of these are indicated by the manner in which the toga is draped. Western dress would need to be changed to indicate such a variety of things. The Ethiopian system of

> changing the appearance of one and the same piece of clothing . . . [is] more flexible and manageable. . . . However . . . this kind of nonverbal communication by means of relatively slight changes in clothing can only be . . . achieved in . . . cultures in which interrelations among persons are either formed or ritualized. (Ogibenin 1971, p. 27)

Although Western symbols usually are less detailed, they are nonetheless important, as witness the embarrassment we experience when our dress is inappropriate for a situation. Behavior should also be congruent to costume. Imagine a man in a suit and tie with neatly polished shoes and a thin attaché case. His demeanor will be brisk and serious as befitting an executive. His hair will be trim and controlled and his handkerchief clean. He may wear a ring, a watch, and a tie tack or clip; a gold bracelet or neck chain is less likely though possible, but earrings or a large necklace will not be worn. His nails will be clean and trimmed to an appropriate length. All of this because of his awareness, whether intuitive, formally taught, or self-taught, that certain clothes go with certain behaviors, from speech to gestures. On the other hand, the

> black-jacketed motorcyclist who wears steel-studded gauntlets and an obscene swastika dangling from his throat completes his costume with rugged boots, not loafers or wing-tips. He is likely to swagger as he walks and to grunt as he mouths his antiauthoritarian platitudes. For he, too, values consistency. He knows that any trace of gentility or articulateness would destroy the integrity of his style. (Toffler 1970, p. 307)

However, he too will be unlikely to wear earrings, since a man's wearing earrings has been associated with homosexuality. Our appearance is dictated by, and in return dictates, our lifestyles and values. This relationship is evident in our verbal language when we show lifestyle or values through dress symbols such as white collar, blue collar, blue stocking, or hard hat.

We also use dress symbols to show attitudes—to "throw down the gauntlet" or "throw one's hat in the ring." Hats are doffed in respect, gloves are given in pledge, rears are exposed in derision, hair is let down in relaxation and spontaneity.

Our mood can be communicated in our clothing. When appearance is untended or careless, the individual is probably either depressed or unhappy. When appearance is most "dressed up," the mood is probably upbeat. Dark colors are associated in the West with somberness. White is sweet and innocent, with the purity of the virgin. Imagine a girl wearing a white dress, white shoes, and a white ribbon in her hair. If she should curse it would be far more discordant than it would were she wearing a bright red dress, red shoes, and a red ribbon. Add lace to the description of the white dress and a pale pink sash and white stockings, and the cursing would be even more discordant. Add tight and low cut to the description of the red dress, black fish-net stockings, black boa, and dangling earrings, and the cursing would be almost expected.

Both roles and status can be indicated by dress. Trophies are used, for example, to indicate prowess, usually in hunting or fighting. An Indian warrior's deerskin shirt could be a citation of valor with his battle history painted or embroidered on it. A Sioux warrior's costume in the Smithsonian Institution's collection has such a shirt adorned with scalp trophies. Other trophies are

Figure 4.2 A chief's decorations. (Library of Congress)

a plume of eagle feathers, a necklace of bear's claws, and a hair ornament of a cross within a circle, which was a heraldic device symbolizing the saving of a friend under the fire of an enemy (Krieger 1928). To an American Indian warrior every item of dress from head feather to "the wolf-tail dragging at the heel of a moccasin . . . gave publicity to [his] . . . feats of valor" (Lowie 1929, p. 82). Both warriors and hunters have worn parts of their victims, human or other animal, including scalps, shrunken heads, teeth, and bones. When an enemy could be carried off and eaten, the Marquesan warrior kept its head for a trophy.

> These skulls were carefully prepared, and were worn at the belt at dances and on war parade. Hands of victims were also sometimes dried and worn as waist orna- ments. If a warrior acquired too many skulls to be worn conveniently in this fashion, he would cut them up and wear only a section of each. If the victim was a woman, the warrior might not keep the skull, but he would cut off the genitals, dry them, and wear them attached to a lock of his hair. (Linton 1974, p. 178)

It is not an uncommon belief that the trophy enhances the wearer's power. Flugel (1930) suggested that this power was phallic and that the removal of the body part was a symbolic castration. His hypothesis may have had some merit in certain instances, as with the Ethiopian soldiers who attached the testicles of their fallen enemies to their lances. It may also, if one accepts phallic symbolism as an aspect of tattooing, be accurate for groups such as the Kalenja in the Philippines, who tattooed themselves each time they took a head. However, military decorations, taking the weapons of one's enemy, wearing jewelry to denote each kill, or notching one's weapon typically seem to lack any phallic association.

Lots of jewelry or feathers could indicate prowess if the wearer might need to defend his right to wear them. In fact,

> It came to be taken for granted that the Chief was entitled to more decoration than the ordinary warriors and in time the system crystallized, first into an unwrit- ten sumptuary law and then into the insignia of rank. This is the Hierarchical Principle which still makes it seem natural that the red band round the hat of the general is out of place round the hat of the private. There is an element of class-consciousness in the very earliest developments of male attire. (Laver 1969, p. 4)

Wearing feathers, teeth, or the like sometimes has symbolized a man's ability to shoot game, which was evidence that he was a good provider. As a result, the trophies could even become sexual attractants. A bear's tooth, for example, indicates hunting prowess and ability to provide; it also has aesthetic interest because of its sheen and color. Its rarity enhances its value; and since it is associated with a powerful animal, it may also be seen as a method of increas- ing the wearer's strength. "If a man owned a great number of these teeth it might be assumed that he possessed one or all of these qualities to a superior degree," which would make him a more attractive sexual partner or mate (Hiler 1930, p. 36).

Figure 4.3 Trophies. (Library of Congress)

Figure 4.4 Mongolian woman with a headdress indicating that she is married. (National Anthropological Archives, Smithsonian Institution)

Marital status is socially important. Single individuals interested in finding mates must be able to indicate their availability just as the married indicate their removal from the courting arena. Most cultures have specific dress showing whether an individual is single or married or has any interest in a sexual involvement.

Dress has often been used to denote group affiliation. Reference groups are most apt to be shown. By distinguishing the group from other groups in the society, the common bonds of the members are stressed. The individual is reminded by his dress of the expectations and norms of the group. He will feel the group's approval and acceptance of him and his dress. This helps to strengthen intragroup ties and to reduce the probability of ties formed with individuals outside of the group. When a group uses dress to differentiate itself, the dress requirements tend to be rigidly defined and stable. This is especially so for groups such as reference groups with voluntary membership. Such a membership entails a stronger commitment to the group. Only when a nonvoluntary group, such as a racial group, is threatened will such a commitment be directed to it. Thus, membership is more often shown by dress when a small group is attempting to prevent its assimilation into a larger one, such as, for example, the Japanese Ainu and the Hasidic Jew. Rigid definition of any group's dress generally increases when that group is threatened. The dress of the hippies in the late 1960s and early 1970s was an assertion both of their affiliation with "hippiedom" and all that that entailed and of their rejection of the rest of society. While their norms were antisocial, conformity to that norm was demanded. Even though their antisocial dress reduced their effectiveness in producing the social/political changes they desired, they continued to wear the same attire. Blue jeans, the basic unit of their wardrobe, ultimately lost their antisocial meaning once they had become an accepted dress form and could be worn in restaurants or at school, for instance. Where first they had symbolized militant conformity, they finally merely showed conformity.

Morris (1977) hypothesized that membership in a large group such as "citizens of the United States" is insufficient for meeting the need to belong. Such a group is too large and impersonal to provide its members with the sense of belonging. Thus, the individual must form smaller subgroups whose members are well-known to her. Clubs, gangs, unions, fraternities, sororities, cliques are more effective ways to meet the need to belong. Most individuals "belong to at least one of these splinter groups, and take from it a sense of tribal allegiance and brotherhood." All of these groups develop "territorial signals," such as badges and costumes, that indicate the group's identity (p. 128). These signals are often the only overt symbol of membership. An athletic group will have some special dress insignia differentiating it from other athletic groups. School uniforms, ties, rings, and pins all distinguish one school from other schools. The Girl Scouts and Boy Scouts and similar organizations have their own special and distinguishing uniforms.

Tribal, clan, or family membership has historically been indicated by dress in those societies in which they were the primary social affiliation. The totem,

Figure 4.5 This family uses dress to visually represent their interconnection.

animal or plant, symbolizes both the spiritual and social kinship of a group's members (Frazer 1935). Dress has been a primary way to indicate this totem in primitive societies. Family crests have been used by primitive peoples such as the Tsimshian Indians, feudal peoples such as the Japanese, and the modern Western family. Special scars, jewelry, patterns of cloth such as tartans and kente are other ways that have commonly been used. In the Aran Islands, the women of sea-going families knit their family members' sweaters with a personalized stitch to facilitate the identification of bodies washed up from the sea. Modern dental records have provided a more accurate means of identification so that such personalization is no longer needed.

Until World War I, national costumes were common throughout much of Europe, with each local area having its own unique attire. In Ireland such differences began around the sixteenth century. Prior to that a tribal government existed that attempted to maintain the old traditions in dress. The effort was assisted by the cultural teachers, such as poets and historians

> who traveled from tribe to tribe to encourage development and maintenance of a unified culture. These two factors probably were responsible for the maintenance of uniform dress throughout the country; however, by the sixteenth century, warring resulted in destruction, devastation, and a breakdown of the old tribal government. Royal power of England increased so that by the end of the sixteenth century almost the entire island was under the central authority of England. As a result, custom and tradition probably began to break and dress became less uniform throughout Ireland. (Meurisse 1970, p. 140)

Figure 4.6 The girls' dress identifies their Dutch affiliation. (Library of Congress)

The Hutzuls of Ukrainia could determine from which village each person came through subtle variations in dress such as color, kind of embroidery, and accessories (Warnick 1974, p. 116). The same thing was also true in Moravian Slovakia, where there were twenty-eight general costume districts. Within each of these districts the dress differed according to the individual community in such small ways as the number of buttons used or the number of folds in the women's head scarves or the arrangement and color of the men's hat decorations (Bogatyrev 1971, p. 54). Primitive peoples have also developed such nuances in dress. For instance, the Dyaks of Borneo show the part of the tribe to which they belong by the length, color, trim, and method of wearing of a man's waist cloth. American Indian tribes whose members wore moccasins could be told apart from other tribes by tribal peculiarities in the moccasins' shape (Krieger 1928). The Indian tribes also had unique hair styles so that from a distance they could tell enemies apart from fellow tribesmen.

The decline of such folk costume has been a concomitant of increased industrial production of clothing and changes in the patterns of government. Which has had the greater influence is unclear. It is clear, however, that this decline has been associated with a decrease in local or community identification as the provider of a major sense of belonging. Clothing has continued to become more uniform and less able to distinguish social data.

> This can be taken as a sign of a general step forward—the disappearance of social barriers, a rise in the level of culture and information—but it is also an indication that the individual has lost his ties with the members of a group in the bosom of which he had been integrated in his own right.
>
> To live in the costume of one's province or of one's nation insures the sense that one is an individual element in a group where one plays a role as one's proper self, and also insures a sense of opposition to other groups. To live in a standardized human uniform prefigures a broad interchangeability of individuals as so many units in a universal macro-organism. To make clothing symbols uniform means that a man acquires a planetary self-awareness and loses his relative independence as an ethnic person. (Gourhan 1970, p. 155)

Dress Communicators

Dressing, both selecting items and putting them on, is a behavior, and all behavior is communicative. Much, perhaps in some instances even most, of this communication is unconscious. It occurs because the observer sees the behavior and interprets it. How accurate such interpretation is, therefore, is determined by the degree of congruence between the observer's perceptions and the performer's intention, conscious or unconscious. This congruence generally increases as the level of overt consciousness rises. Thus, for example, Marilyn Monroe's beauty mark was an effort, either conscious or unconscious, to relate something about herself to the rest of the world. Had she verbally expressed what the beauty mark meant to her she would have heightened both her own and the observer's awareness of the mark and its meaning. In the seventeenth century such marks had a conscious meaning; they were words with agreed-upon definitions.

In London they were even used as political devices, the right-wing Whigs wearing them on the right cheek, and the (then) left-wing Tories wearing them on the left. The simple black spots soon grew into fancy shapes, such as crescents and stars, and at the court of Louis XV the precise position of these facial adornments became loaded with meaning: the corner of the eye indicated passion, the centre of the cheek gaiety, the nose sauciness, the forehead majesty, and so on, around the face. (Morris 1977, p. 227).

The fan is an item of dress that has also been part of an agreed-upon communication system in most societies that have commonly used the fan. By gesturing with one's fan, one could send messages from the specific, such as arranging a tryst, to the general, such as indicating one's mood. Wildeblood and Brinson (1965) analyzed the language of the fan in seventeenth- and eighteenth-century Europe. They found, for example, that one way of communicating with the fan was by touching its tip to different parts of the face. For instance, at the lips it meant "be quiet," at the right cheek it said "yes," at the left "no," and at the tip of the forehead it meant "you're crazy." Today eyeglasses may be used in a similar fashion. For example,

Figure 4.7 In his painting, *The Letter Writer–Seville,* John Philip shows the fan used for privacy. (Library of Congress)

> Throwing down a pair of glasses . . . expresses anger and hostility. . . .
>   . . . When you don't see eye to eye with someone, you will often remove your glasses while you're talking. It's a subtle, unconscious way of getting the message across.
>   However, this assumes that the person wears glasses because he is nearsighted. A farsighted person will remove glasses in order to see more clearly, and the removal will have an entirely different meaning. (Fast 1970, p. 167)

The two elements of dress most universally used to communicate are color and hair style. Both are aspects of all costumes. Hair style is the most universal element of dress since even the naked person has a hair style. It would seem that every hair style, whether done consciously or unconsciously, does communicate data about the individual, his or her culture, and his or her relationship to it.

Color, while not an element of dress for the naked person, is probably the element of dress with the most common meanings. White, black, and red have been the colors most frequently used in rituals that, it has been suggested, reflect their association with "body products and fluids associated with the process of living" (Vlahos 1979, p. 21). Colors have had specific meanings within a culture, particularly in primitive societies. The Thompson Indians, for instance, designated north with white, east with red, south with yellow, and west with black. The Zulu girl writes love messages in her beading of her necklace. Since these bead love letters are worn, anyone who knows their code can read their message. They are read by interpreting the beads, which usually stand for letters; the threads of beads, which stand for words; and the pattern of beads, which indicate a sentence or "complete thought. The sentence may have a double meaning. . . . In reading a message, therefore, one takes note of the meaning of the colors of the bead, its position in the pattern, the background on which it is fitted, the sex of the person to whom the message is addressed . . ." (Twala 1951, p. 115). A girl's first "love letter" is usually all white to show her pure and waiting heart. To show interest in marriage, she adds black at the sides and a red band.

White has symbolized innocence and purity in many cultures, others have commonly used it to connote hostility and war, mourning and death, winter, milk, and semen. Red has usually meant blood, life, health, and, less commonly, indicated war, speed, autumn, and transcendence of the normal world. Black has been used to show evil, night, cold, death and mourning, dirt, and rain. The Tchikrin Indians used black to indicate transitional periods or states "where normal clear-cut structures of ideas and rules of behavior are 'blacked out' " (Turner 1969, p. 70). Gray has been used for the world of spirits and for death. Green has meant spring, energy, youth, and earthiness. Blue has denoted sky and truth and loyalty (true blue). Yellow has spoken of sun, warmth, summer, peace, and cowardliness. The modern American's use of colors is more personal or idiosyncratic, although there are some very generalized associations between mood and color.

Figure 4.8 Zulu girls wearing beaded love messages. (National Anthropological Archives, Smithsonian Institution)

SUMMARY

Communication is the least likely theory to explain the origins of dress. It is, however, the most universal *result* of dress and may currently be the most universal function of dress. As a medium of communication, dress communicates social information such as economic status, social roles and status, group affiliation, and personal identity in terms of lifestyle, values, attitudes, mood. Thus, dress enhances society's efficient functioning and facilitates social interaction. Societies with more stable and unvaried fashions have a more precise language of dress.

Perception is the process of taking in sensory data and identifying, organizing, and interpreting it. It is an intrinsic part of communication, yet no two people can ever perceive any one thing in exactly the same way owing to a variety of variables that come together to cause us to perceive data selectively and analyze it uniquely. Person perception is the individual's perceptual process of other humans. The first step in person perception is the formulation of first impressions. These impressions are based primarily on demeanor, especially appearance.

Both the selection of dress and the method of wearing it are behaviors that communicate. The more conscious this effort to communicate is, the more apt it is to be accurate. Unfortunately, much of Western clothing behavior is unconscious as is the use of dress in analysis of others. Yet, because dress is a visual statement, it is impossible to avoid its impact in visual situations. It is this inevitability of the communicative function of dress that makes this aspect of dress so much more powerful than any of the other functions.

Solution to problem, page 106:

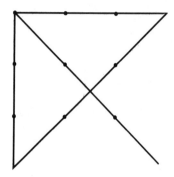

5 | Roles

Roles define the individual in his or her society by describing the special tasks or functions he or she has in that society. In this chapter we shall analyze typical kinds of roles, their function in personality development and in society, and how dress relates to roles.

Roles are learned. The behavior norms pertaining to a role are internalized by the individual so that he or she performs the role in a predictable and standardized mode. The more clearly defined and enforced a role is, the more likely its associated dress will be specialized and formalized; this is typical in societies with strongly authoritarian governments. As roles become less well defined, their associated dress will become less role specific, more flexible, and, therefore, more useful for other roles. Since one individual will have many roles, multi-role dress will have an economic (time and money) advantage. Role flexibility expands the area for one's potential interpersonal relationships, since interactions with people in a wider range of roles become more probable.

Roles in modern America are becoming less clearly defined. Adherence to one's role is not legally enforced but is controlled through social or peer pressure. The result is that behavioral norms of roles have become less universal, although there are some roles that are still quite standardized. With these more formal and standardized roles, there is greater social distance between those in the role and those not in it as well as between the individual and the physical environment. For example, individuals who wear informal work clothes, which will not be ruined if they become dirty, can more easily interact physically with their environment (Goffman 1963).

The language of clothing is particularly well developed in the area of role-related dress. Such standardized knowledge of what to expect from others facilitates social interactions; for example, should a person in a police officer's uniform stop our car, we would expect certain behaviors. This expectation has been used by some criminal elements to commit crimes by wearing police dress in order to gain the initial trust and concomitant lack of wariness of the victim. Even so, the overwhelming odds remain that someone in a police officer's uniform will protect rather than attack.

EFFECT ON THE INDIVIDUAL

Roles can be ascribed or achieved. Ascribed roles are those that are given rather than chosen or worked for; age, sex, race, and birth circumstances (son, only daughter, oldest child) are examples of ascribed roles. Achieved roles are roles to which we may have aspired and for the attainment of which we have taken specific actions; career, marital status, and avocation are examples of achieved roles. Ascribed roles generally are more pervasive than achieved roles; they often determine what other roles we can assume and even the manner in which we assume them. The most pervasive role in modern American society is sex, an ascribed role. Some roles may be extremely limited in their impact on our other roles. For example, if a person is only a weekend tennis player, the role of tennis player may have no impact on any of his other roles.

The roles that we have can affect our personality development. People react to others partially on the basis of their mutual roles, and it is from the reactions of others to oneself that the self-concept develops. As we mature, we will play or act out different roles in an effort to ascertain with which ones we are comfortable and from which we get the positive reactions of others. This role playing may be formalized; the student being given on-the-job-training is learning to play the role for that job in a formalized setting. However, much role playing is informal, such as the soon-to-graduate college senior's experimentations with dress.

SITUATIONAL INFLUENCE

Roles can conflict with each other if we cannot meet the demands of all the roles that we must perform at one time. In such conflicts we generally choose to meet the demands of the most valued role. For example, when the chairman of a corporate board of directors is chairing the annual stockholders' meeting, she must be impeccably dressed. Taking her child to his day-care center where the child wants to show "Mommy" how he learned to build a sandcastle may conflict with her corporate-role dress needs. Women filling a traditionally male occupational role often feel role conflict between their sex and their occupational roles. Army women's fight to wear earrings probably reflected this conflict.

We often change our clothing as we change our role. Clothing can even symbolize a changing role. In parts of Southeast Asia and Australia women adopt male dress if they are performing a masculine role or are no longer deemed feminine because of widowhood or age. When the clothing associated with any role changes, the role itself will be changing. For example, as American women became more involved in the labor force and in activities outside the home, their dress became simpler, less voluminous, and shorter. It has even been suggested (Bush and London 1960) that the changes in modern sex and age roles, their lack of specific definition, and the frequent conflict within those roles have brought about the great variety of clothing styles for women and for adolescents. While clothing expectations are often less rigid where roles are less clearly defined, confidence and social success frequently depend on our skill in accurately predicting the appropriate dress for our role in a specific situation. For example, between social transactions one might wish to change clothing, even if that change is as small as (in the case of a man) loosening or taking off one's necktie. However, if someone loosens his tie when others present feel more formality should be maintained, he will decrease his chance for success in the situation. Church dress—Sunday-go-to-meeting clothes—is among the most formal daily wear. Work dress also tends to be more formal. At-home dress and social dress are usually more informal. Informal or casual dress often so reflects an individual's avocation that Zweig (1952) found after-work attire actually showed how a man spent his after-work hours.

The complex interrelation between role and dress is evident today primarily in shoes, which have been found to change according to role more than any other dress item. Specific shoe styles have been designed for various types of activities—sports, social, at-home, school, occupational, travel. These style areas vary according to such factors as sex, age, status, values, season, and geographic location. In earlier times most items of dress were equally involved. The English gentleman of the early nineteenth century, for example, needed six pairs of gloves per day, from reindeer gloves for a hunt to embroidered white lambskin gloves for dancing. By the turn of the century, the Edwardian woman needed five different outfits per day for breakfast, walking, resting, dressing or lounging, and dinner. Of course, at that time in rural pioneer America, activities were limited primarily to work-related ones, and one outfit was sufficient throughout the day.

Informal dress for outside the home is generally cleaner and/or newer than housewear. Bogatyrev (1971) analyzed the functions of everyday dress as opposed to holiday dress and found that while many of the functions are the same, their degree of importance differs. It is especially illuminating to note

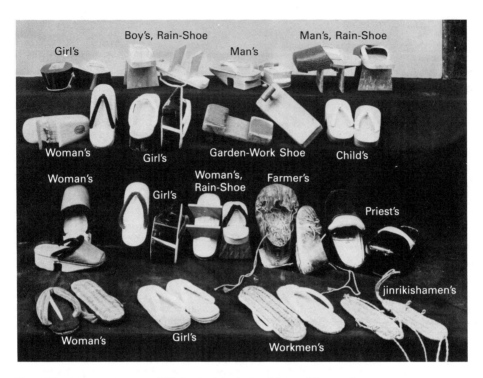

Figure 5.1 Japanese shoes, ca. 1900, for a variety of roles. (Library of Congress)

Bogatyrev's Functions of Dress*

EVERYDAY DRESS	HOLIDAY DRESS
1. Utility	1. Ceremonial
2. Social status	2. Aesthetics
3. Aesthetics	3. Ritual
4. Group belonging	4. Group belonging
	5. Social status
	6. Utility

*Listed in order of importance
From Bogatyrev 1971, p. 43.

that two of the most important holiday dress functions, ceremonial and ritual, are not even a consideration in everyday dress. Utility, the prime function of everyday dress, is the least important for holiday dress.

SEX ROLES

Sex and age roles are the most universal. Of the two, sex is generally more important, perhaps because of its greater influence on family and occupational roles. In some societies dress is extremely different between the sexes while in others it is fairly similar. If the cut is the same, the detail will probably differ.

In societies employing only corporal adornment, the amount, kind, or placement of the adornment may differ. All of these differences are maintained by social taboos or laws, civil or religious, against wearing the dress of the opposite sex. Sometimes one sex is allowed greater freedom in this respect. The American female, for example, is able to wear male dress without receiving social disapproval, although the American male would be ridiculed were he to don dress and heels.

The dress differences between the sexes tend to reflect the role differences between them. For example, the modern Western woman has been, and to some degree still is, judged by how capable she is in attracting and keeping a man. Thus, most women have invested considerable time, effort, and money into increasing their attractiveness in terms of the aesthetic standard of their culture and time. There may be, therefore, some truth in the old adage that women dress to attract men. However, it is probably equally true that men dress to attract women. The difference is in how the sexes attract each other. Traditionally, women have attracted men through their physical beauty, whereas men have attracted women through their occupational/financial success. Thus, the woman has emphasized her physical appearance while the man has stressed his socioeconomic level. But both behaviors have been manifestations of the same goal.

Pregnancy is involved solely with the female role as is child rearing in most cultures. Maternity dress is, in part, determined by normal wear. A Japa-

Figure 5.2 Bedouin female dress is suitable for pregnancy and breast feeding. (Library of Congress)

nese woman, for example, can wear her kimono during pregnancy but not her obi; thus, the pregnant woman wears a special obi with her regular kimono. American Indians whose dress was loose fitting were also able to use their normal dress for maternity wear although breast feeding sometimes required the opening of a side seam. The Zulu woman wears a full-length antelope-skin apron over her traditional attire. Her husband killed the animal for this apron and his father prepared the skin (Tyrrell, 1968). The Eskimo woman can wear her normal dress because it is designed for pregnancy and motherhood. The wide hood and full, broad-shouldered jacket are ideal as a pouch in which to carry the baby or toddler and under which the child can be passed from the back carrying position to the front for breast feeding. The Eskimo male's parka fits more tightly and uses bigger skins (so that it has fewer seams through which air or water can enter) than the female's because the men are out of doors more. In those cultures where men are more involved in public interactions and activities, men tend to be more decoratively attired. After all, they will be the ones seen and, therefore, evaluated in terms of the family's degree of success.

One of the differences between the sexes, which has often been used as a basis for discrimination, is menstruation. In most societies there is a negative association with menstruating women. This is also true in modern America, where a spot of blood on one's skirt is extremely embarrassing to the woman and any observers. Tampons have allowed women to feel more confident since tampons have no tell-tale bulge or odor associated with them. It has even been suggested (Schroeder 1976) that technological advances in menstrual pads and

Figure 5.3 Eskimo woman with her baby. (The Estate of Dr. Cook, courtesy of Janet Vetter)

Figure 5.4 The telephone company linewoman dresses for her work role in clothes like these worn by her male counterpart. (Southern Bell)

tampons have had more to do with shorter hemlines and fewer petticoats than emancipation has!

As sex roles become more similar, sex differences in dress decrease. Today's more unisexual dress reflects both greater sexual equality and the fact that in modern society there is less need for male and female sex-role differences. For example, birth control has allowed modern individuals the luxury of determining whether pregnancy and child rearing are roles they will assume. When both parents freely choose parenthood, then both will probably participate more fully in the consequences of that choice. Thus, differences in parenting behaviors should be less radical, since each parent should be more willing to assume the duties parenthood brings. Both sexes are more often working in the same office area so that the weight differences between male and female dress have had to decrease; constriction differences—at the neck, for instance, from a starched collar with tie—are also declining.

Unisexual Dress

Unisexual dress was evident in the nineteenth century when pioneer women and women in groups such as the Oneida Community began to wear trousers as they worked side by side with the men. However, in most urban communities the adoption of male dress was not accepted. Dr. Mary Walker, a Civil War surgeon, dressed in trousers worn under a full-length tunic. She soon adopted the male's frock coat for day wear and tails for evening (with perhaps a flower

Figure 5.5 Women going to the Klondike in 1897 wore more masculine dress. (Library of Congress)

Figure 5.6 (a & b) Dr. Mary Walker's dress became progressively more unisexual. (Library of Congress)

a   b

Figure 5.7 Early 20th century bifurcated skirt. (Library of Congress)

in her lapel) and cut her hair quite short. Frequently arrested for impersonating a man, she fought in the courts for the right to dress as she pleased. By the early twentieth century, fashionable women were wearing a tunic over pants. Trousers increased in popularity in the 1920s and 1930s as women continued to assume more roles outside the home. Female factory workers in World War II put the final stamp of acceptance on female trousers.

One of the few examples of unisex dress adapted from traditionally feminine attire was that of the late 1960s when young men let their hair grow long and began to sport colorful, full-sleeved shirts; tunics; flared trousers; jewelry; and higher-heeled shoes. However, in 1983 when a high school in Florida banned shorts while still allowing miniskirts, only about twelve young men could muster up sufficient courage to protest by wearing miniskirts. Of course, the school administration would not allow miniskirts to be worn by the boys, who gave in when threatened with expulsion. The rarity of feminized unisexual dress may reflect a dichotomy in sex-role changes. Although men are assuming more traditionally female roles, public interest in role changes and acceptance of them have rested primarily in women's assumption of traditionally male roles. This dichotomy seems to be symbolized in modern unisexual dress.

AGE ROLES

In modern America age roles are next in importance to sex roles since age is also a factor in family and occupational roles. While age extremes are identifiable, many age differences are not as easy to distinguish as are those of sex. But

Figure 5.8 Age roles are evident in the styles of dress worn by the adult female, young girl, baby girl, and male toddler.

when dress is obviously inappropriate to age, the incongruity will be noted, although it will probably not be directly mentioned to the offender. In other cultures wearing of age-appropriate dress may be more rigidly enforced.

Early Childhood

Infant wear generally shows fewer sex differences, perhaps because the sex roles of an infant are less specific. Traditionally, blue has been the American color for boys and pink for girls. In other cultures different colors are used—for example, red for girls and white for boys among the Andes Indians. Diaper folds are also different with the girls having the thickest padding at the back and boys at the front, although disposable diapers do not reflect this difference. However, most infants' and children's wear reflects age rather than sex role. Since infants do not like to be dressed and undressed, their garments should be simple to put on and take off. Snaps instead of sewn seams, for instance, allow babies to be dressed without pulling a garment over their heads, arms, or legs. Infant wear also must take into account a baby's lack of toilet training. Some cultures do this by not dressing their babies; most modern American parents dress their babies in disposable diapers or rubber pants. However, in cultures where babies are dressed and either wear no diapers or cloth ones, infant wear should be rapid-drying and dye fast. It also needs to be warmer since an infant's physiological thermostat does not function as efficiently. There should be no buttons or decorations that could be pulled off by the baby and swallowed to cause choking. However, permanently attached cords or strings can be stimulating and safe adventures.

Toddlers' dress must be practical for their active days now that they have achieved mobility and must be easy to put on to encourage "self-help" skills involved with dressing themselves. Clothing should be easy to fasten with velcro, zippers, or big buttons; have as few places needing closing as possible; and have all closings in the front. Walking is easiest for the barefooted novice. Those high-topped baby shoes make it more difficult, as do slippery booties or socks. Children often prefer familiar dress items and this is particularly so for toddlers, who will like best the clothing over which they have the most mastery. Toddlers are building their language skills and exploring their world; therefore, various textures, colors, and sartorial adornments are useful.

All children's wear should be durable and easy to care for. "Growth room"—by purchasing a size too large, or an item with large seams and deep hems,—is another consideration, especially for families with limited budgets. Shoes, on the other hand, should not be bought with growth room but should fit as well as possible. Children can remain the same size for several months; however, when they are in a growth spurt, they can change several sizes in only a few months. Thus, clothing purchases should be made for the child's current use and size rather than for some future need. Pockets appeal to many children, as do hats. Dress allowing for easy movement is important; although at the end of the nineteenth century children were still garbed like miniature adults, with little girls wearing corsets, tight waists, and low-cut bodices.

Children explore their world through play, and one of the most educational play forms is role playing, more commonly known as dress-up. Such play enables the child to learn about different roles and to discover, through experimentation and imitation, the behaviors appropriate to a specific role. While the actual clothing props are not required for successful role playing, they do facilitate the game, especially when a group of children are playing, and dress cues can provide an instant, visual reminder to all the children of each child's specific role.

Puberty and Adolescence

In most cultures there is some ritualistic ceremony recognizing a child's transition, at puberty, into adulthood. The Cuna Indian girl cuts her hair, which is thereafter kept short. Until the 1920s the American ceremony primarily involved dress; a boy changed his short pants for long trousers, and a girl could finally wear her hair "up" in, for example, a bun or chignon. In the 1950s girls celebrated "maturity" with make-up, nylon stockings, and high-heeled shoes. Some societies celebrate puberty by putting clothes on the pubescent child/adult for the first time; in other societies the change is to more revealing clothing. Many primitive cultures use body-alteration techniques such as tattooing or scarification. These techniques often have some purpose other than mere adornment or communication of status. Frequently this is done for protection; for example, the Balinese file the adolescent's teeth to fend off characteristics like laziness, lust, materialism, and vanity. Some rites are designed to complete the transformation into adulthood. The scarification ceremony of the New Guinea male adolescent, for example, is believed to remove the inferior female part of him, a part created by the mother-child bond.

The American teenager's interest in clothing increases as he or she matures and becomes more interested in attracting the opposite sex. Teens, especially young teens, also use dress in a kind of role play as they struggle to establish their own identity. Thus, a teenager may insist on a clothing purchase that his parent recognizes as inappropriate. However, if the teen is allowed to make this mistake (with the consequential reduction in his clothing budget), he will learn from the reactions of his peers whether it is or is not suitable for him. If young people, even as early as seven or eight, are allowed to fully participate in part or all of their clothing expenditures, they will be able to learn to use their budget more wisely.

Adulthood

The casual dress of the modern young adult is remarkably similar between the sexes. Their dress reflects their wish to fit in and be part of the group, as well as their desire to be attractive to members of the opposite sex. Just as teenagers do, they want to demonstrate both their independence from their families and their sophistication or worldliness. Thus, one is more likely to find an outrageous "costume" on a young adult than on an older person. It is in young adulthood that the female is most likely to be so heavily made up that one has no idea what she really looks like, and the male is most likely to have his ears pierced or get a tattoo.

As we mature, our dress becomes more predictable because we develop our own unique style. This style is not apt to be radically different from the norm; the differences will be reflected in color choices, accessorizing, trim details, or the like. During the years of middle age (35–60), the majority of people are at their most attractive in terms of their dress. Since divorce has become more acceptable, adults tend to work harder at maintaining a youthful appearance so that their mates will not need to exchange them for a younger model. Thus, we find more middle-aged women and men dieting, exercising, and receiving the benefits of cosmetic surgery. Compounding this is our society's emphasis on youth and antipathy toward aging. Unwilling to accept the inevitability of physical deterioration and death, Americans spend a great deal of effort keeping away from the aged and the dying. Old age is, of course, a relatively new phenomenon as an experience for the majority. In eighteenth-century Europe the average life expectancy was thirty-seven; in America at the turn of the century it was fifty; yet today's baby can expect to live to seventy-eight or even longer. Thus it is only recently that society has had to address itself to issues relating to an aging population. Since our society is fast-changing, the old are considered to be less well informed and are therefore less valued as a group. But as they increase in numbers, they will also increase in power, both political and consumer. Dress designs for the elderly are likely to become a prime investment area in the future. Such designs should reflect the physiological changes of the aging human body. For example, because the body's thermostat becomes less efficient as it ages, the elderly get cold more easily, especially at night, when the rate of the body processes tends to reduce. Thus, clothing for the elderly should be designed to provide greater warmth than the same item for a younger person would. Fire-retardant fabrics are also more important for old hands and slower reflexes. The elderly tend to like familiar, more traditional styles. Since they sit more, designs with a bulky area in the lower back or buttocks would be less appropriate. As agility and flexibility decrease, wrap-arounds, front fasteners, and velcro closings are easier to handle. Garments should allow for size fluctuations due to water retention, a common problem among many of the elderly. Designs that hide the widening waist and sagging skin areas (upper arms) are more attractive—like a long-sleeved A-line. Perhaps designs developed to "fit" the aging body and the aging individual's roles would help to change the spending patterns of our elderly, who currently spend considerably less for clothing than do their younger counterparts.

OCCUPATIONAL ROLES

Dress has been and is frequently associated with occupational roles. In modern American society this association influences interpersonal judgments since it is a common, though unstated, belief that we are what we do. This belief is

Figure 5.9 (a & b)   Just who is the mistress and who her maid is obvious—from their dress. (Library of Congress)

a   b

evident in the typical first question asked of a person one has just met in a social setting: "What do you do?" However, dress historically has often indicated occupation. The Chinese, for example, indicated occupation by the color and shape of a man's head covering.

The dress expectations of a job must be learned in order for successful performance. Promotions can change dress requirements, and success may depend on one's adopting the expected new dress neither too soon nor too late. Such dress expectations are standards, implicit or written into a dress code, which are commonly held by all the workers within a field or company. They may reflect safety requirements, identification concerns, economic issues, or efficiency factors.

White-Collar Dress

Businesses usually try to adopt the most widely acceptable dress style with the more conservative businesses adopting more conservative dress. For example, when the successful executive of a firm engaged in medical research became the director of a bank, he was asked to wear the traditional suit, shirt, and tie in conservatively muted colors. Such a business suit symbolizes seriousness, efficiency, and "get-ahead Americanism." It is the versatile modern example of the sack suit, which became popular because it was suitable for wear throughout the day. Business dress is associated with office work, with the white-collar worker who uses dress as a symbol of occupational success. More prestigious and influential positions will relate with both greater quantity and better quality of clothing. Dress will be selected to impress the public as well as fellow workers. As women entered the business world, they began to adapt the business suit to a skirted version. The result was a simple, practical style that ultimately resulted in short skirts and trousers. The tailored dress of the office is more classic in style than fashionable.

However, while men's business dress is not stylistically much different from less formal suits or from year-to-year designs, women's business dress does have significant differences. This may reflect the fact that a woman's sex role is still generally seen as different from the role of a successful business executive, whereas the male's sex role equates the two. Thus, women may feel a conflict in the tailored, masculine look of business and the frilly, feminine, female stereotype. However, it is unlikely that ultrafeminine street-length skirts could ever again become popular for day wear *unless* the primary female role returns to the home. Computers could conceivably enable such a return if white-collar workers become able to perform their tasks at computer consoles located in their own homes.

Blue-Collar Dress

Laborers or blue-collar workers dress to fit in with their fellow workers. Their clothing choices are utilitarian: practical, economical, durable. Since the mid-nineteenth century, when women mine workers in Britain wore trousers like those worn by the male miners (Lucas 1979), women laborers have often adopted masculine work dress. Many modern female "hard hats" wear jeans or work pants with a practical top like a T-shirt or sweatshirt. To feminize themselves, they use perfume, cosmetics, and brighter-colored shirts.

Workers involved in physical labor cannot wear too many clothes or tightly fitting ones that might impede physical movement or the evaporation of sweat. Many laborers wear aprons or coveralls to save their street wardrobe. Others, such as firefighters and radiation workers, choose their dress primarily for safety reasons. As more women began to work in factories during World War II, safety issues in women's wear were raised, such as ease of physical movement, particularly in bending, stretching, and climbing, and measures to keep garments or hair from being caught in machinery. To meet these safety requirements, women could not wear high heels; open-toed shoes; loose, long hair; long sashes; jewelry; or full sleeves or skirts while at work in factories.

Uniforms

Occupational dress, such as uniforms, may be worn for quick identification. They are often a way to differentiate employees by specific role or rank. This differentiation may ultimately influence interpersonal interactions within the occupational environment (Lafferty and Dickey 1980). Courtesans and prostitutes are an example of people who dress for occupational recognition. In ancient Rome prostitutes had to be blondes, natural or bleached. Prostitutes have usually been more made up, depilated, bathed, scented, coiffed, and breath sweetened than the average woman. Priests and nuns, doctors and nurses, police and military are some other examples.

Uniforms are a "fixed" or traditional clothing, which will rarely change. Any changes that do occur will probably be small. This is true even for social or activity uniforms like those of the Boy or Girl Scouts. However, when a role changes, so may its associated uniform. Lafferty and Dickey (1980) found that those nurses who viewed nursing most traditionally were more positive toward traditional dress symbols of nursing and wore them more frequently: cap, school pin, white uniform. Nurses who viewed nursing nontraditionally, especially those with a B.A. degree, were the most negative toward these symbols and wore them least frequently. Many workers involved in service roles (such as porters, stewardesses, waitresses) also dress so as to be easily recognized by the public.

Certain professions wear the vestiges of uniforms historically associated with them. This is particularly true in societies where tradition is respected and maintained, in England, for instance. Students may wear a uniform (or school tie) to indicate their school allegiance. Professors and scholars may wear academic robes or other designators. The English scholar's dress is a more complete costume; the color of the robe designates both the subject area of the degree and the college granting it. The level of the degree has many symbols: the bachelor's has a long, pointed sleeve and three-foot hood; the master's has a long, slit sleeve and three-and-a-half-foot hood; the doctoral has a long, bell

SALLY FORTH   by Greg Howard

Figure 5.10   Subtle dress differences can communicate radically different roles. (Field Enterprises)

sleeve, velvet trim, gold tassel on the cap, and a four-foot hood. England's legal profession still uses legal wigs, which have, when worn correctly, an equalizing and dignifying effect. It has even been suggested that these wigs enhance performance (Woodforde 1971). In court the modern American lawyer wears no wig but a conservative suit and plain shirt or blouse, which is neither shabby nor too expensive looking. The judges will probably be wearing black robes, like those worn by judges since 1714, when they wore black in mourning for Queen Anne. However, black is not mandatory, and some judges have opted for other colors, such as purple in Wyoming. The defendant and his or her family should be dressed conservatively in a wardrobe that suggests middle-class values and a secure but not affluent economic level. Such dress is designed to suggest to the viewer, a juror in this case, that the wearer has a lifestyle and value structure similar to his own.

LIFESTYLE

Dress has also symbolized lifestyles. For example, religious dress, representing a religious lifestyle, is designed to shield the wearers against the temptations of the world by keeping them somewhat isolated from those not sharing their religious views and dress. The "artiste" or bohemian dresses to assert his uniqueness from the mundane rest of the world and his similarity to other sensitive intellectuals. Since old men have been associated with philosophy, many male philosophers have emphasized their masculinity and maturity by wearing a beard. The rebel will indicate his or her rebellion by wearing dress that is antifashion and similar to that worn by other devotees to the particular cause.

Sportswear

The majority of modern Americans use sportswear for everyday dress to symbolize their casual, informal, and egalitarian lifestyle. It would seem likely that sportswear has developed from participation, either as a viewer or player, in sports. Sports and leisure activities created a new need for clothing and a new function. Most active sports roles, from umpire to ball boy, have some clothing items associated with them. America has made sports clothing a fashion influence throughout the world, but these garments began to evolve at least as early as ancient Greece.

Riding and hunting were probably the earliest sports participated in by adults of both sexes in Europe. The usual dress of the aristocrats was too inhibiting and ornate to be worn for such activities. Men's dress was modified for riding and hunting by cutting out the front of the coat and leaving tails in the back for ease in sitting, making the boots sturdier and higher, and reducing the size of the hat brim. Women, unfortunately, were usually forced to ride sidesaddle, a precarious position indeed. If astride, they had to wear skirts of extreme width so that their legs would remain covered. Some riding skirts had buttons and loops at the back to fasten the excess skirt. It was not until the late nineteenth century that bifurcated riding skirts were introduced in the United States and later adopted in Europe. By the 1920s most women rode astride in jodhpurs.

Archery and croquet became popular in the 1860s. Since clothing did not greatly interfere with croquet competency, normal streetwear was worn. However, lawn tennis, which developed soon after, was more difficult to play wearing normal dress. Women's clothing was especially handicapping since their gowns were tight, with a bustle in the rear and leg o'mutton sleeves. They did have special shoes that had one-inch heels and soles of India rubber—and were black to hide grass stains. Tennis aprons protected the dresses from dirt and also provided big pockets for carrying the tennis balls (Warren 1982). Edwar-

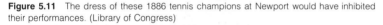

Figure 5.11 The dress of these 1886 tennis champions at Newport would have inhibited their performances. (Library of Congress)

dian dress was looser and had no bustle, making tennis easier to play and thus more popular. Since tennis was played in summer when white was the most popular color, and white showed perspiration less, white became the predominant color for tennis wear. In 1919 Suzanne Lenglen played at Wimbledon wearing a scarf on her head, a calf-length pleated skirt, a short-sleeved blouse, white stockings, and no corsets or petticoats. Lenglen, who related lawn tennis to ballet, had been influenced by the Russian ballet. Soft fabrics complemented her gracefulness and gave her greater freedom of movement (Tinling 1977). This was the beginning of modern tennis wear.

> Gentlemen tennis players suffered relatively little from the restrictions of fashion.
>
> In the 1880's and 90's, gentlemen wore well-cut, cream or white flannel trousers and long-sleeved shirts, buttoned at the cuff. From this time and well into the early 1900's, the "Owe Forty" or blanket coat was worn to and from the track, almost like the Victorian equivalent to the track suit of modern times! From the beginning, gentlemen's tennis wear was casual, combining comfort and ease. Neatly rolled sleeves became the convention, until short sleeves appeared with shorts in the 1930's. (Warren 1982, p. 23)

But tennis did not have as much influence on fashion as bicycling. The latter, it has been suggested, was the major force for freedom in women's dress. Biking began as an upper-class activity, so dress innovations were likely. By the 1890s women bikers were commonly seen wearing bloomers or another form of bifurcated skirt. Biking tops were tailored and often masculine.

Figure 5.12   The female cyclist's dress made cycling a more dangerous sport for her. (British Columbia Provincial Archives)

Team sports use uniforms in order to be able to quickly identify their fellow team members. The importance of this instant recognition factor was seen in the 1982 NCAA basketball final between Georgetown and North Carolina. In the final seconds of play, with Georgetown leading by one point, a Georgetown player passed the ball to North Carolina's Worthy, who made the winning basket. The highest-seeded team in each tournament game wore white, and until the final, Georgetown had worn white. Thus, under pressure in a situation in which he had to react instantly, the player threw to a man in white, perhaps because he had associated the white uniform with his own team in all of the previous games.

CEREMONIAL DRESS

Some roles are ceremonial in nature. The most universal characteristic of ceremonial clothing is its newness; new clothes may symbolize the new life change that is being ritualized (Crawley 1960). Ceremonial dress usually differs from daily wear in quantity or level of ornateness. European ceremonial dress has been heavily imbued with centuries of tradition. For example, the English Parliament opens with a ceremony at which the nobles wear bands of ermine to indicate their specific rank. Members of the House of Commons wear knee breeches like those worn during the reign of William II; their coat design dates from the early nineteenth century (Hurlock 1976). Some religious ceremonies also use dress to indicate the type of ceremony; for instance, the priest's vestment indicates the kind of mass. The two most universal ceremonies, celebrated throughout most of the world since recorded history began, are the recognition of a marriage or some similar union for procreation and the recognition of a death.

Weddings

In most societies weddings are among the most joyous celebrations. After all, a wedding represents the creation of a new family unit, potential growth of the society, and a strengthening of ties between two family groups. The last is evident in the exchange of gifts between the families. The groom and his family often give clothing to the bride and her family, which may include all or part of her wedding costume; for example, the American bride and her mother are given their flowers by the groom. Frequently the dress will have been made by the groom or his relatives; thus, the Hopi bride's trousseau is made from cloth woven by the groom.

Most dress associated with weddings is symbolic of fertility or of strength; for example, orange blossoms, cowrie shells, and wheat sheaves often symbolize fertility, while boars' tusks and rings may symbolize strength. Protection or good fortune are also "enhanced" by wearing certain items. The veil was originally intended to protect the bride from the evil eye. In order to convince any evil powers that the bride and groom are not worthy of their attention or are too powerful for it, bridal couples have dressed variously in mourning clothes, in the dress of the opposite sex, in dirty clothes, in the attire of royalty, or in the same dress as others present at the wedding (to confuse evil). The colors chosen are sometimes designed to repel evil. Good fortune may be invited by the bride's wearing a sixpence in her shoe or a combination of "something old, something new, something borrowed, and something blue."

White, originally used for mourning, replaced red for the bride's dress after Anne of Brittany wore a plain white satin gown for her wedding to France's Louis XII. It came to symbolize the bride's virginity so that it was thought appropriate only for first marriages when the bride was not pregnant. This association with virginity has decreased as sexual values and behaviors have altered. The bride or someone in her family may make part or all of her gown, or she may gather the flowers she will carry. She may choose to wear a dress worn by her mother, grandmother, or some other family member or close friend. Whatever her choices, her final selections will reflect the personal symbols of her values and interests. Some symbols are less easy to understand but probably represent an important aspect of marriage or the wedding ceremony. For example, the Molgal in Korea wash their faces with urine before they marry; the bride wears an uncomfortable shirt of hemp, while the groom is attired in pigskin with a fur hat adorned by a tiger or leopard tail (Osgood 1966).

Mourning

Mourning, or the recognition of a death, is a sad or frightening occasion in most societies. Special clothes for mourning have been used throughout the world, primarily to demonstrate or symbolize grief or to protect the living from death or evil brought by the spirit of the deceased. People have attempted to gain protection by painting their bodies or by giving a portion of themselves—a finger joint, part of the ear, or hair—to the corpse in order to satisfy its desire to "get" the donor.[1] Frequently, the dress will be physically uncomfortable as a reminder of one's grief or to placate the deceased; smeared mud or clay mixed with ashes results in a coating that dries, cracks, and flakes in an uncomfortable process. In one area of New Guinea the mourner wears numerous strings of necklaces that weigh, depending on the wearer's closeness to the deceased, up to thirty pounds. One necklace is taken off for each day of mourning. Cutting the body, sometimes in ways to ensure scarification, was practiced by the Australian aborigines and some American Indian tribes. The aborigine men did not have to subject themselves to this process if the deceased was a child or a woman. Another practice has been to wear coarse, rough cloth, like sackcloth or coarse hemp cloth, which acts as a constant irritant to the skin.

---

[1]Evidence of amputation of body parts exists from Paleolithic times and has been quite common among some peoples, for example, the Australian aborigines.

Figure 5.13 Mendi woman in mourning necklaces. (Malcolm Kirk)

Psychological discomfort is sometimes induced by wearing "abnormal" dress during the mourning period. For example, the Korean woman's head rope or the man's belt is twisted in the opposite direction from normal wear. Some Andes Indian women wear their skirts inside out. Men and women have limited their decorative dress; drabber colors and materials have been used by many groups; frequently societies limit the color of dress for mourning to one color, perhaps white or black. One Australian aborigine tribe uses black when mourning a member of "one's own generation-line which includes grandparents and grandchildren . . . while red is the color for persons of the parents' and children's generation" (Elkins 1964, p. 314).

Another aspect of mourning dress is its use as a method of maintaining the exclusion of the bereaved from the rest of the society. Usually it is widows who are excluded since a widower must go about his daily affairs outside the home. This exclusion has sometimes been rather extreme. In Melanesia, some widows used to have their legs wrapped so heavily in vines that walking was difficult. However, since they were walled up in a tiny room for several months and could go out only for short periods twice a day, mobility was not important (Vlahos 1979).

During the two World Wars morale in the United States might have decreased if everyone had dressed in mourning, as could have happened. Thus, the custom changed, and the use of mourning wear has become increasingly rare. Today mourning might be indicated by wearing a black band on the sleeve. In the United States a veil is sometimes worn at the funeral by a widow when the deceased was a public figure and the family is on public display. In

Europe a veil is sometimes worn for as long as a year. Some rural European widows still dress completely in black, the color of mourning in the West. As the mourning period continues, the black may be relieved by a touch of white and can finally be exchanged for gray or lavender. The length and intensity of the mourning period has tended to vary according to the closeness of one's relationship with the deceased, from one day for the funeral of a family friend to all of one's remaining life for one's spouse.

Memorial jewelry, especially popular in the Victorian era, was worn as a token in memory of a deceased. Just as the Mt. Haganer man wears a wig made from the hair of his dead male family members, this jewelry frequently contained hair from the deceased. Hair is one of the only body parts that can be both easily taken from the body and maintained. In colonial America funerals were big social occasions, especially in rural areas where get-togethers were rare, and memorial tokens such as a scarf, a ring, or gloves were given by the deceased's family to those in attendance at the funeral.

SUMMARY

Roles serve to add order to society. Primitive societies usually have fewer and more clearly defined roles than more complex societies. Such definition provides the individual with a strong sense of security in his or her interpersonal interactions because he or she is fully aware of what is expected of each participant. Thus, the behavioral parameters provided by roles facilitate the functioning of both the society and the individual.

Roles describe the special tasks of the individual within society. They are learned patterns of behavior, which may be more or less clearly defined and enforced. The less well-defined a role is, the less specific and more flexible its associated dress will be. Some roles are given, such as age or sex, while others are earned, such as occupation. Given or ascribed roles tend to be more pervasive than achieved or earned roles. Dress can facilitate the assumption of a role both by aiding the individual's actual performance and by persuading others that he or she belongs in the role. Thus, roles facilitate human interactions.

6 | Status

Status is the value placed by society on a role or group of roles. A status is relative to the value placed on other roles within a society so that each society has a kind of status hierarchy or—in those societies with a vast array of roles—a group of such hierarchies. In modern American society there may be a discrepancy between the many statuses an individual has. John Kennedy, for example, had the high status of youth, political power, physical attractiveness, and education. His wealth was high in dollar value but low in type and source because it was from the "ill-gotten" gains of the previous generation. A compounding factor was his even lower status as a Roman Catholic of Irish descent. His overall status was therefore not as high as one might have expected.

The desire to impress others seems to be universal, as is the use of clothing to express one's "superiority." In fact, of all the various functions of clothing, comparative anthropological study suggests that status display is the most universal (Keesing 1958). Some primitive people wear no clothes when they are passing from one status to another; because they are believed to have no status at such a time, they consider dress inappropriate, since its purpose is to show status.

Throughout history societies have reserved some clothing items for symbols of power and status (Sybers and Roach 1962). Such symbols are important because of the considerable influence status has on social interactions. This

145

Figure 6.1 Eichholtz's picture, *An Incident of the Revolution,* depicts an incident in which Gen. Charles Lee had ridden ahead of Gen. Washington and the troops. A kitchen maid mistook him for a servant and made him work for a meal. When the troops arrived, the girl realized her mistake, and Gen. Lee pointed out that a hole in one's coat had such significance that a general could be mistaken for a scullion. (Museum of Fine Arts, Boston)

influence is one way dress provides a more ordered and more homogeneous society. In order to conform to social expectations and to achieve higher status, we must conform in our dress to the standards or norms of our society. It is this potential to produce social conformity that is the most significant power of status and of dress as a status symbol.

> There is no power without clothes. . . . Strip its Chief to the skin, and no State could be governed; naked officials could exercise no authority. . . . Clothes and title are the most . . . formidable influence, in the earth. They move the human race to willing and spontaneous respect for the judge, the general, the admiral, the bishop, the ambassador, the frivolous earl, the idiot duke, the sultan, the king, the emperor. No great title is efficient without clothes to support it. (Clemens 1905, p. 321–22)

In this chapter we shall examine the relationship between status and society as well as the importance of dress as a status symbol. We shall analyze the effectiveness of dress as a visible status cue, its versatility in quickly denoting any status changes, and its convenience.

STATUS SYMBOLS IN INDUSTRIALIZED SOCIETIES

In primitive societies status symbols are more pronounced than they are in modern cultures. This difference is probably less a reflection of need or desire than it is of mass production. Standardization of products, a necessary facet of mass production, limits the status potential of clothes. Blumberg (1974) hypothesized that status symbols must be both desirable and scarce. Mass production has enabled a more equitable distribution of goods so that a state of material equality has been able to be more closely approximated. Thus, fewer consumer goods, including dress, are now scarce enough to serve as status symbols in industrialized societies.

Anspach (1969) suggested that mass fashion in America identifies status levels through the "hierarchical relationship between high fashion, mass fashion, and past fashion" (p. 28). She noted that these fashion types reflect American values of time: the future and high fashion have high status; the present and mass fashion, medium; and the past and past fashion, low. The garment maker, especially if a couturier, has been a source for status, although his or her name used to be—at most—printed on a label discreetly sewn inside the garment. Exterior placement of labels or symbols of a label, such as Izod's alligator or Lauren's polo player, which the consumer was led to believe stood for quality and the high status of "designer fashions," was a phenomenon of the 1970s. But most individuals of high status would not have used their bodies as free commercial space for clothing manufacturers. They probably did not purchase such mass-produced ready wear, considered "designer wear" only by virtue of its label. They would not have wanted to wear garments that "anybody" might be wearing. Thus, they would have selected dress that had not been mass produced.

The current lack of sharply defined, visible clothing differences related to status might make it appear as though status display is no longer a major function of dress. However, closer examination suggests that the reverse is actually the case. Modern America, with its emphasis on materialistic values and its desire for social mobility, judges the worth of individuals primarily on their ability to have control over economic resources, their ability to consume, and their purchasing power. This is partly a result of urbanization, which has led to frequent segmental contacts with strangers. Thus, appearance, especially in cities, has become one of the major cues to status, which

> may be temporarily appropriated by the "correct" display and manipulation of symbols, while in the small town it is more permanently manifested by the direct enactment of rights and duties. The bestowal of status in the city is often an inference from symbolism to social position; in the small town the bestowal of status proceeds from the evaluation of rights and duties appropriate to social position, and the relevant symbolism is basically symptomatic. (Form and Stone 1957, p. 504)

When higher status symbols than reflect one's actual status are worn, what is revealed is the status the wearer desires. Morris (1969) called such behavior dominance mimicry. He noted that a true status symbol is affordable. A dominance mimic, however, causes some degree of financial sacrifice; it is purchased in spite of its being too expensive for the purchaser. A dominance mimic provides only a transitory elevation of status, which is only provided by strangers. This mimicry threatens status symbols. Since laws preventing such imitation are no longer acceptable, high-status individuals have had to find a different way to prevent this competition. They have sometimes done so effectively by producing cheap and obvious imitations of status items, such as rhinestone earrings for diamond ones. A low-status woman might be able to save enough to buy small, poor-quality diamond earrings. This dominance mimicry would be a threat to the higher-status woman and would cause diamonds to lose their effectiveness as a status symbol. However, if obviously fake diamond earrings are made and marketed inexpensively, and if they are attractive enough so that the lower-status woman purchases them rather than diamonds, then dominance mimicry can be prevented.

> On the surface this is not apparent. The low-status wife, sporting her flashy fake . . . *seems* to be mimicking her dominant rival, but this is an illusion. The point is that the fake . . . is too good to be true, when judged against her general way of life. It fools no one, and therefore fails to act as an aid in raising her status. (ibid., p. 66)

IMITATIVE NATURE OF FASHION

Veblen's (1934) theory of conspicuous consumption or competitive emulation is still applicable today. We copy those of higher status with whom we are competing, and we do so as obviously as possible. Thus, just as some Africans wear all the fabric they possess, even when doing so limits their mobility, the modern American can be found wearing unnecessary layers of clothing. American women have far more clothes in their wardrobes than they need. Although they generally indicate that they use these clothes to be sexually attractive, Ellis (1962) suggested that their real motive—one they don't even admit to themselves—is likely to be the desire to instill envy in other women. Another example of conspicuous consumption would be the woman wearing a fur coat in a warm climate that does not require the warmth of fur. In such a case the purpose of the fur coat is to display status. However, this type of ostentatious display does not necessarily symbolize high status; it may only show desire for such status. The modern individual with true high status would be more apt to dress according to the principle of inconspicuous consumption as exemplified by costumes like blue jeans worn with a classic silk blouse. Inconspicuous consumption is a way of indicating that one is above material things or too secure to need the safety of material possessions. Most of us are not so secure. Hoult (1954) found that 52 percent of male purchasers of sport coats made their selection for reasons of attractiveness and prestige. What would they think was attractive or had prestige? Something similar to an item worn by someone with a higher status. Their choice reflects their desire to compete with the individual(s) they are emulating. Of course, they might also choose to copy someone they admire without considering his status. Such reverential emulation has the same result as the competitive, but the motivating factor is quite different.

A third form of emulation is negative emulation, which is possibly more powerful than either of the others since its essence is the power of custom or habit. One must behave as one is expected to behave, and that expectation is based on custom. In order to flout custom, an individual must have either extremely high or extremely low status. For example, in America—with the exception of Jewish males, for whom it is a religious requirement—circumcision is no longer done for any reason other than custom. The mutilation continues because the vast majority of American males have been circumcised and to not be would make one different, against the custom.

Even among peoples such as the Eskimos, where clothing traditionally has had a strong utilitarian function, status display is becoming the most important factor in clothing selection. Eskimo girls have adopted "mainland" dress codes even when that dress has been less effective in keeping them warm (Hughes 1960). This Westernization of dress has often been associated with status. Thus, it is not surprising that the first garments adopted have usually been the exterior, most visible, ones. In Afghanistan, for example, one can find traditional dress slowly being exchanged for Western. A suit jacket worn over the traditional costume has usually been the first Western garment to be adopted. Among Afghani villagers, wearing a suit symbolizes literacy; if an illiterate man wore one he would be subject to ridicule, as would the educated man who wore traditional Afghani dress (Wilbur 1962).

PRESTIGE SYMBOLS

America is a prestige-oriented society, with its citizens striving to gain higher prestige, or public esteem, in order to prove their superiority. Prestige distinctions facilitate social interactions by indicating the amount of deference an individual should be given. For example, it is crucial for a person in the mili-

Figure 6.2 "Now remember—the more stripes they have, the more you mind them." (Library of Congress)

tary to be able to quickly determine who his superiors are so that he may regulate his behavior appropriately. To be mistaken in that behavior could lead to disciplinary action. Traditionally, there have been four primary ways to indicate prestige through dress: quantity, quality, size, and workmanship.

Quantity

Quantity of dress or of one item of dress has been used in many societies and can be related to the conspicuous-leisure and conspicuous-consumption theories. Generally "more" has meant higher status. The quantity of clothing in many primitive societies has depended on an individual's success in hunting or fighting. In more "advanced" societies, it has sometimes depended on such factors as the number of wives or slaves one had to produce clothing or the financial resources one had to purchase it.

In Africa, status dress is conspicuous and often audible. Abundance is the key, whether in the form of beads, cloth, paint, or other clothing. When the abundant items make a noise as they touch, there is the double pleasure of status being heard as well as seen. If the accumulated treasures are uncomfortable, the discomfort itself may gain status. A high-status Ibo woman waddles from the weight of her anklets, but without them she continues to waddle to symbolize her right to them and to the prestige they indicate (Sieber 1972).

But quantity has not been a symbol of high status just in exotic or "primitive" cultures. In the first half of the nineteenth century there was a trend toward wearing greater amounts of clothing (this trend reversed itself during the last half). This movement toward greater quantity may have

> symbolized the rapid rise in prosperity and general increase in the standard of living occuring in the nineteenth century. The rise in well-being, the increase in purchasing power on the one hand and the decline in the prices of fabrics on the other, were the conditions out of which competition to wear more and more clothing might well have grown. So, during the [18]20's women began to add more fabric; then, later, in the [18]30's, more garments, particularly more petticoats, so that by the latter [18]50's there were women who wore as many as thirty thicknesses of cloth about their waists. . . . In some indirect but nevertheless effective manner, the number of petticoats was taken as the measure of success, social rating and other "honorific" qualities. (Nystrom 1928, p. 275)

Thus, the individual with the most layers of garments would have been accorded the highest status.

High status has also been associated with a greater number of—for example—necklaces or beads in a necklace. Hottentot women once wore up to one hundred leg rings made from sheep or calfskin; these rings—smooth, hard, noisemakers when moving—protected the women's legs from vegetation as they foraged for food. In times of economic distress they could even be eaten. However, their major purpose was to indicate status: the more rings, the

a   b

Figure 6.3 (a & b)   Compare the dress of this woman of the Hindu court with her peasant counterparts. (Library of Congress)

higher the woman's status. Similarly, Eskimo men of high rank have had a greater number of holes pierced in their ear lobes and ear rims.

Beads or shells have been universally popular ornaments that have also often been used as a medium of exchange. The beaded individual in such a system is essentially wearing his or her bank statement to establish an instant level of credit. In some cultures different materials, from feathers to gold, have been worn for the same purpose. In one African tribe, women wore valuable brass neck rings weighing from forty-four to ninety pounds. After a woman died, her body was decapitated so that her wealth could be inherited (Hiler 1930). Bedouin women have traditionally decorated their clothing with gold or silver coins. While such a use may appear impractical, since it is noninterest bearing, we must remember that the benefit is from others' increasingly recognizing one's higher status. It also provides the Bedouin woman with some financial security, since females may usually keep their jewelry, while lands and other investments may be inherited only by men. Furthermore, wearing one's jewelry and other valuables has been an easy way to keep them with one when traveling. In times of social unrest jewelry becomes a popular investment since one can leave one's home, if necessary, while easily carrying one's wealth. Wearing one's wealth is no longer prevalent in many modern urban areas, where the threat of robbery has placed an effective damper on the practice.

Figure 6.4 Bejeweled Bedouin woman. (Library of Congress)

In cultures stressing quantity for status the lowest-status individuals, such as servants or children, would be nude. Consistent with this principle are rules similar to that of a Pacific Northwest American Indian tribe, whose chief could never be seen nude by a slave. Generally, a higher-status indiviudal *must* have a greater quantity of clothes on than a lower-status individual in his or her presence. In 1983, however, the mayor of Sweetwater, Florida, had a policeman suspended because while off duty he appeared at a city council meeting wearing shorts. The mayor's belief that such brief attire indicated a lack of respect for his office is consistent with modern American attitudes. While quantity still indicates status, it is generally more subtle and less visible, demonstrating this more in the variety and quantity of items in one's wardrobe.

Size

The use of size or scale of all or part of one's costume to show status is also compatible with the "more" principle; the bigger the size the higher the status. The size of an Eskimo's labret, for example, shows his wealth and social importance; the most VIP labret would be about four inches long by three inches wide. Size also relates to conspicuous leisure since long sleeves, trains, and floor-length gowns, for example, all inhibit physical labor as do high heels, elevated headgear, poulaines with twenty-inch points, and shined shoes (which limit walking if they are to be kept shined). In general, the greater the size of one's costume, the higher one's rank.

Figure 6.5 Who has the highest status? (Library of Congress)

When height, as achieved through elevated headgear, has been used as a status indicator, the removal of one's hat in the presence of one's superior demonstrates one's awareness of one's own lower prestige. However, the superior, to show humility, is expected to request the "doffer" to "regain his status" after the initial lowering.

Quality

The quality of materials has also been used to indicate status. Generally, high-quality items are those that are rare or have either intrinsic (i.e. beauty) or extrinsic (i.e. cost) value.[1] Dye or color can give quality. Usually, higher status has been associated with brighter and/or more unusual colors as well as with their number (quantity). For example, purple had the highest status association in ancient Greece and Rome because it was obtainable only in small quantities. In the Polynesian Islands red was associated with the gods, so it had the highest status; but when yellow feathers became rare, they replaced red in the status hierarchy. When aniline dyes first became available, they had a higher status association since they fixed more firmly and came in more hues. Today the softness of natural dyes, when available, denotes a higher status, as does creative use of colors.

Fabrics with the softest texture and/or the greatest sheen have generally had the highest status. Thus, among those South American Indians who had both bark cloth and woven fabric, bark cloth was worn by those of lower status.

[1]Veblen (1934) suggested that to be beautiful an item has to have economic value.

Figure 6.6 This 1925 Reville court gown, designed for the wearer's presentation at the Court of St. James, is of platinum and silver brocade woven in a moire design and embroidered in diamante. The Manteau de Cour is of silver cloth with diamond tassels. (Library of Congress)

Incan nobles wore vicuña clothing; those of lesser status were limited to cotton or llama wool. As a material becomes more common, its status decreases. Polyester had become such a low-status fabric in the 1980s that Nancy Reagan rejected a proposed official engraving of President Reagan, because it appeared as if he were wearing a polyester suit when in fact he only wore suits of English or Italian wool (Herald Wire Services 1982). Newness and higher price are also associated with high status; thus when buttons became fashionable in the thirteenth century, they were expensive symbols of high status.

In modern America many of the traditional quality materials have been imitated by fakes, which are sometimes even superior to the originals. Ultrasuede, for example, is easier to care for than suede is, yet it looks like "the real thing." Thus, furs, leathers, and silks and other luxury fabrics, as well as precious stones and metals, have become less precise prestige indicators. Furthermore, conservation efforts and humane concerns for animals have given some of these traditional quality materials a negative connotation. Women wearing the skin of an endangered animal or of an animal that was killed in an unacceptable way—for instance, the harp seal—may get a negative reaction from others to their insensitivity, rather than a positive one based on their high status. With the movement away from obvious status symbols of privilege, and toward the high status associated with being able to look like one's poorer compatriots, the "poor boy" items, such as well-washed or stone-washed denims, have become high-status symbols of conspicuously inconspicuous consumption.

Figure 6.7 The card in this 1955 window display stated: "Introducing Salonnette Furs! For the 'Not-Yet-A-Millionaire'." Furs have less status today. (Library of Congress)

Workmanship

Workmanship, the quality of the construction techniques, indicated status at least as early as the fourteenth century and is the most "modern" indicator. It has been the selling point of the modern couture industry, as it was with the tailoring of past centuries. For example, a finely tailored coat has not always been available to just anyone. Couturiers, of course, also select quality fabrics, like the silk failles produced by Abraham and Cie. But the quality of the workmanship itself has, supposedly, been one of the major cost differences. Fraser (1981) enumerated the many figure-flattering techniques used in James Galanos's designs: a fitted, low-waisted bodice over a bias-cut skirt; tucks at the breast; capelets over the upper arms; discreet gathers at the waist; and interesting back treatments such as bias-cut capes. Galanos's meticulousness in finishing a garment was rare among designers, even other couturiers. His workmanship employed such techniques as hand-rolled hems; hand piping and facing; bias-cut cuffs; chiffon linings; and a molded, rather than darted, bustline.

As industrialization of clothing production began to be refined, the perfection of machine-made clothing caused it to have a higher status than handmade. However, as handmade clothing became increasingly rare, since it was too time consuming to be cost effective, its one-of-a-kind quality finally brought it higher status. Clothing imported from certain countries has had higher status in the United States owing to a belief that it has been made with greater care. French blue jeans, for example, have had higher status and cost than their American counterparts even though they have been a poorer-quality product.

Today prestige is also derived from cleanliness. Pale colors and whites must not have a spot or stain; when an item does become spotted, even with a tiny mark, continuing to wear it is a sign of low status. The individual of high status whose clothing has become spotted or slightly frayed or has merely been worn for one season often gives it to a lower-status individual or donates it to a charity, which will resell the item in a thrift shop or rummage sale. But the lower-status individual will not gain the original prestige value of the garment. That will have been lost by the spot, the frayed area, or the age of the item.

Comfort and health, or physical fitness, also can give prestige. A tennis outfit would have a higher status than a t-shirt and shorts, for example, since the tennis outfit also indicates leisure time spent productively. Another prestige indicator is wearing the latest, most fashionable style *until* it has begun to be imitated by those of lower status.

POWER SIGNALS

Some status signals indicate power as well as prestige. Power is the amount of influence one wields in a particular situation. In authoritarian governments the ruler has the greatest power and will have certain clothing items that are reserved for him or her alone. For example, Chinese emperors wore a front-facing, five-clawed dragon on all their robes. The Incan king wore the biggest ear plugs and a multicolored headband with a fringe. However, prior to his investiture and during the period of preparation for it, he wore the shabbiest, dirtiest clothing so that he would remain forever aware of the horror of poverty (Joyce 1969). Imagine if that were a prerequisite for holding political office today!

Some power signals derive their symbolism from strengths attributed to an aspect of the garment; the Swazi queen mother's skirt is treated with fat from "the cattle of a sacred herd attributed with supernatural power" (Kuper 1973, p. 355). Catlin (1965) noted that among the American Indians only a chief or warriors of exceptionally great power could wear the buffalo-horn headdress, and even they could wear it only for special occasions. The horns were attached loosely enough that they could move forward or backward depending on the tilt of the head.

> By an ingenious motion of the head, which is so slight as to be almost impercept-ible—they [could even be] . . . made to balance to and fro, and sometimes, one backward and the other forward like a horse's ears, giving a vast deal of expression and force of character to the appearance of the chief . . . wearing them. This . . . is a remarkable instance . . . for its striking similarity to *Jewish customs*, to the kerns. . . the horns worn by the Abyssinian chiefs and Hebrews, as a *symbol of power* and command; worn at great parades and celebrations of victories. (p. 104)

One of the unique power symbols is the gold nose ring worn by the Cuna Indian women of Panama, who were descended from female slaves captured in raids on other tribes. The slaves were taken by the Cuna men, who would string them together with a cord passed through a hole in their septums. Purportedly the slaves learned the Cuna language but also retained their own;

Figure 6.8 Yellow Shirt wearing a horn head-dress. (Library of Congress)

Figure 6.9 Cuna girls. (National Anthropological Archives, Smithsonian Institution)

they taught these languages to their daughters. Ultimately, only the female descendants could communicate with everyone; the rest of the people understood only the Cuna language. This gave the women power over the rest of the Cunas who, ironically, were finally controlled by the descendants of their own slaves. The string, which had evolved into a gold nose ring, ultimately became a power symbol.

In modern America power dressing is more subtle though just as important. Morris (1977) noted that modern royalty displays pomp without power while the powerful do the reverse. Thus, the most powerful corporate officer is the one without a briefcase. The underlings, who carry attaché cases, show their relative power by the width of their case, the thin leather portfolio denoting the most power. But since women are newer to power positions in business, they show power by carrying a large briefcase, as long as they do not carry a handbag as well (Korda 1975). Powerful people tend to wear plain shoes in classical styles. A faddish style is associated with a lack of power (ibid.). However, the most powerful individuals may be the ones who dress as they choose, even when their choices go against the accepted standards. In business, after all, if they did not have power, they would already have been fired.

In the United States prestige is associated with economic power and occupation, but economic power is no guarantee of high social status. A wealthy criminal, for example, has economic power without high status, except among the criminal population.

Clothing has been used by the powerful to maintain their power. For example, the uniform of the African native man in domestic service to a white was an apron, which was associated with women, worn over shorts, which were associated with children (Kuper 1973). Clothes have also been used to compensate for low status. Status compensation has been one of the factors in dress choices of black Americans. Dardis, Derrick, and Lehfeld (1981) found that households headed by blacks spent from 20 to 30 percent more on clothing than comparable households headed by whites. This finding is consistent with data from the 1950s. Clothing has been one of the few avenues of conspicuous consumption open to blacks and other economically disadvantaged minorities whose inability to compete for other restricted-consumption status symbols has been compensated for by increased clothing consumption (Schwartz 1963).

STATUS AND GENDER

Most societies use clothing to distinguish the sexes. Even in cave paintings there is evidence of dress differences according to sex. While such differences may reflect role characteristics, the status assigned to the sex and its roles may have been a greater influence. Among primitive peoples men have tended to have the higher status and to wear the more decorative dress. As women's status has increased, so has the decorative quality of their dress. Dress has been more unisexual in societies where men and women have equal status. Patriarchal

Figure 6.10 The difference in status between the sexes is evident in this dress, ca. 1860. (Library of Congress)

societies tend to have more differences in dress between the sexes than do matriarchal. It is not known if one of these conditions is healthier for society or for the individual. But it seems probable that the specific requirements of a society will determine which type of system is "best."

There are many theories as to why sexual distinctions are universal in dress. It is possible that the physically more powerful male assumed greater status by virtue of his physical dominance over the weaker female. Then by associating that higher status with all the masculine roles, he was able to maintain his higher status even after physical power was no longer a prerequisite for social power. There is some evidence to support such a theory since status symbols have often been exaggerations of masculine-gender signals. These have taken natural, physical-dominance characteristics, like greater height or wider shoulders, and emphasized them by such things as high headgear, elevated footwear that did not impede mobility, and shoulder pads or epaulettes. However, many gender signals, such as hair length or the use of make-up, are invented. These symbols have a shorter life span and are culturally related. They are also universal and extraordinarily common, in spite of the fact that they are physiologically unnecessary. Neither naturally nor biologically do they relate to either sex. For example, both sexes are biologically capable of growing long head hair; but in most industrialized Western cultures long hair is a feminine-gender sign. It has been suggested that this Western association of short hair with masculinity may reflect the military requirements for short hair (Morris 1977). The arbitrariness of such signals can pose problems for the cross-cultural visitor. Imagine the confusion of an American couple visiting a culture in which make-up is viewed as masculine. Each representative of the two different cultures could evaluate his or her counterpart as a transvestite.

It is unlikely that dress differences have been needed as visual clues to the sex of the clothed body, since most societies have sex-distinct dress even when their dress does not cover the primary or secondary sex characteristics. For example, women of the Chavantes Indians of Brazil wear a leaf loin covering and a bead necklace, but their bare breasts easily reveal their gender. The men wear ear plugs; cord wrappings at their ankles, necks, and wrists; and a yellow penis cone. The penis cone does not hide their sex from the viewer, it draws attention to it. Obviously, sexual identification is not the reason they dress as they do. The Chavantes male wears more items, and his items all *seem* decorative. Was Langner (1959) correct in his hypothesis that such differences stem from a masculine wish to assert male superiority over females, thus keeping women in servitude? In order to determine the validity of this assumption, we would have to know the value of the dress, which sex was the first to wear anything, and what the first item worn was. Those societies with dress styles that hinder female mobility, however, would appear to support such a hypothesis, since limiting a person's movement is an excellent method of maintaining control over him or her. Most Moslem women are covered from head to foot so that their vision is restricted, and they are prevented from independent travel except by foot. The sidesaddle similarly hobbled the skirted Western woman,

Figure 6.11 These chopines, ca. 1550–1650, from Venice, Italy, effectively hobbled their wearers. (Museum of Fine Arts, Boston)

whose dress made it difficult for her to mount astride; for her, riding was difficult and dangerous. In both cases women have been made more dependent on men. Even the bonnet and some hats have impeded movement by reducing peripheral vision. But most hobbling techniques have involved the feet or legs. The Chinese lily foot, high heels, and chopines are examples of dress that has effectively limited foot movement. Leg hobbling has been achieved by such means as having women wear leg or ankle ornaments which by sheer weight—up to fifty pounds per leg—limit movement, attaching a woman's legs together with a chain (which sometimes might have bells attached as an "alarm" should she try to wander off), or having women wear leg ornaments with serrated edges or edges that extend out from the leg up to eight inches in every direction. Corsets and other restricting garments are also hobbling techniques. In the early twentieth century there was even a dress style called the hobble skirt, which fit so tightly at the knee that a wearer could move only in small, mincing steps; a short version of this style enjoyed brief popularity in the late 1950s. All of these techniques were successful, at least in part, because they reflected socioeconomic as well as sexual status. Only the rich could afford to be so incapacitated, and since most people seem to be striving for a "superior" status, the adoption of such styles gave the wearer a sense of higher status than those lesser and unfortunate free movers. Need can reduce such hobbling, as has been the case with nomads, who can have no immobile people, and with Chinese farmers who, needing wives to help in the fields, purchased their wives from families in provinces where feet were not bound.

Stone (1970) hypothesized that since knowledge of another's gender is made visually, "sex is, in fact, a universe of appearance. Adopting sexually distinctive dress commits one to a social world" (p. 256). Certainly the dress of each sex reveals information about it as well as about its interrelationship with the other sex; the dress of each sex reflects its needs and the needs of the other (Broby-Johansen 1968).

While gender symbols have often been positively associated with higher male status, they have sometimes given a superficially higher status to women. For example, in the nineteenth century the large skirts and sleeves of the antebellum female fashions provided powerless females with a profound social presence. Their dress enabled them to command a large area of personal space and thus become a person to be recognized. At the same time this dress style was visual testimony to the limits society had placed on these "fragile and dependent creatures." That women voluntarily wore such inhibiting dress is, perhaps, the most conclusive evidence of their actual status (Smith 1981).

In most societies the female derives her status from the male with whom she is most closely associated. Thus, a lower-status woman can elevate her status by marrying a man from a higher-status level. She catches this man, in part, by accentuating her physical, feminine appearance so that she has greater appeal as a sex object. In this way she enhances her value in the sexual marketplace. For this reason, a lower-status female who is single is apt to spend a large proportion of her income on the accoutrements of "beauty." (The upper-status female can use her dress to meet other needs.) (Hurlock 1976). The paradox of being a subject (mind) and an object (body) has created much anxiety in the modern woman. While she may exercise her mind (subject) options while attempting to create a more "meaningful" lifestyle, she will still generally experience anxiety about her basic sexual desirability, herself as object. This anxiety can be allayed only by successfully attracting *and* keeping a man. Thus, the American female continues to try to enhance her physical attractiveness through her selection of clothing and her use of make-up. Her efforts are designed to make herself, as closely as possible, into a stereotype of the cultural ideal of feminine beauty rather than to enhance her own unique physical appearance.

The operative phrase in western culture seems to be "I must put my face on," since "face" refers both to an aspect of the self as individual and to the self as stereotyped image that must be presented to others in the correct way. Insofar as "skin" and "face" are then considered synonymous, we arrive at the point of the mind/body dichotomy once more, since face is an aspect of the body, as opposed to the mind, in our symbol system. Why, then, don't men also put on cosmetics every day? (They are, of course, allowed after-shave, but anything that smells too much is regarded as inappropriate.) The answer is that men are not seen as ambivalent subject/object creatures, but rather are presented as subjects, who establish their identity through their acts rather than simply through being looked at and admired. They gain prestige from doing rather than being, and it is an aspect of the created "being" that cosmetics celebrates. That things are, however, rather more complicated than this in practice, and that women's actions in dressing and the use of cosmetics can also be seen as the deliberate acts of subjects, can be guessed from a controversy in Britain surrounding Anna Ford, a prominent television personality. Ms. Ford rightly objected to newspapermen who concentrated in their accounts of a public meeting that had to do with the position of women in society on photographs of her split skirt rather than on what she said. A possible ambiguity in the dispute was pointed out by a letter writer to the *Guardian* when he asked why Ms. Ford had worn the skirt at all if she indeed had not wished to attract that kind of attention. In effect, unspoken male appreciation of the skirt might have disposed male listeners to praise what the speaker had to say, but public acknowledgement of this element instead shifted the primary focus to consideration of Ms. Ford as a decorative object, and this made further *serious* consideration of the issues she was raising impossible. My intention here is not really to comment on the actual dispute but to indicate that its basis lies in the symbolic value of the body as opposed to the mind in our culture. The form of dress announces, "I am a woman" and this is *opposed to* the other message, "I am a person who can speak on an intellectual topic of public interest. . . ." Generalizing, we may say that the model of "woman" here is that of the "culturally modified natural object," while that of "man" is the "naturally active cultural subject." (Strathern 1981, p. 36)

Gender Symbols

In most cultures specific dress items have become associated with each sex. These gender symbols vary from culture to culture, reflecting each culture's sexual ideal. In America today jeans are among the most universally popular leisurewear; their unisexual nature may symbolize the lack of clarity in modern American concepts of the ideal male or female. While jeans have many practical assets, they are sexual, especially when tight fitting so that they reveal the contours of the body. This sexuality was recognized in the Calvin Klein jean ads of the early 1980s. Skirts, while predominantly feminine attire in the West, are worn by men in certain limited, and usually private, circumstances; the terry cloth, aftershower wrap-around skirt for men is such an example. Pipes, large cigars, and jock straps are associated with males, bras with females; colorful underpants, once the domain of women, are now worn by both sexes. Facial hair is deemed masculine, and women with an excess of dark facial hairs usually attempt to remove them. In the United States body hair has also been viewed as masculine, a perception spreading to many other countries, where women have begun to shave their legs and underarms.

Another difference between masculine and feminine dress in the West is that women's clothing has been made and designed by men as well as women whereas men's wear has been designed and tailored primarily by men. (Women have been involved in the mechanics of sewing as long as this did not require any fittings.) (Byrde 1979).

There are fewer gender symbols today, and dress is becoming more unisexual. It is women who are adapting or adopting masculine dress. This may reflect the traditionally inferior status of women to men, the more inhibiting character of much female dress, and/or the common social-ego ideal that men are serious but women are frivolous (Lundberg and Farnham 1947). As the differences between gender-related dress continue to decrease, some of the artificial separations between the sexes may also decrease. This could reduce intersex suspicions and hostilities and pave the way for fuller, more open interactions between the sexes.

STATUS AND AGE

It is a universal practice to assign various levels of status to different age groups. In most societies there will be some ceremonial "rites of passage" to indicate the change from childhood to adulthood. Other age-related passages tend to be less clearly defined and are frequently less celebrated. In those cultures where the children are nude and adults are clad, the achievement of the adult status is marked by the assumption of dress. In those cultures where both children and adults wear clothing, the child assumes adult dress as he or she assumes the adult status.

Females are apt to mark this passage with a purification ceremony preparing them for their social role of wife and mother. Adult males tend to have rights to greater knowledge, competency, and therefore power. It is these rights that make the male's passage into adulthood a celebrated event. The Bororo male at puberty receives a penis sheath symbolizing his right to the secret knowledge of adults. Among some tribes, such as certain of the Australian aborigines, a boy's rites of passage into manhood involve several stages and can extend over several years. These stages usually have different dress rituals associated with them. Until the 1940s the Western rite's visual symbol was the

Figure 6.12 (a & b)   Note the differences in the dress of the man and the boys in these two photos. (Edward D. Storm)

a   b

long pants on a boy instead of short ones. This easy passage perhaps signified the lack of real status difference at puberty.

Freedman (1969) hypothesized that since a beard indicates maturity and age, shaving symbolizes youth or indicates the negative value of aging. He suggested that a beard tends to increase the social distance between two men; but because women find beards sexually suggestive, the social distance between a woman and a bearded man is decreased. However, such symbolism is not universal; in some cultures the beard symbolizes virility or masculinity rather than age. Among the Tchikrin men, who associate hair with sexual power, puberty marks the end of the hair cutting that began at weaning. Their long hair represents their right to fully participate in sexually based relationships (Turner 1969). In Korea marriage signified a male's achieving manhood and was symbolized by his putting his hair up into a topknot.

In some cultures men do not reach adulthood until they become fathers. The Kayapo mark this attainment by replacing their small lip plug with a saucerlike plate to symbolize both paternity and maturity. Since oral aggressiveness is the right of the mature male, this symbol relates to both the phallic and oral aspects of the Kayapo ideal of mature masculinity (ibid.).

Old age is valued in many nonindustrial societies. Elderly Nuba men, who are the leaders and the decision makers, have the highest social status. However, the aging body is not valued, and after the body loses its youthful firmness, body painting for adornment ceases and the practice of covering the body with cloth begins. In modern American society, where youth is so valued, there is a kind of shame and anxiety experienced by most aging people. Everyone is striving to be happy, and happiness is associated with youthfulness. There is also a double standard of aging in that women lose status as they age, while men maintain theirs—and can even gain. A woman gets old when she grays; a man gets distinguished. For a woman, whose value has often been determined, at least in part, by her physical appearance, aging holds a threat to her actual sense of self-worth. Some great beauties have even become recluses as they lost their youthful glow. We in America have a shallow and mistaken view that aging, sagging flesh is ugly. Thus, the aging woman uses clothing to ameliorate or camouflage the reality of nature. Since the 1960s the older woman's style of dress has no longer varied radically from the popular style of the day. Fraser (1981) wondered whether this will help modern young women turn fifty or sixty more calmly than women have done in the past.

> Perhaps there will be less anxiety about the loss of youthful good looks than there was in times when capturing a husband and bearing and rearing children were the principal choices for a woman's life. Some of our culture's ideas about aging women—a "fading beauty" being a more tragic reminder of mortality than an aging man or an aging horse—may have depended on seeing a woman's function in society as being done when she had raised her children to maturity. Time will tell how much of women's traditional distaste for their wrinkles will really disappear, and to what extent the old anxieties will be augmented by the new. Women are no longer obliged to dress to show financial dependence on

men—parading evidence of a husband's or father's money-making skill—but they do not, for the most part, choose to look unattractive to men. In a time of flexible or unstable relations between men and women, anyone may be shopping for a new partner at any time, so window dressing is more important than ever. And the competitive career world sets great store by attractiveness, a look of youth and vigor. Far from seeing women free themselves from the promises of the cosmetics industry, we are seeing male Senators having hair transplants and male executives getting face-lifts. Much of what both men and women accepted as their lot in the stuffy, sometimes wise, old world has no place in the brave and "ageless" new one. (ibid., pp. 248–49)

SOCIAL DISTANCE

Social distance, the degree of informality or intimacy between individuals, is determined by the status of the individuals and—since one can have a different status in different situations/groups—the situation. One of the kinds of status that most modern Americans recognize as regulating social distance is marital status.

In most monogamous societies marriage limits the number and kinds of informal interactions an individual can have with members of the opposite sex outside his family. On the other hand, the single adult who is interested in marriage may be quite free in those interactions and may even wish to symbolize or advertise his or her availability. Among some American Indian tribes, for example, paint (cosmetics) was only used by single women wishing to advertise

Figure 6.13 Her coin decoration indicates her single status. (Library of Congress)

Figure 6.14 The unmarried Hopi woman's hairstyle. (Library of Congress)

their availability and their willingness to engage in sexual activity. In many societies the single maidens wear brighter colors or garments made of more sensual materials; they may wear their hair long and unbound to symbolize their virginity; they are more likely to be bareheaded. Hopi maidens wrap their hair around cornhusk frames into large coils or spirals on either side of the head to symbolize an immature squash blossom. After they marry, they will wear their hair in a braid to symbolize the mature squash vine. Single Swazi adults have complete freedom in their hair styling until they begin courting, when they must let their hair grow so that it will be long enough to wear in the style of marriage. The marriage hair style changes from district to district, but each involves putting the hair up into some form of cone. The style is changed for mourning; if the deceased was a woman's husband, she even shaves her head. Urban Swazi women have detachable cones or topknots, which they wear when dressing up; otherwise they simply braid their hair. But regardless of the style, for a woman to cut her hair prior to her husband's death always shows dissatisfaction with her marriage (Tyrrell 1968).

Marriage often has five steps of status states: (1) betrothal, (2) wedding, (3) marriage, (4) parenthood, and (5) widowhood. The betrothal stage is when the couple (or their families) makes their first commitment to each other. In modern society such commitments are sometimes made by young people, who exchange pins, rings, or some other symbol of their "going steady." But an engagement is usually symbolized by a man giving his intended a ring to serve as notice to other single men that this woman is spoken for—she is off limits. In societies where a maiden's long, loose hair symbolizes virginity, an engagement or wedding may be symbolized by her cutting or putting up her hair.

Weddings are essentially rites of passage from a single status to the married. As with most rites of passage, there are strongly adhered-to traditions involved with weddings and wedding clothes. The wedding ceremony of the Hutzals involves elaborate dress since the bride and groom are treated like royalty for the day. Both have symbolic crowns of plaited periwinkle wreaths, which are removed by the bridal attendants after the ceremony. The bride then puts on the cap of a married woman. After her wedding, she may not expose her hair except to her husband (Warnick 1974). Veils are also used in many wedding ceremonies to symbolize purity; rings are commonly given or exchanged to symbolize the union.

After the wedding, the marriage itself begins. In most societies the wife is under the authority of her husband, who is the only man with whom she may be sexually active. Thus, visual symbols of her social status as a married woman are necessary to serve as instant reminders of the required social distance. In the last century there was an effort to keep people from taking off their wedding rings to fool other people into thinking they were single; some Americans even suggested that wedding rings should be tattooed on for more permanency. The Hindu woman's nose ring, the Mohave wife's three vertical lines tattooed on her chin, the Namba wife's knocked-out front teeth are all instantly observed symbols of their married status.

The relationship between the husband and his mother-in-law may also involve dress. For example, since the Navaho husband is not allowed to come face to face with his wife's mother, he wears little bells to warn her of his approach. When adornments are used to attract the opposite sex, married women generally wear fewer adornments. Except for her wedding ring, however, the modern Western wife wears nothing indicative of her marital status. In fact, she may even wear especially revealing dress, which might sometimes be intended to give her husband additional status by showing what a fine piece of property she is (Langner 1959).

Figure 6.15 The hair style of married women of the Yao-tin-pan tribe reflects the inhibition required by marriage. (Library of Congress)

Widow's weeds are rarely worn anymore in the West. Widowhood is a complex state since the widowed spouse is now single and may or may not elect or be able to elect to remarry or reunite in some way with a member of the opposite sex. Some societies view a widow or, more rarely, a widower as someone outside of the society, who is not and should not be a full participant in normal living. Most societies hold such a behavioral norm for a widow following her spouse's death; but after a period of "confinement," the widow is free to alter her appearance. She may wear dress symbolizing her decision not to remarry, or she may wear something to symbolize her desire to rewed. The widow in Greenland wears a black ribbon in her hair to indicate her loss. Eventually she may add a red ribbon to signify her interest in, and availability for, remarriage or switch to a white ribbon to show disinterest in another union. Widows in most cultures wear less ornamental dress; their dress becomes more decorative and more similar in style to that of married or single women as they move back into society.

SUMMARY

Status is the value placed by society on a role. Clothing is a universal cue to status; it is a status symbol. Because rapid identification of status is both more important and more difficult in urban societies, clothing is an important status symbol today. Fashion is an imitative behavior; its emulation may be motivated by a desire to compete, to show positive identification with the norms of one's society, or to conform to them.

Prestige symbols indicate the amount of deference an individual should be given. There have been four primary ways to indicate prestige through dress: quantity, quality, size, and workmanship. Modern methods are basically through variety of wardrobe, cleanliness of attire, and the comfort and newness (fashionability) of one's costume. Power symbols indicate the amount of influence or authority an individual wields. Traditionally, dress was reserved for each status level, with the more powerful individuals wearing the more ornate and luxurious dress. Currently, the most powerful individuals tend to be fairly inconspicuous in their dress. In modern societies clothing has often been used as a compensatory device by individuals of low status, who have been able to consume more conspicuously in this area than in other visible areas, such as housing and transportation.

Differentiation of status between gender and age groups has been universal. Men have generally been accorded a higher status than women, whose status more nearly approaches parity with men's in matriarchal societies. Many of the most consistent and universal status signals are associated with physical, male-dominance characteristics; but some gender signals have no relation to actual differences between the sexes. Such symbols have sometimes superficially increased the status of one sex over the other. Age status changes have usually been celebrated or recognized in some kind of ceremonial rite of passage. Such rites have been most elaborate and distinct in the recognition of the passage from childhood to adulthood. Social distance is determined by the relative status of one individual to another or to a group of individuals. In modern America marital status is the status with the greatest impact on social distance, since the married adult must maintain a greater social distance from members of the opposite sex than would a single adult.

By indicating status, fashion helps to produce a more ordered and homogeneous society. It is this potential to produce conformity within a society that is the power of status and of status symbols such as clothing.

7 | Social Class

Social-class systems are relatively recent structures used to organize social power and status. Thus, the use of clothing to indicate and maintain social class—the primary focus of this chapter—is also a relatively new phenomenon. Small, primitive societies were composed of kinfolk, and status was granted according to age or prowess rather than by a social class or caste system. A caste structure was the first major organizational scheme for societies complex enough to stratify the distribution of power. Today this system is found only in rural societies (Rose 1961). The caste structure is a rigid hierarchy into one layer of which an individual is permanently placed by virtue of his or her birth or social role. Interaction between castes is limited to service contact between an inferior and his superior, and communication outside role requirements does not occur. Intermarriage between castes is rare, even when legally possible. Class systems, based more on economic than social power, allow a greater degree of mobility and communication between classes, although the degree of cross-class interaction has varied from, for example, the nearly open urban American structure to the more rigid class system of seventeenth-century Europe. All societies with a class system have used clothing as at least one of the symbols designating specific class membership. How it is used has varied according to technological factors, the kind of class system, and the society.

In this chapter we shall analyze social class systems, the three major theories of fashion flow or fashion dissemination, types of symbols of upper-class membership, and class differences in spending power and motivation for expenditures.

RIGID CLASS SYSTEMS

Generally, in societies with a rigid class structure, fashion changes slowly, and those changes that do occur are not substantial. The limited cross-class interaction in such systems prevents individuals from gaining information about classes other than their own. Experimentation with symbols such as dress of a class other than one's own is prohibited by law, with penalties even as severe as capital punishment. Because of the relative lack of both contact between the classes and social mobility, the individual tends to accept his or her lot. In such a system each class "really constitute(s) a society in itself, the whole collection of societies living together in a state of symbiotic interdependence" (Linton 1964, p. 110). Since the individual's social identity and, therefore, her behavior is clearly defined, this type of structure can provide her with a sense of security or comfort and reduce the conflict inherent in decision making. Classes are more unified and conforming, and there is a greater sense of unity.

In societies where dress was defined for, and unique to, each class, there was no need for frequent fashion changes to indicate class status. In fact, such changes would have led to confusion. Those societies were therefore best supported by having stability in their fashions, with each class having its own unique set of rules for dress. Thus, dress was a visual label of class membership, serving to more clearly differentiate each class from the others and detering their assimilation of or by "outsiders." Ultimately, therefore, a rigid class structure promotes the maintenance of the existing social structure.

In aristocracies, which were frequently set up by a conquering people whose culture was different from that of the conquered, attempts were made to preserve the status quo by maintaining differences between the nobility and the commoners. One of the methods they used was to enact legislation to prevent dominance mimicry—the aping of one's superiors. In the sixteenth century, for example, it was the fashion among the European aristocrats to decorate their shoes with a rose, which as the fashion continued grew larger and more ornate, with jewels and embroidery. The typical cost of a modest pair of these shoes was a working man's average weekly wage. A luxurious pair could cost as much as an average family's entire annual income! The courts and the legislature tried to prevent the "common man" from wearing these shoes and appearing to have a higher social position (Rossi 1976). However, such efforts were usually so difficult to enforce that another method was needed to indicate class superiority and maintain the status quo. The technique of using constantly changing status symbols became more effective and led to the development of fashionable dress.

Three factors have made this technique effective in societies with rigid

a   b

Figure 7.1 (a & b) Role differences between the aristocracy and the peasants in the early fifteenth century are clearly evident in their associated clothing. (Musée Condé)

classes: (1) rapidly changing symbols (which has made emulation more difficult and expensive in time and labor); (2) using expensive gems, fabrics, or metals that could not be cheaply imitated; and (3) making the production of the dress itself more difficult (patterns have even been destroyed to prevent exact reproductions).

OPEN CLASS SYSTEMS

Societies with more open class systems are more conducive to fashionable dress, and when an open class system is found in conjunction with a downward dissemination of wealth, fashion seems inevitable. As the upper class reduces its proportionate share of consumer power and the middle class raises its portion, it becomes more difficult for the upper class to prevent dominance mimicry. The elite will be less able to afford garments too costly for the rising business-person to copy and less able to enact and enforce laws to limit the behavior of an increasingly powerful middle class. Thus, they must find some other way to demonstrate their superiority, and traditionally they have resorted to frequent and often major fashion changes.

Such a situation began to develop in seventeenth-century England, where the middle class businessman had considerably more economic, social, and political power than his Continental counterparts. Robinson (1963) suggested that the British dominance of male fashion in Europe and the United States since the mid-seventeenth century has been due to the relatively greater power of the British middle class.

> The middle classes of other countries must have felt infinite frustration because they could not achieve a social or political position as much to their liking as had their British counterparts, nor could their governments so unfailingly support their enterprises. This sentiment gave rise to slavish imitation of the English gentleman's dress, itself an odd compromise between chivalry as retained in the riding habit of the country squire, and resurgent industry, as exemplified in the Puritanically sober worsted of the city dweller. (p. 25)

However, in open class structures, especially those with greater economic parity between the classes, there will be less sharply differentiated classes and greater social mobility; and dress will be less indicative of class membership.

FASHION DISSEMINATION

Social class structure is reflected in three major theories of how fashions begin and become popular. A fashion is created by the innovator—the designer—of a garment. However, if no one buys the design, it will not become part of the fashion. Thus, this design must be appropriate to the taste(s) and needs of the era in order for the second step—the initial purchase—to occur. The individual, or small group of individuals, who first buys the design is the leader of fashion *if* his wearing the garment helps to persuade others to adopt it or a style similar to it. The final step is taken by the emulators, or followers, whose en masse adoption of the garment enables the style to become fashionable.

Trickle-Down Theory

The trickle-down theory of fashion, the oldest theory of fashion flow, is based on a clearly defined social class hierarchy in an open class system. According to the trickle-down theory, when the highest class adopts a fashion, the class next to it, wanting to move up or even to appear to have already moved up, will proceed to adopt the new fashion. The fashion will continue a downward adoption through the classes until it reaches the lowest class economically able to afford it. As the fashion marches downward, its reproductions are usually made with less desirable materials and poorer workmanship. In some cases, like that of the full skirts of the mid-nineteenth century, even the quantity of fabric used is reduced with each downward diffusion. By the time the fashion has been adopted by the majority, it is no longer a sign of class status, and the highest class will have already begun the process over again by adopting a new fashion. A trickle-down fashion flow appears to have begun in the late Middle Ages, when a merchant and business class began to flourish in the cities of Europe. The Industrial Revolution of the late eighteenth century further accelerated the development of a class structure supportive of a trickle-down fashion flow. Urbanization also contributed to this flow because crowded cities increase interpersonal contacts of a limited or superficial nature. Limited knowledge about all or most of the people with whom one comes in contact leads to increased opportunity to appear to be socially "better" than one is. Imitating the clothing of the dominant class has been the easiest way to accomplish such a charade. Exemplifying this would be the costume or artificial jewelry worn by middle-class women of the Georgian and Victorian periods in place of the family jewels of the upper class, or the more modern use of watches that look like a Rolex but cost much less.

In the trickle-down system the fashion leader, the first person to adopt the eventually prevailing fashion, will have high status within his group and be admired by his peers and, perhaps, even his inferiors. For example, when the fifteenth-century Duke of Burgundy became ill and began to lose his hair, his nobles cut off their own long hair to show their love for him. Some leaders are copied not out of respect or fondness but out of a desire by the emulators to best the leader or another early adopter of the fashion. A third form of emulation stems from the psychological need to belong, to be integrated with one's group. This need for the acceptance that comes with being "in fashion" seems the most powerful currently of the emulation motivators.

The trickle-down theory appears less appropriate to current fashion dissemination. Today the upper class consumer patronizes the private designer, whose fashions are intended to appeal to the socially elite. Mass-market styles are adapted from successful haute couture designs. Since these copies are so quickly marketed that they are available within a few weeks, it seem unlikely that a designer's customers would be spending large sums of money for clothing that can indicate upper class status only for a few weeks. The desire to be "first" or the need to be "in" would seem more likely motivations.

Upward-Flow Theory

The most recent theory of fashion flow is the upward-flow theory, which posits that fashions originate with the lower class, especially the young. They are then adopted by the youthful members of the upper and/or middle classes, and finally are adopted by the rest of the population. In the period following the French Revolution, such an upward flow was evident. The dress and leisure

Figure 7.2 Châtaignier's 1975 engraving shows the dress of the periods both before and after the French Revolution. (Library of Congress)

values of the old upper class were rejected by all the classes, and the new upper class, the nouveau riche, wore dress evolving from that of the common working man. Langner (1959) predicted that such a flow could occur in America if men lost their social discipline and that if it did, it would stimulate a deterioration in work performance. A revolutionary movement toward casual dress began in the early 1960s, when the American worker adopted more casual clothing. At the same time, productivity rates were dropping. Were these changes related? The evidence is not yet clear as to whether there is in fact a relationship between dress and work performance. Among the early leaders of the 1960s casual revolution were England's Beatles, who were members of the lower or lower-middle class. Their fashions were more hedonistic than the staid and somber traditional dress of the middle class male. However, rather than causing that change, the adoption of "Beatle fashion" more likely reflected a value change that had already taken place. Beatle fashion, which roughly coincided with the deterioriation in worker productivity and the focus on more hedonistic values, was not adopted while the Beatles were struggling artists, members of the lower class trying to move up, but after they had already met with success, demonstrated their upward mobility, and could no longer be considered lower class. During these same years, Japanese workers retained their adherence to a powerful work ethic. They also dressed in uniforms or job-related attire so that, from their dress, one could successfully predict their occupation. Sportswear, even a sport coat, was not suitable attire for office boys, let alone businessmen. Women had not adopted the pants look and wore heels and hose during their working hours. Currently, the Japanese are adopting more casual dress. It will be illuminating to observe whether Japanese work performance deteriorates as their dress standards change.

The urban cowboy look of the mid-1970s and the motorcycle or greaser look of the 1950s are also examples of upwardly flowing fashions. In all of these examples the wearer has had to be clearly distinguished from the lower-class originator for the dress to have been considered fashionable.

> The clothing signals must transmit the perverse message that: "I approve of 'poor boys,' but I am not one myself." This is done in several ways. The first is to wear the sweaters or denims in just those social situations where the true "poor boy" would be climbing into his "best clothes." The second is to have the "poor" clothes beautifully tailored and elaborately styled, without robbing them of their superficial "poorness." The third device is one that belongs exclusively to the modern world of mass media, and could not have existed before it. This is the famous-face contrast. Anyone who is rich and well known, and whose face appears regularly in newspapers and magazines and on TV and cinema screens, can afford to wear the scruffiest of "poor boy" clothes to even the most glittering occasions. He is then, by the contrast between his famous face and his faded denims, making a violent silent attack on his affluence-oriented culture. If he is carefully photographed alighting from his gleaming Rolls-Royce, while wearing his crumpled, "poor boy" clothes, he must be forgiven for the inconsistency. (Morris 1977, p. 220)

Figure 7.3 The "poor boy" look.

Horizontal Theory

The third theory of fashion flow—the horizontal theory—suggests that fashion originates or is adopted within a class level rather than from a class above or below it. The development of folk costume for the lower classes in rigid class systems would be a historic example of separate fashions moving in a horizontal flow. This flow would appear to be most appropriate to rigid class systems, where the dress of each class is quite distinct and changes in dress are infrequent and minor.

However, most evidence supporting a horizontal flow stems from politically and socially advanced nations that lack a strong class emphasis and have fashions that are visually similar for all classes, although the quality and number of garments may be different. The classes in such societies tend to be less differentiated and hold more common values; it is this value unity that would seem the most likely cause of a horizontal flow. However, the similarity in dress between the classes may also, in part, reflect mass production, mass marketing, and the influence of the mass media. Fashion leaders have been found in each class (Grindereng 1967); they are all exposed to the same introductory process at approximately the same time with the same media and marketing information as well as the same "standardized" mass-produced dress items. They are emulated because they select from all of this data the look that best "fits" the taste of the times. Depending on how common the experiences and lifestyles of the different classes are, this taste may be shared by all the classes. Since American classes tend to be economic entities sharing values with some members of all the classes, it is not surprising that the "in" fashion look is also shared. Only the upper-upper and lower-lower classes are free from this sharing. The upper-upper class member can be more individualistic in her dress because of her greater degree of social security. The lower-lower, often unable to adequately copy the most "in" look, is free to drop out and dress as she pleases since she cannot successfully compete. Linton (1964) hypothesized that large societies make it more difficult to have common standards leading to self-conscious classes. He noted that the individuals controlling

> big business and banking in this country are probably more conscious of their common interests than the members of any of the other so-called classes, yet there have been very few occasions on which they have been able to present a united front.
> The lack of a definite aristocratic culture which might provide the members of this ruling group with common ideals and standards of behavior and thus integrate them into a conscious society is perhaps the most distinctive aspect of the modern condition. Exploiters and exploited have existed since the dawn of written history, but the only parallel to the modern situation is that of Rome in the days of the late Republic. Here also power came to be vested in the hands of a group of self-made men who had no common standards and no feeling of responsibility to each other or to the state. (p. iii)

These three theories of fashion flow have been accurate for different societies in different eras. For one to be "the one" or the most accurate would assume that all societies having a fashion flow are organized in the same manner and have members with identical motivations and needs. Such an assumption is obviously untenable. In fact, one must assume that there have been and will be still more directions of fashion flow. Adams (1967) suggested that "only in one respect has the history of costume shown a steady progress, and that is in the decline of social differentiation. . . . Steadily, down the centuries, the lower classes have aped the dress of their social superiors" (p. 43), but this fails to recognize that social differentiation occurs in a unique way for each social system. Instead, it views the lower classes as inferior beings who should wish to be like their superiors, a view limited to an early-twentieth-century perspective.

SOCIAL MOBILITY

When appearance is used as a criterion of class, it creates a barrier to social mobility. The removal of such a barrier will increase the ability of an individual to move up or down the social ladder, and this social mobility favors fashion change. The higher the rate of social mobility, the more frequent the cross-cultural contacts, the deeper the individual's understandings and information about the different classes, and the less overt difference between the classes, the more likely it will be that the society's fashion will be changing. Americans believe anyone can move up in social class through occupation; through one's ability and success in occupation as judged by financial gain; and for women, through marriage. The possibility of social mobility does in fact exist, but it is less likely that members of the lower class will manage such a transition, and the probability is that when upward mobility occurs it will be only from one tier of the class continuum to an adjoining level.

The increased incidence of social mobility in the United States may reflect colonial America's lack of an upper class. Europe's lower and middle classes, not its nobles, settled the colonies. In urban areas the upper classes evolved from successful merchants and businessmen, men like Benjamin Franklin. As industrialization produced more and more such self-made men, the upper classes toured Europe looking for contacts with the well-established, aristocratic European upper class and adopting their dress and other behaviors. In more rural communities class was associated with land ownership and length of residence and involvement in the community. The lower class was often composed of "aliens": the newcomers, immigrants, or ethnic minorities. The classes today are a continuum of financial and occupational potential rather than sharply distinct social units. The rate of social mobility has increased with our rapidly changing technology so that "overnight" successes are possible in new fields. For example, in the 1960s and 1970s the fast-food business and computer-related industries mushroomed, and successful entrepreneurs in these fields quickly became members of the nouveau riche, the lower-upper class.

When an individual changes classes, her behavior will change toward that associated with her new class. The most successful socially mobile individuals adopt these new behaviors and values; adaptation, while perhaps psychologically healthier, seems less successful socially.

UPPER CLASS SYMBOLS

Throughout modern history members of the upper class have attempted to maintain their superior positions by differentiating themselves from their inferiors. One of the most popular and most visible means of accomplishing this was by wearing symbols of upper class membership. Veblen (1934) categorized these symbols into three areas: conspicuous consumption, conspicuous leisure, and conspicuous waste.

Conspicuous Consumption

Early fashions were evidence of conspicuous consumption, perhaps because people have equated consumption with wealth or income; wealth or income with occupational position; occupational position with social class; and, thus, consumption with social class (Barber and Lobel 1952). Such consumption is evident in the wardrobe list of an American woman making a weekend visit to Napoleon's country palace: eight day dresses, one hunting costume, five tea gowns, and seven ball gowns. Each gown cost between 1,500 and 4,000 francs at a time when a dinner could easily be purchased for 2 francs (Brubach 1983).

But as more and more of the population have been able to consume conspicuously, the fashions of the highest class have tended to reflect inconspicuous consumption. As early as 1843 Pendleton noted that when a fashionable man discovers that an item he has been using is becoming popular, he drops it. "But it is not often that even the most dressy of our men of fashion originate any thing outré, or likely to attract attention; of late years their style

Figure 7.4 This attractive outfit's understated elegance does not attract attention; this would be an example of upper-upper class dress. (Fairchild Visuals)

has been plain, almost to scrupulosity" (p. 230). Members of modern America's upper-upper class would not use the snob appeal of labels or insignia worn as visible signs of consumption; rather, their dress is symbolic of such security that they do not need to compete. It is the individual who is attempting to be upwardly mobile who will tend to "consume" more of the status items associated with the class he or she wishes to enter. The well-established members of the class do not need to rely on appearance.

Conspicuous Leisure

Today's new members of the American upper class generally have acquired their position through their occupational achievements; but historically most societies placed high value on the individual who did not have to work. In both cases, however, manual labor has been associated with the lower classes. Thus, dress that clearly demonstrates the wearer's inability to perform manual labor has been a status symbol for the upper classes. The Chinese bound foot is a good example of this symbolic function of dress. The female child's foot was bound when she was around seven to nine years old, and the painful process was completed by the time she was marketable as a wife. The tinier the foot, the higher valued a commodity for marital negotiations a girl would be. Her bound feet made it impossible for her to perform labor involving walking, since she could merely hobble. Thus, she demonstrated her husband's ability to provide for her economic needs. As was pointed out in an earlier chapter, the practice, because of the status it conferred, continued into the mid twentieth

Figure 7.5 The Korean aristocrat's dress differs from the peasant's in ways that indicate his not engaging in manual labor. (Library of Congress)

Figure 7.6 Elevated footwear was used in China by women of high status whose feet were not bound. Library of Congress.

century despite its being periodically outlawed. Elevated footwear has accomplished the same thing without permanent disfigurement. In the fifteenth century the chopine was adopted in Venice. Chopines were shoes with wooden or cork soles up to two feet in height; a woman wearing them could not walk unassisted. Chopines were popular during the Renaissance in other parts of Italy, in France, in Spain, and, to a lesser degree, in England. Examples of elevated shoes can be found in many cultures throughout history. The platform shoes of the 1940s and 1970s were lower versions that, while not preventing walking, made it more treacherous as did the spike heels of the 1950s.

Long fingernails have been another popular way to demonstrate leisure. The Chinese had nails several inches long with even longer nail protectors. Zulu upper class adults wore their fingernails an inch or more in length to indicate their upper class status. However, since members of their upper-middle class had to do some work, they could wear these long nails only on their left hands (Bryant 1970). A few modern women have attempted to match the Zulus and Mandarins.

Instead of long nails, Victorian women desired small hands as a sign of their inability to work. Thus, they wore tight gloves both in and out of doors.

Clothing that fits so tightly as to impede movement, that cannot be securely fastened, that requires manual holding, or that is so flimsy it cannot withstand the stress of movement has also been used to symbolize conspicuous leisure. Another, perhaps more subtle, symbol has been dress that would be disturbed or dirtied by manual labor. Thus, until the introduction of modern fabrics capable of holding a permanent crease in men's trousers, the crease informed the observer that the wearer neither was nor had been involved in physical labor. The shirt has been the primary indicator of class status for men. A shirt of white linen or some other fabric easily soiled and difficult to clean and press has traditionally indicated the superior status of upper class membership, membership in the leisure class. However, modern wash-and-wear fabrics have removed the symbolic power of the white shirt. But symbols of cleanliness are still a social boost. This is evident in "ring around the collar," which is only a social "sin" if it is both noticed and commented upon by someone outside of the family.

The milky-white skin prized by women until this century demonstrated their not having to work. However, when work moved into factories and offices so that it promoted a pale complexion, the tan became a status symbol. The area of untanned skin must be small enough to indicate that the wearer got his or her tan during leisure or vacation time. In the north a winter tan has more status than a summer tan, since it indicates that the northerner could afford to travel to the sunny south for a winter vacation.

In the same way, certain informal leisure clothes have achieved higher status because many businesses that are generous with their bonuses and salaries expect employees to work long hours in return—law firms, for example— so that money has become more plentiful than leisure time. Thus sports clothes can have the same status as a tan. Higher status is conferred on sports that require considerable expenditure of both time and money, such as polo. The associated dress should not be ostentatious and it must be related to an "in" sport. Since the French Revolution, leisure clothing has been worn primarily by women. A successful man has had to be gainfully occupied; idleness has been a condition of retirement or unemployment, neither of which commands respect in current America. However, as women have entered the job market in greater numbers, their use of leisure clothes for status seems to be changing to an evening or weekend dress code, with more formal dress for the professional woman's working day.

Conspicuous Waste

A third aspect of dress symbolic of upper class status in materialistic cultures has been conspicuous waste. Since the nature of fashion is change, it is intrinsically wasteful. The ability to maintain or be in fashion indicates having sufficient economic resources to afford waste.

Not only have individuals had to be able to afford ornate, luxurious dress that would impede their physical movements, but they have had to limit the number of times they wore a specific item. Empress Eugénie, for example, had a white satin crinoline dress with 103 tulle flounces, which was so fragile that it could have been worn only once (Binder 1953, p. 171) even though the gown was obviously quite expensive. Since dresses generally tended to be simple during the Empire period, however, most women demonstrated wastefulness by changing gowns several times during the day. At the beginning of the twentieth century, American pioneer women, unable to obtain a wide variety of fabrics for a large and varied wardrobe, indicated their wastefulness by selecting fabrics that could not be washed and would therefore have a limited span of wear. Even today there are women who will wear a dress only a few times.

Riley (1958) found an example of conspicuous waste in a well-dressed upper class woman's closet that contained:

  6 cloth coats, 6 jackets (1 mink and 1 chinchilla), 1 fur-lined coat
  2 stoles, a mink and a sable, 1 floor-length mink opera coat ($28,000)
  1 autumn-haze everyday mink coat, 1 nearly black dressy mink coat ($14,000)
  1 mouton coat ($2,000), 1 broadtail coat and suit
 14 short evening dresses ($500–$800), 28 long gowns ($950–$2,500)
 29 sweaters, 42 blouses, 19 suits ($800–$1,000)
 10 winter day dresses ($500–$700), 8 summer day dresses ($500–$700)
  3 dress-and-coat ensembles
  8 short printed silk-and-chiffon cocktail dresses ($500–$850)
 35 housecoats and negligees, 37 nighties, 8 bed jackets
 37 hats, 225 pairs of gloves, 89 pairs of shoes, 28 handbags
  1 pair of rain boots, 3 umbrellas (no raincoat)
 93 scarves, including 5 custom-made Alençon lace stoles ($185 each)
 23 slips, 8 half slips (handmade in Paris of satin and Belgian lace at $150 each)
 18 bras, 4 strapless bras (custom-made in New York of heavy silk lace backed with marquisette at $58 each)
  5 dozen pair of stockings
 16 panties (made of fine English silk knit at $20 each)
 17 girdles ($60 each), 117 hankies
 45 pairs of earrings (all the jewelry set with precious stones) 38 necklaces (3 diamond), 16 bracelets, 28 pins

At each of her other four homes, she had wardrobes about one-third the size of the above list, which varied by style according to location. Yet such conspicuous consumption and waste has not been limited to the upper classes. Lewis (1965) found a substantial wardrobe among lower class women. One of these wardrobes contained, in part, twenty-seven dresses, three suits, eleven skirts, eleven blouses, eleven slips, sixteen panties (identical number to her wealthy counterpart), seven pairs of shoes, and two wrist watches.

In cultures that value conservation of resources and/or tradition, such as the Japanese, conspicuous waste has not been a status symbol, and fashion has been remarkably static.

SPENDING POWER AND MOTIVATIONS

Modern American dress shows few overt class differences; however, variants remain in spending power and in motivations for specific consumer expenditures. The upper-upper class is the well-established monied class whose prestige is based on their family connections and political power as well as their financial power. Not needing to demonstrate their class membership, their clothing reflects inconspicuous consumption—high in quality, but traditional rather than high style. This inconspicuous consumption may also reflect a need to seem secure enough not to *have* to compete with the members of any social group, including their own. Although members of this class have a high level of clothing awareness and dress appropriately for any occasion, they tend to put the least value on clothing and be the most independent of the "newest" fashion. In fact, an antifashion attitude is actually evident in their use of timeless, classic styles. The lower-upper class, composed of the nouveau riche, or money without family connections, is a class whose members have moved, during their current generation, to this class level. Since socially mobile individuals tend to be more insecure in their status position, clothing has greater importance to them. It is visible proof, for those still unaware of it, that the nouveau riche have socially "arrived." Thus, they conspicuously and competitively consume the high fashion of haute couture. They must do this without ostentation, which would indicate a lower class background, yet in a "money is no object" manner.

Figure 7.7 (a & b)   Guy Laroche's classic suit of Fall 1982 is much less attention demanding or status-stating than Chlóe's suit for the same season; Chlóe's design is more suitable for the nouveau-riche. (Fairchild Visuals; Chlóe)

a   b

The middle class has an acute awareness of status dress cues and generally evaluates both the dress of others and others by their dress. Respectability or social acceptance seems to be the primary motivation for most middle-class clothing behavior. However, status motivation is still important for those desiring upward social mobility, which may be at least an unconscious desire in the majority of Americans. The middle class, wanting to fit in, selects dress that does not stand out. Polhemus and Procter (1978) suggested that because of this, the middle class "must constantly change its attire in order to maintain its distance from the epicentre of fashion" (p. 69).

Lower class individuals, though they cannot afford to, also engage in conspicuous consumption. They may be more ostentatious in their display because they are likely to have fewer opportunities to achieve status in areas such as education or occupation. It is only in the marketplace that they are truly equal. For them consumption becomes a method of compensating for the social status that is denied them or made unusually difficult for them to obtain. Unable to compete in quality, they often resort to ornateness to indicate that they need not make consumer choices primarily on the basis of utility, practicality, or durability (factors evident in upper class clothing selection). Because of transportation costs, lower class consumers are often forced to shop in fewer stores and closer to home. Exposure to the mass media makes them aware of the clothing cues for status, and any inability to dress as they feel is appropriate can cause stress and heighten feelings of deprivation (Kelley et al., 1974).

The relativity of poverty is an important factor when evaluating class membership. For example, within a slum community there will be varying levels of economic ability. Those community members with a relatively higher income may feel fairly economically secure if they are unexposed to individuals of a still higher economic level. In the same way, an upper-middle-class family living in an upper class community may experience a sense of greater financial difficulty or lack than they would were they residing in a less affluent neighborhood. It is because of this relativity of poverty that the American poor are apt to feel most deprived in spite of their having a higher income than the poor of most of the rest of the world. And the more affluent Americans, noting the relatively good level of dress of the American poor, wonder why these people are complaining when they seem to have it so good.

Hartmann (1949) applied clothing to the American ideals of liberty, equality, and fraternity. His conclusions were an indictment of the American society's lack, at that time, of clothing provisions for the poor:

> Liberty implies in part freedom to vary and to experiment, and some conservatives in women's wear would say we have had more than enough of that freedom; but if freedom also includes positive opportunity to appear "not ill-clothed," then it remains true that one-third of this nation is denied that simple form of genuine liberty. Equality, as Horace Kallen brilliantly phrased it, is really "the parity of the different." But here again we find clothing still insolently employed as a badge of snobbish exclusion and discrimination, much to the resentment and deep hurt of broad masses of our citizenry. Similarly, fraternity is denied in the common per-

Figure 7.8 Poverty. (Library of Congress)

version of clothing as an instrument to express the many fine shades of "superior" and "inferior" which afflict a stratified and class-ridden culture. Every literate adult can add his own examples of the numerous ways in which clothing artificially reflects or confers status and prestige in the complex and far from equitable social system of our day. (p. 297)

Is Hartmann's evaluation still pertinent to American society? Most of us, from our middle or upper class vantage points, would probably reject his interpretation as being an accurate reflection of our society. Yet, through the wonders of television, which usually presents even middle class people living and dressing rather luxuriously, and through increased interaction between classes and the promise of upward mobility, the modern poor may feel greater disparity than they would have felt in Hartmann's America. Thus, dress continues to be a common and powerful method of differentiating the lowest class from the middle and upper classes.

SUMMARY

There are two kinds of class systems. The rigid class structure has sharply defined classes with limited cross-class interaction. Individuals are prohibited from wearing clothing representative of any class but their own. Fashion changes slowly, and those changes that do occur are minimal. Open class systems are more conducive to fashionable clothing, especially when they are associated with a downward dissemination of wealth. Fashion flow also reflects class structure. There are three major theories of how fashion flows or is disseminated: the trickle-down theory, the upward-flow theory, and the horizontal theory. Each of these theories has accurately described the fashion flow for at least one period in Western civilization.

Historically, upper class membership has been symbolized by wearing clothing that clearly shows that the wearer does not engage in manual labor and has sufficient resources to fully participate in consuming, and even wasting, the goods available to the society. However, there are few overt class differences in modern American dress. Those that do exist tend to reflect differences in spending power and motivations for expenditures. While these differences may be less visible, individuals with a smaller share of resources are often acutely aware of their reduced clothing choices. Therefore, it would seem that clothing continues to indicate and maintain the social class hierarchy.

8

Economics

An economic system is a social structure used to determine how a society's resources are to be utilized. In this chapter we shall examine the four basic kinds of economic systems: subsistence, barter, central, and market. These systems lead to different strategies and decisions in the prioritizing of resource allocation and the production, distribution, and consumption of goods and services. We shall also investigate aspects of worldwide economics relating to the international textile trade and of personal economics relating to individual income and clothing expenditures.

SUBSISTENCE ECONOMIES

The subsistence economic system is found in primarily agrarian or hunting, preindustrial societies having a technology powered by animals (including humans). Since agrarian societies are not nomadic, they have tended to develop greater role specialization and accumulation of material goods than have the hunting or gathering groups. The family is the basic social unit; small, isolated groups of families may form a loosely bonded community. Because of the isolation of such a group, the members have more similar experiences in their world and their reactions to it; they are more homogeneous. Tradition is the source of knowledge and education; therefore, the older members of the society are considered the wisest and receive the most respect.

In subsistence economic systems the group is able to produce only enough to meet its own needs. Individuals will be able to make just enough clothing for themselves and perhaps their immediate family. Wardrobes are small with little variation except for sex and status symbols.

Dress is produced from materials that are easily found in the environment and that can be used without much processing. A leaf or feather, for example, can be worn just by finding a way to attach it to the body or to suspend it. The simple processing of fibers to make yarn, cord, or fabric is also found in some subsistence economies. Cords made from twisted hair (human, buffalo, dog, goat) can be worn by tying them to the body. A girdle of "human hair braided into fine sennet and wound into a skein 200 yards in length" was collected from a northern California Indian tribe (Krieger 1928, p. 642). The grass skirt of Oceania and New World peoples required the attachment of blades of grass to such a cord. Leaves and stems and other nonspun fibers could be plaited or crudely woven without a loom. The Iroquois, for example, plaited cornhusks.

Animal skins were also used for clothing. The Aleuts wore robes of bird skin, particularly that of the tufted puffin. Their rain gear was made of the

Figure 8.1 These men of Oceania are elaborately garbed with everyday items requiring little processing (shells, seeds, and bands and cords of crudely woven vegetable fiber). (National Anthropological Archives, Smithsonian Institution)

intestines of sea animals, whale tongue skin, or halibut bladder (Gunther 1972). Tailored skins were used in Europe from at least the late Stone Age. But they were especially common among Eskimos and northern American Indians. Tailoring has generally been found only in societies with a method of treating skins to make them more supple. Such methods were among the earliest technological advances and increased both the incidence of skins in dress and the complexity of that dress. These methods were often time consuming. For example, the Eskimo sometimes chewed a scraped skin until it became soft. Each time it got wet it had to be rechewed. Skins treated with fats, oils, brains, bone marrow, dung, or urine will stay supple even when wet, as long as they remain oiled. Tanned skins treated with vegetable substances containing tannic acid retain suppleness even after being wet.

Cloth can be made from bark with a mallet as the only needed tool. The bark is dried and its inner layers, separated from the outer bark, are stripped into fine fibers which are redried. The fibers are then smoothed and sorted so that they lie in one direction; the strands are placed in perpendicular layers, which are repeatedly soaked, dried, and pounded. It is finished with a final drying and bleaching in the sun. It can be dyed or block-printed. The Hawaiians developed fine tapa cloth, which ranged, by virtue of the plants used, from gossamer to fairly thick (Clark 1963). They scented their tapa and increased its water resistance by rubbing it with oil in which seeds or wood from aromatic plants had been soaked. They were able to produce a faint design rather like a

Figure 8.2 Ugandans making bark cloth. (Library of Congress)

watermark by using patterned mallets for the pounding process. Unfortunately, wet tapa is subject to tearing and is neither as insulating nor as soft as most woven fabrics.

BARTER ECONOMIES

A barter economic system is found in societies similar to the subsistence societies except that there is slightly less isolation between groups and production is sufficient enough in some area to enable the group to trade product(s) or service(s) with another group. Both ancient Greek and certain American Indian women, for example, wove standard squares of cloth, which they used to trade for other goods. Looms made such excess production possible, and the squares were sufficiently standardized, functional, and sturdy that they were used as a kind of currency (Linton 1969). The ease of transporting cloth has been another asset in its use as a medium of exchange.

In some groups the trading of goods was for social rather than economic reasons. Big exchanges were made among the Kwakiutl and some other American Indians at the time of major life events like death or birth. Such trading was not done to meet survival needs but as a form of a competitive "surpassing the Joneses" by "aggressively demonstrating the consumer's own social position to the public and if possible even of enhancing it during competition with rivals in the form of a challenge" (König 1973, p. 107). Each trader would attempt to outclass his opposite. Status appears to have been a primary motivation for these trades. Such a link with status is not uncommon in barter economies. People in many cultures carry their shoes when walking over rough ground

Figure 8.3 Mexican peasants carrying their sandals. (Library of Congress)

that could damage or scuff the shoes. Clearly the shoes function more as a status symbol than as a foot protector. Status has also resulted from the trading of specific resources. One American Indian trading post, for example, traded iron collars for the Indians' animal skins. Since the collars were only traded for the best pelts, the collars themselves became status symbols, and the trading post was offered only the finest skins.

Rural colonial America is an example of a somewhat sophisticated barter system. The rural colonial family tended to be isolated; even when they were close to a village, getting to it required considerable preparation and expenditure of time. They grew or foraged for most of the resources they needed and made most products they required. Westbound pioneers took many clothing items with them, but their clothes wore out quickly or were traded with the Indians for more suitable attire such as moccasins. Once settled, the family members had few clothes; two working outfits—one to wear when the other was washed—and one "good" costume was the norm. Wool, heavy cotton, and linsey-woolsey (wool and cotton blend) were used for winter and light cottons for summer. Every bit of material was used, and everything was used and reused until it was worn out. When mother created a new skirt for herself, she would do as little cutting as possible. Gathering, for example, was used to give shape at the waist. Then when the skirt could no longer be remodeled (or turned inside out), it would be taken apart and the cloth used for a child's garment. The child's outfit would be cut extra large with big seams so that she could still use it as she grew. When there was no child small enough to use the remaining cloth, that fabric would be used in patching, quilting, rag rugs, or the like. Even feed and flour sacks were used as dress material. Garments had to be simple; European peasant immigrants did not have the time to continue the elaborate embroidery of their dress. The high value of dress is evident when one examines old wills in which clothing was among the more important bequeathals.

A true barter system does not use coinage or other forms of money. For our purposes, however, we will consider those that have money but use it only rarely as barter economies. The Indian's wampum was a form of coinage. The kinds of shells—and later, beads—used and the length of the strip had a specific, common value. The use of clothing as a medium of exchange—ornament currency—is not uncommon when there is no monetary system and when the clothing has intrinsic value or is rare.

A variety of shells, feathers, and teeth have been used for exchange. The Mt. Haganers of New Guinea determine the value of a shell by its iridescence. The most important items in their ceremonial dress are shells, feathers, furs, hair wigs, and aprons. They trade for the shells and feathers. When the Europeans used shells to pay the natives for food and work, the superabundance of shells resulted in an inflated economy. After inflation, some shells, such as the cowrie and nassa, lost popularity as adornments; yet others, such as the bailer shell, retained their decorative importance. It is not the wearing of the valuables themselves that indicates wealth but rather the wearing on one's chest of a bamboo stick tally to show participation in the traditional system of wealth exchange. This tally represents the number of groups of shell valuables the wearer has given to his peers. Prestige is achieved by such gifts, which are actually investments since the recipient will lose prestige unless he makes a return gift of even greater value (Strathern 1981). These trades set up loose alliances or friendship patterns, which have served to maintain peace and cooperation among the different family groupings.

In a barter economy family members produce sufficient clothing for their family's needs, although they may trade for some clothing items. The small wardrobes will be more varied than in subsistence economies. Clothing is produced from materials easily found in the environment, but these materials may undergo a simple processing, such as spinning and weaving. Weavers have been primarily agrarian or pastoral people since the preparation of fibers and the weaving process is lengthy. However, the Chilkat Indians of the Northwest Pacific coast, a tribe of hunters and gatherers, wove cedar-bark robes, which "required the coordinated efforts of both men and women, the use of imported materials, and the export of the products" (Coon 1971, p. 272). The cedar bark was imported from southern coastal regions; wool of the Rocky Mountain goat used to wrap the cedar bark warps and for the wefts was obtained in the mountains by the men, who also set up the looms. A loom consisted of a single bar suspended from two forked sticks. "The men also made pattern boards . . . and . . . measuring sticks for the women to use in copying the designs off the boards" (ibid.). The women did the spinning, dyeing, and weaving, sewed the woven panels together and bordered the sides and bottom by braiding (ibid.).

While the technology to make fabric existed early in the evolution of clothing, the resources and time elements required for its production often made the finished material quite valuable. People were loath to cut woven fabric, even when they were technologically able to, since they could not afford the waste that cutting involved. Thus, most early garments of woven fabric were made of uncut rectilinear pieces sewn together, for instance, the kimono; of one uncut piece of cloth with an opening for the head woven into it; or of one uncut piece of cloth, for instance, the sari and toga.

CENTRALLY PLANNED ECONOMIES

Centrally planned economic systems are those in which production and distribution are determined by a central government, as in the Soviet Union and other Communist countries. This system has also been found in other societies having a powerful central government, as in feudal Europe. The government is the most powerful social unit, more important than the family. Tradition is revered, and the old are given great respect. However, this respect for tradition and the elderly decreases with industrialization and most of these economic systems have industrialized. Textiles are the major source of clothing, but fabric is used conservatively since its production involves the consumption of time, labor, and resources in a consumer- rather than government-interest area. Because the government's purpose is to meet its own needs and interests, consumer concerns such as fashion have tended to have a low priority. If the technology is limited, fabrics will probably not be cut. Dress styles will change infrequently except for the dress worn by those in the top social level(s).

In the Soviet Union the distribution of consumer goods follows the same procedure as in the United States: from factory to wholesaler to retailer to consumer. However, both the wholesale and retail levels are generally controlled by the state on either the national or local level. At the retail level there are government stores, both department and specialty, in urban areas and cooperative stores in rural areas. Each of these has its own wholesale system. There is also a state mail-order system to provide more goods to rural areas. Warehouses from which goods are shipped to stores are often attached to factories, although they may be independent entities.

Production is not determined by consumer needs and desires but by plans that were predetermined by the state. These plans include factory size and location as well as the quantity and specification of the products. The factory has no direct links to the market; its production must please the planner rather than the consumer, who, having few or no alternatives, is forced to buy. Styles have been chosen because they were the easiest to produce even though they were unattractive or uncomfortable. The little advertising that exists is designed to mold consumers into wanting what has been produced even though the production determination was not based on consumer interest. Clothing has sometimes been produced that has so ignored consumer interests, tastes, and comfort that it has been unsalable. When innovative designs have been proposed, the products have too often been unsuccessful because the factory ignored stylistic specifications in favor of maintaining a high level (and ease) of production. These problems, among others, have forced the government to begin decentralizing the administration and planning of some consumer products in order to improve consumer goods (Vasilyeva 1981).

Pricing is not competitive since it is set by the state. In rural cooperative stores prices tend to be higher than they would be in city stores, which have a greater number of product choices. Prices generally are double the production costs. About 20 percent of the half unrelated to production cost is to cover distribution costs; the rest is designated surplus value belonging to the state. This "turnover tax," which provides a large part of the Soviet budget, is used to regulate demand. By keeping prices higher than necessary, the government makes sure that citizens will not have too much money for the limited availability of consumer goods. When consumer goods that the government wants to discourage are plentiful, such as jewelry, they are given an extremely high price. Lower prices can encourage certain kinds of consumption, for instance, of children's wear. However, practicality and availability of a consumer product does not necessarily mean a lower price. In the 1960s, for example, the turnover tax on a pair of plain adult shoes was nearly 40 percent of the production price (Goldman 1966). Because the Soviet Union has stressed the development of heavy industry, consumer goods have had limited availability. In the early 1960s Russian consumers used about 60 percent less material and about 50 percent fewer socks, stockings, and shoes than their American counterparts had in the 1890s (Bergson and Kuznets 1963). But difficulties in acquiring fashionable dress have not prevented the development of a fashion interest among the Soviet citizens. Their interest created a black market in clothing and ultimately has forced the government to divert more resources into clothing production. Thus, for example, in 1981 Zaitsev, one of the first Soviet fashion designers since the Great Depression, was named supervisor of a new fashion house in Moscow whose mission was to supply stores with a variety of clothes in styles to please the consumer (Vasilyeva 1981).

Procedures for inspection of goods have been instigated, but quality has remained a problem. In the 1960s Khrushchev (1962) noted that the quality of some goods was so poor that they could not be sold. Over one and a half billion rubles' worth of shoes were unsalable in spite of the fact that the demand for shoes was greater than the supply.

Both centrally planned and market economies depend on production exceeding need, which leads to specialized labor and an urban work force, and on a means of distributing the surplus goods.

MARKET ECONOMIES

In a market economy and in most current centrally planned economies people generally obtain all or most of their wardrobes by purchasing mass-produced clothing from the mass market. However, styles in a market economy change frequently, waste is valued, and wardrobes are larger and more varied than those in societies with the other economic systems.

The major difference between a market economy and a centrally planned one is that production, distribution, and consumption are determined by free market forces in the first case and by a central government in the second. It is the market system, therefore, that is governed by the principle of supply and demand. When the supply is less than the demand, the cost of the product or service will increase. Production will thus be stimulated, and as the supply begins to increase, the price will start to decrease. This cycle is a result of a constant search for equilibrium between supply and demand. In such a system the group with the most demands *and* sufficient financial resources to meet them will be the consumer group with the greatest influence on production and distribution. For example, fashions in the last fifty years have focused on the demands of young people who have had, for the first time, sufficient purchasing power to make their demands important. As money is redistributed more to the elderly, who are increasing in number and political clout, their fashion needs will, theoretically, begin to be met more frequently. Individuals alone exercise little power; it is when a large number of individuals have a common demand that they gain importance in such decision making. Obviously, a market economy will be stimulated by a wider distribution of wealth since more groups will form, with different demands and the financial ability to meet them.

The market economy (and many modern centrally planned) is a system of mass: mass production, mass distribution, mass marketing, mass communication. These "masses" are a result of automated, high-technology industry, which necessitates standardization of products. While the population may be quite heterogeneous, as in the United States, the lifestyles will be surprisingly homogeneous because of this standardization.

Labor is highly specialized and an individual's work role may be quite different from his or her social roles. Thus, work dress may be distinct from social dress. A policewoman or other uniformed career woman may change from her uniform to a wide variety of clothes designed to fit her social roles: a tennis outfit, bathing suit, cocktail dress, street dress, housecoat, and so on. In each of these roles, her status will be determined by her role-related achievements.

Production of new styles depends on their appealing to consumers so that they will purchase the new style *and* discard the old. This respect for the new and dismissal of the old is also evident in the society's relative placement of value by age group; it is the young who have the greater importance. New styles are not designed because they are "better"—more beautiful, functional, comfortable (Borsodi 1929). They are designed because a market economy, dependent on meeting consumer demands, must constantly create new or different demands. Fashion, the popular mode, is critical to a market system since the "essence of fashion is wastefulness rather than utility" (Gordon and Lee 1977, p. 166). Change is valued and accelerated. Materialism, waste, and stylishness will be valued rather than quality, practicality, conservation, or functionality, which are valued in the other economic systems. Products will, by design, have a limited life or planned obsolescence. Demands or wants will reflect nonsurvival motives; one doesn't *need* this year's newest look in order to physically survive but one needs it to enhance some area of social or psychological "appearance." For example, to be "in" one must have what is "in," what the mass media have designated as necessary. Because of these values modern society has seen an expansion of the structure of human wants.

We see this in the struggle of the "have-not" nations to copy the "have" nations, to achieve a high level of living for masses of the people rather than a few. The drive for *economic democracy* may have begun (a condition the United States has almost achieved). Poverty has two aspects: (1) the lack of better things for better wants; and (2) the lack of better wants for better things. However, the degree of satisfaction derived from the consumption of the same goods under varying conditions cannot be measured and will be different for each person involved, for "the good life" is a relative concept. (Anspach 1969, p. 40)

MASS PRODUCTION

Because mass production, an aspect of all market and most centrally planned economies, requires a large labor force having easy access to the production and distribution facilities, urban communities are necessary. Urbanization brings the individual into contact with a greater number of people and at the same time leads to a depersonalization of human interactions. Thus, one's judgments of others must rely more on their appearance since intimate knowledge is unlikely; the social-communication potential of dress, therefore, becomes a more important factor in the urban setting.

The need of industrial societies for a mobile population in urban areas has contributed to four powerful social changes: (1) decreased importance of the kinship system, (2) increased social roles, (3) association of status with occupational achievement, and (4) increased social equality. This last has been especially evident in dress which no longer serves as an obvious symbol of class. Theoretically a sense of social equality should enhance the individual's self-image. We do not know whether this is in fact the case, although the demands for political equality made by women and many minority groups seem to support this assumption.

Technological advances that have made clothing easier to care for have given women more equality in their life options. Imagine, for example, the mother who used to have to hand wash, line dry, and iron her family's clothing; her housework actually entrapped her in the home. But the laundry can now be done in very little time, and the housewife is free to pursue other activities, such as a career. The furthering of social equality has also had a revolutionary impact on economic, governmental, stratifying, and religious institutions. In fact, most world changes in the last two centuries can be directly or indirectly attributed to advances in technology.

The specialization of labor found in industrial societies has caused people to depend on others to meet many of their needs for goods and services. Few modern Americans, for example, grow their own food and none are likely to make their own clothing from fabric woven with yarn spun from a fiber they have harvested. In fact, more and more Americans are becoming less and less aware of even how such products are made and what natural resources are used in their production.

One of the uncertainties facing market economies today is whether their labor force must be cheap. In the past the factory worker has been poorly paid and often worked in less than ideal conditions (textile and apparel workers have been lower paid than most other major industry workers). Since the 1960s, however, this has been changing so that today's factory worker expects a salary higher than many college-trained professionals, excellent working conditions, and benefits such as health and life insurance. No successful market systems have had to deal with such demands, and one cannot be sure whether the system will be able to survive, let alone thrive, in such a situation. One response by some manufacturers has been to move their facilities to other countries with lower wage and production costs, fewer restrictions, and more favorable tax structures.

Mass production is not a creative process, even in the design of a product. The mass producer of women's dresses, for example, examines a couturier's new design, which is a limited product, to differentiate those cost-efficient aspects with a wide appeal from those with a limited one. She will produce an adaptation of the designer's garment that will incorporate the wide-appeal aspects (from one or more designs) with less expensive materials. The cut or structural detail of the garments will be fairly standard; differences will be limited primarily to fabric and trims.

The United States has led the world in mass production and consumption. Owing to the general belief that better clothing enhances the wearer's view of herself or himself, dress has been considered an important consumer product. We use more synthetic fibers than any other economy as well as an abundant amount of natural fibers such as cotton and wool. When the natural-fuel shortages began in the 1970s, synthetic fibers like polyester, whose major ingredients were petroleum or natural gas derivatives, became more expensive than natural fibers. The textile industry began looking for ways to cut production costs. Thus, they began to emphasize natural fibers, which had been somewhat ignored in the previous decade. However, these are often blended with synthetics so that the easy-care qualities expected and needed by modern consumers have been retained.

The materialistic values of the American culture stem, at least in part, from the market economy, which has continually created new and more demands for goods. Businesses have a great interest in new-product research and development. More economical products will enable them to be more competitive; more goods will provide consumers with more choices, more avenues for spending their money. Underlying this never-ending search for material goods is the American assumption that quantity is an asset, "that if 'some' is good, 'more' should be even better" (Anspach 1969, p. 19). No other form of economic system stresses the production of consumer goods that are not needed for survival. Instead of attempting to promote a desire for more, other systems try to promote a sense of less being quite sufficient and even good. Choices are more limited, both by having a smaller range of options available and by making acquisition of the goods more difficult.

Technology has enabled us to be so wasteful. The mechanization of fabric production, for example, has led to relatively less expensive fabrics that are used in greater quantity and variety and are available to more people. This has led to ever more rapid fashion changes so that obsolescence occurs more quickly, even when unplanned.

In an industry-based society, change is inevitable. Advancing technology alters wants for material goods by introducing new or more efficient products and by lowering the cost of existing items. It breaks up expected status characteristics by introducing new occupations around which status symbols are formed. It redistributes wealth. By various means, technology initiates and supports social change. A technological nation must reinforce a desire for mobility and change within the society. (ibid., p. 39)

All of these changes in technology have led to a fashion and human revolution: the democratization of fashion and, therefore, of the humans who wear the fashions. And as industrialization and other Western technology spread to more and more cultures of the world, so spreads Western clothing; "fashion," still constantly changing, is becoming more uniform worldwide. This uniformity, whether ultimately a positive or negative force, is bringing at least a superficial (or sartorial) human equality. Such a sense of equality will have tremendous repercussions on the individual's psychological development.

MASS MARKETING

Beginning in the 1950s, the family in market economies has been replaced more and more by the mass media as the unit that forms the values and attitudes of the individual. Modern individuals, faced with the vast array of choices presented to them through the media, find choosing difficult. But the media, by stressing certain options, help to make them seem more "correct," more natural. Advertising begins before a product is available so that consumers will have become accustomed to the "new" by the time they are able to choose whether or not to purchase it.

Use of the mass media is the first step in mass marketing. The ready-to-wear clothing industry began in the eighteenth century with the marketing of used clothing. There were 225 such businesses in France by 1844 (Garland 1971). In the late eighteenth century tailors were making garments during their lax periods that they would sell, with some alterations, at a lower price than a custom-made garment. Westward expansion in America created a greater demand for a quick, inexpensive clothing alternative. This came as the technology for mass production developed and a cheap labor source, new immigrants, was available. Later in the nineteenth century as women began to assume more roles outside of the home, they required more clothing. Distances in rural America were too great for easy travel to a seamstress or a visit from her for selecting a design, taking measurements, and having fittings; thus there was a need for ready-to-wear clothing.

Urbanization made mass marketing a realistic concept and mail-order companies, like Sears, Roebuck, made mass marketing appropriate even for rural areas. The mass media have become one of the major ways that modern societies "educate" their citizenry. Through the mass media, individuals learn how to behave so that they "fit in" with the needs and expectations of their society. The media message in a market economy is for "more," and consumers are bombarded with a vast array of "new" and "better" products, which they "need" in order to be "happy." The media message of the industrialized, cen-

Figure 8.4   The New York City Old Clothes Market, ca. 1910. (Library of Congress)

trally planned economy is quite different since it is promoting less consumer expenditure and less acquisition of material goods. Thus, for example, in October 1980 there was not a single fashion picture or fashion advertisement in the Soviet newspaper *Pravda*. Compare that to any newspaper in the United States during the same time period.

ECONOMIC CONDITIONS

The cost of clothing and the economic times were also important factors in the development of the American ready-to-wear industry. The depression of 1873 caused financial problems for many of the wealthy, who had to cut back their expenditures. One of the ways they chose to economize was to purchase more ready-to-wear clothing, especially men's trousers. Their desire for ready-to-wear goods increased the total sales in this marketing area and, more important, the producers upgraded the quality of their product in order to enhance its sale potential.

> The period of depression of 1893 to 1895, and, again, the panic of 1907, had similar effects in driving additional numbers of people who had formerly patronized tailors to ready-to-wear retail stores. In each case there resulted decided tendencies toward developing better grades of clothing. This movement, however, seemed to have reached its climax with the panic of 1907, for during the business depression of 1921 the clothing industry, in common with practically all industries suffered a serious decline with no change in demand such as had been noticed in the previous periods of hard times. (Nystrom 1928, p. 412)

Economic conditions can influence the kind of clothing produced as well as the method of its production. The Great Depression of the 1930s, for example, led to the development of the cocktail dress. Since entertaining costs had to be curtailed, the large cocktail party developed as an inexpensive alternative to the dinner party. Because the hostess did most of the setting up for a cocktail party, she could not be efficient and comfortable in a floor-length dinner gown.

Since World War II theorists have speculated that a relationship has existed between the length of women's hemlines and economic conditions. Short hemlines have been associated with rising stock prices, while hems have dropped as the market has fallen. The short hemlines of the 1920s and their drop in the 1930s and the miniskirts of the 1960s and their disappearance in the 1970s are cited as examples of this esoteric market barometer. However, skirts had begun to lengthen before the market crashed in 1929 (they were only truly short from 1925 to 1927). During World War II skirts were shorter because of conservation requirements necessary to meet the war's demands. After the war Dior's New Look featured a long hemline which rose only to about midcalf by the mid1960s. Yet during the 1950s the economy and stock market experienced numerous swings. Laver's (1952) hypothesis that women's waistlines move from the waist or disappear altogether during periods of economic instability is also inconsistent with fashions since then.

DISSEMINATION OF ECONOMIC RESOURCES

The degree to which the wealth of a society is distributed influences the distribution of its products and services. The more widely disseminated the economic resources are, the more widely distributed the products and services will be. Wealth began a downward diffusion in the West during the fifteenth century when the European nobility began to decrease their assets through expenditures for wars and luxurious lifestyles. At the same time the merchants were accumulating a greater portion of the economic pie through the selling of goods to the nobles and through the establishment of new trading routes. The Industrial Revolution accelerated this redistribution.

Economists in the eighteenth century promoted higher wages believing that they (1) were an incentive for increased worker productivity, (2) helped to spread the economic resources, and (3) stimulated consumer spending, consumption, and therefore production (Freudenberger 1963). The United States soon had the highest wages and therefore the most effective dissemination of economic resources. Her citizens became the best dressed population in the world as more and more Americans were able to rise above a subsistence level of clothing and into a world of fashion. However, there were still great disparities in the early twentieth century. Wealthy men and women could spend a great deal of money for clothing; a gown by Worth, for instance, could easily cost $600 and a fine petticoat as much as $150. As one went down the income scale, clothing expenditures obviously had to decrease. A society woman with a

a   b

Figure 8.5 (a & b) Class disparity is evident in the dress of these women in the 1890's. (a) The affluent woman's dress was impractical as well as expensive. (b) Her counterparts, chainmakers earning about $1.25 for a 60-hour week, wore more practical dress. (Library of Congress)

marginal income could economize on clothing by spending only $150 per season. In *The Lady* of 1902, an advertisement purporting to appeal to those forced to budget gave the following list of necessary wardrobe expenditures for one season:

Hairdresser	$6	
Millinery	$10	for three toques or hats
Boots and shoes	$6	for 1 pair walking shoes, 1 pair boots, 1 pair evening shoes
Gloves	$4	for 10 pairs suede, 6 pairs kid, 2 pairs long evening gloves
Mantles and ruffles	$19	
Petticoats and hosiery	$5.50	
Parasols	$4.50 for 2	
Gowns, blouses, etc.	$75	
Odds and ends	$13	

(Gernsheim 1963, pp. 86–87)

Yet at this time the average Boston shopgirl earned about $5 per week and women sewing at home averaged 30¢ to 40¢ a day; southern mill workers—men—got less than $6 per week (Allen 1952). These wages only come to about $100 to $300 per year!

By the end of World War II there were fewer families of great wealth and power; economic extremes had been reduced as the average income had increased. The great wealth once held by a small number of families was now shared by a growing middle class. However, there still exists a sharply skewed curve of income between the poor, the middle class, and the wealthy. The disparity in net worth—one's assets and liabilities—is even greater than that in incomes, and while actual incomes have approached parity, inflation has made real income—the purchasing power of one's money—decrease. This decrease is particularly deleterious to the poor, who also increasingly suffer a psychological poverty, a sense of despair that they will ever have enough money to live comfortably. As the relativity of poverty causes the American poor to feel even poorer, the rest of the society believes that current poverty is less poor and affects fewer individuals.

> Clothes make the poor invisible too: America has the best-dressed poverty the world has ever known. . . .
> This is an extremely important factor in defining our emotional and existential ignorance of poverty. In Detroit the existence of social classes became much more difficult to discern the day the companies put lockers in the plants. From that moment on, one did not see men in work clothes on the way to the factory, but citizens in slacks and white shirts. This process has been magnified with the poor throughout the country. There are tens of thousands of Americans in the big cities who are wearing shoes, perhaps even a stylishly cut suit or dress, and yet are hungry. It is not a matter of planning, though it almost seems as if the affluent society had given out costumes to the poor so that they would not offend the rest of society with the sight of rags. (Harrington 1962, p. 5)

Instances of people whose poverty is obvious from their dress are rare. Why do the poor dress well? Perhaps it is because a positive appearance is an aspect of a positive sense of oneself, of a positive mood, and of a sense of belonging to or fitting in with one's community. Any of these powerful needs would be a sufficient motive for greater concern with and attention to one's appearance. The importance of appearance in nonverbal communication and in interpersonal relationships is far greater than is the importance of other needs such as housing or food.

Society's Level of Affluence

It has been suggested that a society's fashions symbolize its level of affluence. For example, sixteenth-century Spain was a highly affluent society, and gold was used heavily in dress, while in Japan as late as 1969, a four-person urban household had an average income of only $270 (a rural household had less). The kimono was suitable to the low income. Its style never changed; its size allowed one to change in girth without having to change wardrobe; it was easy, quick, and economical to produce (it wasted no fabric since it was rectilinear); it could be stored in minimal space, which was important since that same family

a   b

Figure 8.6 (a & b) The differences in dress between Queen Elizabeths I and II, in these two photos, visually parallel the difference in level of affluence in England between the 17th and the 20th centuries. (Library of Congress)

of four would live in a home with three hundred square feet; it required few accessories; it could be cleaned at home; and it required infrequent cleaning because it was worn over undergarments that protected it from the body's oils (Sakata 1973).

PERSONAL DRESS EXPENDITURES

Many variables influence an individual's expenditures for clothing. For instance, the low income of many of the world's peoples prevents them from purchasing those consumer goods, including dress, that are available. In the 1960s the income of the average American family increased, and as it did, so did their clothing expenditures. Some of this increase in clothing purchases may have also reflected demographic changes that were taking place. Since population size was increasing, there was a natural increase in demand for clothing. The urban population was increasing, and the size of the family was decreasing (urban families tend to be smaller than rural ones). Urban families generally spend more money as well as a larger proportion of their income on clothes; they will have more clothes and the clothing items will cost more.

Sex is another factor that influences clothing expenditure. While women have traditionally had, and continue to have, lower incomes than men, their dress requirements and costs have often been similar. Especially as they have assumed more roles outside of the home, they have required even more clothing. Today's women tend to buy more clothes than men, but men pay more per garment. Career women generally have larger wardrobes than homemakers and, if married, spend more money on clothes than homemakers do. Because working women have less time for shopping, their husbands tend to shop more for their own clothing.

Family size and life stage also affect clothing expenditures. A beginning family—newlyweds—tends to have low clothing expenditures. The couple generally have purchased new clothing prior to their wedding and their income priorities are more for home-related goods and services. The expanding family spends a greater portion of their income for clothing than any other family. From the first pregnancy, which requires the purchase of a maternity wardrobe, to the birth of the first child, who requires frequent clothing purchases in his or her growing years and more expensive and more varied clothing during adolescence and young adulthood, clothing expenditures have to increase. This need frequently results in the parents having to "make do" with older styles for themselves. However, in the upper-middle and upper classes, parents will generally require more clothing for themselves. The contracting family's children are leaving the home and becoming part of a new family—thus, the parents are able to spend a greater percent of their income on clothing for themselves. However, as the adults reduce their roles through such events as retirement or the death of a spouse, they also usually reduce their clothing expenditures. Young people, on the other hand, tend to be expanding their roles, and thus their role-related clothing needs are increasing. As the size of the average family decreases and the size of their income increases, a greater amount of its larger income will be spent for clothing. This is even more true when the family's raised income lifts them to a higher status or class level since they will buy better, more fashionable, or more expensive clothes in order to demonstrate their new status.

The geographic location of a family and its degree of geographic mobility also influence clothing expenditures. Cold climates require clothing, often wool, that is usually comparatively expensive but will wear well. Warm climates require less expensive and a smaller quantity of clothing; but that clothing will wear out more rapidly owing to the need for more frequent cleaning and the effects of heat, humidity, and sun on the fibers (Tate and Glisson 1961). Heating and cooling systems are to some degree ameliorating these differences, but clothing worn out of doors is still affected. Data on clothing expenditures indicates that they are higher in the Northeast than in the South or the West. A family either residing in a locale with cold and hot temperature extremes or able to travel to an area with an extreme different from their own, will have to purchase more clothing in order to meet the varied climatic needs.

TEXTILE AND INTERNATIONAL TRADE

Regardless of the type of economic system, the clothing industry—from fiber processing to cosmetics and accessories—is a major economic factor for modern nations, especially the developing ones. It is vital to both domestic and international commerce. The French government was among the first to recognize the importance of the textile-related industries. Business led the way in England (Freudenberger 1963).

The resources used in textiles are a major aspect of the agriculture industry. Animals which provide wool, silk, and leather are raised on ranches or farms, as are most of the vegetable fibers, such as cotton or linen. For primarily agrarian nations, the production of such products can be critical to the national economy. In Pakistan, for example, the textile industry is the largest industry; it employs one-third of the industrial workers and produces 20 percent of all industrial output and 60 percent of exported goods (Ehrlich 1983).

International trade in fibers is important because of the geographic limits of the distribution of natural-fiber resources and the unique qualities of each of these fibers. Eighty percent of cotton, the most heavily used natural fiber, is produced in India, Mexico, Egypt, the United States, and the Soviet Union. Flax and silk are even more geographically limited. Even wool, while grown throughout the world, has a limited area of commercial yarn production. These limits have an enormous impact on production of goods. For example, when silk stockings became the rage in the 1920s, American stocking manufacturers had to import great quantities of silk. Twice a month a special twenty-one-car train carried twenty-eight tons of silk from Vancouver, where it had been brought by ship from Japan, to New York. Because the work forces of factories were dependent on the arrival of this silk, the train took precedence over all other trains. There was even a $1,000 per hour penalty for each hour the train ran behind its scheduled arrival time (Hall 1972). A 1954 United Nations Food and Agriculture Organization survey of natural and synthetic fibers found that sufficient clothing resources are found in countries that have only about 15 percent of the world's population: the United States, Canada, Argentina, Uruguay, Australia, New Zealand, and Western Europe. Such resources were profoundly lacking in most of South America, Central America, Eastern Europe, Southern Europe, Russia, China, India, Southeast Asia, and Africa. Thus, the world's fiber production would have had to increase by about 25 percent in order for a per capita consumption of ten pounds per year to be achieved. Yet that per capita consumption was only one-quarter the rate in the United States at that time (Holtzclaw 1956).

Although natural resources are not unlimited, their scarcity is relative and depends on human demands. Those natural resources in great demand must be cared for in ways that will extend the supply. This can be done by finding substitutes for the resource, by augmenting the natural yield, by using the existing supply more efficiently, or by lowering or changing the lifestyle of a people. For example, should wastefulness be rejected by the American people, conservation of many natural resources would automatically begin. Many of the so-called have-not countries reuse the waste products of the haves. Rubber tires, for instance, are used to make footwear in India, where there are sixteen factories devoted to this reclamation, and Indians have even been investigating international markets to try to find more sources of used tires for import (Vogler 1982). Yet in spite of conservation efforts, the principle of diminishing returns means that

> at any given time, increasing use of labor and capital combined with a fixed amount of land will produce progressively smaller yields. . . . In years past consumers have partially escaped the consequences of this principle through discoveries of new lands. This outlet is now closed, however, because there is no undiscovered land on earth and the moon has been found to be barren. . . .
> [Today] the supply of goods and services falls far below the volume required to satisfy all current consumer wants at prices all can pay. (Gordon and Lee 1977, p. 33–34)

This problem is further compounded by the use, in many societies, of current money supplies to create more money rather than more products.

SUMMARY

There are four basic kinds of economic systems, although elements of each can be found in all of them. The subsistence economy is found in primarily preindustrial societies. Their dress is fairly homogeneous, though it may differentiate for sex and/or status. It is made from materials easily found in the environment and that do not require much processing. Societies that have a barter economy are similar. However, they produce more than they require in at least one area so that a group can trade product(s) or service(s) with another group with which they have contact. The centrally planned economy is one in which a central government determines the production and distribution of goods. Unlike the barter and subsistence economies, in which the family or clan is the most important social unit, the government is most powerful in this system. Textiles are the major source of clothing, although fabric production may be limited. This limit leads to infrequent changes in dress styles and conservation of fabric. In a market economy, free market forces determine production and distribution. The principle of supply and demand can be applied to this economic system. The market economy is found in technologically advanced societies, which have mass production, mass distribution, mass marketing, and mass communication. Fashion—changing styles—is a critical force in such a system since it helps to create artificial consumer demands.

The degree to which a society's economic resources are diffused through its populace has a major impact on clothing. The more widely disseminated they are, the greater the demand throughout the society for its products. Demographic factors, and family size and life stage all influence clothing expenditure.

The clothing and textile industries are important to the economies of all nations, and natural fibers are a major aspect of the agricultural industry. However, the geographic distribution of natural fibers and their relative scarcity mean that most nations have to import at least some textiles. Thus, clothing is also an important factor in international trade. Through such trade all textiles are becoming available to all nations. This commonality of textiles is leading to a decrease in the diversity of the world's clothing.

9 | Government

In this chapter we shall examine how governments, the established systems of political administration, influence clothing and how clothing influences governments. We shall analyze the influence on clothing of different forms of government, international relationships, and political leaders. Clothing's role in political ideologies, rebellions, revolutions, and wars will also be investigated, as will sumptuary laws.

The power of clothing is evident in government's use of it as a tool to demonstrate the power and authority of government. Langner (1959) suggested that complex systems of government could not even exist without military and police uniforms since it is the military and police who dominate or control the larger population through an authority indicated by their uniforms (p. 127). Such a uniform symbol can be a complete costume or merely an insignia like a sheriff's star or marshall's badge.

Clothing can even help to establish authority through tradition. Thus, when William, son of Prince Charles and Princess Diana, was christened, he wore the same Honiton lace christening gown worn by Queen Victoria's son Albert (later Edward VII) at his christening in 1841. The wearing of this gown is traditional for any baby in line to ascend the British throne. It is a visual, public affirmation of the child's right to the authority of the crown and thus his

Figure 9.1 Coronation robes, such as these worn by King George V and Queen Mary, visually attest to the legitimacy of the monarchs. (Library of Congress)

or her right to govern. Clothing has even been a factor in the initial establishment of authority. A Zulu chief, for example, achieved power by developing a spear for close combat that made the old spear and shield obsolete (Tyrrell 1968).

MAINTAINING OR CHANGING THE SOCIAL ORDER

Governments have used clothing to maintain the social order as well as to cause a desired change in it. After the Communist government took power in China, the sexless, utilitarian "Mao suit" was mandated to symbolize the philosophy of the new social order—classless, nonsexist, nonmaterialistic, and organized for the common good. This costume assisted the Chinese in making the massive changes required for their new social order. Like all uniforms, it helped to build a sense of belonging and of group identity among the many regionally unique Chinese peoples; it also helped to maintain a uniformity in values and, therefore, behavior. The Soviet Union has used clothing in a similar way, although their clothing has not been quite so standardized. However by controlling all fashion production, the Russians have theoretically been able to reduce sexism, increase the seriousness and work ethic of their citizens, and maintain the subordination of the individual to the state. But rising consumer demands and unique social needs have prevented them from consistent success in this effort. For example, their attempts to control money expenditures by limiting fashion changes, cosmetic production, and beauty services had to be tempered when the birth rate began to decline in the 1930s. When consumer demands increased but production capabilities were required in other areas, such as the military, a black market developed to meet consumer demands. This infringed on the government's control, and to reduce that threat, Moscow's House of Fashion was founded, to provide women with a legal way to dress more fashionably.

Feudal Europe maintained its social order through dress differences, which enhanced its system of social stratification. Dress in the different classes became more alike at the same time that greater political parity was achieved between them. It is not possible to know if either of these factors caused the other, but both would have been mutually reinforcing.

FORMS OF GOVERNMENT

In dictatorships or monarchies power is held by one individual who is all powerful. That leader's fashion preferences are often adopted by those able to afford fashionable dress, but the dress of those from the higher tiers of society will be recognizably different from that of the lower stratum. Uniforms have been an important means of indicating a monarch's authority, and in the eighteenth and nineteenth centuries uniforms became the most common form of

Figure 9.2 John Leech's cartoon of Louis XIV, entitled "Ludovicus Rex—Clothes Maketh Man," is a humorous depiction of the ability of dress to cloak the wearer in power and authority. (Mansell Collection)

court attire. Only the French and Spanish monarchies resisted the uniform in favor of the elaborately embroidered court jacket. The French embroidery industry was so heavily involved in the production of this older "habit habille" that the court had to continue to use this luxurious dress (Mansell 1982).

Communism, on the other hand, favors a common fashion since all citizens are considered equal. However, such parity has not become a reality under current Communist governments, and differences in quality, quantity, and adornment are evident between the leaders and the general population. Since communistic governments have complete control of consumer goods, including imported items, they can effectively control the consumer's purchasing power and general use of money as well as limit the goods available for purchase. Thus, manipulation through dress is easier under a communistic form of government.

Democracy is also predicated on a belief in the political equality of all citizens. It does not espouse economic parity, although some democracies with socialistic economic systems do. However, all citizens in a democracy are thought to have an equal opportunity to achieve economic power. Fashions in democratic countries tend to be similar throughout the social levels; differences generally are in the quality and quantity of dress. The direction of fashion flow tends to be more varied in a democratic system. Since individuals are not subordinate to the state, they are freer to express themselves in their dress. Laws or other restrictions on clothing tend to be fewer and, when they do exist, harder to enforce.

Young (1956) hypothesized that the striving for upward mobility and higher status, combined with the high value of the individual, prevents mass society from destroying fashion. But the danger of such destruction, Young suggested, is inherent in the standardization necessary for mass production and in the "stress upon conformity and unity in mass society" (p. 321). A freedom-giving government rather than one that is highly regimented and authoritarian may help to reduce this danger. However, one should not disregard

> the dictatorial aspects of fashion itself . . . the kind of mass demand and mass control which comes with being in the fashion . . . [But such] domination . . . is not quite the same as that which we might envisage if we had an authoritarian control that would predetermine the clothes and styles which people wore (ibid., p. 321).

REFLECTING INTERNATIONAL RELATIONSHIPS

The way that a people dress is often related to their nation's power and rank among other countries with whom their government is involved. As a nation's power declines or during eras of overwhelmingly complex social or political problems, such as high crime rates or major balance-of-payments difficulties, the dress of its people often becomes more flamboyant.

Nations influence the dress of other nations important to them, even when that value is negative. For example, the political weight of the Soviet Union in the Western world has caused periodic Russian influences on Western fashion in the post–World War II years. This influence tends to increase with greater cultural contact; thus, the movie *Dr. Zhivago* had quite an influence on Western dress styles. Likewise, American fashion—blue jeans, T-shirts, combat jackets, military patches—has had an influence on Soviet styles. The Soviets, however, have opposed many of these influences. Jeans, available on the black market for up to $200, have represented American cultural elements and have been status symbols to Russian youth. The government has viewed the wearing of such American dress as unpatriotic. Thus, it has mounted "letter to the editor" campaigns urging young people to spurn their unpatriotically attired peers.

The greatest influence on dress generally comes from nations aligned out of common interests or from nations with which such an alliance is desired. Today, as a nation takes an equal position with other countries, say, at the United Nations, it tends to adopt dress styles typical of industrialized societies since that dress generally symbolizes progress. The adaptations may be unique; for example, there have been cases where neckties have been worn before shirts have been adopted.

Such new dress is unlikely to be functionally superior to the old except for its psychological power to represent the perceived progress of the emulated nation (Gordon and Lee 1977). Similarity of dress is increasing throughout the modern world; this increasing commonality may lead to a greater commonality in other areas and could increase international understanding by making other peoples seem less alien. However, a national style reflecting the essential beliefs and values of a nation—its social identity (Anspach 1969)—is usually retained in these westernization efforts. Elements of the other culture(s) that fit in with the existing one are adapted rather than adopted. When national costumes and uniforms are lost in this process, it reflects ethnic disintegration.

Imperialism—political or economic control of one nation by another—can have an influence on clothing and textiles of both nations. British control of the American colonies, designed to benefit England, required that all goods (except for some foods and servants) be imported into the colonies via England regardless of the country of origin. Imports from other countries were further limited by high import duties on items such as French silk. These duties, collected by and for England, made foreign exports profitable for Britain. When the colonists tried to smuggle in French commodities, the English forbade foreign ships from entering the colonial harbors. Colonial exports were also controlled. Textile products could be exported only to England or its colonies.

Since the purpose of these acts was to maintain a profitable balance of trade for England, colonial domestic manufacturing also had to be regulated and limited. Woolen tools and workers could not leave England for the colonies. Production of anything other than a poor-quality fabric for personal use was discouraged and even outlawed in certain instances. What manufacturing was allowed had stringent limits on it. For example, one could not train to be a hatter, and transportation of hats from or between the colonies was prohibited. Such economic domination caused the colonists to revolt. But revolutions are neither easy to begin nor easy to carry out successfully. Imperialism still exists because powerful nations continue to try to maintain their power over, and at the expense of, the less powerful.

POLITICAL LEADERS

Political leaders and their families, by virtue of their frequent public performances, have often assumed the role of a fashion leader. They may be emulated either because the public admires them or because others wish to appear equal in status to them. In Europe these leaders have usually been members of royalty. For example, in the second century A.D., the Roman Emperor Hadrian grew a beard to hide his facial scars; Roman men also adopted beards although beards had not been worn in the preceding four centuries. When Francis I cut his hair after it had been scorched, the royal court followed suit (Cooper 1971). Royalty's influence, however, has declined as its power has decreased.

Queen Victoria had a lively interest in fashion and a strong influence on it. Patronage was no longer practiced during her reign, and designers and artists were eager to learn her opinions as inspirations for new designs. At the same time the French Revolution had left a vacuum in jewelry making, which the more poorly trained English jewelers filled. Thus, the sphere of British influence became more international (Curran 1963). During her Diamond Jubilee celebration, Victoria's Scottish background led to a popularization of the tartan and kilts, as has also happened in countries where Queen Elizabeth II has visited.

Around the turn of the century, Victoria's daughter-in-law Alexandra, the Princess of Wales, popularized the dog collar and short, curly hair. The Duke of Windsor had tremendous influence on men's fashions during his years as Prince of Wales. He popularized, for example, the zippered fly, the dinner jacket—or tuxedo—worn with a white tie, Shetland knitted sportswear, the Windsor knot, snap-brim hats, blue shirts, and plaids. Princess Diana has had a similar influence on British fashion, particularly right after her marriage to Charles.

The courtesans, or mistresses, of European kings often had greater fashion influence than did the queens, whose royal dress could not always be legally copied. Agnes Sorel, mistress to Charles VII of France, led the fashion with her low-cut necklines, high headdresses, and diamonds. The Marquise de Pompadour, mistress to Louis XV, hid her unattractive throat with a ruff, which soon became the rage. She also popularized the pompadour hair style. Courtesans have had greater influence during periods or in cultures in which women have had low status since they have been the only women allowed to be glamorously attired; thus, geisha girls have usually worn the most attractive kimonos and adornments.

In the United States the president's wife has often had the role of fashion leader. Jacquelyn Kennedy was especially emulated, perhaps because of her youthful image, strong fashion interest, and well-defined taste. She influenced hair and hat styles and focused attention on American designers.

POLITICAL SYMBOLS

Political causes, ideas, and ideals have been both supported and suppressed by clothing. In 1782 George III was presented with a petition asking for an end to the war in the American colonies. The Whig member of Parliament making the presentation wore a country outfit as a symbol of his disrespect for the king. Six years later, English politicians demonstrated their allegiance to the Whigs by wearing blue and buff and to the Tories by wearing blue and red. One of the simplest forms of support is political campaign dress. From plastic hats with a candidate's name on the band to simple button pins with a name or a slogan, people proudly "wear" their choice, especially when at the parties' nominating conventions. Clothing has even been symbolic of a candidate. In the 1950s, for example, Adlai Stevenson's presidential campaign was symbolized by a shoe with a hole in the sole after a news photo caught him wearing such a shoe. His 1956 vice-presidential candidate, Estes Kefauver, was associated with a coonskin cap representing his home state of Tennessee. He had made it his trademark during his senatorial attack on organized crime. In nations having a high illiteracy rate people have worn a picture of the candidate rather than his or her name or a visual symbol of their party rather than its name.

The t-shirt, embossed with a slogan, has become an "advocate" for modern young Americans, who have "worn" their stands on a wide variety of issues. The civil rights movement of the early 1960s was associated with "working" clothes like t-shirts, bib overalls, blue jeans, and sneakers. When the Vietnam War protest displaced civil rights as the major arena for young people's political activism, the same clothes continued to be used to indicate opposition to the social/governmental status quo. Civil rights finally received support from most national leaders, but the war protest began with almost no such support. The protest was viewed by both "hawks" and "doves" as a more antisocial movement. Thus, the appearance of the protestors also became more antisocial as they refused to meet society's basic grooming expectations. Some protestors even adopted an unworldly rather than merely an antisocial stance by, for example, shaving their heads as a symbol of their rejection of the material, social world. Such clothing symbolism was a conscious message, a political tool. Abbie Hoffman, a political activist in the Vietnam era, said, "Costume *is* politics. . . . If you're a freak . . . people are afraid of you." Hunter Thompson, an

Figure 9.3 Suffragettes used dress to symbolize their struggle for political equality. (Library of Congress)

unsuccessful candidate for mayor of Aspen, noted, "We use clothes politically . . . and they are our finest way of mocking power and authority" (Sabol and Truscott 1971, pp. 123–24).

Mahatma Gandhi wore a native dhoti of hand-woven cloth to boycott British fabrics (and other products) and to symbolize that India was Indian, not British, and belonged to the Indian people, not the British. Merely by rejecting British dress, he was able to show his rejection of Britain itself. This same principle was applied in another way by the last shah of Iran and in the 1920s by the king of Afghanistan, both of whom wanted their people to embrace the more progressive, industrial West. Western dress was given high status and symbolized philosophical, intellectual, and industrial progress. In Afghanistan those not wearing Western dress were ridiculed. When Western dress was mandated, disobedience was punishable by a fine which precipitated a revolt ending the king's reign. The civil war in the mid-1920s brought in a more fundamentalist Afghani government until King Nadir, nephew of the former king, regained the throne in 1929 and put the country back on a *slowly* progressive course. Women, who had returned to wearing the traditional chadri after the civil war, were encouraged to attend schools and to wear Western costumes under their chadri. Once again Western dress became positively associated with an outward rather than a traditional orientation (Dupree 1978). Since the late 1950s the voluntary removal of the chadri has been supported by the government.

The Shah of Iran was overthrown in the late 1970s by a fundamentalist group, who returned women to the traditional chador. He might have been able to retain power had he allowed some cultural retrenching in a return to

Figure 9.4 Children in Nazi dress at the Fallersleben Celebration. (Hugo Jeager, *Life* Magazine © Time Inc.)

more traditional dress. The massive social changes Iran was experiencing were threatening to many individuals. Such threats to social boundaries have been associated with individuals having greater concern with their body boundaries; competing groups have even selected appropriate body imagery as a banner for their cause (Polhemus 1973).

Europe in the 1930s and 1940s had many examples of clothing that was used to support the Nazis. The Hitler youth movement, for example, was based on a reward system of uniforms and badges in its successful efforts to indoctrinate and control the youth of Germany. While adults can be responsive to such a system, adolescents are particularly vulnerable because of their greater concern with their appearance and their powerful need to "fit in" and win approval. Nazi Germany was remarkable in its awareness of these adolescent needs and its ability to manipulate dress to meet them.

POLITICAL REBELLION

In the late 1960s the Tanzanian government, in an attempt to assimilate and modernize the Masai tribe, outlawed public nudity. The Masai, whose nudity symbolized their attempts to preserve their unique identity and culture, were able to manipulate the law so that assimilation was not forced upon them. Mazrui (1970) hypothesized that the Masai's refusal to change typified one of

Figure 9.5 Masai men. (Library of Congress)

five forms of political rebellion or political assertiveness. The other forms are more subtle assertions than was the Masai's stubborn refusal to conform. Adopting parts of the new culture or lifestyle while still maintaining parts of the old to serve as residual cultural distinctiveness is exemplified by the Japanese's use of the kimono at home and for special occasions while wearing Western-style dress for street attire. The Iranian rejection of Western dress for the chador is an excellent example of the ritualistic rejection of a foreign dress that had earlier been adopted. Imitating the dress worn by a foreign group having similar revolutionary affiliations is exemplified by the adoption of Chinese dress in Tanzania. A militant response by nationalists to laws governing dress enacted by conquerors was evident in the Algerians' use of the veil in the 1960s to show their identity and affiliation with the Algerian nationalist movement. When the French tried to force the Algerian women to unveil, veils were worn even by women who had not previously worn them. All of these examples are evidence that clothing can both support and repress a political cause. However, repression is often less effective because it may cause one of these assertive responses. Thus, when the Scots were forbidden by the English in 1745 to wear the tartan, the tartan became a symbol of Scottish nationalism. Men began wearing a kilt and women a shawl with their clan's tartan as the clans united in response to the repression.

Unfortunately, attempts to repress an ideology seem inevitable when the group in power believes that an ideology threatens its retention of power. Repressive measures have ranged from social ridicule to death. Paradoxically, it may be that fashion adopted as a political rebellion or assertion to such repression is actually antifashion because it is designed to accomplish a specific change, while fashion's essence is continual change.

> True fashion never comes to rest; it is permanent revolution. . . . Utopian styles are anti-fashion rather than fashion in that they advocate a single change to a new status quo rather than change itself. They are always attempts to assert and publicize symbolically a particular ideal society . . . [to] represent society *as it is, as it ought to be or,* in the case of distopian styles. . . . *as it should not be.* (Polhemus and Procter 1978, p. 25)

The Afro of the 1960s and 1970s was an example of an antifashion for how society should be—nonracist—as was the 1970s flower-child look, which symbolized pacifism and nonmaterialism. A "what is" representation is exemplified by the blue Mao suit, which as was mentioned earlier, is symbolic of the supposed equality of all Chinese regardless of sex or family background. Blue jeans may have served a similar purpose since the 1960s, when they were adopted by young people who were fighting for human equality.

REVOLUTION

Revolutions have usually involved clothing as a cause and/or symbol. The Puritan Revolution led by Cromwell was partly caused by the nobility's luxurious and extravagant lifestyle as exemplified by the wearing by the Duke of Buckingham of a suit valued at over $150,000 (Langner 1959). The Puritans reacted by asserting such qualities as purity, sexual repression, and unworldliness. But the revolution never really accomplished long-term change since there was a quick return to the old ways after Charles II regained the throne in 1660.

The American Revolution had less ideological involvement with clothing than most revolutions have had; however, it was more accurately a war for independence than an ideological revolution. Its major impact on fashion was economic: the reduction in British imported goods forced the colonies to rely more on domestic production and on French imports. Because of their limited domestic production capability and their difficulty in getting French imports, clothing design had to be simplified during the revolutionary years. After the Revolution dress became more elaborate, but American fashion retained a French flavor, especially after Lafayette's visit in the 1820s.

Figure 9.6 Visual support for the American Revolution. (Library of Congress)

Figure 9.7 *The Original Macaroni*—Matthew Darly's 1772 print of Charles James Fox, a fashion leader and the first Macaroni. The British used the song "Yankee Doodle" as a put-down of the poorly clad American militia. However, the Americans gladly adopted the song as a put-down of the "foppish" dress of the English as represented in the extreme by the Macaroni Club. (The British Museum)

The French Revolution

The French Revolution is a better example of a true revolution and it produced real change. The abuses and extravagances of Queen Marie Antoinette for the sake of "fashion" were one issue leading to the Revolution. The queen spent about $700,000 "on clothes in 1785, a year in which she had supposedly lost all interest in fashion" (Bernier 1981, p. 119). Yet her official dress budget was less than half that amount and a yearly income of less than one-fifth that sum was considered large. When the royal family attempted to escape from Paris, Marie's clothing trunks were so heavy that the coach was unable to attain enough speed for them to avoid capture. Their subsequent return to Paris was so frightening that the queen's hair turned white overnight. Yet in spite of this experience with terror, Marie continued to order new clothes, which she billed to the new Republic of France. However, she did cut back; she spent only the equivalent of $132,000 for dresses in 1791 (ibid.).

Louis XVI's refusal to wear the uniform of either the National Guard or the military may have contributed to his overthrow. His luxurious and expensive traditional court dress visually identified him with the most wealthy and idle of his aristocrats even though he was ideologically supportive of many of the reform efforts. Had he finally donned the National Guard's uniform, the guard might have remained at the palace, in which case his flight from Paris could have been prevented (Mansel 1982).

Prerevolutionary dress was used to differentiate between the wealthy, the noble, and the common men. The revolutionaries used dress as a powerful, visual symbol of their opposition to the status quo; they simplified dress and brought it closer to working attire. Thus, the visually defiant emblems of the Revolution were the laborer's rough trousers and a coarse scarf; the battle cry was "sans-culottes" (aristocratic knee breeches) or "sans-cravates" (the tie). The red cap, adopted from ancient Rome and Greece, where it was supposedly a badge of liberty, symbolized their republican sentiments.

Figure 9.8 (a, b) (a) French pre-Revolutionary dress and (b) Revolutionary garments. (Library of Congress).

a   b

After the Revolution, fine jewels were patriotically donated to the public treasury; such a donation could protect an aristocrat from being arrested or even guillotined. The best jewelry no longer was set with precious or semiprecious stones but contained a piece of stone from the Bastille. Many aristocrats rejected the old ornate jewelry, dress, wigs, and shoe buckles but did risk a symbolic declaration of their royal affiliations by wearing a black velvet collar on their coats as a sign of their mourning for Louis XVI.

Because the French silk industry had been decimated during the Revolution, silk had to be replaced. The new sheer cotton and muslin replacements were most suitable to the loose, easy-flowing Empire style. Sheer formal gowns, weighing less than a pound, were worn over little or no underwear. The bulky, high headdresses of the rococo period gave way to short haircuts and small hats or even none. The Empire look was an almost childish, prepubescent look, perhaps a warning to women that they had not achieved a true increase in status. Without a real change, women's fashions soon began to regain their more elaborate form. Male fashions, however, reflected a real change: a positive social value placed on work and the positive social judgment, therefore, of men who worked. Their new styles were most suitable to the merchant class, the new elite. Menswear, reflecting the Anglomania of the period, was that of the English country gentleman. The clothing-conscious male indicated his fashion interest by being perfectly dressed in high-quality garments.

The Russian Revolution saw a similar change in dress, particularly for women, whose sex roles did, in some respects, change dramatically. However, dress became more feminized in the late 1930s after the birth rate began to decline, until World War II forced a return to more masculine styles. In the 1950s women demanded more feminine clothing and beauty products. A black market grew to meet this demand, which forced the government to allow beauty shops, more cosmetics, and more feminine and fashionable clothing styles.

WAR

War has an impact on clothing. It is a serious business that creates death and grief; thus wartime fashions tend to be somber and simple. But they are also patriotic in order to build and maintain a high national spirit. In general, warlike nations tend to have warlike fashions, with more elaborate styles in menswear than womenswear (women's postwar fashions are more ornate). The American Civil War created a large demand for better-fitting menswear. This led to some standardization of sizing in men's ready-to-wear. We have had enough wars to have accurately sized menswear today. However, since the sizing of women's and children's wear has not been affected by wars, their standardization of size remains inexact.

Clothing also has an impact on war. In fact, Langner (1959) argued that since wars require uniformed armies, the most effective disarmament might be one that simply bans the use of military uniforms. Should the next war be a nuclear conflict, however, uniforms will have less importance, as the opposing armies will never be in visual contact with each other. The morale aspect of a uniform will not be a factor either in such a quick, impersonal battle. In the disorder of the aftermath, uniforms will probably play a role, whether negative or positive one cannot know. The Sukhomlinov effect is the hypothesis that the victor of a war will be the side whose leaders had the least ornate uniforms. Beaumont and James (1971) analyzed wars, beginning with the English Civil War, to see if this effect could be consistently applied. They found that the side with the simpler uniforms won in twenty cases, although in the Russo-Finnish and Spanish Civil Wars the ornate side won. The effect could not be applied to either the War of 1812, where both sides were equally ornate, or to the Korean War, where both sides were equally drab.

Many theorists have argued that wars, revolutions, or other great social/ political upheavals cause massive changes to the predictable fashion trends and styles. However, Cunnington (1941) suggested that only wars perceived as picturesque or colorful—wars that are of short duration and create few shortages (and thus create little to no social upheaval)—have great impact on fashion. Because television can bring war and its grim reality into the living room of the modern civilian, such "picturesque" conflicts may be limited to those taking place in remote areas where television access is limited, such as the Falkland Islands. During the first year of the Korean conflict, perhaps the last of the great "little wars," conical hats, adapted from Korean straw headgear, were fashionable as were white cotton high-necked coolie coats, mandarin necklines, and heavily padded coats (Binder 1953). The Crusades, a truly "romantic" series of conflicts, brought a Middle Eastern influence to European fashions by introducing styles like the hennin headdress, turban, and poulaine as well as fabrics like damask, felt, and muslin. From other "little wars," fashion has gotten the raglan coat, tassels, the Garibaldi blouse, zouave jacket, the colors magenta and khaki, and cigarettes.

World War I

Laver (1940) hypothesized that those major wars that do create social upheaval lead to corsetless, waistless dress styles; short hair; and promiscuity. At first glance, the fashions of World War I (1914–18) would seem to support his contention; however, the major style changes followed the war by nearly a decade. While the war may have had some influence on these changes, it was not the only—or even necessarily the major—influence. Changes in sex roles and sex status, fought for long before 1914, were more significant factors in the fashions of the post–World War I decades. War shortages did lead to a simplification of women's dress, but postwar fashions had to provide more physical freedom since women were participating in a wider range of occupations and public activities. The postwar couturier collections emphasized silk since the French cotton and woolen industries had been extensively damaged during the war.

Women's fashions became increasingly youthful in keeping with typical postwar fashion, which generally emphasizes the female's reproductive capacity. However, the fashions soon reflected women's increasing freedom rather than their fertility. The cloche hat of the 1920s was probably not, as Laver (1940) suggested, an adaptation of the German infantry helmet, but rather an aspect of the Eastern influence of designers like Erté or, even more likely, simply the most appropriate style for the fashions, short haircuts, and mobile lifestyles of the period.

War shortages had a more direct impact on menswear; drawers were shortened, and undershirts, because of the wool shortage, were made of different fabrics, such as cotton, merino, llama, flannel, and silk (Benedict 1982). Civilian men, ostracized for their lack of military participation, dressed more informally in order to draw attention from their lack of obvious involvement in the war effort.

World War II

World War II (1941–45) created massive shortages, as do most protracted conflicts. War is hard on clothing, particularly in the infantry. Thus, the raw materials, production capabilities, and labor supply are all adversely affected for consumers by increased military demands. For example, conserving fuel by lowering thermostats and driving less created a need for warmer leisure wear and sturdier shoes.

In World War II men were needed to serve in the armed forces; women replaced them in the work force. Thus, women's incomes were generally increasing. But prices were also rising because of the limited availability of consumer goods; some goods were further limited by a rationing system. A limited clothing supply meant that new designs had to be more versatile.

After the fall of Paris, New York became the center of American fashion, and casual or sportswear lines grew. The Nazis, who recognized the power of clothing, unsuccessfully tried to persuade the French couture industry to move to Berlin or Vienna (Green 1981). However, they ignored the importance of clothing when they sent their army into the Russian winter without good foot protection from the cold. It is interesting to speculate on whether the outcome of the war might have been different had Hitler thought to supply his foot soldiers with the felt inner boots that their Russian counterparts wore. Certainly, the Russians were aided by not having to cope constantly with frostbitten feet.

War demands for improved textiles led to increased government-sponsored research into the development of new fibers and the improvement of existent ones. The t-shirt and duffle coat, both introduced by the navy, and the army's tropic shorts and Eisenhower jacket have remained popular civilian wear, reminders of World War II military fashion.

Immediately after the war clothing materials were still scarce, so fashions like the collarless blazer were introduced. The scarcity of traditional shirt fab-

Figure 9.9 The battle jacket was adapted to civilian attire. (Library of Congress)

rics led to the use of other, sportier patterns as supplements. Thus, the divisive white shirt, symbol of the white-collar worker and the genteel classes, was replaced by sportswear, the great equalizer. Shortages were a problem in England for an even longer period and, in order to limit the use of materials, the Labour government in 1947 tried to enact a law to regulate the length of women's skirts. But the power of fashion, as usual, was greater than the power of government and the New Look's lowered hemlines won. The New Look reflected the principle that postwar women's fashions must be feminine and sexually revealing because the usual postwar male shortage forces women to compete more for a man. Society needs that competition to be successful in order for it to replenish its depleted population. This principle has been applied as far back as ancient Greeks and Romans, who enacted laws forcing women to adopt more revealing dress, for instance, by slitting the sides of their togas (Hurlock 1976).

SUMPTUARY LEGISLATION

The laws affecting fashion that were passed by the Greeks and Romans are examples of sumptuary legislation, legislation designed to regulate people's personal or private lives as opposed to their public lives or their conduct as members of their society. This type of legislation has been used in many cultures and was particularly extensive in Asia—the Japanese have used it throughout their recorded history—and in Europe during the Middle Ages and the Renaissance. The paternalistic, feudal government structure was particularly well adapted to such legislation because of its absolute power over all of its subjects (Phillips and Staley 1961). However, sumptuary legislation is not merely an oddity of history; it is a method still used by most modern societies. There have been many motives for such laws, but the primary ones have been the following:

1. To maintain status/class distinctions and status/class separateness
2. To control morality and limit extravagance, luxury, and the resulting self-pride
3. To encourage domestic industry and encourage a balance in international trade by controlling expenditure for foreign goods
4. To promote savings
5. To control population growth
6. To maintain the status quo

These motives have varied in their relative importance in different cultures and different eras.

Maintaining Status/Class Distinctions

The maintenance of status/class distinctions and separateness seems the most universal reason for such laws and has been evident in Western cultures since ancient Greece. Legislation for this purpose is most needed when money begins to be diffused downward so that more people can afford to try to imitate the dress of their superiors. Thus, in Europe in the Middle Ages, as the feudal system began to collapse and a merchant class began to acquire more of the resources of the nobility (who had spent much of their money on personal displays such as clothing), the ruling nobles began enacting sumptuary laws designed to prevent the merchants from copying their lifestyle. As early as the thirteenth century the French had laws regulating by rank the number of dresses one could own and the value of the materials used in them. The laws, however, were ineffective, and the extravagances in dress continued.

The English had an enormous number of detailed laws beginning in the early fourteenth century. Many of their laws were designed to enable immediate identification of rank by dress and thereby prevent individuals from pretending to belong to a higher class. However, enforcement was difficult and imitation was common.

The ancient Romans, Irish, and Koreans legislated the color, both number and kind, and the materials used by the different classes. From about 200 B.C., the Chinese legislated status-related robe adornment, thus also controlling expenditures for such adornment. All details of their ceremonies were so regulated that a powerful set of traditional behavior and predictable psychological responses developed. The armed forces are one of the only modern structures where there is any resemblance to the Chinese tradition of ritual and of detailed regulations. In the late tenth century specific colors were mandated for each level of the mandarinate hierarchy. "However these regulations soon fell into disuse, because the court granted the right to wear purple indiscriminately to officials of all grades" (Gernet 1967, p. 128). Laws limiting the use of the round, blue-green, silk parasols were similarly ignored after the court allowed some officials and women of the court to carry them (ibid.). By the mid-eighteenth century rank was demonstrated by legislated color and external adornment. The emperor's robe had twelve imperial symbols; the focal point was a dragon facing frontward with five claws shown. Lesser nobles could wear only the profile of a dragon with four claws (Kefgen and Touchie-Specht 1976), although the right to wear five claws could be conferred.

Regulating Morality

In many cultures the control of morality has involved hiding the female form. For example, a nineteenth-century Chicago law made wearing knickers or revealing one's stockings illegal for women bicyclists. Identification of prostitutes has also been a recurrent theme. Prostitutes of Venice, for instance, were not allowed to wear pearls so that no matter how they were dressed they would be easy to differentiate from other women. The fourteenth-century London prostitute also was easily distinguished since "no known whore should weare . . . any hood, except reyed or striped of divers colors, nor furre, but garments reversed or turned the wrong side outward upon paine to forfeit the same" (Baldwin 1926, p. 34). One of the few examples of laws to control male attire was an English act of 1463 passed to prevent knights under the rank of a lord from wearing, when standing erect, a garment not long enough to cover their buttocks and genitals.

Sumptuary laws have been used to maintain segregation between religious groups. In Europe such laws began in Spain in the late thirteenth century with legislation requiring specific clothing to be worn by Jews. Earlier in that century Jews had been required to wear a badge when they were in areas where they could not be easily recognized by their dress. By the fifteenth century such requirements were common, although they were not uniformly enforced. Money, for example, could frequently buy an exemption.

> The Badge was usually in the shape of a ring. . . . and the regulation colour was yellow, although other colours existed. . . . The usual position was the breast but sometimes it had to be worn on the shoulders, the back or the hat or in two positions. . . .
> In England the Badge consisted of a piece of white material shaped to represent the Tablets of the Law. . . . Used at first as a means of extracting money the wearing of the Badge was more strictly applied after 1253 when Henry III issued a fresh series of Statutes based on ecclesiastical canons, thus falling into line with the decrees of Innocent III. Usually the Badge applied to men, women and children but a special distinction for women was a veil with two blue stripes. (Rubens 1967, pp. 114, 118)

Extravagance in dress has often been believed to lead to vanity, and laws have been enacted to deal with that. For example, Puritan immigrants to the New World had many sumptuary laws designed to prevent extravagance in dress; for instance, the width of sleeves was limited. Other laws were designed both to curb extravagance and to indicate class; only the upper class could wear gold or silver buckles or lace, ruffs, embroidered caps, and slashed sleeves. Women were not allowed to dress in a manner better than one expected on the basis of their husband's incomes.

Greenfield (1918) suggested that the proclivity toward clothing-related legislation in middle Europe reflected the opportunity dress offers for self-display. People's attempts to stand out from the norm by purchasing the finest fabrics in the showiest colors to be made into the most fantastic styles were so extravagant that city fathers were constantly worried that citizens would overspend their personal budgets. However, some laws actually promoted excess, as did the fourteenth-century French laws limiting the length of poulaines to six inches for a commoner, twelve inches for a wealthy merchant, and twenty-four inches for a noble. Obviously, if one could flaunt it one would, so the points were at the maximum even when that length was impractical. The English version, which limited shoe points to two inches except for nobles, was a more effective means of reducing excess.

Occasionally one finds an individual oddity among sumptuary laws. Queen Elizabeth I, for example, enacted laws designed to promote her own vanity. She had more than six thousand garments at her death, but there would have been no copies of any of them, at least no legal ones. Many of her gowns had large ruffs to hide her scrawny neck; other women were forced to wear ruffs of smaller size, and should their ruffs be too large, the guards at the London gates cut off the excess. Elizabeth wore dresses of exotic colors; other women were limited to more subdued hues. The queen's thin, sparse hair was

Figure 9.10 The poulaine. (Museum of Fine Arts, Boston)

kept from unfavorable comparison by a law forbidding other women to wear their hair either curled or long. The queen's laws were not enforced sufficiently to suit her; in 1597 she proclaimed that although she had charged the authorities to uphold her laws limiting excess in dress, such enforcement had been lax owing to their negligence and the overt contempt and disobedience of the offending subjects. Such disobedience, she contended, was resulting in an increase in crime, since the poor had to steal in order to get fine clothes; a deterioration in hospitality, since money was spent on dress instead; and difficulty in accurate identification of rank (Baldwin 1926). Had the queen been a better student of history, she would have realized that extravagance curbs, never popular with those whose behavior they try to limit, had always been difficult to enforce. After the many repressive Elizabethan laws, English commerce needed the stimulation James I provided when he repealed most of the sumptuary laws.

Controlling the Economy

Many sixteenth-century French laws enacted under Henry IV were designed to encourage the domestic silk industry and to discourage a negative balance of payments that was caused by French money going for Italian silk. Other French sumptuary laws of the seventeenth and eighteenth centuries attempted to accomplish this same purpose in different industries. This stimulation of industries producing silk and other luxury goods led to France's position as the primary European producer of luxury products (Freudenberger 1963, p. 140).

The English had many laws designed to stimulate the wool industry (and sometimes to prevent foreign expenditure for items such as silk). In the late eighteenth century Sweden's Gustav III ordered his subjects to wear a national costume of Swedish wool in order to encourage the domestic wool industry. Serendipitously, class differences in dress decreased. In the same period Polish people were required to wear only Polish goods, but style differences according to class were also retained by law.

Promoting Savings

Laws designed to promote savings were not common in pre-twentieth-century legislation. However, promotion of savings was one of the purposes (easy movement was another) of the Amir of Afghanistan's late nineteenth-century decree to end the wearing of gigantic sleeves and trousers. Until that decree, just a pair of trousers could require about fifteen yards of material (Dupree 1978).

Controlling Population Growth

The control of population growth has been attempted primarily through sumptuary laws to control reproduction and/or marriage. One European city, for example, limited the number of expensive dresses a bride could have in her trousseau so that more girls could afford a trousseau sufficient for marriage and, consequently, reproduction (Freudenberger 1963). A New Jersey law that imposed the penalties for witchcraft on any woman who married a man whom she had manipulated through the use of perfumes, cosmetics, high-heeled shoes, or dentures, may also have had a deterrent effect on population growth.

Maintaining the Status Quo

Many governments have enacted sumptuary laws designed to help them maintain their internal authority or their international position. Venetian sumptuary legislation, for example, attempted to preserve the status quo by forcing nobles to dress in inconspicuous, simple black garments to prevent the lower classes from realizing how few nobles there really were (Hurlock 1976). The English used sumptuary laws to assist them in maintaining their control over Ireland. In the fourteenth century they outlawed the wearing of Irish national dress (by the Irish or the English), tonsured hair (which had been a popular Irish man's hair style), and moustaches. By the fifteenth century the Irish were forced to wear English dress. However, enforcement was primarily directed at aristocrats so that the lower classes still wore the national dress and in the sixteenth century the most common shirt color was still saffron, even though it was forbidden by law (Meurisse 1970).

Enforcement

Enforcement of sumptuary laws has been supported by penalties ranging from fines to confiscation of offending items, public humiliation, imprisonment, and death. Ignorance of the law has been no excuse (Greenfield 1918). In some German states the church cooperated with the state by annually reading from the pulpit any new sumptuary laws (Vincent 1935). But enforcement has often been difficult or lax. Each of the Swiss laws was prefaced with a concern that they might not be obeyed, even though enforcement efforts are apparent in the number of dress-related court cases. In one city there were 289 such cases:

> 133 persons were cited for unlawful clothing. Out of this 133 there were eighty-six presented for house dress, lack of lacing, or exposed arms on the street. Sixteen others wore their jackets without proper overgarment; and 2–7 more, mostly servants, had to answer for fur, laces, or ribbons. Only 7 men were called up for dress, and 4 of these wore excessively large wigs. (ibid., p. 104)

Enforcement was often a reflection of the government's power; the greater the power, the greater the enforcement. Roman sumptuary laws, for example, were strictly enforced until the empire began to decline (Binder 1953).

Peasants have been able to circumvent many sumptuary laws by developing a national dress that was externally adorned with embroidery or other handwork and, less overtly, splendid in its ornate underwear. The underwear

Figure 9.11 A Hungarian national costume. (Library of Congress)

was visible with (thus perhaps caused by or causing) the twirling and spinning of their folk dancing. The Japanese common folk used tattooing as their foil to the sumptuary legislation that attempted to limit their sartorial splendor.

Modern Sumptuary Legislation

Since the French Revolution, sumptuary legislation has been increasingly liberalized to grant more and more individual freedom. However, such laws are still used. In the United States, since the late nineteenth century when their constitutionality was questioned, fewer of these laws have been enacted *except* in times of increased demand on government, such as wartime.

The sumptuary legislation enacted during World War II, the most thorough modern American example, was primarily in response to shortages created by defense needs. The Textile, Clothing and Leather Division of the War Production Board, headed by Stanley Marcus of Neiman-Marcus, determined the amounts and ways of using textiles and leathers in consumer goods. Fabric was rationed throughout the war; shoes were rationed from 1943 to 1945. Luxury items were subject to high taxes, which made them even more desirable as status symbols. Price ceilings were set by the Office of Price Administration, which did not tie the price into the quality although it was intended that prices should be lowered if a garment's serviceability was decreased (Van Syckle 1943). The disallowment of unit pricing for two or more articles seemed to disturb the retail industry more than any other single aspect of the legislation.

Dyestuffs were limited; dyes were conserved by using less dye-consuming shades, so that colors were lighter, and by limiting the range of hues. In 1942 "one mill made six different shades of navy blue. . . . This year [1943] the mill makes only one. There are three or four medium blues instead of a score, and other shades have been cut down in proportion" (Blaker 1943, p. 74). Since colors in prints were applied with copper rollers, the copper shortage forced a reduction in the number of colors in a print.

Those aspects of the limits that pertained to women's fashions were considered by the War Production Board to be potentially the most controversial and least likely to be obeyed. Therefore, they summarized the decree in an "eighteen-page press release (single-spaced, on both sides of the paper) [to assure] the ladies that no style 'freezing,' or standardization is involved," and those fashion changes they directed were designed to be quite small so that current wardrobes would remain stylish (Hemline of Battle 1942, p. 32). Skirt widths (two yards, six inches for daywear and four yards for evening) and lengths were limited; hems and facings could be no wider than two inches. No yokes, large sleeves, french cuffs, pleating, tucks, overskirts, patch pockets, pocket flaps, double collars, double-breasted coats or jackets, culottes, or epaulettes were allowed.

Wool restrictions were the earliest limits, since the army's wool requirements plus a reduction in the availability of imported wool necessitated cutting the consumer's 1942 wool consumption by half. Banned were wool evening clothes, wool linings, and wool plaids cut on the bias.

Figure 9.12 The garment on the left did not meet the requirements of the War Production Board because of its overlapping bodice, high collar, and full skirt. The dress to the right was suitable. (Library of Congress)

But shortages touched almost every facet of clothing. The rubber shortage caused restrictions on elastic for baby pants, surgical bandages and hose, and sanitary belts; encouraged the use of scrap elastic; and influenced the manufacturing of corsets and brassieres. The leather shortage caused restrictions such as no multicolored or leather-on-leather shoes; no new patterns or trims; only black, navy, white, or brown shoes; and no platform shoes over 1 3/8″ high or heels over 2 1/8″ high. Silk was in such short supply owing to the demand for parachutes and ammo bags that it was banned completely from consumer goods. The hosiery industry was most affected by this ban and the ban on nylon. In place of silk and nylon, rayon and cotton were used, but even stockings made with those fibers were restricted in color, amount of reinforcement, length, and gauge. Men's dress socks were also restricted. Cotton work clothes for women were limited to four models or styles per year of overalls, coveralls, work slacks, work shirts or blouses, work jackets, work dresses, and work aprons.

Early in the war a law was passed restricting the quantity of toiletries and cosmetics produced, but it was revoked after only a few months. Metal, also in short supply, was regulated in hair- and bobby-pin production by limiting the quantity produced, the number sold in a packaged unit, and the length of the pin itself.

More typical of modern sumptuary legislation are laws regulating public attire. Most communities have indecent-exposure laws making public nudity illegal, although some have beaches where nude bathing is permitted. Many communities have ordinances requiring shoes and/or shirts to be worn in certain kinds of public or retail buildings. Cigarette smoking is banned in some public areas, although the accouterments have always been allowed. Dress impersonation of, for example, the military, police, or the opposite sex is not allowed in many municipalities. While schools and businesses sometimes dictate skirt length and other aspects of dress, few communities still attempt such control. In the mid-1920s, when hemlines shot up, several states mandated a minimum skirt length; but enforcement was too difficult for the legislation to be effective. Military uniforms, however, are still effectively regulated by the government.

Many communities have laws governing the days and hours stores can be open, and some still dictate the kinds of goods that can be sold during certain hours or days. Other aspects of clothing production and marketing are still legislated. In 1981 President Reagan repealed legislation banning the home manufacturing of knitted outerwear; similar bans on the home manufacturing of jewelry, gloves and mittens, buttons and buckles, handkerchiefs, embroidery, and women's clothing were retained.

In the United States the federal government also regulates clothing through the use of tariffs, quotas, and nontariff barriers designed to favor the growth of domestic industry. Other federal laws, attempting to conserve dwindling resources, limit or ban the use of materials such as alligator and certain other animal skins, tortoise shell, and ivory.

Some modern laws are intended to protect the consumer from dangerous or shoddy products; such legislation was rare prior to the twentieth century. The Wool Products Labeling Act of 1939 forced manufacturers to give the percent of wool actually used in a garment. In the late 1950s the Textile Fiber Products Identification Act required such data for all fibers used in a garment. In 1953 the Flammable Fabrics Act was passed; this act has been amended by several additional standards that regulate the degree of flammability for specific items, such as children's sleepwear. Deceptive fur names were banned in 1951 by the Fur Products Labeling Act; labels indicating appropriate care for a garment were legislated by the Permanent Care Labeling Act of 1972. There has even been an effort to standardize the symbols used on the care labels of imported garments. The Wheeler-Lee Act of 1938 protects consumers from false advertising.

Some nations in the 1960s and 1970s increased their sumptuary legislation. Sometimes it was done to promote "progress," which was usually considered becoming more westernized; Indonesia's Sukarno, for example, decreed that women would have to wear blouses (enforcement of this law was difficult, particularly in rural areas). Other sumptuary laws, such as Oman's outlawing the wearing of glasses, seem less ideologically motivated. In certain cases, as in Pakistan and Iran, new regulations are attempts to return the people to their traditional lifestyle. How effective they will be may depend on how acceptable the traditional values still are and on how the nation will be able to cope with the exigencies of a modern world, which in many ways is antithetical to those traditions.

SUMMARY

Clothing both influences government and is influenced by it. It has been used to demonstrate governmental authority and to change or to maintain the social order. In dictatorships or monarchies fashions in dress often have tended to reflect the ruler's preferences and there has been a disparity in clothing between social levels. In Communist countries equality in dress is favored, and complete control of fashion production and distribution is exercised by the state. This control has enabled Communist governments to more easily manipulate their citizens through dress. In some Communist countries, dress has been completely standardized. Democracy favors political but not economic parity. Styles in democracies tend to be similar on all social levels, although individuals are freer to express themselves through their dress. Under all forms of government, political leaders, their families and/or their sexual partners have sometimes had an unusually profound impact on fashion.

Clothing often reflects national power, both political and economic; international relationships; and international identifications and alliances. However, a national style is generally maintained despite these influences. Clothing also has been a symbol of political beliefs and even a form of political rebellion. Revolutions and wars have had an effect on clothing and have been affected by it. Governments have legislated certain aspects of clothing or its production. Some of the primary reasons for such legislation have been to maintain status/class distinctions; to control morality, extravagance, and vanity; to encourage domestic industry; to encourage a balance in international trade; to promote savings; to control population growth; and to maintain the status quo.

10 | Religion

Religions are social structures reflecting people's relationship with the supernatural and organizing their ethical codes, philosophies, and moral conduct. Each of the world's religions embraces its own unique set of beliefs and practices. Many of the peoples of the world practice religions that "civilized" men and women would call magic, demon worship, or nature worship.

> The thing that religion and magic have in common is ritual. Whether one looks upon it as something instituted by gods or executed by magicians, ritual provides a way for everyone to have a share in divinity. . . .
> . . . Performing a ritual means opening a door to another world by carrying out gestures and uttering words that have always proved to be efficacious. . . .
> The aim of all ritual, whether magical or religious in nature, is to throw a bridge between the two banks of a river that some call life, others, death. (Virel 1980, p. 129)

Corporal adornments, such as scarification, tattooing, and circumcision, have frequently been associated with the practices of such "magic" religions and with religious ritual. These kinds of religious uses of dress we have examined in the first chapter.

In this chapter we shall examine the uses of dress in the major world religions. We shall also investigate the relationship of dress with morality, since individuals who are uninvolved with any organized religion will still have a code of morality that reflects their ethical code and philosophy and determines their moral behavior.

SACRED DRESS

Clothing can be divided into two broad categories, the sacred and the profane. Profane or secular dress is dress that is not related to a religion or to religious matters; sacred dress is involved with religion. Crawley (1931) identified four kinds of sacred dress: sanctity, priestly, godly, and sacrificial.

Sacrificial

Sacrificial dress is quite rare today. Our examples and understandings of it come primarily from primitive religions, cults, or history. Common themes in sacrificial dress are dress designed to please the god or power to whom the victim is being sacrificed and dress to consecrate the proposed victim. For example, in the Aztec religion, which had many gods demanding frequent appeasement through human sacrifice, children to be sacrificed to Tezcatlipoca were consecrated by being painted red and black. In some religions human sacrifice finally became symbolic; thus the female victim might simply cut off her hair and sacrifice it to the god(s).

Godly

The dress of the god(s) in most primitive, polytheistic religions has been dress like that worn by the believers (inventors?) of the religion and the god(s). Buddha's princely birth status, for instance, was reflected in his long earlobes, his monastic lifestyle, his shaven head, and his simple garb. These dress symbols were consistent with those of his peers.

In modern monotheistic religions God is generally not viewed as in a body and thus he/she needs no clothing. When God is represented as dressed, the representation is usually somewhat masculine, with a nebulous but flowing robe. Bifurcated dress or dress having a strong sexual connotation is not used since God (unlike the Greek gods and goddesses) is not perceived as a sexual entity with sexual body parts. The only incidence of human dress worn by a god of a major monotheistic religion is the dress of Jesus who was, according to Christian beliefs, the son of God living among men as a man. The dress of Jesus has been represented as simple dress appropriate to the region of Galilee at that time. However, the shroud in which Jesus was wrapped during his days in the tomb is believed by some to be godly clothing and has great impact in the modern religious world. Thus, dress, one of the most powerful means of human communication, might contain the "proof" of God's existence for which humans have searched.

Priestly

Priestly garb is used to stress the uniqueness of the priestly role from that of the congregants. In cultures like the Aztec, where religion has been the largest institution, the religious leaders or priests have had a status equal to, or parallel with, that of the nobility. Thus, their dress has included symbols of their high status. Roman Catholic priests originally dressed like their male congregants. However, when fashion made a significant change in the sixth century, the priests remained with their traditional garb. Their dress has evolved to indicate the cleric's order, role, and status and has become a means to control his moral and sexual behavior.

Removal of "maleness" from priestly dress has been a recurrent theme in many religions. Roman Catholic monk and priest novitiates have their bishop cut off a lock of their hair to symbolize their rejection of wordly desires and goods. Most priests wear no facial hair, to symbolize their voluntary departure from the sexual arena. Some orders shave the crown of the head; such symbolic castration may be the modern equivalent of the actual castration done to priests of the goddess Astarte. A priest's shaven head may symbolize celibacy, or his matted hair may indicate total detachment from the sexual passions (Cooper 1971). The shaven head of a woman entering into or a member of the Roman Catholic and Buddhist sisterhoods may also symbolize her turning away from worldly pleasures for a life of celibacy, self-sacrifice, and eternal penance.

Figure 10.1 Franciscan monks with tonsured heads. (Library of Congress)

Priestly dress often reflects the priest's life of poverty. Buddha admonished his followers to give up luxurious living. Thus, Buddhist priests wear a simple robe; if they have been given a fine robe, they will cut it into pieces, which are then indiscriminately patched together. The role of the Catholic monk has often included a rule of poverty, which required a multipurpose, uniform garment with wide "fitability." But priestly garb for those of high church status has often been ornamental and elaborate rather than pious or humble. Priests, for example, have worn elaborate vestments studded with precious stones; yet the vestment symbolizes the priest's donning of divine character, an experience that might seem more appropriately viewed as humbling and self-effacing.

Most modern ecclesiastical daily garb is no longer radically different from secular dress, perhaps because the clerical role is similar to the occupational roles of many of the congregation's members. In some denominations the major difference is the Roman collar, an ever-present reminder of the priestly requirement for moral uprightness.

Priestly dress may include a special relationship of the priest to his god(s) or to spirits or events. Thus, the medicine man's or woman's dress indicates his or her power or control over, for example, the spirits causing an illness, and the Pope's dress indicates his closeness to God. The Taoist priest wears a simple kimonolike robe except at special ceremonies requiring him to increase his power. To achieve greater faculty, he wears a cape-like vestment that gives him a universal power through its symbolic depiction of the cosmos with decorative symbols of all aspects of the universe: the yin and the yang; the earth's directions; the Eight Taoist Immortals, the path to immortality; and the parts of the earth, sea, land, and sky (Cammann 1979). There are some instances where the priestly garb itself is believed to have some sacred power. Thus, before a Greek Orthodox priest pronounces absolution, he places his stole over the shoulders of the penitent who has just confessed.

The modernization of some Roman Catholic sisters' habits also reflects a concomitant decrease in the amount of differentiation from secular garb as the sisters' roles have differentiated less and less from the roles of single women within the congregation. For centuries some sisterhoods have worn either no habits or habits that differed very little from secular dress. In most cases this was due either to political reasons or to the nature of the particular sisterhood's work (Plogsterth 1975). The new habits also reflect the sisters' increasing ability to be productive, to work, to be taken seriously. But they still symbolize sexual bans, group identity, humility, poverty, and simplicity. The Ursulines' habit modifications reflect many of the changes: the dark colors, symbolizing their seriousness, and the tightness, symbolizing their uprightness, have been retained. The volume of their garb, representing aloofness and a "distrust of the human body and unwillingness to be involved with others" (Lucas 1971, p. 49), has been decreased. Habits that are distinct from secular dress tend to cause others to approach the sister as a "what" rather than a "who" (ibid.). However,

Figure 10.2 (a, b) A Taoist priest's robe from nineteenth century China (front and back). (Philadelphia Museum of Art)

a

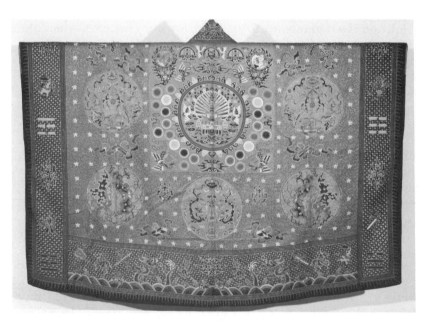

b

treating sisters as a "who" may lead to religious understandings based more on individual interpretations and could create confusion and uncertainty in some members of the congregation.

Sanctity

Dress of sanctity is designed to differentiate the wearer, in his or her consecration, from the profane. It usually accomplishes this by employing different color and/or form from that of the secular. Thus, the ascetic often wears dull-colored dress of coarse fabric in an extremely simple style; it may even have a worn-out appearance; and his or her hair will be opposite in length to that of the norm and generally will be unkempt. Sacred dress is often associated with ceremonies involving the Christian sacraments of baptism, communion, marriage, and ordination. These sacraments, and their associated dress, symbolize the individual's religious development. The baptism consecrates the individual to God. Baptismal dress is often an ornate, white, long gown with matching bonnet. For their first communion, girls traditionally wear an ornate white dress with a white veil or hair covering, and boys wear a blue or white suit. Marriage is the institution that ultimately helps to maintain the church by enlarging its membership. Its dress is designed to symbolize the virtue of the two individuals being "eternally" united.

Dress has been used to designate a temporary state of sanctity. This may reflect participation in a special religious event such as a pilgrimage, a special interaction with a supernatural being(s), or participation in a religious ritual or service. Thus, the Moslem pilgrim making a hadj to Mecca, one of the five acts required by Mohammed, wears a special dress that has such importance that it is often finally used as the pilgrim's shroud. The Armenian Christian pilgrim to Jerusalem tattooed himself with his name and the date of his pilgrimage. Many

Figure 10.3 A woman being tattooed to commemorate her pilgrimage to Jerusalem. (Library of Congress)

pilgrims wear items designed to make them uncomfortable, such as stones in their shoes, as a constant reminder of the individual's relative lack of importance. Humility, awe, or respect can also be shown to the supernatural being one is approaching by the removal or donning of clothing. The Mandan Indian braves cut off the little finger of their left hand to show their respect and love for their Buffalo god. To indicate extreme piety or sanctity they would cut their chests and tie the edges of the wounds with rawhide. The rawhide would be attached to a pole from which they were suspended while being spun. The resulting scars were a strong sign of the individual's sanctity.

Some dress of sanctity is used to get the attention of a busy spirit. The farm women of southwestern China's Miao tribe wear an elaborately bordered, full-skirted dress. The embroidery of the squares composing the border is so intricate and time consuming that the Communists offered, for the sake of saving time and increasing crop production, to machine print the borders. The women kept refusing this offer because the borders were not decorative in nature. They were a carefully designed prayer designed to get aid from the gods by informing them, through the placement and pattern of each square, of just what crops the peasants were growing. Since the women wore their "prayers" each day in the field, the gods had ample opportunity to receive an accurate understanding of the help that was needed for each crop (Binder 1972). Even more familiar religions use special dress for times of communication with their god. In Orthodox Judaism, for example, a married man must

Figure 10.4 Late-nineteenth-century Jews arrayed for prayer. (Library of Congress)

wear a prayer shawl when praying in the synagogue. The specific spirit or god one follows can also be shown through dress. Some Hindu forehead marks indicate which god the wearer follows. Siva worshippers, for example, honor the long penance endured by Siva by adorning themselves with ashes from a funeral pyre or from the holy cow's dung.

Probably the dress of sanctity with which most of us have the greatest familiarity is that of the worshipper or "church goer." At times, however, Protestant clergy have been concerned with the prevalence of material values over spiritual as indicated in the luxurious and vain church dress of their congregants. In modern America church garb is frequently one's most elegant and newest but otherwise is like secular dress. The hats and gloves worn by women to church until the mid-1960s have largely vanished as indicators of church attendance. It is only in the synagogue that we in the West still consistently find such symbols. The yarmulke, worn by most Jewish men—reform Jews often dispense with it—shows the wearer's reverence of God. However, the Hasidim use more dress symbols in their effort to prevent assimilation with non-Jews among whom they dwell and contamination from the less orthodox Jews who no longer uphold all of the laws of the Torah. The male's dress indicates the intensity and frequency of his religious observance on a scale of 1 to 6. Men of the least intense class, the yiden, wear double-breasted suits that button from right to left. The rebbes, men of the most intense class, wear beards with sidelocks, large-brimmed black beaver or sable hats, long overcoats, long silk coats with pockets, breeches, and black slippers with white socks. The classes in between have correspondingly fewer articles as they decrease in religious intensity. However, the subtle differences in dress are often meaningless to the non-Hasidic observer, who only notes the more obvious items such as the sidelocks in categorizing the wearer as Jewish or Hasidic. The more Orthodox women wear wigs when they marry to cover their shaved heads, and their hair thereafter is not to be seen in public. Prior to her marriage, the Hasidic woman is only required to modestly cover her entire body. However, since hose, for example, can cover while still revealing, this requirement no longer prevents the single woman from conforming to normal secular fashions.

There are other religions whose worshippers indicate in their daily dress their religious affiliation and devotion. The saffron tika forehead mark of the Hindus symbolizes their purity from performing the daily ritual bathing and indicates their soul's location. Sikhism, a Hindu sect rejecting idolatry and the caste system, requires all male Sikhs to wear five items indicating their faith: short underpants, an iron bracelet, a wooden comb, unshaven beard and uncut hair, and a special knife around which their hair is rolled. The Moslem worshipper removes his shoes before entering a mosque so he will not soil his holy house; thus, a slipper shoe style is normal, as it is easy to remove. The fez worn by many Moslem men allows them both to respectfully cover their heads and to touch their foreheads to the floor in prayer; their full-seated trousers enable them to sit cross-legged in contemplation and prayer (Gordon and Lee 1977).

Figure 10.5 Moslems at prayer. (Library of Congress)

DRESS IN MAJOR RELIGIONS

Clothing has been used in two primary ways by organized religions: to maintain the religion's traditions and customs and to control the moral thought and conduct of its adherents. Obviously, both serve the even more important purpose of helping to perpetuate the religion itself. When clothing is used to maintain tradition, the clothing generally will undergo fewer changes, and those changes that do occur will take place very slowly. Thus, fashion, the essence of which is change, has been consistently viewed as evil and opposed by most organized religions. High clothing interest has, in most of these religions, reflected an immodest attempt to glorify oneself rather than one's god(s).

Hinduism

In Hinduism, a major polytheistic religion that encompasses all parts of one's life, it is the inner self that has the highest value. Worldly life is seen as temporary, whereas the spiritual is eternal. The Hindu believes in reincarnation as he moves through the various stages of moral development indicated by his caste—the higher the stage, the higher the caste—until his karma allows him to finally enter and remain in the spiritual world. Contemplation is required for an individual to get in touch with his inner self which he must do in order to enter this final world. Since Hindus have little interest in, or need for, consumption (which is used for the external self), dress has had relatively little importance. Adornment, when used, has been supposed to be intended to please a god(s) or indicate the believer's devotion to his god(s) rather than to beautify the individual. Thus, Hindu dress has reflected this by being an unchanging classic style rather than one of fashion. It has been used primarily to show three things: caste, level of piety, and the specific god to which the individual is devoted.

Judaism

In Judaism, the oldest of the major monotheistic religions, dress has had more importance. The ancient Jews had many symbols involved in their dress; for example, the division of the pure upper body from the impure lower body was indicated by wearing a girdle. Moses forbade nudity, reflecting the Jewish connection of dress with morality, and he forbade adopting non-Jewish clothing styles, reflecting the Jewish desire not to assimilate. Today, however, only a minority of Jews wear clothing that does not conform to the general secular style. Perhaps the most important Jewish belief pertaining to clothing has reflected their belief that humans are a celebration of God. Thus, people should dress in a way to be attractive and pleasing to God; dressing attractively has not only been accepted but has been one's religious duty.

Christianity

Christianity has conflicting views and values pertaining to dress. Since the afterlife is the eternal life, this world is seen as less important than the next. Meekness and humility are valued; self-display is not, although modest dress has been emphasized more for women than for men. Renbourn (1972) hypothesized that this double standard reflected the patriarchal nature of the European cultures in which Christianity evolved. However, it may also reflect the church's projection of the male's sexual guilt onto the female in a form of "she tempted me" (Flugel 1930). Women (Eve) were seen as the source of man's (Adam's) fall from grace; they were evil, sexual creatures who could only contaminate the lofty thoughts and ideals of the superior male. Women were taught to feel shame about their bodies and their sexual functioning. They had to prevent additional sin, carnal lust, from arising in men and to atone for the general sins of the female body and "guilty Eve." A woman's head or hair was thought especially provocative, and by the third century, the church required adherence to St. Paul's admonition that women cover their heads when attending church.

Similar attitudes were still evident in the seventeenth century when an anonymous papist wrote:

> There is always danger in attentively looking upon a naked Breast; and there is a kind of crime in beholding it with attention in the *Churches.* . . . for *Jesus Christ* being then in so eminent a manner to be rembred by us, methinks, to prefer a Woman to him, or at least to divide our attention, and perhaps our vows, beween him and her . . . is without doubt a great injury. (A Papist 1678, p. 15)

Baring a breast was no worse than adorning oneself with a wig—"borrowed hair"—and baring one's "Arms and Necks, to catch and ruin those souls which Jesus Christ hath redeemed by his blood" (ibid., p. f).

Calvin and Luther turned Christianity toward greater drabness in dress. Bright, ornamental clothing was viewed as leading to the sins of pride and sensuality, while somber dress showed the sinner's humility on his or her road to God's salvation. Sinfulness in dress was believed to lead to other sins, such as living above one's status and means. The hoops that could blow upward to reveal the female's drawerless legs and thighs were deemed as suggestive of illicit sexual activity (Tyrrell 1975).

The Puritans and Quakers were anti-ornament, frivolity, or female body exposure in dress. They even tried to make dresses to conceal the shape of the bust. They were also interested in dress that was practical. The Quakers adapted current styles but omitted excessive sartorial adornment and used simpler color schemes. Puritans, fearing spontaneity, wanted their clothing to be drab (Taylor 1954) as well as practical. During Cromwellian times "the most devout English Puritans practiced fetishism in their fixation on the Old Testament, wearing sacred texts next to their skin under their coarse shirts" (Binder 1953, p. 10) or embroidered texts on their coarse underwear—which they kept clean against the admonitions of St. Jerome, who asserted that purity of one's body and one's garments indicated impurity of one's soul.

The Amish, Hutterites, and Mennonites, all Anabaptist sects, wear somber, simple, modest clothing in styles similar to those worn in colonial America (although some communities wear colorful underwear). Their clothing shows their value of the spiritual and traditional rather than the material; their rejec-

Figure 10.6 The Mennonite beard, symbolic of pacifism, is characterized by a bare upper lip. (Library of Congress)

tion of the modern, technologically and materially oriented world and their attempt to remain apart from it; and their pacifism. Their simplistic interpretation of the Bible has led the Amish to adopt some unique dress requirements; for example, lest the devil grab a buttonhole for a free ride, they have no button closures.

The modern Christian has developed a separateness between sacred and secular dress. Perhaps this reflects the emphasis the major Christian religions place on the individual over the group. One achieves redemption by one's efforts. Because of this stress the individual has been more resistant to the strictures of the church. Only when one examines those Christian religions that stress the importance of the group over the individual do we still find dress that conforms to religion's stricture and dogma.

Mohammedanism

The newest of the major religions is Islam, or Mohammedanism. This religion emphasizes the group over the individual, and it requires much daily religious involvement by its followers; thus, its clothing strictures have had great impact on the behavior of its congregants. The Koran enjoins women to dress modestly and cover their hair in public; self-display is prohibited, and the dress of the women often would seem to suggest that this is strictly adhered to. However, Fertile-Bishop and Gilliam (1981) noted that the veiled Saudi women frequently exploit "the art of dress, coiffure, and make-up. The perfume stocks of stores in the Jeddah suq are reputed to be the largest in the world" (p. 26).

African Moslems have adapted Islam to their ancestors' more animistic religions. Thus, they still attempt to control God through amulets; but now the amulets are texts from the Koran worn in metal cases rather than herbs or the like.

In the post–World War II period many of the Moslem countries made great strides in industrialization. As they adopted Western technology and ideas, Western dress and its adaptations became more common. The Islamic fundamentalist movement reflects a concern for these changes and an attempt to return the societies to more traditional garb and behavior. It will be interesting to see whether women will really be able to return to the greater confines of purdah and the veil. If the fundamentalists can convince the women that such dress is necessary for gaining heavenly admission, they may be successful, for many peoples have submitted to seemingly negative dress customs in order to attain an afterlife.

RELIGIOUS SUMPTUARY LAWS

Most religions have used sumptuary laws to attempt to regulate the conduct and expenditures of their members. Jewish sumptuary laws were of special importance in the sixteenth and seventeenth centuries; however, they restricted dress in other centuries during times of trouble. Most of the laws were directed at women and designed, for the social good, to prevent the adoption of new fashion and to curb extravagance and envy. Both the Roman Catholic church and the Moslems created sumptuary legislation to prevent Jews from assimilating in Catholic or Moslem communities; thus, they insisted that Jews wear clothing indicating a Jewish heritage. The Moslem laws pertained to all Dhimmis—nonbelievers—and were first instituted around the eighth century, when Arabs began to adopt the fashions of other cultures (Rubens 1967). These laws were fairly nonexistent by the nineteenth century.

Roman Catholic sumptuary legislation was primarily intended to maintain class distinctions. The church's support for a class hierarchy with a ruling class has resulted in frequent conflicts between revolutionaries and the church (Binder 1953). Roman Catholic laws have also been used to control sexual behavior by, for example, regulating skirt length.

Moslem sumptuary legislation generally has followed the Jewish proscriptions against tattooing, nudity, and the potential idolatry of representing the human form in pictures. The modern Islamic fundamentalist movement has

Figure 10.7 (a, b) In Tunis, a Jewish woman's garb (a) was markedly different from her Moslem counterpart (b). (Library of Congress)

a   b

Figure 10.8 Ecclesiastical scrutiny. (Library of Congress)

provided us with the most recent examples of sumptuary laws, especially in Pakistan and Iran. To some extent this legislation may reflect an attempt to maintain the integrity of Moslems by preventing their assimilation into Western ideology. Such attempts have been made by many religions throughout history with various degrees of success. In Europe, Catholics and Protestants attempted to prevent assimilation, and the gayer dress of the Catholic was in stark contrast to their somberly clad Protestant neighbors. Some differences not consciously selected or legislated have helped to maintain group differences; for example, the Hindu man buttons his tunic on his right side, the Moslem on his left; the Hindu man wears a dhoti, the Moslem a lungi; the Moslem man wears a cap, the Hindu a turban or no head covering; the Moslem man is bearded, the Hindu shaven. These differences reflect the enmity often found between geographically common religious groups.

Langner (1959) suggested that "no great civilizations have existed without the goal of superiority imparted to mankind by religion and clothes co-acting to influence man in his belief that he is akin to the gods" (p. 125). Perhaps of equal or greater importance has been the security humans have gained by the daily order and stability religions have given. Those whose dress is completely dictated by religion are able to perform the daily ritual of dressing without having to make decisions. Those whose dress reflects their religious identification and involvement are provided, and provide others, with another reminder of a part of their social identity.

MORALITY AND BODY EXPOSURE

Although not everyone is involved with an organized religion, everyone's dress will represent his or her moral code of conduct. Morality has often been associated with the degree and kind of body exposure. Philosophic writings of the seventeenth to nineteenth centuries frequently connected sins of lust and temptation to the body or body part(s), and as late as 1926 the archbishop of Naples attributed the great earthquake at Amalfi to God's anger at women's hemlines rising to show their knees. This view was consistent with the principle, adopted by many Western societies, that the greater the degree of body exposure the greater the level of immoral behavior; and it reflected the Western association of sexuality with morality. Dress covering the female body's erogenous zones, which at times have included nearly all the body parts, was believed to reduce the male's nearly insatiable sexual appetite; revealing such an erogenous part was thought to serve as a sexual stimulant. The early Christians viewed the female body, clad or nude, as a sinful temptress of men. Women, therefore, were to dress humbly. That this belief in the power of the female body to tempt men is shared by many modern Americans is evident in our frequent questions pertaining to the attire of a rape victim; the victim is often believed to have enticed, in some physical way, the rapist, who is thereby deemed the ultimate victim.

The principle of body exposure relating to immorality appears inconsistent with evidence from cross-cultural testing, since many societies, such as the New Britains or some Amazonian peoples, are extremely virtuous or strict in matters of sex even though their members wear nothing. The American Indians from the northwest coast demonstrated no increase in immoral behavior during the summer, when they removed their clothing in favor of naked comfort. In cultures like the Yoruba, where children are naked as are adults engaged in physical labor, there seems to be no increase in immoral behavior during the adults' working hours, and the naked children appear to learn the morality codes and behaviors of the—clad or naked—adults. In those cultures where only one sex is nude, as in the Upoto, Guaycurus, and Curetu, the behavior of the naked sex seems no less moral than that of the attired.

Nude greeting of visitors to one's home, as practiced by the seventeenth-century Irish, some American Indians, Eskimos, and other peoples, indicated a high level of trust given and expected. Clothing, a vehicle for possible concealment of weapons or other evils, had a dangerous side while nudity offered a sort of purity, sincerity, or honesty. In fact, the available evidence could support the argument that moral or modest behavior has been reduced as the amount of body covering has increased.

When Western civilization, represented by its religious missionaries, came into contact with different cultures, they based their judgments about the new cultures on the Western belief that lack of dress relates to immorality. Natives were required to "go foreign" by covering their bodies in order to expose their souls to Christianity. In the 1820s the missionaries insisted that Polynesian

Figure 10.9 The dress of these women at a Tanzanian market gives no indication of their moral code, although the rear tassel of the Kaverondo woman in the foreground does show that she is married. (Library of Congress)

Figure 10.10 Western dress was adopted by these Liberian natives along with Christianity. (Library of Congress)

women wear Mother Hubbards or holoku. These gowns, unsuitable to the hot, damp Hawaiian climate, were designed to reduce sexual thoughts by completely hiding the figure. The missionaries believed they were conducting an experiment to improve human morality. However, their success seems questionable since the islanders often went naked when they were out of the Westerners' view and, when involved in physical labor, the women would roll their Mother Hubbards to their waists (Howe 1977). In those cultures where the wearing of clothing was seen as immoral behavior or associated with it, the missionaries' efforts to garb the natives were even less successful than they had been in Hawaii. However, most natives have adopted Western dress along with Western religion.

Even some body coverings have been perceived as immoral. For example, Charles II believed that female underwear was immodest since it increased male curiosity. This reasoning is perhaps more realistic than we might think since prudery is a psychological defense mechanism to protect prudes from their intense interest in "it." The prude will see sex or sexual innuendo in a large number and wide variety of objects or topics; he is, in fact, fascinated by sex. But because of his inability to accept his own fascination, he is determined to prevent others from expressing their less extreme sexual interest (Cunnington 1941). Thus, Gill's (1931) admonition to have public nudity in times of prudery and modest dress in times of wantonness may be very good advice. Certainly he was wise in asserting that "prudes cannot decide who are wantons, nor can wantons decide who are prudes" (p. 8).

NORMS OF MORALITY

Many societies, particularly in the West, have believed that their moral codes govern sexual relations and procreation. In those societies that have also seen a relationship between morality and body exposure, the degree of body exposure has been controlled by norms of morality in dress. Generally, during periods of strict morality, dress has been more ascetic, even puritanical. Correspondingly, when moral codes have been relaxed, dress has also become "looser." Those not conforming to their society's code of decency in dress have received social disapproval or even more severe social sanctions. In modern American society these norms of decency in dress seem related to the taboo zones of the body— those body parts that are not to be touched by others.

> Each of us has a sense of body-privacy, but the strength of this varies from person to person, culture to culture, and relationship to relationship. Above all it varies according to the part of our body which is experiencing physical contact. If a companion touches a "public zone," such as the hand, then no problem arises; but if the same companion reaches out to make contact with a "private zone," such as the genitals, then the result can be anything from embarrassment to anger. Only lovers and parents with babies have completely free access to all parts of the body. To everyone else there is a graded scale of body-contact taboos.
> In general . . . the body zones nearest to sexual features [have] the strongest taboos, and those farthest away . . . the weakest . . . (Morris 1977, p. 204)

These taboos appear to apply to visual as well as physical contact so that public zones may be exposed to view while seeing a private zone will create embarrassment or even anger in the exposed or the viewer. For example, the intentional infliction of one's private zone(s) on a viewer by an exhibitionist generally results in anger in the viewer whereas unintentional exposure, such as the wind lifting a woman's dress, generally results in embarrassment in the exposed and embarrassment, sympathy, or discomfort in the viewer.

Both the Victorian era and the late 1960s were periods of moral confusion that was reflected in dress. Victorian female garb was tight, restricting women to an upright posture and reminding them of their moral obligations, as did the Victorian male's stiff white collar. However, since the pulled-in waists emphasized the bust and the hips, which were also stressed by the bustle, the clothing was actually a sex stimulant. The emphasis on the leglessness of women (even pantaloon advertisements pictured the advertised garment folded so that the viewer could not see the pantaloon's bifurcation) made any exposure of the leg above the foot a titillating and sexually stimulating experience for the viewer (the exposed would have been as embarrassed as today's woman might be over the exposure of her nipple). Since the sexes could not have skin contact, gloves were worn for dancing and other situations in which a heterosexual handclasp was expected. Imagine the sexual power of a bare finger simply touching the bare palm of another's hand in such a restrictive period. During the turbulent late 1960s and early 1970s, when American youth was questioning traditional morality, they often went braless or wore see-through fabrics. However, they rejected styles along the lines of the topless look introduced by Gernrich. Such body exposure, however, was not something new to Western fashion. Napoleonic France saw women with breasts and nipples exposed and the female form obvious beneath translucent fabrics often wetted down in order to better cling to the wearer's body. In Renaissance Europe women's arms had to be kept covered, yet men, until James I, wore a cod-piece to inflatedly or decoratively hold their penis. Some inflation is achieved today through jockey shorts, sales of which did not overtake those of boxer shorts until the 1960s, thirty years after their introduction, when the young were more open in their talk and their appearance of sexuality.

MORAL CONFORMITY

Dress has been used to indicate society's disapproval of a person's behavior. Individuals have been punished by society by being forced to adopt dress designed to embarrass, cause discomfort, force conformity to aberrant dress, or a combination of these methods. Modern prison garb forces conformity to

Figure 10.11   The canque. (Library of Congress)

anomalous dress to remind the inmates that their actions have been judged to be outside the social moral code. Yet garb causing physical discomfort, such as the Chinese canque or the European body barrel, is rarely used in modern Western penal systems.

The Chericahua, an Apache tribe, are believed to have used nasal mutilation to punish females guilty of infidelity; and throughout history and in many cultures women have had their heads shaved to indicate illicit entanglements. Both of these punishments would be more emotionally charged responses than the punishment inflicted in Hawthorne's *Scarlet Letter* since they change the woman's actual appearance, with or without clothing, and they either cannot be undone or cannot be undone until nature slowly cures the condition. The trauma of head shaving is evident in a case in France of a woman who, after her hair was shaved at the end of World War II because she was friendly with the Nazi troops, never again left her home.

Individuals can themselves choose to wear clothing to remind them of their own (past, present, or future) immoral behavior. These penitential garments usually have been made of rough fabric, such as horsehair or sack cloth, that irritate the skin. Today penitential clothing is more common among cults such as the fakirs than among congregants of the major religions.

The chastity belt is perhaps the most obvious use of clothing as a protector of morality. Popular in the Middle Ages, it was rarely, if ever, actually used.

Figure 10.12 An Apache woman whose nose has been mutilated purportedly as punishment for infidelity. (National Anthropological Archives, Smithsonian Institution)

Figure 10.13 This French woman's head has been shorn to visually proclaim her guilt as a German collaborationist. (Magnum Photos, Inc.)

The requirements of basic hygiene prevented its long-term employment. However, there were still firms in the 1930s doing a thriving business in chastity belts. Less publicized were the chastity cages used on sons by anxious fathers who had the small, spike-lined devices fitted to their son's genitals. The cages were locked onto the son each night so that, should he engage in immoral behavior leading to an erection, the parents would be notified by a bell connected to their room (Taylor 1954). The corsets worn by Victorian women to symbolize their moral "uprightness" bound the torso so tightly that the uterus was pushed down, distorting the cervix. This caused dyspareunia, or painful intercourse. Thus, since humans tend to avoid any stimulus that causes pain, it seems likely that, serendipitously, corsets were a kind of chastity belt (Davies 1982).

Societies have used masks to hide the identity of someone who was engaging in immoral or illicit activities. This practice, however, has sometimes helped to identify the "looser" members of the society to those of like morals so that together they could engage in immoral activities. Groups whose behavior differs from their society's standards have used dress to differentiate themselves, as some motorcycle gangs have done with items like leather jackets or gauntlets or some Cuban "tuffs" have done with tattoos on the lips or between the thumb and the first finger.

Even literature has employed clothing to show the moral fiber of characters. Thus, one has Cinderella, whose honest foot could be detected from all others by a glass slipper; true love depended on a shoe! And of course, every

Snow White is garbed in clothing of "pure" white, while the universal witch must wear "mysterious" black. Reality has much in common with fiction, and in the modern West we still determine the moral character of strangers primarily through our perception of their appearance—their clothing.

SUMMARY

Organized religions have used clothing to perpetuate themselves by maintaining their traditions and customs and by controlling the behavior of their members. Fashion, therefore, is antithetical to most religions since it promotes change rather than tradition. In most religions sacred dress is used to indicate the priestly role and to denote a state of sanctity. In the modern West, however, sacred dress is becoming increasingly less differentiated from the secular as religious and secular lifestyles become more alike.

Cross-cultural evidence does not support an association between immoral behavior and body exposure. Instead the evidence suggests that morality is adversely affected by the adoption of body covering(s). In spite of this, most Western societies equate "loose" clothing, clothing that reveals the sexual body, with "loose" moral standards and behavior. Societies tend to punish individuals whose dress behavior deviates from the social norms for decency. They also use dress as a method of preventing behavior that is outside the social norms and for identifying individuals whose behavior does not conform to such standards. Dress still has so many associations with morality that it is often thought to indicate the moral character of its wearer.

11 | Individual Development

Individual development is so massive a topic that it would be impossible for us to even summarize it in just one book, let alone one chapter. Thus, we have chosen to focus on only two theories. We have selected the two that seem to have the greatest significance to individual development: self-concept theory and Maslow's needs theory of motivation and development. If we can apply these theories to ourselves so that we become more self-aware, we can become more sensitive to, and understanding of, our world and all the people in it. An understanding of these theories will provide us with a foundation of sufficient scope to enable us to interpret individual dress behavior. Thus, for example, we will be able to understand the following vignette reported by Lucius Beebe (1966). The *Titanic* sank on a

> Sunday evening when not all passengers dressed for dinner, [thus] a number of fastidious persons who would have had it otherwise faced eternity in business dress. Unwilling to make an exit on this note of informality, the aged Benjamin Guggenheim summoned his valet and retired to his stateroom, presently to reappear in full evening dress with tails and his best pearl studs. "Now we are dressed like gentlemen," he said, "and ready to go." (pp. 245–46).

THE SELF-CONCEPT

There is little agreement on just what the *self-concept* is although there is widespread agreement that, whatever it is, it is important. As we will use the term, the self-concept is the individual's mental system of organizing his perceptions and concepts about himself, his attitudes toward and appraisals of himself, and those beliefs, feelings, and ideas he has that are related to himself. While much of this is conscious, some is unconscious. For example, the role of the self-concept in interpreting new data is predominantly unconscious, although the interpretation itself is conscious. This reflects the relationship of the self-concept to the process of perception. As the self-concept gets more differentiated and more inclusive, it adds a new dimension, the *peripheral self*. The early formation, "me" as a special and distinct self, becomes the core of the self-concept. This stable core, which houses most of the unconscious aspects of the self-concept as well as many conscious, maintains our inner consistency and unity. It changes rarely, and usually any changes proceed from changes in the peripheral self. This latter is entirely conscious and easily subject to change. It is data from the peripheral self that individuals self-report or use in defining "me." It is intrinsically associated with our social identity, our various social belongings; it identifies the "me" in social roles. For example, the bright child from a brilliant family may feel intellectually inferior at home where she is the least competent. However, when she enters school where she will be among the brightest students, she will learn to see her peripheral self as intellectually adequate or even superior.

It is primarily from the peripheral self that the individual selects a public presentation of her self. This *apparent self* is a chameleon that can make radically different presentations from one person or group to another. It usually reflects the individual's best guess as to what her audience would be most receptive to. Although this may seem like an act looking for applause, it is not. It is more like an impressionistic self-portrait painted to please a specific viewer.

The foundation of the self-concept is composed not only of both conscious and unconscious *perceptions* but also of conscious *conceptions*, which are the meanings the individual attaches to her perceptions. There is also an *attitudinal* component, which is largely conscious although it may have an unconscious element. The attitudinal component consists of the values the individual places on her perceptions, the judgments she makes about them, and her concepts of them. It is in this component that the individual develops feelings about her worth, her value, her adequacy.

The *phenomenal self* is the term generally used to indicate the conscious self, although some theorists have referred to it with other terms, such as the real self. Because it is conscious, it is our true identity to ourselves. However, this is only a psychological truth relative to the individual's unique perception of reality. It incorporates the peripheral self as well as the conscious elements of the stable core. It is the essence of what we mean when we say "I" or "me."

"Its physical boundaries are roughly the skin or clothing surfaces" (Combs and Syngg 1959, p. 43), although its psychological boundaries may extend to other people or objects with which the individual has so identified that she has incorporated them into her "me." Most members of one's nuclear family assume this significance. Many people also incorporate their clothing into their "me" so that they feel personally rejected if someone makes a negative comment about their dress or personally praised if the comment is positive.

Part of the self-concept is the *ideal self,* which is the way we would like to be. This is our model self, and in childhood it is usually based on a concrete model, someone with whom the child has strongly identified. In most children the ideal self is congruent with the behavioral expectations and standards of their parents. As our circle of interpersonal relationships grows, we gain more models so that the ideal self of a teenager or an adult will be a prismatic composite of traits from a fairly large number of individuals interwoven with his beliefs about himself and his environment. Disparity between the ideal and the phenomenal selves is one of the primary causes of anxiety. For example, when you feel anxious before a test, the anxiety exists because your phenomenal self is not confident that your performance will be as brilliant as it should be, according to your ideal self. Students who do not have test anxiety usually feel that their performance will approximate their ideal self. Congruency between the phenomenal self and the ideal self is what is meant by self-acceptance. Gibbins (1969) hypothesized that it is the ideal self or an image between the ideal self and the self-concept that people try to express in their clothing. When the clothing being selected is not actually going to be worn, we are even more apt to select the clothes that are most congruent to our ideal self. Gibbins's research supported these hypotheses.

Self-concepts fall on a continuum from negative to positive. When an individual's self-concept is predominantly positive, she will expect to succeed in most of her endeavors. This expectation will allow her to be more open to new situations since they are not threats but avenues for new success. She will be motivated to stride into experiences and try with all of her ability because if she tries, she expects to succeed. Unfortunately, the individual whose self-concept is predominantly negative believes that she is unworthy and inadequate and therefore expects to fail. New situations are threatening to her so that she enters them defensively, prepared either to fight or to withdraw. Thus, her ability to achieve is actually reduced. If by some mistake she should succeed, she will quickly degrade her positive accomplishment by saying or thinking such things as: "Boy, did I fool them" or "That was a lucky mistake."

Self-concepts are not always realistic but can be placed on a continuum from realistic to unrealistic. Stout people, for example, have been found to perceive themselves as thinner than they actually are just as some thin people feel fat. Most of us know someone whom we perceive to be quite attractive although that individual feels unattractive. This feeling of unattractiveness persists in spite of the fact that she is often told how attractive she is. Why is this? Why would an attractive individual continue to feel unattractive in the face of evidence to the contrary?

Figure 11.1 "I'm sorry, but I just can't go through with the sale." (Library of Congress)

Function of the Self-Concept

The answer to the question above is the core self's ability to maintain inner consistency. It does so by distorting anything that is inconsistent to make it more consistent and by determining our expectations. Remember the self-fulfilling prophecy? It also applies in this case so that what we expect will be is probably what will be. For example, take an individual who feels that he is not worthy or even likable. He expects rejection. Thus, each time he is faced with meeting new people or a new person, he begins to prepare for that rejection. He enters the new situation defensive, hostile, or with resistance. Years ago a young man jumped off the San Francisco Bay Bridge. After the body was identified, the police went to his residence, which was about two miles from the bridge. They found a suicide note, which read in part that he was going to walk to the bridge and if no one smiled at him before he got there, he would jump from it. Life was not worth living in a world of unsmiling people. Experiment with this notion. Take a similar walk two days in a row. The first time walk along looking angry. Glare at each person who passes by. Remember, they are going to let you down. They aren't going to smile at you. If one should smile, look around to find out who he was really smiling at and keep going. A misdirected smile doesn't count. If the person persists in smiling at you and even says "hello," quickly cross to the other side of the street, but keep an eye on him because he is getting ready to mug you! All of this trip is, of course, an example of distorted perception combined with negative expectations. On your second trip walk along looking happy and smiling and greeting each passerby. Remember, everyone is as super and special as you are, and you are fantastic. You will discover what that young man in San Francisco overlooked. Smiles expect smiles and they get them. Think about your own behavior when you enter a new situation. Do you walk in with a smile, a greeting for each new person, and an introduction of "Hi, I'm _____!"? It is the people who do enter with this attitude who get a positive response in return. That is the reason one of the most universal characteristics of popular young people is friendliness.

Thus, it makes no difference whether individuals whose self-concept is negative are accurate in their self-assessment. Their belief makes it so. We humans are so clever at maintaining inner consistency that it is very difficult to change the core self-concept. It cannot be changed through logical thinking or cognition because its purpose is to maintain itself as it is, and it will distort the logic to make it congruent. It cannot even be changed by providing it with new perceptions since its self-reinforcement skill lets it influence our perceptions, through selection and distortion, to make them more congruent to it.

Development of the Self-Concept

To change the self-concept requires rebuilding it. It is a lengthy process as it will probably take longer than it took the self-concept to develop in the first place. It also must resemble the original building process. Thus, the revised self-concept must come from personal experiences, both social and individual. These experiences must either have an affective component *or* must be serial and repetitive. Much of the self-learning is the result of the process of social interaction, especially interaction with people who are significant or important to us. This process, which is both reflective and reflexive, is a feedback system. The individual acts; the other person reacts; that reaction is perceptually processed in the individual, who then reacts to her perception of the other's reaction, and so on. Data interpreted as "me" during the perceptual process is stored in the organizational system, or the self-concept. The amount of data stored pertaining to a trait or its affectiveness determines the degree to which it is adhered or believed, whether it is stored in the core of the self-concept or in the peripheral self. Incidents involving a significant other are more affectively charged and therefore need fewer repetitions to become part of the core. Some self-learning occurs by our being aware of other people's reactions to people so that our self is viewed more within its cultural context. Such learning takes place through an indirect process involving the comparison of one's self to others or to social norms and standards. Another major avenue for self-concept learnings is the individual himself. He can discover aspects of himself when alone, either through introspection or through experience.

All of these learnings are internalized and assimilated into the self-concept organizational structure. Some will be conscious while others will be stored in the unconscious. The core self-concept appears to be formed primarily during the individual's early childhood years. The individuals generally most important in its development are, in order of typical importance, (1) parents, (2) siblings or other family members living at home, (3) peers, and (4) other adults such as teachers.

Multidimensionality

The self-concept is multidimensional. It covers all of the constituents of the self, such as the physical self, the social self, the intellectual self, the emotional self, the loving self. Negativity in any one of these many areas can undermine the overall self-concept. However, the dimensions vary in their relative importance according to the situation and the individual's stage of development.

Body Image

One of the major constituents in the nonphenomenal as well as the phenomenal self is the body image (Fisher and Cleveland 1958), which includes our attitudes toward our bodies as social objects and toward their physical characteristics.

Currently, the somatic self—one's body image—is thought to be one of the earliest parts of the self-concept to develop. If that is the case, then body image may be the beginning, the foundation of the self-concept. Of course, appearance is such a significant part of the way others see us that its impact would be powerful regardless. In fact, there is considerable evidence to support the contention that a negative body image can undermine the general self-concept, especially of a woman (Fisher, 1973), just as a positive body image can enhance it (Secord and Jourard 1953; Jourard and Secord 1955).

DEVELOPMENT OF THE BODY IMAGE. There are at least three major avenues for the development of the body image: direct feedback, secondary feedback, and self-comparison to aesthetic norms.

Secondary feedback, which seems to be the most significant in modern American culture, is social reactions to the individual based on a physical body characteristic(s) but not attributed to it. For example, unattractive children have been found to be more severely punished than attractive children (Berkowitz and Frodi 1979). The major characteristics involved in secondary feedback are skin color, primary and secondary sex differences, and beauty according to the society's aesthetic ideal. Of all our physical characteristics, these have the most impact on our development. In our society, for example, the aesthetic ideal has been the Caucasoid. People from different racial heritages are viewed as more deviant from that ideal. They have even judged themselves according to this ideal. Their adoption of an aesthetic ideal that is unrealistic and unattainable for them may be one factor to explain why research has consistently found that American blacks tend to have more negative self-concepts than American whites. However, this tendency may be changing since, among col-

Figure 11.2 Their dress shows that these South American Indians do not judge their bodies like modern North Americans do. (National Anthropological Archives, Smithsonian Institution)

lege women in one of the more recent studies, blacks were found to have a higher self-esteem than whites (Ford and Drake 1982).

Sex differences in self-concept are somewhat more complicated. While the female has been viewed more negatively from the standpoint of cognitive, social, and person functioning, the male has been viewed more negatively as a physical body. Of course, his body's functioning is not a negative; he is deemed physically stronger and more capable. It is his body's aesthetic beauty that is his drawback. The naked male body is not celebrated by our culture as a whole. Instead it is viewed with a distaste akin to repugnance. The male's form is fine except for one tiny flaw, his penis and scrotum. These we insist he cover. Our insistence is so strong that many girls and some women to whom a man has unexpectedly and inappropriately "exposed" himself are traumatized by the experience in a way not imaginable if the exhibitor was a woman exposing herself to a male. Who would scream and avert his eyes to a female revealing her body? Even our art work has traditionally reflected this difference, and the nude male is either in a pose that effectively hides the offending part of his anatomy or is "wearing" a fig leaf to protect the viewer from so unaesthetic an experience. Thus, it should not be surprising that American men tend to be more modest and less comfortable with their own bodies than women are. Men's bodies, however, appear to be less important to their overall self-concept than a woman's is. This may reflect the fact that "a woman's body [has been] somewhat more important to her attainment of acceptance and security than a man's body [has been] to a man. Men in our culture may have [had] more avenues of attaining security through [other] traits of self" (Jourard and Secord 1955, p. 136). We should not be surprised, therefore, that females have consistently been found to have more negative self-concepts than males.

Sheldon hypothesized that body type, or somatotype, is "a primary determinant of behavior" (Hall and Lindzey 1967, p. 344). It is the biological or genetic factor. He proposed that there is a continuum of at least eighty-eight body types, arranged along a triangle with a distinct type at each angle. These three distinct somatotypes are (1) the ectomorph, who is linear, fragile, thin, and lightly muscled and has a large brain; (2) the mesomorph, who is hard and rectangular with a muscular build and sturdy bones; and (3) the endomorph, who is soft and spherical with underdeveloped bone and muscle. He also suggested that there are three temperament components: (1) the viscerotonia, (2) the somatotonia, and (3) the cerebrotonia. The viscerotonia involves such traits as tolerance, sociability, placidness, slow reactions, and a love for comfort, food, and people. The somatotonia includes such traits as aggressiveness, insensitivity to others, loudness, braveness, physical activity, and daring. The cerebrotonia involves such traits as inhibition, restraint, secretiveness, self-consciousness, and introversion (pp. 357, 359). Sheldon's research findings with adults indicated that somatotype was related to temperament in the following ways: (1) the endomorph was high in viscerotonia; (2) the mesomorph was high in somatotonia; and (3) the ectomorph was high in cerebrotonia (p. 360).

Studies of American children have found differences in the self-concepts of children with different somatotypes (Felker 1974, p. 16). However, these differences in temperament do not appear to be an inherent part of the somatotype. Rather they seem related to the individual's perception of society's expectations of him or her, the same expectations that can give, for example, the obese child a more negative self-concept. In cultures with different aesthetic ideals, different self-concepts would be associated with the somatotypes. For example, in a culture with a fat ideal, it would probably be the skinny ectomorph who has more negative body image and self-concept. Thus, somatotype appears to be a trait that influences body image and self-concept in much the same way that race and sex do.

The second avenue for the development of body image is the direct feedback (verbal and nonverbal) from others that pertains to the individual's physical appearance. For example, children learn that there are certain parts of their bodies or specific bodily functions that should neither be discussed nor touched in public. These are then associated with a sense of shame, which often continues throughout the individual's life. Thus, many women fail to examine their breasts each month and do not know enough about their vaginal region to detect any changes in it. Since both of these omissions are life threatening, why do the women fail to perform them? They fail because they would experience extreme psychological discomfort at touching or exploring these shame-associated body areas. Children who are teased about some part of their body or its functioning tend to be dissatisfied with their body (Berscheid, Walster, and Bohrnstedt 1973). Such teasing is especially prevalent during puberty as the body develops secondary sex characteristics. During this period young adolescents tend to have increasingly more negative and less stable self-concepts (Simmons et al. 1979).

Self-comparison of one's body to one's culture's aesthetic ideal, which is generally congruent with one's own ideal, is the third major avenue for body-image development. That modern American culture places a great deal of emphasis on physical appearance "is obvious in terms of the widespread expenditure of time and effort that is given to altering the body's appearance" (Fisher and Cleveland 1958, p. 23). We are wise to make these efforts since there is abundant evidence that attractive people are judged more positively and therefore treated more positively. They also develop more effective social skills, are physically healthier, and live longer. We even call the people who have achieved great success (wealth) the Beautiful People. We expect individuals, especially women, to make themselves as attractive, according to our aesthetic ideal, as possible. Our mass media are filled with helpful hints at such self-enhancement. In our culture the media bombard us daily with the aesthetic ideal for the female body. This ideal includes the following (italics indicate traits that are either impossible for people to attain if nature hasn't endowed them with those attributes or impossible to maintain): (1) **Thin** with no fatty deposits; (2) **Firm** torso, legs, arms, buttocks, underchin, and neck; (3) *long neck and legs;* (4) long fingernails; (5) *large, erect breasts;* (6) *thick,* wavy hair; (7) perfectly straight, *white teeth with no obvious spaces between them;* (8) *perfect skin without wrinkles, pimples, scars, stretch marks, or even pores;* (9) *skin that is taut and does not sag;* (10) rosy cheeks; (11) arched eyebrows that end above the ends of the eyes; and (12) no visible body hair. Half of our list is impossible for most women to attain and impossible for any woman to maintain. This ideal induces insecurity by making "it virtually impossible for any contemporary woman, no matter how psychologically secure she may be, not to have a wide-ranging and deep-ranging horror of several of her own physical attributes" (Ellis 1962, p. 16). She tends to feel that she is too heavy, especially at her hips, waist, and/or thighs, and that her breasts are too small. In a 1983 survey of *Glamour* readers, 75 percent reported that they were too heavy even though only 25 percent were actually overweight, and most were "measurably underweight" (Maeder 1984). What is particularly disturbing about this apparent sense of body dissatisfaction is that there appears to be a relationship between body satisfaction and self-esteem (Burger 1976, Snyder 1975) so that theoretically we could safely predict that women who feel dissatisfied with their bodies will have a lower sense of self-esteem.

Another aspect of body image, aside from physical appearance, is physical functioning or competency. Research suggests that when the individual has a physical handicap, he or she tends to have a more negative self-concept (Krider 1959). This appears to be more pronounced for female adolescents having a highly visible handicap (Meissner et al. 1967), which suggests that appearance also continues to be a factor for females and, in fact, may be the more important one (Feather et al. 1979). Again, the actual appearance is not the issue; it is the individual's perceptions of his or her appearance and of how others view it that is important. Therefore, individuals living in a community that does not react negatively to them on the basis of their handicap would not be expected to view their handicap as such a negative. But in most communities dress that reduces the visibility of a handicap would probably help the individual to develop and maintain a nonhandicapped self-concept. That may be why handicapped children have been found to be more aware of clothes than the nonhandicapped (Cannon 1969).

However, when the handicap impedes the individual's ability to function, then it may be a factor in his or her development of a sense of competency and self-esteem. Dress that promotes competency in dressing one's self would therefore be an asset to the physically handicapped individual's development. Center-front openings, velcro fasteners, and trouser legs with a two-way separating zipper in the side seams are examples of the assets that could help in this regard. As much as possible, this clothing should fit in with that worn by the individual's peers. Buying a garment and adapting it in ways that minimize the differences would be best from a developmental point of view. For example, velcro can be used for the opening of a button-down dress or blouse, but the original buttons should be sewn over the button holes so that the outward appearance remains the same (Hoffman 1979). As with any child, the handicapped child's involvement in selecting her clothing appears to enhance her sense of competency and independence and thus her self-concept.

BODY BOUNDARY. Fisher (1973) has proposed that there is a relationship between a sense of body boundary, an aspect of body image, and body security. This sense of body boundary is a nonphenomenal part of the self-image, except in those instances when the boundary is threatened by something that disturbs its functioning, such as may occur in schizophrenia or certain perceptual disturbances. The latter include temporary disorders resulting from sensory deprivation. It appears that the average American

> learns, in the course of growing up, to have a certain amount of trust in the protective power of the flesh that girds the periphery of his body. What we have found is that some people clearly visualize their bodies as possessing a boundary, or border, that separates them from what is out there and is capable of withstanding alien things that might try to intrude upon them. But there are others who have trouble perceiving their bodies as separate or possessed of a defensible border. They feel open and vulnerable (ibid., pp. 20–21)

An uncertain body border, thus, leads to insecurity.

American women appear to have more definite body boundaries than American men. Again, this may reflect the exceptional emphasis that our culture has placed on the female's body. It may also reflect women's greater awareness of their body feelings and their more positive acceptance of them (Fisher 1972).

Most of the research on body boundaries has investigated the phenomenon in Western culture. However, Postal (Ogibenin 1971) looked at the issue in two American Indian tribes, the southwestern Hopi and the northwestern Kwa-kiutl. The Kwakiutl seem to lack the feeling of having a secure body boundary. Dress is one of the various techniques members of the tribe employ to reaffirm their border and thereby gain protection from external threats. Taking off or getting rid of clothing is seen as a removal of part of one's identity, whereas putting on clothing bestows a new identity. The Hopi, on the other hand, appear to have a strong sense of border security. It is their own internal abilities that provide them with safety or security, not their clothing.

Dress has been used by some modern Americans to reaffirm their body borders. For example, Compton (1964) found that psychotic, institutionalized women who lack a feeling of a secure body border prefer "bright, more highly saturated colors, and stronger figure-ground contrasts in selecting clothing fabrics" (pp. 42–43). This suggests "that subjects with weak body boundaries tend to define or reinforce them through their clothing fabric choices" (p.44).

Applications to Dress

Clothes are tools that can be used by individuals to express or to conceal and/or enhance their self-concept. Of course, we will reveal our assets and conceal our debits. Thus, the more positively we perceive ourselves, the more we will use dress to reveal this wonderful "me" and vice versa. Dress can boost our confi-

Figure 11.3 This King of Waveri could have been the African chief who told Esther Warner that he wanted a hat; the pill-box hat he had was only a roof for his head. When she offered him her pith helmet, he refused it, saying that her hat was a turtle hat which would make him feel as though he crawled on the ground—such a hat made him feel low. He wanted a high silk hat which would make him "tree-tall;" in such a tall hat he was as tall as a tree and felt enlarged. (Warner, E. S. *Art: an Everyday Experience.* New York: Harper & Row, 1963, pp. 22–23) (Library of Congress)

dence and thereby temporarily enhance our self-esteem. Clothes become valuable when they have a positive effect upon us. Thus, the subjective worth of an article of dress

> is proportionate to its contribution to some sort of extension or differentiation or enrichment of the self. The self with that piece of clothing must become a better self than it is without; otherwise the item either makes no vital difference or fails to fulfill its function (Hartmann 1949, p. 296)

For example, Gibbins (1969) found that affinity for a particular outfit related to the degree of similarity between the impression the outfit gave and the individual's ideal self. Dress that assists us in more closely approximating our ideal self is preferred. That is the reason behind the need for mirrors in dressing rooms. Both men and women generally try on several dress items before they select the one they feel makes them look the best. We know they are not choosing primarily for comfort or for utility since they need a mirror to do their selecting. The mirror would be unnecessary for determining comfort or utility.

We would expect the individual with a positive self-concept to be more conscious in choosing dress for self-expression, whereas the individual with a negative self-concept would use dress in ways to prevent self-revelation. Many of the latter's concealments and/or false revelations would be unconscious attempts to increase behavioral congruence with the ideal self. As Bergler

Figure 11.4 In 1914, this woman's dress was experimental and attention-getting even for a costume ball. This suggests that she had a positive self-concept. (Library of Congress)

(1953) noted, in this case the individual must convince himself as well as the environment that he is more okay than he truly believes he is. For example, Guthrie (1976) noted that silvered sunglasses or dark-lensed glasses serve as shades to hide the eyes. They prevent us from understanding the wearer, whose eyes may reveal what his words conceal. Research findings support the association of self-revelation with two aspects of self-concept: self-esteem and body satisfaction (Ford and Drake 1982).

Individuals with high self-esteem and a positive self-concept are less judgmental, less dogmatic, and more receptive to the new and the different. Thus, we would expect them to be innovative and less conforming in their dress. Evidence from research tends to support these hypothetical relationships (Pasnak and Ayres 1969). We would expect the individual with a positive self-concept or positive self-esteem to be more experimental and spontaneous in her use of dress and more willing for it to call attention to her than the individual with a negative self-concept, who would be more cautious and conservative in her dress. This too has been supported by research findings (Drake and Ford 1979, Ford and Drake 1982, Humphrey et al. 1971, Reeder and Drake, 1980).

Sontag and Schlater (1982) hypothesized that clothing would be an important factor in an individual's judgment of the quality of her life if she related her clothing to her feelings about herself. They investigated the question of whether individuals actually perceive their clothing to be close to or remote from their phenomenal self. Their findings suggest, among other things, that (1) "clothing is one aspect of the self as an organized picture existing in awareness with both positive and negative values attached to it" (p. 4); (2) clothing is one aspect of appearance used both to establish and validate the self and to express it, or express parts of it, or mask it; (3) "clothing facilitates role-taking. . . ." (p. 4); (4) clothing affects feelings that may influence behavior to be more congruent with those feelings; (5) "clothing may compensate for body dissatisfaction; or body satisfactions or dissatisfactions may be translated to clothing and affect self-esteem" (p. 4); (6) "the nature of the link between clothing and self varies with sex and may be related to social roles and norms" (p. 5); and (7) the degree and kind of closeness of clothing to the phenomenal self varies from individual to individual. One of the questions this last finding raises is whether these individual differences reflect the degree to which the individual's body image is nonphenomenal or phenomenal.

How much we identify an individual with his or her dress can perhaps be effectively demonstrated by asking you to picture: (1) John F. Kennedy, (2) Michael Jackson, and (3) Dolly Parton. Now remove these images and picture: (1) John F. Kennedy bald and with pierced ears; (2) Michael Jackson with a crewcut and a three-piece suit (no glove); and (3) Dolly Parton with a flat chest, two gold front teeth, and long, straight, brown hair. Could the new Kennedy have the same charisma? Could the new Michael receive the same adulation from his fans? Could the new Dolly have fit her roles in *Nine to Five* or *The Best Little Whorehouse in Texas?*

MOTIVATION

One important aspect of individual development is motivation. There have been many theories proposed to explain why individuals act as they do. One is Abraham Maslow's (1962) theory of individual development, which is unique because it is based upon the study of healthy, fully functioning people. Maslow suggested that the environment's role in an individual's development is ideally to foster self-actualization of his potentialities.It does not *teach* him or *mold* him into its image of what he should be but allows him to become as fully as possible that which he is by nature. It must also provide the individual with controls, limits, and discipline so that he will be capable of responsibly actualizing himself. This actualization of the self, Maslow hypothesized, is the primary motivation for the individual's behavior.

Hierarchy of Needs

To achieve self-actualization, the individual seeks—is motivated—to meet certain needs. Maslow arranged these needs in a hierarchy showing how each level is prepotent over the next. For example, the base level is the basic physiological needs. These must be adequately met in order for the individual to be motivated to attempt to meet the next highest need for security and safety.

The first four needs Maslow called becoming, or deficiency, needs because he believed they represented deficits that have to be met by other people before the individual is able to reach self-actualization. When he is self-actualized, his inner nature can be fully expressed and personally accepted, and he will be able to "fully function" so that his human potential and capacities can be used. He will be able to be more inner-directed, whereas when he was working on his becoming needs, he was forced to be more outer-directed since he was dependent on other people for meeting his needs. This inner-directedness inherently involves an element of resistance to his culture. Thus, the individual becomes more species or human in orientation than nationalistic or tribal (p. 11).

Maslow did not believe that every individual meets these needs in exactly the same order, although most meet them in this order. For example, an individual might meet her love and belonging needs before her safety and security. Clearly, however, the basic physiological needs, survival needs, must be met if the individual is going to have sufficient energy to try to meet any of the other ones. Unfortunately, for many of the peoples of the world these physiological needs are so difficult to meet sufficiently that people are primarily involved with them (Cantril 1963). In modern American society most individuals have these needs sufficiently met during their infancy. However, a need can cease being adequately met so that the individual will once again direct her energies to meeting it. For example, when an individual becomes very ill, her physiological needs are often inadequately met (for example, severe illness can create a state of malnourishment). In such a condition the individual focuses on

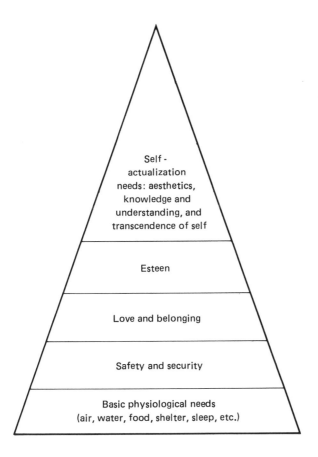

Self-
actualization
needs: aesthetics,
knowledge and
understanding, and
transcendence of self

Esteen

Love and belonging

Safety and security

Basic physiological needs
(air, water, food, shelter, sleep, etc.)

her basic needs. Clothing that protects us from external physical dangers assists us in meeting our basic physiological needs.

Security and safety needs involve both psychological and physiological security and safety. These needs are met by providing the individual with a stable and orderly environment. In our society most people have these needs met by the time they are about three. Being dressed and groomed at specific times in predictable ways helps to meet these needs.

The love and belonging needs are generally met within the family. We use dress that fits in with the norms of the group, first family and then peer, to enhance our sense of belonging. Dress also can provide us with this sense for most of our social identities.

The esteem need—developing a feeling that we have value or worth and are respected by others—is the need that Maslow believed most people in our society are trying to fill. Why is the meeting of this need so difficult for the individual in America? It may be an inherent condition of a competitive society that values *the* winner and dismisses all of the losers. It seems sadly amusing to hear and read American commentary on sporting events because implicit, if not explicit, in it is the belief that "there can be only one winner." This aura of winning and losing is not limited to sports. The first thing most students say to a friend and classmate from the previous semester or quarter is, "What did you get?" No one asks, "What did you learn?" or "Did you try out any of the ideas from the course?" Ultimately, the course comes down to a grade because that grade presumably tells you whether you are a winner or a loser. Of course, that is not what the grade means since it is merely one person's evaluation of specific performances on tests and/or projects. But to most students that grade is an indictment or a validation of their intellectual capability. Anything less than an *A*, therefore, implicitly carries the message that the student is a loser. Unfortunately, few of us get straight *A*s or play on winning Super Bowl teams or receive a steady stream of feedback that tells us we are winners and so have worth and value. *Yet that is precisely what we are!* Thus, our particular form of social stress on competition and winning prevents most of us from realizing how terrific we really are. It has been suggested that only 15 percent of the American population are able to meet their esteem needs sufficiently to become self-actualized (which is, however, better than most, if not all, other major societies). Dress that gives us recognition as being in some way "better" or as having higher status can help us to meet our need for esteem.

After the becoming needs have been sufficiently met, the individual is believed to be self-actualized.[1] He is able to begin to meet the three needs associated with self-actualization: (1) transcendence of the self, (2) knowledge and understanding, and (3) aesthetics. Transcendence of the self means the ability to enlarge one's self and put aside one's selfish concerns, to be able to forget one's self and be, for example, problem centered, spontaneous, absorbed. For the self-actualized person, perceptions will be more accurate because he will be able to see other people or things without judging or interfering with them. He will be able to understand something or someone without having to try to connect it or them to himself. Some of the other characteristics Maslow believed were present in self-actualized individuals are (1) more accurate perceptions; (2) greater openness; (3) increased spontaneity, expressiveness, objectivity, and creativity; and (4) more thorough sense of self (p. 148).

The individual is inherently motivated to try to travel up her hierarchy of needs and achieve self-actualization. Therefore, her specific behaviors, such as dress, are more easily understood if we frame them within the context of the needs hierarchy. For example, it has been found that adolescent girls with low self-esteem try to use their clothing as a way of gaining social acceptance. Further, as their freedom to dress as they choose increases, they tend to use their clothing as a way of gaining recognition, which is another effort at meeting esteem needs (Lutwiniak 1972).

---

[1]Self-actualization has been repeatedly experienced by this time since the individual is self-actualized for brief periods, called **peak experiences,** whenever his or her becoming needs have been fulfilled.

Application to Dress

When an individual's esteem needs have not been met, he would be less self-accepting and therefore could be expected to try to be less self-revealing. This, then, would be the individual who uses dress to camouflage or mask his self or the individual who uses dress for self-enhancement. Both of these responses are examples of using defense mechanisms. A defense mechanism is a response to anxiety produced by a situation the individual perceives to be threatening. It is a temporary response allowing the individual to reduce the anxiety and thus to cope more effectively until he is able to deal with or solve the problem. It is healthy as long as it does not prevent the individual from being aware of his purpose and of the deficit it represents or from ultimately attempting to deal with the problem rather than just cope with it.

Research has found that self-actualized individuals tend to exhibit less personal clothing interest (Aiken 1963; Perry et al. 1983), although they continue to be aware of, and interested in, the clothing of others (Perry et al. 1983).

Developmental Needs and Age Groups

As we discussed in Chapter 5, different age roles are associated with differences in dress. Some of these dress differences are also related to the developmental needs associated with the different age groups.

CHILDHOOD.   For example, infancy is the period during which the average American child is meeting her basic physiological needs. Dress can help to meet those needs by keeping the infant warm and dry. The toddler can enhance her safety and security needs through dress that allows her to develop competency or mastery and a sense of importance. Short garments that cannot be tripped over or bare feet, which help her in her efforts to walk, will also facilitate this. Dress that promotes her sense of mastery by enabling her to dress herself will foster a more positive self-concept and a greater capacity to love. Therefore, front openings, easy fastenings, marking the fronts of garments, and marking a right or left shoe to help her put her shoes on the correct feet would all be assets toward more positive self-development. It is difficult for the very young child to feel important but such a feeling is a factor in his meeting his love needs. Involving him in the selection of his dress will assist him in developing feelings of both competency and value because his opinion will count and be important. If the choices are wild or exotic he may be dressing to get attention (Barr 1934) which he needs to help him feel more important. Dress that will help him in his exploration and discovery of the world would also be a bonus to his self-development. Various textures, colors, and sartorial adornments will assist him in this as will pockets and dress for playing "dress-up." Since dress is one of the clues the child uses in identifying and learning about roles, and since he acts out his understandings of these roles in play—role playing—dress associated with various roles can facilitate this important play. There are two types of roles involved in this play.

> First, there is a genuine *anticipatory socialization* in which the child acts out roles that might quite realistically be expected to be adopted or encountered in later life, such as parental roles, common occupations, or customer. Second, there is a process of *fantastic socialization* in which the child acts out roles that can seldom, if ever, be expected to be adopted or encountered in later life—cowboy and Indian, for example. (Stone 1962, p. 109)

Boys tend to play out more *fantastic* roles, while girls are more involved with the *anticipatory* ones. This may reflect differences in the activity levels we expect of females and of males, although Stone suggested it reflects the difference in the importance and frequency of contacts with men and women. The boy, he contended, is forced to reside in a female-dominant world and remains fairly unexposed to many of the male-associated roles or to any of them in depth. Thus he can choose to role play roles he knows are identified with females, or he can select fantasy roles associated with a male. By age five children have already developed a body image, which usually has some negative elements, particularly for any parts of their body that are different or are "bad" (those that the child has been told not to show or touch, for instance). The child, just as the adult, may select clothes that hide or minimize these perceived defects.

In middle childhood most children are working on their love and belonging needs and esteem needs. They will still benefit from being involved in selecting their daily clothing as well as in its purchase. A tendency to select a style that is too grown-up may give a child a sense of competence he associates with older individuals who serve as a reference group. Since children have relatively little power, and therefore value, in our society while adults are identified with power and worth, many children identify with adults or "bigger" children. By copying their dress, a child may feel he is also assuming some of their power and esteem. During middle childhood children tend to define physical attractiveness on the basis of dress, including hair, with particular emphasis on its quantity. "The emphasis on the *envelope of the body* is so overwhelming one has the impression that children consider beauty something one puts on and takes off with clothes and cosmetics, and not an *inherently intrinsic part* of the body" (Spiegel 1950). In this case the child is somewhat more insightful than the adult, since the child recognizes that beauty is not some absolute "inherently intrinsic" quality but is associated with clothes that help all of us in our attempts to meet our culture's own unique ideal of beauty. But this recognition increases the importance of dress to him. The typical child is desperate to have dress that fits in with that of his peers since this is the only way that he believes he can become attractive. To force him to wear something he has rejected may be, for the child, the equivalent of moving one of his eyes to the center of his forehead or making an adult male wear a woman's hat.

ADOLESCENCE. The teenager's self-concept undergoes a change as his or her body sexually matures. As the body changes, the teen tends to be more narcissistic and egocentric and less satisfied with his or her appearance. These relate to feelings of self-dissatisfaction, especially body dissatisfaction. In one study two-thirds of the teenage girls expressed such dissatisfaction (Williams and Eicher 1966). Adolescent boys also have been found to be increasingly interested in their appearance and dissatisfied with it (Kitamura 1954). These findings may reflect the fact that the teenager's body is becoming sexually mature so that it is now, for the first time, comparable to the aesthetic ideal. To most teens their body seems woefully inadequate. Of course, these feelings are reinforced by the turbulent emotions brought on by the teen's struggle to develop heterosexual relationships. At the same time he is attempting to assert his independence from his family. He uses his peer group as support in this struggle, and the group becomes the primary source for new models. His dress becomes one of the ways to increase the support he receives from his peers (Creekmore 1980; Kelley and Eicher 1970; Williams and Eicher 1966) and to more fully participate in their activities (Creekmore 1980; Drake and Ford 1979; Kelley et al. 1974; Vener and Hoffer 1965). This psychological weaning of the child from the parents is a major (and healthy) task of adolescence. It paves the way for her ultimate physical departure from the home. Yet this task is full of danger, the danger that it will create so much conflict that the parent-child relationship is intrinsically damaged rather than inexorably changed. Dress is a safer way to demonstrate the teen's independence since it is primarily, if the parent allows it to be, a method of passive resistance. By avoiding a direct confrontation or power struggle, the potential for either the parent or the child to become more defensive, and therefore more rigid, is reduced. We would expect most teens to be involved with their esteem needs so that they would frequently use dress as a way to gain recognition as well as assert their belonging. This appears to be supported by research findings (Evans 1964; Hambleton et al. 1972; Humphrey et al. 1971) as well as by the popularity among teens of status-related dress, such as the status jeans of the early 1980s. If a teen's family is his primary reference group, he will probably dress to please his parents. If his peers are his primary reference group, he will probably dress to please them. Research findings support the accuracy of these expectations (Evans 1964; Williams and Eicher 1966). The teenager uses dress as part of teenage role playing. Of course, this is not considered play, but it is a kind of acting. The teen tries out different roles to see how others react to them. Dress facilitates this role acting. For example, it would be difficult to try the role of femme fatale in sneakers, jeans, and baggy shirt (the baggy shirt is used to decrease the appearance of the blossoming breasts either because they aren't blossoming enough or because they've "overbloomed"). This role is more easily assumed by borrowing a mature dress from Mom or an older sister or friend. Profuse make-up, high heels, and dangling earrings complete the teen's concept of a sophisticate who can strikingly attract oodles of ogles. One of the roles adolescents may be trying out is the role of leader. There is evidence suggesting that success in assuming a leadership role is related to clothing awareness and attractiveness (Creekmore 1980; Morganosky and Creekmore 1981).

ADULTHOOD. The adult's needs may not be so different from the adolescent's if Maslow correctly hypothesized that only a small number of American adults fulfill their esteem needs enough to move into the "being" needs. However, the tasks associated with the different life stages of adulthood could be expected to produce differences in the use of clothing. For example, the young adult is generally concerned with establishing both a career and a family, while the aged adult has usually ended his career, his family has often decreased through death and geographic mobility, and he is concerned with an aging body and his own impending death. We would hypothesize, therefore, that the young adult would be interested in clothing that represents competency and success and is attractive to the opposite sex. She would want to fit in but to do so in a manner that would be slightly better so that she would be noticed in a positive way. The elderly adult, on the other hand, would be more interested in clothing that deemphasizes the appearance of aging; protects her body from deterioration by, for instance, temperature control; is easy to don; and is comfortable. The mature, self-actualized adult would be most apt to have a unique clothing style that expresses himself. Since he would have less need to focus his attention and energy on himself, his clothing would not be used for recognition or status. He would be more innovative or creative in his dress although he has been found to be less interested in fashion (Perry 1983). The self-actualized adult has also been found to be a more socially conscious consumer (Brooker 1976). He will not knowingly make purchases that could contribute, for example, to the extinction of an animal species or the lack for future generations of some other resource. His clothing purchases will be economical and ecologically sound.

SUMMARY

The self-concept is the individual's mental system of organizing his perceptions and concepts about himself, his attitudes toward, and appraisals of, himself, and those beliefs, feelings, and ideas he has that are related to himself. The core of the self-concept is stable and acts to maintain the individual's inner consistency and unity. The peripheral self is primarily conscious and easily subject to change. It is the part of the self that identifies the individual as a social being. Self-concepts fall on a continuum from positive to negative. How positive the self-concept is will determine the degree to which an individual, among other things, expects to succeed, is open to new experiences, and is motivated to try difficult things.

The self-concept is learned from personal experiences that either were serial and repetitive or had an affective component. Much of the learning is from social interaction, particularly interaction with significant others; however, some of it takes place in solitary experiences.

The self-concept is multidimensional and negativity in any one dimension can undermine the overall self-concept if that area is of great significance to the individual. Body image is one dimension and may be one of the earliest developed. There are three major avenues for its development: (1) direct feedback, (2) secondary feedback, and (3) self-comparison to aesthetic norms. Body image has great significance to most modern Americans because our society emphasizes physical beauty. Unfortunately, we have an aesthetic ideal of the female body that is impossible for most women to attain and for any woman to maintain. Thus, we induce insecurity and a more negative body image.

Clothes are tools that can be used by the individual to express or to conceal and/or enhance his or her self-concept. Individuals with positive self-concepts tend to use their dress to reveal or express themselves. However, individuals with more negative self-concepts will use dress more for concealment or enhancement of their perceived deficits.

Maslow's theory of individual development is based on the assumption that the individual has certain needs, which, if met, will allow him to achieve his human potential and, further, that the individual is inherently motivated to attempt to meet those needs. The first four needs are deficit needs because they depend on having other people meet them. The higher needs are the self-actualized needs, which the individual can meet by himself. Individuals working on their deficit needs will be more outer-directed since they are attempting to get help from others, whereas the self-actualized individual will be more inner-directed. The deficit need that an individual is attempting to satisfy may be reflected in his dress since dress is a tool he can use in his attempt to meet his needs. Thus, since different age groups are generally working on specific needs, the dress associated with each group will also reflect the need associated with it. Dress is therefore a tool that assists the individual in meeting his developmental needs and in expressing or enhancing his self-concept.

12

Group Dynamics

In this chapter we will examine some aspects of group dynamics, specifically of how groups function in the dissemination of fashion. We will look at two methods of learning a culture—socialization and diffusion—and at fashion as a collective behavior. We will examine the concept of collective taste or aesthetics and look at some of the factors that influence it. We will look at large, impersonal groups, such as the American society, and small, intimate groups, such as the family. Most smaller groups tend to be homogeneous. As they encompass a larger number of people, this homogeneity is diminished. In the American society there exists an enormous variety of subcultures representing the diverse lifestyles and values of their members. Each of these smaller groups has a number of activities so that it is impossible for one citizen to participate in most of the society's activities. This complexity or heterogeneity and limited ability to participate has made it difficult for the individual to feel a sense of belonging to the large group. Many people feel alienated from our society or believe that they are unimportant to it. Thus, they begin to look to one or more of these smaller groups for cultural learnings.

CULTURAL LEARNINGS

Learning a culture, including data about its dress, occurs in two major ways. The first is socialization, or enculturation, which is the teaching of a culture to its members. The second is diffusion, which is the dissemination of cultural information from a culture that is not the individual's or is hers by adoption.

Socialization

The socialization process begins in the family whose task it is to teach its children about their culture. The parents are usually the primary agents for this process in a child's preschool years. When the child begins to attend school, the school reinforces and adds to her previous learnings. She is also socialized by her peer group, although that is not a true purpose of the peer group. Other groups to which she belongs, particularly when they are reference groups, also help to socialize her. The specific individuals who guide the child in this regard are called *significant others*. This title reflects the method by which socialization is taught: *identification*. When we identify with someone, we like her and want to be more like her. We will, therefore, imitate her. That is how we are socialized. The baby will identify with the parent who has become significant to him. This identification will motivate the baby, throughout his childhood, to continue to

Figure 12.1 Imitation of a parent. (British Columbian Provincial Archives)

imitate the parent. Thus, the parent socializes by being a model, and the child is socialized by imitating the model so that he will be more like the significant other. This is the process of socialization. It is the way we learn values congruent with our society's; socially acceptable behavior patterns, including dress; social norms; cultural customs and traditions; and roles and their associated behaviors.

The typical child has learned most of his values and attitudes by the time he is three to five. For example, by then he will have acquired any prejudices he has been exposed to, for instance, against specific ethnic groups. Boys will have learned to shun girls and activities associated with girls. By the time he is ten, the typical child will have learned and be able to successfully adapt his behavior to socially accepted norms and patterns of behavior.

Diffusion

Diffusion is the spreading of an element or a number of elements of one culture to a member or members of another. It involves three steps: introduction of the new element, acceptance of it, and its integration into the adapting culture (Linton 1964, p. 334). This has been

> a process by which mankind has been able to pool its inventive ability.... It has stimulated the growth of culture as a whole and at the same time has enriched the content of individual cultures.... It has helped to accelerate the evolution of culture as a whole by removing the necessity for every society to perfect every step in an inventive series for itself. (ibid., p. 324)

When an individual attempts to learn an entire other culture, the process is called acculturation. Complete acculturation is not possible because diffusion is basically adaptive rather than adoptive, since we cannot substitute a new behavior or attitude without filtering it through our own perceptual process. Thus, it is incorporated so that it is more congruent with our past experiences and beliefs. In the *Seven Pillars of Wisdom* (1938), T. E. Lawrence recognized his inability to acculturate himself to the Arab culture.

> In my case, the effort for these years to live in the dress of Arabs, and to imitate their mental foundation, quitted me of my English self, and let me look at the West and its conventions with new eyes: they destroyed it all for me. At the same time I could not sincerely take on the Arab skin: it was an affectation only. Easily was a man made an infidel, but hardly might he be converted to another faith. I had dropped one form and not taken on the other ... with a resultant feeling of intense loneliness in life, and a contempt, not for other men, but for all they do. (pp. 5–6)

Lawrence tried to give up his culture in its entirety, both the valued and the despised, and to assume another in its entirety. But it would have been as impossible for him to totally divest himself of his Englishness as it would have been for him to incorporate into himself complete Arabness.

Increasingly today we find cultures seeming to attempt such total acculturation, primarily to become like Western culture. We in the West too often assume that a Westernized culture is so completely like our own that we believe

Figure 12.2 T. E. Lawrence (Lawrence of Arabia). (Trustees of the Tate Gallery)

Figure 12.3 (a & b) (a) The American Indian began adapting Western dress as he came into contact with it as is evident in this 1913 photo of Winnebago Indians. (State Historical Society of Wisconsin) (b) In the same way, Western culture has also been influenced by Indian dress, as evidenced in the window display of "squaw" dresses and moccasins. (Library of Congress)

a

b

we should have a more perfect understanding of it. However, adaptation makes such an understanding impossible. Complicating this further is the other culture's impact on our own. Each culture not only alters any element it adapts but influences the parent culture.

The diffusion of Western culture throughout the world is due to the increased contact. Whenever there is cross-cultural contact, the potential for diffusion exists. The greater the contact, either greater by number of cultural representatives or by the amount of time for the contact, the more probable it is that diffusion will occur. The West has exported its technology to many other cultures. This exportation has usually involved visits by Western representatives to those cultures to assist them in setting up and effectively using the new technology. But perhaps even more significant has been the exportation of Western media such as magazines, movies, and television shows. These have been potentially more important because they demonstrate so much of the private lifestyle of the West. That these demonstrations are often inaccurate is unimportant to the process, although it is highly significant to the results.[1]

Linton (1963, 1964) has provided us with some principles of diffusion. These may also help to illuminate the predominant spread of Western culture.

Geographic proximity promotes diffusion. The Japanese, for example, were strongly influenced by the Chinese, the Koreans, and after 1868 the West. However, isolation, owing either to geography or rigid social stratification, will restrict or retard the probability of diffusion. Thus, efforts at increasing our cross-cultural contact with societies more alien to our own should help to reduce differences. Developments in transportation and communication[2] have made geographic isolation an unusual condition and have promoted the speed at which the diffusion process takes place (Linton 1964, p. 325). For example, the importation of Western media into many countries has provided a propinquity, even though the communication is often superficial. In the last two to three years, cable television has brought American culture to many of the geographically isolated islands in the Caribbean. These islands have been going through the first steps of the diffusion process, which are introduction of the element and its acceptance. But they have not yet integrated most of these elements. Thus, many of the citizens are experiencing a sense of culture shock from the apparent displacement of certain elements of their own culture.

Material objects such as dress are more quickly adapted than are nonmaterial ones such as values. A material object can be held and physically examined so that it is easier to understand than an abstract idea that cannot be seen and is often difficult even to describe. The American Indians generally adapted the white man's dress before any other cultural elements (Childers 1938), and this typifies common adaptation patterns. However, the Loyalty Islander who in the mid-nineteenth century wore a European hat and a dress

---

[1] It is because of these media depictions that so many of the world's people believe all Americans to be rich.

[2] Censorship helps to retain isolation.

Figure 12.4 (a & b)   (a) The Japanese adaptation of Western dress is shown in this Sadahide woodcut, *Gate Leading to Foreigner's House.* (The Art Institute of Chicago) (b) The Japanese kimono was one aspect of Japanese dress that was quickly adapted to Western fashion, such as in the case of this dress designed in the early 1900s for the Countess of Yarmouth. (Library of Congress)

a

b

Figure 12.5 This New Guinea woman has adapted some Western dress behavior, although it is clear that she does not understand its true Western purpose. (Magnum Photos, Inc.)

coat but no trousers (Howe 1977) was indicating that he had adapted the artifact without an awareness of the abstract purposes it had in Western culture. This is also a common pattern.

Elements that are functionally related to each other tend to be diffused as a group. Thus, we would expect dress items that related together, such as the trouser and the belt or suspender or the skirt and the blouse, to move together. All of us can cite examples where this was not the case, *but* that it is the normal pattern is exactly what makes those examples so memorable.

Adaptation is more probable for elements that are associated with high status or prestige. Thus, traits that are obviously superior or that come from a group considered superior are more likely to be adapted. This is exemplified in the dress of the South African Sotho boy upon his completion of puberty school. His pantaloons are an "Americanized" adaptation of the tribe's original animal-skin garment; his light blanket that is folded into pantaloons has been dyed a bright red with "ocher from America" and has been decorated with an American safety pin (Tyrrell 1968, p. 93). If the adapter dislikes or feels superior to another culture, he will be less apt to adapt, especially if he is forced to use techniques of passive resistance to show his hostility (Linton 1963). Thus, like the Masai of Kenya, he may continue to wear his native dress to assert the superiority of his own culture. However, if he is made to feel self-conscious, he may adapt. Since many of the American Indian tribes valued reticence as opposed to self-display, they were sensitive to the white man's attention toward such dress customs as women being bare-breasted. In these cases they would adapt a dress style to prevent them from being so noticeable, although they usually continued to wear some dress to proclaim their being an Indian. (Immigrants have often quickly adapted the dress of their new land in an effort to minimize their "alienness" and so reduce the potential for discriminatory reactions.) However, the American Indians' adaptation of white dress was, to some extent, orchestrated by colonial policy and later by national policy. By the early eighteenth century both the French and the British selected cloth and dress items as gifts for Indian emissaries to promote friendship and understanding (Viola 1981). This policy was continued by the American government, which continuously tried to get the Indians to adopt Western dress. For example, when the War of 1812 began, the government invited a delegation of Indians to Washington in the hopes that they would be favorably impressed so that they would not take the side of the English. Each delegate was presented with Western clothing, a blanket, a pipe, a sword, and a presidential medal of peace. The clothes, unless they were a military uniform, were often seldom worn after a delegate had returned home; but the peace medals and military uniform continued to be worn since they were "visible symbols of the owner's status and importance. Bits and pieces of the uniform might become lost or discarded— trousers especially were subject to attrition—but not the coats" (ibid., p. 120). Such a stress on clothing made the Indians more aware of and embarrassed by their "native" dress when they were in urban situations involving the national government (ibid.).

Figure 12.6 An Apache delegation to Washington in 1880 shows delegates in various degrees of Indian and Western dress. (Smithsonian Institution, National Anthropological Archives)

Figure 12.7 Jack Red Cloud, 1899, wearing his presidential medal of peace. (Library of Congress)

Adaptation is more likely to occur when the adapted elements are traits or objects that are compatible with the adapting culture. The dress of the Seminoles and the Florida Creek Indians reflected Highland rather than English dress because the kilt was more similar to their traditional skirted garb and because a short skirt was more suitable to their wet environment and their travel by canoe. Since well-established customs or habits decrease the possibility of diffusion, it was unlikely that they would have adopted trousers, which they associated with helplessness and effeminacy (Downs 1980). In fact, most of the men did not adopt trousers until the 1930s (Downs 1979).

Adaptation is more probable when a trait or object is useful. The Greenland Eskimos adapted Danish methods of clothing construction because they were so much easier than their own, but they retained their own traditional clothing styles (Krieger 1928). Ease of production was one of the reasons many American Indian tribes used the white man's calico shirt in place of their skin tunic. Trousers, however, were too physically restraining to be useful for many of the tribes and therefore were adopted much more slowly. In the early 1930s, Japanese women had become more active and were taller and bigger-busted. Thus, Western dress styles were more useful to them as well as more flattering than they had been earlier.

Inertia and/or a fear of change will restrict or retard diffusion, and adaptation is more likely to occur when a society is open to change. Thus, American society, where change is a value for most people, could be expected to show the evidence of much adaptation as the result of diffusion. In fact, the American culture has been one of the most adaptive. It is an amalgamation of elements of nearly all the cultures of the world, as the elements were presented by their immigrating representatives. Since the Native American was actually an immigrant from Asia, there really is no American element that has not been adapted from another culture.

Let us briefly apply these principles of diffusion to the spread of Western culture. The exportation of Western media and technology has provided a kind of propinquity that essentially replicates the conditions of geographic proximity that favor diffusion, and combined with exportation of Western material goods, from Coca Cola to steel, it has presented a picture of economic prosperity and technological superiority for the West. Thus, the importing cultures are more likely to adapt elements of Western culture since those elements often have status. Each adaptation of an element paves the way for further adaptations since other elements in the donor culture will be compatible with the already adapted element(s). Thus, diffusion is a process that is self-reinforcing so that adaptation makes further adaptation more likely.

FASHION: COLLECTIVE BEHAVIOR

Fashion is always a collective behavior since it means dress that has become aesthetically pleasing to most of the people in the society or culture. The individual's interpretation of fashion is an individual behavior; but fashion will determine the adequacy of that interpretation and whether it is to be rewarded by acceptance or punished by ridicule or rejection.

Fashion assists society in developing a common reality. It provides a means of reconciling the needs for freedom of individual expression and for social conformity by being a safe outlet for individuality and freedom, and concomitantly it creates an illusion of freedom and individuality. It helps a rapidly-changing society to maintain order through uniformity in much the same way that custom maintains order in a stable society (Blumer 1969). Yet it also promotes change and assists the individual in adjusting to change. For example, in the period following the French Revolution the aristocrats were forced to dress in styles like those worn by all the citizens. Dandyism helped them adjust by letting them "make up in cut and elegance what they had lost in visual splendor, and so helped acclimatize the *frac* [the new style] among them" (Mansel 1982, p. 12).

Massive changes in the collective taste "denote a change in the way people feel about themselves and the world about them" (Carter 1977, p. xiv). Thus, the victim-style dress of the punks in the late 1970s and early 1980s may have denoted their difficulty in finding the meaningful jobs they had believed were awaiting them. The young jobless individual was, therefore, forced to look to his leisure pursuits for his self-fulfillment (ibid.).

Certain factors promote fashion or even make it inevitable. They are somewhat similar to the factors that promote diffusion. Fashion is promoted by (1) openness to change; (2) abundance of economic and natural resources; (3) social mobility in an open class system; (4) greater distribution of economic resources throughout the population; (5) cross-cultural contact; (6) technological change; (7) social change, especially in roles; (8) increased leisure time; and (9) mass marketing, including advertising. Modern American society embraces all of these factors.

Fashion is restricted by (1) fear of change, (2) shortage of economic and/or natural resources, (3) a caste system or a rigid class structure limiting social mobility, (4) inequitable distribution of economic resources throughout the population, (5) isolation from cross-cultural contact, and (6) strong values for tradition and custom.

AESTHETICS: COLLECTIVE TASTE

Aesthetics is the group's ideal of what is beautiful in form and style; it is their collective taste. There is no absolute of beauty. There are only social standards of beauty, so that we think something is beautiful because our society or group has said that it is. This social relativity of aesthetics explains why, as research (Barr 1934) has shown, aesthetics is an important factor in dress and is related both to the desire to be attractive *and* to conform. The fashionable dress of one culture or era may be aesthetically displeasing to another.

Fashionable dress is, in one sense, never flattering to the natural human form since each unique body must wear the same style in order to be fashionable, and no one dress style can look equally attractive on the variety of bodies with which the human species is blessed. Yet the majority will adopt the fashionable style—that is what makes it fashionable—regardless of how flattering that style is to each individual. They adopt it in order to meet their need to belong. Since fashionable dress is the dress that is selected by most of the members of a group, it would seem that fashionable dress is a cultural universal, although the rate of fashion change may be extremely slow or the degree of change may be as minimal as the color or type of bead(s) worn.

There are some perceptual relationships with aesthetics that seem to be tentative generalizations. We humans tend to perceive more readily and to prefer those stimuli that contrast with the surrounding stimuli. Thus, for example, both the "primitive" and the "culturally advanced" individual are most apt to pick up a stone that is shinier than the surrounding stones or the color that is brighter than the surrounding colors. However, if all the stones were shiny or all the colors bright, both would be more apt to select the dullest stone or the least intense color. We prefer the unusual stimuli and, in fact, we tend to ignore those stimuli that are always present, that are the norm. Thus, we notice the rose while usually being unaware of the grass or trees around it. As individuals have more experiences with a greater variety of stimuli, they increase their perceptual ability to distinguish among the stimuli. Thus, young children and others with limited color exposure tend to prefer the red color class, are unable to perceive the complexity and variety of hues within that class, and prefer color combinations with considerable contrast. Everyone tends to prefer tactual stimuli that are cool, as opposed to hot, and smooth, as opposed to rough.

Ideal Beauty

The ideal for beauty is frequently quite different between cultures. Compare, for example, the ideal American female beauty as exemplified by most of the Miss America contestants with the ideal female beauty of some other cultures. For example, the ideal Rukuyenn woman of Guiana has a big abdomen; the Payaguan woman, long, hanging breasts. The Ainu woman of Japan tattoos her mouth into the ideal look, a facsimile of giant chapped lips. These beauties would consider our ideal as aesthetically displeasing as we find theirs. However, mass communication and other ways of increasing cross-culture contact have

Figure 12.8 (a & b) Ideal beauties from the same era but two different cultures. (Library of Congress)

a   b

Figure 12.9   An Ainu of Japan. (Smithsonian Institution, National Anthropological Archives)

accelerated the diffusion of the Western beauty ideal into more and more cultures. Even within one culture, the aesthetic ideal is not static. As fashions change, so does the ideal. Thus, what was once aesthetically pleasing may no longer be so, although it may become so once again in the future.

There is one Western fashion style that has been more recurrent as an aesthically pleasing style than any other. This is the classic Greek style based on their draped chiton. The chiton was one piece of uncut fabric that the wearer draped in a manner to be attractive and self-expressive and to suit the occasion. The style remained fashionable for centuries in Ancient Greece where it was believed to be the dress most congruent to the human form. It was quite versatile; easily individualized; and easy to produce, store, and care for.

Collective taste does not develop in a vacuum but within the context of a culture and an era. It is because of this contextual relationship that fashion seems to be able to reflect the general lifestyle, the values of a people, and the spirit or essence of their era and culture. Whether or not a specific fashion actually embodies this essence, it will reinforce the Zeitgeist by promoting more commonality of experience. Thus, various cultural elements have often had an impact on the aesthetics of dress. Architecture and interior design, art, literature, and special events have all influenced fashion. We will briefly discuss each of these elements, with some examples of their influence.

Architecture and Interior Design

Heard (1924) hypothesized that stylistic or aesthetic changes occur first in the public domain—in architecture, for instance—and then in the private—dress, for instance. Regardless of which comes first, there is a remarkable congruence between the aesthetics of dress, architecture, and interior furnishings. Imagine, as an example, an Art Deco home with its crisp, geometric lines. Both the furnishings and clothes required a similar geometric sharpness in order to blend in with the architecture. Rococo dress or early American furnishings would insert an element of visual discord; they would be irritating interruptions. Consistency was evident when the classic Greek dress style was revived in the Empire period, and it was associated with neoclassical architecture and interior designs such as the Adams mirror.

The most apparent relationship between architecture and fashion is in the roof type and the headgear of an era or a culture. For example, the Gothic henna is reflective of the era's architectural spires; the Roman helmet is a miniature version of the Roman dome; the Turkish turban complements the minaret; the American Indian's war bonnet relates to the teepee; the Siamese dancer's crown is a replica of the tower of the temple; and the stove-pipe hat corresponds to the smoke-stack skyline of the industrial city.

Ancient Egypt's architecture was closely related to all of its dress styles—both dress and architecture employed the triangle as the basic shape. The pyramid was the solid form used in architecture, and all of the dress fashion was inspired by the triangular, from hair style to costume. In ancient Greece hair and chiton fashions were both mirrors of the columns so prominent in the architecture.

Visual Art

Visual art has also been related to the aesthetics of fashion. It is, of course, an integral part of interior design, but it has had a broader influence. Before there were any public museums and before the days of mass communication, the sphere of influence of art was fairly small. Only the wealthy had access to works of art. Portraiture was one of the primary ways of preserving an era's fashions. Unfortunately, because visual art is an impressionistic and often romantic form, its representations are not always accurate as historical data.

With the development of mass-communication systems and the growth of the great museums, the visual arts have increased in influence. As an example, we will look briefly at two art movements as they related to the aesthetics of dress. Art nouveau was popular around the turn of the century. It was characterized by the use of curves, often with rococolike flourishes, and was supposed to be a return to the natural: the ocean's waves or a woman's long and flowing hair. Dress was fluid and emphasized the body's curves. Soft, unsaturated col-

Figure 12.10 A 1914 Poiret design.
(Library of Congress)

ors were the rule during the early development of art nouveau, but after the opening of the Russian Ballet in 1909, the vivid, saturated colors of Russian folk art took over. The fashion designs of Paul Poiret reflected the influence of art nouveau.

Art deco began in the early 1900s and was the dominating art force from the post–World War I period through the early 1930s. It continued the move toward simplicity of line that had occasionally glimmered through the art nouveau movement and was also evident in the early twentieth century in the Japanese influence on art, known as orientalism. Art deco used sharp, geometric shapes, with an emphasis on the linear rather than the curved line. It also employed pure, bold, saturated colors. Clothing was functional and provided more freedom of movement.

The influence on fashion of an artist or a work of art can easily continue for centuries. For example, our knowledge of Greek dress comes from Greek art works. It is these works that have repeatedly given fashion a classical flavor. Sonia Delaunay, a Russian-born artist and textile designer in the early twentieth century, was influenced by the cubism of Picasso and of her husband Robert Delaunay. She worked with bright colors in her bold geometric designs. Perry Ellis got the inspiration for his fall 1984 sweater collection from two of her paintings that he had hanging in his home (Landers 1984).

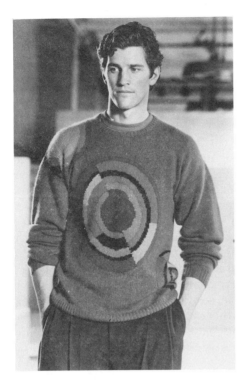

Figure 12.11 The art of Sonia Delaunay inspired this sweater by Perry Ellis. (Perry Ellis, Erica Lennard)

DANCE. Dance had a special influence on aesthetics during the early twentieth century, primarily because of the Russian costume designer, Léon Bakst, and Diaghilev's Ballets Russes. When Diaghilev brought his Russian Ballet to Paris to perform in 1909, the costumes designed by Bakst took Europe by storm. The 1910 performance of *Scheherezade* used the bright and sharply contrasting colors typical of Russian peasant folk art. The harem pants were an immediate novelty. Both of these had an almost immediately discernible impact on fashion. When Bakst stopped designing for the Ballets Russes in 1914, his influence on fashion actually diminished (Behling 1979).

The vacuum created by his absence was filled by another Russian, Erté, who designed for the stage, movies, ballet, and Paul Poiret. His designs were seen frequently in *Harper's Bazaar*. He continued to use the colors Bakst had popularized and, to a lesser extent, the Russian folk art designs introduced by Bakst. But Erté also made considerable use of details such as buttons, tabs, buckles, trains, high collars, handkerchief hemlines, and dropped waistlines (Behling and Dickey 1979).

During this same period the American dancer Isadora Duncan was providing innovation in dress as well as dance. She wore a sheer, filmy Grecian-style dance dress and danced in bare feet and legs. Although her styles were too extreme to be copied, their freedom may have helped to acclimate society to the freedom and excitement evident in the work of Bakst and Erté.

Literature and Theater

Literature has served as inspiration to designers and artists. When, for example, interest in classical literature has been high, dress has had a more classical style. This inspiration has been most evident in dramatic literature for the stage, movies, or television. Stage drama has had less influence than the latter two, perhaps because its audience has traditionally been smaller. However, the theater has given us such fashions as the Merry Widow hat from *The Merry Widow* and the poodle haircut from *South Pacific*.

Movies began as a form of mass entertainment that was economically available to most Americans. As the Lynds (1956) noted in 1929, people would go to the movies week after week, "often with an intensity of emotion that is apparently one of the most potent means of reconditioning habits" (p. 82) and were able to observe lifestyles and daily activities that were different from their own. In most cases this difference was made to seem "better." Thus, reasonable viewers would want to organize and structure their lives to resemble the "happy ending" lives of the movie's characters. Dress was often one of the only ways they could find to make a concrete change in that direction.

Changing methods of movie costuming have been a factor in the influence of movies on fashion. In the early years of movie production the cast selected their own clothes. In the 1930s the studios began to hire designers to produce more coordinated costume designs. The designers could market their

Figure 12.12 Fashions inspired by the movie *Little Women*. (Library of Congress)

Figure 12.13 Early 20th century fashions such as this inspired designs in the 1980s. (Library of Congress)

fashion designs just after a movie's opening. This led to an increase in the influence of movies on fashion.

Annie Hall, Urban Cowboy, and *Flashdance* are all examples of movies that have influenced dress styles. However, their influence was basically limited to one or two seasons and directly related to the popularity of the movie. The styles were more like fads than aesthetic changes. Occasionally, a movie can have a more lasting impact. For example, when in *It Happened One Night* Clark Gable removed his shirt to reveal his bare torso, undershirt sales plummeted and remained adversely affected for nearly a quarter of a century until Marlon Brando in *A Streetcar Named Desire* wore a t-shirt—underwear—as outerwear and set a new fashion (Benedict 1982, p. 91). Generally, however, it is when a series of popular movies or television productions have a congruent fashion theme that changes occur in the collective fashion taste. Thus, the movie *Chariots of Fire* and the television series *Brideshead Revisited* spawned a fashion style in the early 1980s for men and women that reflected English fashions from the 1890s through the 1930s. But television alone has also influenced fashions with the looks popularized in series such as *Miami Vice* and *Dynasty.*

Special Events

When King Tut's tomb was discovered in November 1922, the fashion designers had representatives rush to the tomb to provide them with accurate descriptions of the relics that were found. A two-year fashion trend followed, which was aptly called Tutmania. The long, straight mummy-wrap dresses and coats; the Egyptian hieroglyphics used in fabric and jewelry designs; the pale tan shoes and stockings (called Sahara) (Binder 1953); headbands; "the Lotus, the scarab, the sundish, the scroll designs, the wings of the vulture, and the uraeus (the sacred serpent)" used by designers in their creations (Forman 1978, p. 8) are all examples of the fashion influences of this discovery. Aesthetically, they were the final step in preparing the way for the flapper look. In the 1970s, relics from Tut's tomb were displayed in a major exhibit in various cities across the United States. Tutmania returned, although on a more limited basis, and hieroglyphic designs, Egyptian collars, and Egyptian hair styles enjoyed popularity.

Ever since television began to bring the Olympics to all of us, a sports-related fashion theme has evolved in the seasons just preceding the winter games to just following the summer games. In 1980 the cancellation of American participation in the summer Olympics left manufacturers with merchandise that could serve only as a reminder of the boycott rather than of the athletic competition. What was usually an economic windfall became an economic diseaster.

In the early years of rapid industrial development there was an explosion of technology. New products and processes were often presented to the public at world's fairs or expositions, which were also gazetteers of products from around the world. Such exposure made these fairs important events that influenced fashion by expanding fashion interest and desires. For example, a theme of the New York World's Fair in 1939 was "fashions for the future." Exhibits stressed "freedom of dress, adaptable clothing, figure idealism, and modern art." The international exhibits also "provided much inspiration and became interesting features of [American] fashion developments . . . in the early forties" (Hornback 1967, p. 29). More recent fairs have provided us with less new information and fewer ideas. Thus, they no longer have a significant effect on fashion.

Museum exhibits have also been sources of inspiration for fashion designs, particularly those exhibits organized by the Costume Institute of the Metropolitan Museum of Art.

GROUP DYNAMICS

It is through the processes of group dynamics and intragroup interaction that collective taste is communicated and demonstrated. Groups vary in size, in purpose, and in the degree and frequency of direct contact between members. But regardless of these differences, all groups are communication networks; the variables determine how the network is structured. The most important function of a group is the provision of its members with "*meanings* for situations which do not explain themselves" (Katz and Lazarsfeld 1964). The group defines "reality" for its members when it cannot be demonstrated by concrete facts. Thus, what is "real" is so because it is what most of the group believe to be real.

> This is the way that stereotypes develop; and it is one of the reasons why ideas about what is real in religion or in politics vary from group to group. So many things in the world are inaccessible to direct empirical observation that individuals must continually rely on each other for making sense out of things. (ibid., pp. 54–55)

It is the reason for collective taste and for differences in cultural ideals of beauty.

Small and more intimate groups, such as families, peers, and social clubs, are usually reference groups. They form interpersonal alliances of mutual attraction, which appear to be " '*anchorage' points for individual opinions, habits, and values*" (ibid. p. 44). They can inform, model and exert social control on their members' behavior.

To some extent this "anchor" phenomenon is a result of the socialization process. However, for the already socialized adult, socialization does not appear to be a sufficient explanation for this powerful role of "anchor." Illumination of this process might be enhanced by examining groups, especially group roles involved in the dissemination of ideas. We will limit our investigation just to the process of fashion dissemination and those roles involved in it.

Innovator

All groups have an innovator, although the role may not be active all of the time. The innovator is the first person to do something or suggest something. The innovator role can be filled by several group members, who may be innovative at different times, in different ways, or in different areas. In small-group fashion dissemination, the innovator is the first one to suggest such things as wearing some item, putting a costume together in a special way, or shopping at a specific store or in a certain way. In one group, for example, an innovative dresser in 1960 made earrings out of her husband's fishing lures, wore maternity blouses over her tight ski pants, bought her blouses from the boy's department, and combined a brightly colored embroidered Mexican skirt with a turn-of-the-century camisole as a blouse. In some cases, as it was with this one, the innovator is the only member to behave in this way. In other instances some or all of the group members may elect to imitate the innovator.

In large-group fashion dissemination, the innovator is usually a designer or, less often, a manufacturer, who serves as the group's interpreter and determines which of the variables that could influence the collective taste are most apt to do so. They look at past and current styles and at fashions of other cultures. But their most important sources appear to be a result of their

Figure 12.14 Baroness Von Winterhead designed her own clothing, such as this boudoir gown with crepe-de-chine trousers trimmed with swansdown, a brocade jumper, and a lace veil. (Library of Congress)

intimate familiarity with the most recent expressions of modernity . . . in such areas as the fine arts, recent literature, political debates and happenings, and discourse in the sophisticated world. The dress designers [are] engaged in translating themes from these areas and media into dress designs. (Blumer 1969, p. 330)

A fashion house in Paris, for example, might present over one hundred designs for women's evening dress, of which they can expect that only six to eight of their designs will be chosen by the buyers (ibid.). Thus, their interpretations will be broader than the resulting collective taste will be. The innovator also may be someone else, such as a buyer who purchases an item of ethnic apparel that is not being used by the designers and/or manufacturers, or a store-display artist who innovatively accessorizes a particular outfit.

There is some evidence that suggests that fashion innovators in small, intimate groups dress more to please or stimulate themselves, enjoy experimenting with dress, spend time in clothing-related activities, have decisive attitudes about clothes, are more tolerant of ambiguity, are more inner-directed and self-accepting, and are oriented to the present (Pasnak and Ayres 1969).

Leader

Most groups have one or two leaders, although there can be groups in which all the members are leaders, such as a group of business executives or political leaders. However, even in these groups only one or two people will probably lead at any one time. An individual may be a leader in one group or situation but not in another.

There are two types of leaders: the opinion leader and the action leader. One person, however, may fulfill both roles. The fashion action leader is the first person to adopt a specific dress behavior. Thus, he or she may also be an innovator, but not all innovators are leaders. Leaders are leaders only if they are followed or copied. The innovator with the fishing-lure earrings, maternity blouses, and so on, was not followed by the members of her group, although they did adopt similar styles when those styles were popularized just a few years later. Thus, she was only an innovator. The ideas she initiated had to be diffused into other groups through their leaders before becoming fashionable in her own group. The fashion action leader serves as a model for the dress behavior of the group members, who fill the role of follower. Usually, this leader is a person the group admires, although he or she may be envied instead. In massive, impersonal groups the fashion action leaders are usually admired individuals who are frequently in the public eye.

The fashion opinion leader is the individual who shares with the group current ideas and styles. This person often reads more fashion magazines and helps to clarify (influence and persuade) as well as to present that information to the other group members. Most are also fashion action leaders (Katz and Lazarsfeld 1965; Schrank 1973), since they have strong views about fashion issues. However, there are circumstances, such as economic deprivation, that could prevent them from fashion action.

Both types of leaders have a high interest in fashion, although the opinion leader's interest is even greater (Schrank 1973). Both maintain a high level of awareness of the latest fashion developments. They also must be attuned to the spirit or feeling of their era and culture so that they are able to select fashions that will be congruent with it and therefore become fashionable. Their tendency toward self-confidence (ibid.) and their inner-directedness (Katz and Lazarsfeld 1965) enable them to act or to express their fashion opinions. The opinion leader also believes in conformity to the group's dress norms (Schrank 1973). In a massive, impersonal group, in the United States for instance, the fashion opinion leaders are usually the fashion writers and the buyers for department and clothing stores. It is the buyers who select from the season's designs those they believe will be most attractive to the public. By being immersed in the world of fashion, the world of the collective taste, the successful buyer develops an intuitive awareness of public interests and tastes (Blumer 1969).

Katz and Lazarsfeld (1965) attempted to determine the factors associated with fashion leadership. They looked at life-cycle position, gregariousness, and status level. They found that:

1. Fashion leadership declined with each successive life-cycle position (p. 249) and was most strongly related to this factor (p. 269).
2. Fashion interest declined with each successive life-cycle position (p. 251).
3. Fashion interest was related to fashion leadership *when* the group members were

also interested in fashion and/or when the group members were "an advice-giving source for members of other groups" (p. 255).

4. Fashion leadership was related to high gregariousness (p. 259), especially among older women or women with large families (p. 263).
5. Fashion interest and leadership increased as status level increased (pp. 265, 269).
6. Fashion leadership was related positively to high status and middle status but negatively to low status (p. 265).

Followers

Every group must have some members who follow or who follow at certain times and/or in specific situations. In the dissemination of fashion it is the followers who really propagate a style since they must adopt it in sufficient numbers for it to become "popular" fashion. There are three types of followers: (1) the early adopter, who is quick to follow, (2) the midcycle adopter, and (3) the late adopter, who is slow to follow.

The midcycle adopters appear to be the most conformity prone. They adopt only when enough group members are wearing the style that it has become the norm. In general, it appears that fashion followers dress more for others than for themselves (Pasnak and Ayres 1969). Those who are slowest to adopt a new fashion may be indicating economic inability, inner-directedness, low dress consciousness, low fashion interest, and/or hostility either to the group or to the fashion leader(s).

Most of the research investigating fashion action leadership has not been able to clearly differentiate action leaders from the early adopters. For this reason we add a proviso to the data from these studies that we cannot be certain just how the individuals who fill these two roles differ, if they differ at all. The "early adopters/action leaders" have been found to be socially secure, interested in clothing and clothing activities, and from all socioeconomic levels (Schrank 1973). Theoretically, we would expect the early adopters to have an interest in fashion but to lack leadership or innovation capabilities.

SUMMARY

Learning about a culture occurs in two ways: (1) socialization, which is the process of learning about one's own culture and (2) diffusion, which is the process of learning about another culture or an element of that culture. Socialization begins in infancy, and by the time children are about ten, they will have learned and be able to adapt their behavior to the socially accepted norms and patterns of behavior. Diffusion involves the introduction, acceptance, and integration of an element from another culture into the adapting culture. The westernization of many of the world's cultures is an example of diffusion. Diffusion is more apt to take place when there is (1) geographic proximity; (2)

a material object that is being adopted rather than a nonmaterial, or abstract, concept; (3) the elements are associated with high status or prestige; (4) the elements are compatible with the adapting culture; and (5) the elements are useful.

By nature of its definition, fashion is always a collective behavior. It has social as well as individual purposes. Fashion helps societies to (1) develop a common reality, (2) maintain order, as well as (3) promote change. It helps individuals adjust to social change and reconcile their needs both to conform and to express themselves. Fashion is promoted by (1) openness to change; (2) economic- and natural-resource abundance; (3) social mobility; (4) the distribution of economic resources throughout the population; (5) cross-cultural contact; (6) technological change; (7) social change; (8) increased leisure time; and (9) mass marketing, including advertising.

Aesthetics or collective taste is the group's ideal of what is beautiful in form and style. It is a relative standard and, therefore, differs in different cultures and eras. Collective taste is influenced by (1) architecture and interior design, (2) art, (3) literature, and (4) special events.

Collective taste is communicated and demonstrated in intragroup interaction through the processes of group dynamics. These processes may vary according to the size and type of group. But the dissemination of fashion will always include the following roles to be filled by group members: (1) innovator, (2) action leader, (3) opinion leader, and (4) follower. All these roles must be filled for fashionable dress to exist.

13 | Behavior

Behavior is an instinctive or voluntary reaction to stimuli. All behavior is caused. However, the causes are often so complex and interrelated that it may be difficult if not impossible to isolate them with any precision. We have all had the experience of being asked why we did something and offering "because" as our only answer. Few of us understand why, for example, we "did not have time" to complete a class assignment when if someone had asked us to do something we really wanted to do, we would have had time. Why? Certainly motivation is one factor, but it is unlikely to be the only one. After all, there are times when we do study even though we have been offered more attractive alternatives. The differences between "having time" and "not having time" may reflect a wide variety of factors. The amount and kind of sleep we had, the amount and kind of food we ate, the amount of time we spent sitting versus the amount spent in physical activity, our current health—those are all examples of possible physiological factors that contribute to behavior. Psychological factors are equally diverse and complex, such as one's current sense of self-worth, the last grade received on a project, not getting asked out by someone, getting asked out by someone. Dress can appear both on the physiological and psychological lists. It always has an impact on our behavior. For example, blue jeans have enabled women to sit in places and assume postures they never would have assumed in dresses or good slacks (Morris 1977). Jeans that are too tight may even cause us to stand more than we sit.

In this chapter we shall explore this influence of dress on behavior. We shall examine the way that behavior seems to conform to dress, some psycho-physio factors involved, and the relationship of dress to social participation. Unfortunately, most of our knowledge about the relationship of dress to behavior is based on theory and observation. The complexity and variety of variables that influence behavior make controlled studies extremely difficult to perform. The limited research that has been undertaken has been descriptive rather than experimental, has relied mainly on the technique of self-reporting, and has primarily investigated reactive behavior (behavior responding to one stimulus).

CONGRUENCE OF BEHAVIOR TO DRESS

In spite of the lack of research and the limits of that which has been done, most of us have a sufficient grasp of clothing's effect on behavior to confidently select our dress for most situations, instinctively knowing that our dress will guide our behavior. Parents who do not want their child to behave like a member of a gang, for example, can reduce the probability of such behavior by prohibiting the child from dressing like a gang member. Not only will this decrease the incidence of ganglike behavior, it may also prevent the group from associating with the child or fully accepting him. For parents who are concerned that their fifteen-year-old daughter is dating older boys and is in danger of behaving in a sexually precocious manner, there is a simple possible solution: keep the daughter dressed in a more childlike style without make-up, heels, or hose, for instance. This will reduce the probability that older boys will ask her out and may help her retain a less sexually precocious outlook. In the same way, if we want our young people to take their education more seriously, perhaps we should return to more formal attire for school.

We will usually select dress that will cloak us in the security of "fitting in" with a particular situation. Greater care is generally exercised when choosing dress for situations in which we expect to be with our superiors, for instance, at work. The least care is usually given when we are going to be at home alone. Most work dress is more serious, and it usually requires no additional personal space. Leisure wear will generally offer greater freedom and naturalness, both physical and psychological. Inhibitions can be reduced even more by adopting a mask or some other means of hiding one's identity. Hiler (1930) noted that even individuals representing something sacred tend to engage in more licentious behavior when they are masked.

When dress is appropriate for the situation, individuals tend to feel more confident and competent. Thus, they will participate more fully and will have a greater probability of being successful in that situation. On the other hand, individuals who are inappropriately dressed tend to be less confident and competent. Their feelings of self-consciousness will be heightened since they will be expecting social criticism, disapproval, or even rejection. Thus, they will tend either to withdraw or to more aggressively enter in, each of which will reduce

Figure 13.1 Part of the congruence of behavior to dress is based upon the expectations of others who have relied on dress cues in making their judgments. (Library of Congress)

their probability for success. One aspect of dress appropriateness is that the dress should be correct for the individual's expected role. This relationship of role and dress helps to remind all the participants of the role expectations, promotes the behavior associated with the role, and can therefore facilitate or disrupt the smooth performance of a role. For conventional situations the conventional dress associated with the expected role(s) will *always* enhance the interactions, while unconventional dress will be considered discrepant behavior and can disrupt or even stop any interactions.

PSYCHO-PHYSIO FACTORS

The impact of dress on behavior involves both physiological and psychological factors. Our initial interaction with dress is always physiological since it involves our sensory organs. We hear our dress move in the swish of fabric or the clang of metal or rattle of similar items; we see the color and design of dress; we feel dress touch our skin; and we can even smell certain types of dress. Our perception of this sensory data is psychological. In fact, as noted in chapter 4, we do not even perceive all of the sensory data that is received. The mind is constantly bombarded by sensory data, so much so that if we perceived all of it we should probably be unable to be aware of anything else. But once the stimuli have reached a critical level, the mind refuses to perceive the continuing incoming data. We all have this experience on a daily basis whenever we put on an article of clothing. Imagine the pleasure of putting on the garment that feels the most positive to you. Imagine the feeling of the fabric as it falls over your body. Now try to recall how long you can remain aware of its sensation. Tomorrow morning concentrate on the feeling of what you are putting on and note how long you are able to maintain awareness of the physical feeling of the garment—you will need only two or three minutes for this experiment. Of course, you can increase your awareness by moving so that the garment touches you in a different place or way. However, even that awareness will be fleeting.

The physiological and the psychological factors are *always* interconnected even though some kinds of dress reactions may seem to reflect just one or primarily one. This fact makes research into the relationship between dress and behavior even more difficult. Since no two people will ever perceive anything in exactly the same way, there will always be a quality of uniqueness to each individual's behavior. However, there may be a sufficient commonality of experience to enable rather gross generalizations. For example, putting on a silk garment is physiologically pleasing to *most* people. The silk feels cool and smooth on the skin; it is light and untroubling to the muscles; and it is interesting in its movements when juxtaposed with a moving body. These are all direct sources of physiological pleasure and may explain why Barr (1934) and so many other researchers have found that silk is the fabric purported to give the most positive physiological sensation. However, the research has also found that silk gives the wearer positive psychological sensations or feelings of, for

Figure 13.2   These radium-figured silk lounging pajamas would feel terrific to most people. (Library of Congress)

example, well-being, moral support, freedom, and energy. Some of these may derive from the physiological pleasure but they may also reflect certain psychological associations with silk, for instance, silk's association with high status. Thus, the wearer may feel freer or have a sense of well-being from this association. Belding (1920) even suggested that the affordability and subsequent adoption of the silk shirt by the working class in the early twentieth century reduced both the differences between labor and management and the incidence of physical violence during strikes. Clearly the relationship between silk and behavior reflects physiological and psychological factors.

Kinesthetic Body Consciousness

Kinesthetic body consciousness is awareness of the body's movement, position, and level of muscular tension. It is achieved through perception of muscle and joint movements and through the senses, primarily the tactual; the auditory is also frequently involved, and all of the senses can play a part. Sensory-deprivation studies reduce either the amount or variety of sensory data available to an individual. Their results suggest that sensory stimulation is a universal human need without which mental functioning deteriorates even to the point where one becomes incompetent. Kinesthetic experiences provide a means for the individual to stimulate himself. The Tasmanian aborigines, for example, rubbed red ocher and grease into their hair and worked the mixture into pealike pellets that provided a rattling auditory stimulation with every movement of the head (Roth 1899). Many ankle, wrist, ear, hair, and neck adornments have been made from materials that move and produce a sound. These have all provided the wearer with auditory stimulation. The stimuli may simply provide sensory pleasure. However, the pleasure may be compounded through certain psychological associations. Some American Indians, for instance, wear the rattlers from a rattlesnake so that they will never be alone when walking through dangerous territory; they are thereby able to exert a more powerful presence, as if in a group, in much the same way that we might "Whistle a Happy Tune" whenever we are afraid. Lotze (1885) hypothesized that there are three primary kinds of kinesthetic stimulators in dress: (1) move intensives, (2) tensors, and (3) extenders. The examples I have given of auditory stimuli are instances of move intensives.

MOVE INTENSIVES. Move intensives are items of dress that heighten awareness of the body moving through space. This awareness allows individuals to feel "an expansion of our proper self, . . . the acquisition of a kind and amount of motion foreign to our natural organs, . . . an unusual degree of vigor, power of resistance, or steadiness in our bearing" (ibid., p. 592). Soft fabrics, full skirts, strings, feathers, ribbon, or any other dress item that is subject to frequent and easy movement are excellent move intensives. In fact, all of the baubles and bangles, from bits of bone to chains of gold, from ribbon sashes to cloaks, are worn to expand our existence by creating "the pleasing delusion that it is ourselves that float and wave and sway" (ibid., p.

Figure 13.3 Leg bells provided the same kind of auditory kinesthetic stimulation as rattlesnake rattlers. (Library of Congress)

Figure 13.4 A Tlingit chief in the traditional garb. (British Columbia Provincial Archives)

594). Thus, we experience the joy and energy of such freedom of movement. Dearborn (1918) suggested that even the observers, through empathy, will derive joy and energy. The Tlingit chief's headdress provided him with a visual display of his body movements when he was dancing. He was crowned with a high fringe of seal whiskers extending up from the top of his ornate headdress. The fringe surrounded bird's down that covered the crown of his head (Niblack 1888). Gross body movements such as jumps and spins would cause the down to move, and some of the feathers would escape the whisker fringe to rain their pleasurable caresses upon the chief. Move intensives are often found in dress for dancing. The Swazi men have different degrees of dress-up depending on the importance of the dance. The most dressed up outfit has the most move-intensive items. For the Swazi equivalent to a "sock hop" a Swazi man will wear a leopard-skin kilt with a pleated tail over his regular loin cloth, and he will add wristbands of dangling, teased-out cattle tails. For the "prom" he will also wear anklets like his wrist bands, a large bib of teased-out cattle tails, and a feather headdress (Tyrrell 1968). Each addition will help to expand his sense of existence.

Move intensives may function because of their stimulation of the tactual sense. Everywhere that a garment touches the skin, the body receives tactual stimulation. If nothing has touched our skin, we are even more quickly aware of any item that does come into contact with it. However, once a stimulus has been perceived, we will soon select it out and fail to perceive it as long as it remains somewhat constant. Tactual stimulation was an important aspect of dress to the women in Barr's (1934) study. For them, wool gave the most negative sensations and silk the most positive. This is understandable when one considers that rough or scratchy stimuli rub against the skin's surface and irritate the sensory organs located at the base of the fine hairs on the skin. This physiological irritation becomes a generalized psychological sense of irritation. Smooth textures, on the other hand, are soothing or calming. Soft, light garments that gently touch the skin here and there with every movement provide exciting and pleasant feelings of lightness, frivolity, glee, freedom, sensuousness, and gentleness. Watch a woman (female readers can observe themselves) try on a soft, full negligee, and you will recognize through her movements that she is feeling such sensations. A long, flowing garment will "encourage, if not require, broad, outwardly flowing gestures that cause [it] . . . to balloon, flap,

Figure 13.5 (a, b) (a) This negligee with wings of blue mousseline embroidered with gold pellets demands soft but full movements. (Library of Congress) (b) However, the skirt's fringe and the cowl neckline on this crepe dress by George Samen respond more to quick turns and jerky motions. (Mollie Parnis)

a   b

and swirl" (Sieber 1972, p. 19). Stiff fabrics tend to prevent the equal distribution over the skin of the weight and feel of the garment, and therefore they intrude more into our sensory awareness. Since stiff garments do not conform to the body's contours, they also generally interfere with the body's movements. Thus, they act as irritants and cause the wearer to assume a stiffer posture and make more rigid or limited movements. New denim jeans, for example, can be so uncomfortably restrictive that people have paid someone else to wear their new jeans, have subjected new jeans to innumerable washings, or taken some other action intended to "break them in."

Clothing can reduce one form of positive tactual stimulation. Because it is worn over the body, it reduces the body surface that is exposed to the play of the natural elements—the wind, sun, or water—on the skin. These elements produce a positive, almost sensual, pleasure, which is known as skin eroticism. However, in a clothed society, even the experience of private nudity for sunbathing or swimming, for instance, may be diminished because of the psychological discomfort elicited by such exposure.

TENSORS. Tensors reduce the freedom of movement of the body or a body part either through the material used or the style of dress. Tight sleeves and/or tight armholes, for example, cause the wearer to limit his arm move-

Figure 13.6 Neither individual's dress will allow them to bend enough to retrieve the dropped hankie. (*Punch*)

ments in order to decrease his perception of discomfort. Stiff collars restrict the neck and the entire upper torso, both of which will have to be stiffly held in check. Tight waistlines have a similar effect. Both the tight collar for men and the corseted waistline for women were partial causes of and symbols of the rigid, tight conduct of the Victorian era.

Tensors can also be caused by heavy weight exerting a drag or pull on a body part. Long trains cause an unequal distribution of weight, preventing the body from maintaining normal balance. Women with trains are forced to alter their posture since their bodies are being subjected to a rearward drag. Heavy fabrics or multiple layers of fabrics, especially when in a long or full skirt, can actually cause muscle fatigue, which results in feelings of depression and apathy. They also give a sense of physical impediment or interference. Heavy shoes put an unusual strain on both muscles and joints, and that can also cause feelings of depression. However, foot tensors are generally tight shoes or long slim skirts that impede walking.

Tensors can also result from dress that is so insecurely attached to the body that it requires constant adjustment to maintain its proper position. Garments with straps that easily slip from the shoulders, wide-brimmed hats, or belts that won't stay fastened are all examples of this type of tensor.

Lotze (1885) believed that constraining garments like corsets give individuals a sense of independence and firmness. In this respect, however, it appears that Lotzean theory was inaccurate since such constraint actually causes a decrease in self-confidence and efficiency and an increase in self-consciousness. In fact, whenever a tensor is used it appears to have a negative effect because the individual will have to exert more energy to maintain a stiffer posture. Instead of pleasure, tensors generally cause irritation and the wearer is unable to concentrate fully and is inhibited in her physical movements.

EXTENDERS. Whenever an article of dress is brought into relationship with the body surface, the wearer's personal consciousness or awareness is extended into the article's extremities and surfaces. Thus, a tennis player's racket is an extension of his arm and so much a part of his body that he need not question its position anymore than he need question the position of his arm. When the racket makes contact with any other surface, the player will be aware of that surface through his racket. If the extender is worn on the head, where the sense of pressure is more diffuse, it must be placed slightly askew so that the muscles will have to adjust in keeping the head upright. It is this adjustment that allows the illusion of personal extension to the head/hat.

However, if a garment is so big that it impedes the wearer's body movement, it may cause her to feel smaller (Flugel 1930), less significant, and more inadequate. Imagine a woman of the antebellum period wearing her hoop skirt while walking in a windstorm. It is unlikely that she would have felt positive sensations of enhanced power and awareness as a result of her dress.

Figure 13.7 Extendor dress is evident in the parasol and hat of this woman's costume. (Library of Congress)

Figure 13.8 The full, floor-length skirt was often an impediment to movement, thereby reducing the wearer's sense of adequacy. (Library of Congress)

Confidence and Competence

We have noted that most tensors and some move intensives and extenders can reduce an individual's feeling of self-confidence and decrease his level of competence. In general, they cause such reductions by increasing the individual's level of self-consciousness. The reverse is also true so that when dress decreases one's self-consciousness, it increases one's level of confidence. We can accomplish this latter by selecting dress that is appropriate to the situation, and that gives us positive kinesthetic body awareness. However, confidence can be achieved in other ways as well—for example, from dress that increases our competency. Most sports have some dress associated with them that allows the wearer to perform more competently. Imagine the difference in the tennis performance of a woman clad in a modern tennis outfit as opposed to the turn

SALLY FORTH by Greg Howard

Figure 13.9 (Field Enterprises)

of the century player in her boater hat, leg o'mutton sleeve (which fit tightly over the forearm), tightly fitting neckline, long and full skirt over several layers of petticoats, cinched-in waist, and heeled shoes. Clearly we should expect much greater competency from the woman dressed in the modern, freedom-giving outfit. There can also be a psychological competence boost from dress that makes one feel more capable. The player who finally makes the team and gets the team's uniform will have the same skills he had the day before he got his uniform, but he is apt to perform with more competence because he will feel more capable and confident.

In general, confidence is positively related to competence. Both are related to comfort, which is in turn related to efficiency and the ability to concentrate. Many individuals have one outfit of which they are particularly fond. They probably enjoy it because it is comfortable and because they have received positive feedback or experienced success when wearing it. Thus, they feel more confident in it. Feeling more confident and worthy, they will be more apt to expect to be accepted and less apt to feel defensive or worried that they will be criticized. Thus, they will be more efficient and better able to concentrate on issues outside of themselves. They will also behave more naturally, with a greater freedom and less inhibition. Feeling well-dressed, they will be more apt to interact with others. All of these factors will facilitate the achievement of success in the situation. The individual who is uncomfortably and/or inappropriately dressed will feel the reverse of her contented counterpart and will therefore be less likely to experience success.

MORALE BOOSTING. Institutionalized people often experience a strong sense of depersonalization. That will be especially true in those institutions that force the arriving individual to remove his clothing, shower, and put on institutional garb, which is generally fairly shapeless, worn, and identical to that of the other institutionalized individuals. His own dress and the personal items he needs to maintain his appearance may be taken away from him at the time of his entry. When he leaves the institution, the process is reversed and he gives up the dress to which he has become accustomed for his own original garb or some attire similar to it. In both of these instances the situation itself is inherently full of anxiety and insecurity, each of which are exacerbated by the forced and dramatic change in the individual's daily wear. Such exacerbation decreases the probability of a successful adjustment.

Research in several Western countries has found that recidivism rates have been reduced for women who received attractive clothing, make-up, and hair styling while in prison. Considering the influence physical appearance has on self-concept, these results can hardly be surprising. Recent research has even linked physical unattractiveness with harsher overall character judgments and delinquency. When unattractive boys were compared with attractive ones, the unattractive were found to have lower grades, fewer friends, fewer school activities, more difficulty in their family relationships, lower goals, and more delinquent behavior (Winter 1983). These findings are consistent with some of the findings of numerous other studies, which have shown that unattractive people are judged to be more aggressive, antisocial, and apt to be convicted if accused of a crime, and less intelligent, less popular, and less capable of positive work products. The self-fulfilling prophecy suggests that such expectations will eventually become a behavioral reality simply because of the expectation. We are what we were expected to become.

The success of fashion therapy with the mentally ill should have been predictable for the same reason.[1] The therapy appears to bolster the patient's positive self-regard, boosting their morale. Selecting one's own dress, an exercise in decision making, has added to these positive feelings. It also appears that dress has promoted better adjustment upon the patient's reentry into the greater community (Baker 1955; Thompson 1962). Dress has also been found to have a therapeutic benefit for the sick. For example, Mulready et al. (1982) found that enhancement through cosmetics was "a viable means for improving a chemo-therapy patient's perceived quality of life."

Dress can be a factor in defense mechanisms. These are mechanisms that allow an individual to cope more effectively with an anxiety-laden situation with which he or she is unable to deal. They are not solutions but temporizing discomfort reducers. Many depressed individuals, for example, go shopping for a new article of dress to serve as a temporary spirit elevator. Since depression is symptomatic of dissatisfaction with one's self and/or one's life condition, such purchases produce a temporary change for the better simply by effecting a change in the individual's appearance (Ellis 1962). Samuel Clemens (Mark Twain) was very sensitive to his own uses of dress. When his self-respect would begin to sag, he found that

> there is but one restorative—*Clothes!* respect-reviving, spirit-uplifting clothes! heaven's kindliest gift to man, his only protection against finding himself out: they deceive him, they confer dignity upon him; without them he has none. How charitable are clothes, how beneficent, how puissant, how inestimably precious!

[1] Fashion therapy does not involve the use of aversive conditioners worn in some behavior-modification programs. These conditioners, which give small electric shocks to the patient, are associated with ethical considerations that are beyond the scope of this text.

Mine are able to expand a human cipher into a globe-shadowing portent; they can command the respect of the whole world—including my own, which is fading. I will put them on. (Clemens 1905, p. 326)

For many people one situation that is threatening and calls for defensiveness is having to meet a group of strangers. Some gain reassurance by wearing a special outfit, one providing confidence, or by keeping on their coat or some other item of attire that maintains formality and distance between the wearer and the others.

Such distancing phenomena are quite common as are the similar situational "ers." Morris (1977) called one kind barrier signals. An example is an body-cross as executed by a male celebrity walking toward a group of well-wishers. The celebrity puts distance between himself and the group by crossing his right arm in front of his body to adjust his left cufflink, cuff, or watch. A woman would be more apt to shift her handbag position, finger a button or watch, or smooth her dress. In both instances the individual protectively, but in a socially acceptable way, places some part of his body as a barrier between himself and others (pp. 134–35). Cigarettes may be a more constant way of doing this on a more intimate level. Continuously checking one's cuff would be rude; fidgeting while smoking a cigarette is a more acceptable manipulation, although it is becoming less so. Tennessee Williams protected himself with a long cigarette holder that kept a greater distance between himself and others than a cigarette could (Brown 1983). Cigarettes are also excellent situational "ers." They can fill in a silent moment, during which time the individual can better compose her thoughts. Thus, before answering a question, for example, the smoker may stop to light her cigarette, tap an ash off, put it on an ash tray or lift it off, or take a puff. Pipes can require even more attention, but they may have too strong an aroma so that, like a cigar, they are too powerful an invader of other people's personal space and thus may produce too much distance. Fans and snuff have been used in the same way in those cultures in which their use was common. It is possible that the British use their umbrella and folded newspaper in a similar way.

COLOR.   Color does affect mood in humans. However, one color can have a variety of effects depending on both the individual and his culture. Sensory acuity in color discrimination, for example, appears to be culturally related. Generalizations of color's effect on mood seem accurate more for value and saturation or intensity than specific hue.

Less intense colors are preferred by introverts and are seen as more depressing or more sophisticated and mature, while strong colors are preferred by extroverts (Barrett and Eaton 1947; Ryan 1966). Warm colors—reds and yellows—are more energizing then the cools—blues and greens—and cause the individual to be more receptive to other kinds of stimuli. Cool colors tend to be more calming and relaxing and cause the individual to be less responsive to other stimuli (Bjerstedt 1960). Bright colors are positively associated with efficiency (Flaccus 1906).

SOCIAL PARTICIPATION

Research has found that dress influences how much, where, and when we participate in social situations (Florkey 1976; Kelley et al. 1974; Moore 1972; Vener and Hoffer 1965).

Dearborn (1918, p. 29) hypothesized that our dress determines:

1. How much one "goes out," both into the street, and
2. Into society in general, how many "calls" one makes;
3. The time of day or night at which one goes out when living in town . . .
4. Where one goes, that is, the sort of place to which one goes, both in town and in the country.
5. How much company one invites to his home, and,
6. To some extent, the nature of that company.
7. How much one attends church, disgusting Easter parades, etc.
8. How much one attends the theater, and the nature of the entertainment so designated, whether it be a dark movie among often unfashionably or ill-dressed people, or the grand opera with its brilliant promenade and conspicuous visiting.
9. Clothes frequently help people to get "jobs," and to hold them, but (see below),
10. Clothes help others to miss positions and to lose them.
11. The amount of exercise one takes and its variety . . .
12. How much one sits and where and how one sits. (One thinks here of the attention which the "dude" pays to the creases in his trousers, and even dignified madam to her dress-skirts.) . . .
13. How much one eats and drinks. . . .

People tend not to participate in situations for which they believe they do not have the appropriate dress. This may reflect our tendency to make judgments about others on the basis of their clothes. Because we do this we expect, and rightly so, that others will do the same (Flaccus 1906). Of course, we desire positive judgments; we want to be liked and to belong. Buckley (1983) found that there was a positive relationship between similarity of dress and a judgment of attractiveness, with the most similar dress being deemed the most attractive. This suggests that if our clothing is not going to be similar, to fit in, we will withdraw from participation in order to avoid any possible or probable negative judgments. Such appropriateness may reflect the entire costume including even accessories, such as a tie (Green and Giles 1973).

This relationship of social participation with dress is especially true for adolescents, who are so egocentric and self-conscious that they believe everyone is extremely aware of them. In general, the more secure a person feels in a particular social situation, the less important clothes will be to her and the less they will affect her. This may explain the findings of one study that adolescents who participate in more organized activities tend to dress more for themselves (Drake and Ford 1979). Thus, we would also expect the upper-class individual, who tends to be more comfortable in a greater variety of situations, to be more apt to dress uniquely. At the same time, we would expect members of the lower class to participate in fewer social situations. These expectations appear accurate even, unfortunately, for school participation. Dropouts and their families have reported, for example, that one of the reasons they stopped attending school was their lack of adequate, appropriate dress (Kelley et al. 1974). Langner (1959) may have been correct when he suggested that

> if we want our nation to consist of self-reliant individuals interested in personal as well as national achievements, one of the ways to bring this about is by raising living standards so that all our people can afford to wear clothing which adds to their morale, dignity and self-respect. In the last analysis, a well-dressed population may not necessarily be a happy one, but it is likely to be far happier than an ill-dressed one. (p. 155)

SUMMARY

Behavior is caused, and the causes are complex and interrelated. There is a strong congruence between dress and behavior, and we behave in ways consistent with our dress. The impact of dress on behavior reflects a perceptual response that is an interconnection of physiological reception and psychological perception.

Kinesthetic body consciousness—awareness of one's body movement and position—can be stimulated by three kinds of dress: (1) move intensives, (2) tensors, and (3) extenders. Move intensives heighten awareness of one's body moving through space; tensors reduce the freedom of that movement; and extenders enlarge our personal consciousness into the outer extremities of our dress. Dress can increase or decrease our confidence and competence and therefore our degree of success in a situation or task. It can also elevate our spirits and help to protect us from anxiety. It influences the amount and the kinds of our social participation, and therefore, we may say that dress is a guide to one's general conduct.

14 | Issues and Applications

In this final chapter we shall examine the relation of dress to the issues of (1) values, interests, and attitudes and (2) differentiation and integration. Both of these issues involve the application of group functioning and of individual development. We have chosen these two because they are pervasive and powerful forces in human conduct.

VALUES, INTERESTS, AND ATTITUDES

Values are one's basic beliefs or ideas about what things are important, desirable, good. They determine, either solely or in conjunction with needs, our interests and attitudes, the kinds of choices and judgments we make, and our conduct. Generally, they exert this control on a subconscious level. Interests and attitudes are behavioral manifestations of values. Interests are the things we are motivated (by our values) to act upon, think about, and be involved in. Attitudes are less overt than interests; they are the judgments we make or positions we take (as a result of our values) about issues, ideas, and actions. Attitudes are more affective than interests.

In order for a belief or idea to be a value, it must (1) have been freely chosen from alternatives that were understood; (2) be prized and publicly affirmed; and (3) be a consistent directing force of our interests, attitudes, decision making, and general conduct. An individual's values will generally not change as long as her environment is not significantly altered and her significant others maintain those values. However, they can change. For example, in situations that offer no emotional support, individuals will often change their values toward that of a group that does offer support. These changes tend to occur gradually. Most individuals have few values, probably less than ten. These values are organized into a hierarchy according to their relative importance, with the higher values being prepotent over any lower ones. Thus, when two values conflict, the higher will always be acted upon if the individual is free to act upon it. Most of our values are learned during early childhood, first from our parents and then from other people who become significant to us. It is the learnings from people outside of our family members that expand and alter our values so that they will be unique rather than carbons of our parents' hierarchies. During adolescence young people are often experimenting with values that are different from those of their parents and reflect those of their peers. However, most adults' values tend to strongly resemble those of their parents since we humans seek out and are attracted to other people who share similar values, interests, and attitudes.

Eduard Spranger proposed six basic types of values: theoretic, aesthetic, economic, political, social, and religious. The existence of these types was validated by Allport and Vernon, who found that "people do in fact subscribe to

Figure 14.1 Mary McFadden's dresses are an example of wearable art with the aesthetic a primary consideration. (Mary McFadden)

Figure 14.2 These dresses, inspired by Medici court styles, would appeal to those with high political values. (Mary McFadden)

all six values, but in widely varying degrees" (Allport 1968, p. 53). They also found that these values were not completely independent but tended to covary, the theoretic with the aesthetic, the economic with the political, and the social with the religious. These six types of values have been used in developing theories and carrying out research regarding the use(s) of dress. Table 14-1 represents each of these types of values and the kinds of dress interests and attitudes that have been theorized or have been reported in research findings (these latter are in italics; data pertaining to men is in capitals).

Table 14-1
Basic Values as They Affect Dress Interests and Attitudes

VALUE TYPE	VALUE EXAMPLE	DRESS INTERESTS/ATTITUDES
Theoretic	Truth, order, knowledge	Fiber content and care, *low fashion interest*
Aesthetic	Form, harmony	*High fashion interest, enjoyment of shopping for clothes, pleasing oneself in terms of attractiveness*
Economic	Practicality	Dollar value, utility, *comfort, quality, classicalness of style, high fashion interest*
Political	Power	NON-ECONOMICAL, *impress others, high fashion interest*
Social	Other people	*Conformity*, NON-STATUS DISPLAYING
Religious	Unity with the universe	*Modesty* (when other psychological needs have been met), *conservativeness, low fashion interest*, ECONOMICAL

SOURCE: Based on data from Christiansen and Kernaleguen 1971; Creekmore 1963; Hartmann 1949; Lapitsky 1961; Richards and Hawthorne 1971.

Figure 14.3   These American coeds of 1942 are dressed to conform, which indicates their high social values. Even their knitting—for the boys at war—represents those values. (Library of Congress)

Mass Values

Just as each individual has his or her own unique value hierarchy, so does each culture. In fact, it has even been suggested that culture stems from and expresses mass values (Lee 1948) that are widely held and compatible with the value hierarchies of most of the members of the society. In modern American society most mass values are determined by the middle class, who, unsurprisingly, tends to conform to them more than do the other classes (who do have a considerable value consensus with the mass values). Many mass values are formally taught in institutions such as schools, churches, and families that are responsible, at least in part, for socialization and acculturation. They are informally taught by the mass media and by many organizations and groups such as the peer group or Girl or Boy Scouts. Mass values serve as the cohesive element of a society and, therefore, facilitate the social order and its functioning by helping to increase the level of social conformity.

Some current mass values in greater American society and their impact on dress are presented in Table 14-2.

The success of any fashion depends on its being compatible with the mass values of the era and society. It is this compatibility that is responsible for the Zeitgeistic nature of fashion, its ability to capture the feeling of an era. Ellis (1962) listed six major requirements of dress for the American woman of the 1950s and early 1960s. These requirements reflected the mass values of materialism, youth, and the present and represented the attitudes toward women at that time. The following list presents Ellis's requirements (in italics) and relates them to the mass values. A woman must dress:

Table 14-2
Mass Values as They Affect Dress

MASS VALUE	IMPACT ON DRESS
Materialism	Large and varied wardrobe, current fashions, status symbols, extensive leisure-wear wardrobe
Youth	Styles to suit the youthful body, extensive leisure-wear wardrobe, slimness, hair dyes, marketing techniques designed to appeal to the young
The present	Increased spending on consumer goods rather than saving, extensive leisure-wear wardrobe

1. *Romantically, which may necessitate making her body appear different than it is.* Youth: she must make her body conform to the aesthetic ideal of youth.
2. *Fashionably.* Materialism: she must indicate that she can afford to change her wardrobe for new styles. The present: she must be aware of, and conform to, the latest style.
3. *Distinctively, to outdress her peers without being too original.* Materialism: she must engage in a peer-group rivalry to indicate her superior economic status.
4. *Extensively.* Materialism: she must have a large and varied wardrobe.
5. *Properly, sexy but decorous.* Youth: she must maintain the innocent curiosity of youth.
6. *Sex-invitingly, not to say that she will but that she'd be terrific if she would.* Youth: she must maintain the sexuality of youth.

Fads are fashion styles that lack this Zeitgeistic compatibility and will therefore have a short life span. Both the western and the peasant look of the 1970s were dress fads and had no real relation to the mass values of America during that period. For example, while they were somewhat compatible with youth, they were incompatible with materialism and the present.

In the 1960s many young people in the United States, especially those from affluent backgrounds, rejected the mass value of materialism. It was, in fact, value differences between the young and the adults that caused "the generation gap." The young selected an informal style of dress—jeans and a simple top such as a t-shirt.[1] Some young people rejected other social norms in dress, such as grooming. Their dress was counterculture or antifashion and reflected their counterculture values and attitudes—for instance, their rejection of sex-role stereotyping, premarital sexual restrictions, and the traditional nuclear family—and their political liberalism and social activism (Buckley and Roach 1974; Thomas 1973). Individuals whose attitudes were congruent with the established culture did not consciously use their dress as much just to express their values and attitudes (Buckley and Roach 1974). They did not need to consider their dress in this way since it already conformed to the norms. Neither they nor their dress had to be on the offensive or the defensive.

[1] By the early 1980s, most young people valued materialism and blue jean sales had decreased significantly in spite of the development of "designer" jeans.

However, the counterculture people needed a variety of tools as they attempted to publicly affirm their values. Their use of dress was offensive, yet it often caused them to assume a defensive position and even limited their ability to effect the changes they sought.

Fashion Interest

Everyone has an interest in dress. However, the type of interest and its intensity will vary according to the individual's values and their hierarchical organization. The more interest we have in a topic, the more we will try to be informed about it, even to the point that a strong interest leads to our becoming informed about positions different from or opposed to our own. Interest also reinforces itself, as the more we attend to a topic the more interested we will become in it.

One would expect high-fashion dressers to have the most fashion interest. There is some support for this, since a relationship between high fashion interest and high economic, aesthetic, and political values has been found. Low fashion interest appears to be related to both high religious and high economic values.

However, there is at least one other factor that influences the degree and direction of our fashion interest, and that is our specific needs, as identified by Maslow's hierarchy of needs. If, for example, an individual is attempting to meet either his basic physiological needs or his safety and security needs, he is apt to be most interested in the utility and practicality (economic value type) of his dress. If those needs have been adequately met so that he is involved with his needs for love and belonging, he will probably be most interested in dress that "fits in" with that of his peers and family (social value type). If he has begun attempts to meet his esteem needs, he is likely going to be most interested in dress to show his superiority, to impress others (political value type). Dress to show one's unity with nature and that one is self-effacing (religious value type) would probably be associated with the need to transcend oneself. Finally, the aesthetic needs would be associated with the dress interests reflecting an aesthetic value type, just as the need to know and understand would be expected to correlate with the dress interests of the theoretic value type. Thus, we would expect that an individual's values and interests will probably differ in their priority or hierarchical placement according to his personal development, even though they will probably be held throughout his life. Thus, the relationship, found in some studies, of high fashion interest to certain personality factors can be explained by considering this interrelationship of needs and values with the kind of fashion interest. That the findings have associated high fashion interest with such personality factors as sociability, dependency, maladjustment, conventionality, responsibility, and persistence is not surprising. High fashion interest has been used in most studies to mean high interest in fashionable dress rather than simply high interest in dress. The value types associated with interest in fashionable dress are the political and social, and the personality traits are sociability, dependence, conventionality, and responsibility. This second group of traits would obviously be manifested more (in one direction or another) by those value types. The association of higher fashion interest with teens and some young adults in also a reflection of the uses of fashionable dress for individuals attempting to meet their love-and-belonging or their esteem needs, both of which are typically important during the teen and young adult years.

INTEGRATION AND DIFFERENTIATION

It has been suggested that one of the major human dilemmas is our desire to be unique or differentiated while concomitantly fitting in or being integrated. The average man wants to be unique but not different, outstanding without standing out, in fashion not fashionable. "He wants neither to be mass produced nor lonely, so he seeks solace in being some of both" (Lynes 1957, p. 85). These two desires conflict because of the interdependence of the individual and society and the demand for conformity made upon the individual by society and most other groups. To meet that demand, most of us must give up or inhibit parts of our own belief systems or personality. In his eulogy to Eleanor Roosevelt, Adlai Stevenson seemed to recognize this dilemma and the compromises it entails when he noted that trying to be yourself in a world that is trying to make you someone else means to fight the hardest fight you'll ever fight and to never stop fighting. This fight is harder in modern societies like the American where "the forces making for conformity are ever more powerful" (Crutchfield 1963, p. 208). In fact, we are "indoctrinated, from earliest infancy, to conform. . . ." (Mandelbaum 1963), and most of us seem quite willing to be "someone else." As Lynd and Lynd (1937) noted in their study of small-town America, there

Figure 14.4 (Field Enterprises)

is a struggle between the old pride in localism, in being Middletown, and the opposite pride in being *en rapport* with the "newest," the "smartest," the "most approved by the right people in the big outside world." . . . Mankind everywhere has a deep-seated emotional need to feel itself not peripheral and marginal but central in the scheme of things . . . to "belong" to his world . . . Living as Middletown does today with an unprecedented number of space-binding agencies that bring it to contact with the habits and possessions of authoritative people who "belong" in the wider national culture, Middletown is shifting its centers of "belonging" at a number of specific points to conform to these more distant centers of prestige. (pp. 379–80)

In fact, "every individual displays a good deal of conformity behavior throughout his social life. Inevitably he finds himself in many situations where conformity is the only 'reasonable' or possible form of behavior" (Crutchfield 1963, p. 214). Thus, the conflict between integration and differentiation is more inherent in certain kinds of "situations and at certain stages of the life cycle" (Mandelbaum 1963, p. 242), although those situations may vary in different cultures.

Since this willingness to conform seems quite universal, it may be, of course, that it is more central a part of us than those traits we give up to or for the group. It may, for example, reflect our commonality of cultural experience. Certainly our society with its stress on competition and being the best promotes conformity. In fact, conformity "is the price society exacts for a desired status" (Murphy 1976, p. 27). To win, one must participate in the "correct" way, which is the socially acceptable way. To lose or be in error is to be inadequate. Thus, it is safe and easy to accept social norms and standards, which insulate us from the conspicuousness that too often results in unfavorable evaluation and also enhance the probability of favorable comment or "winning" if we can be just a bit better. This attitude has become so much a part of the American scene that sometimes we seem to admire the average. In schools average, which is the norm and thus should embrace most of us, is often awarded *A*s or *B*s. We have lowered our standards, so the majority will succeed as if it were the excellent minority. In the area of dress we expect people to "put on their best face"—in other words, to conform to the social standard of appearance. That differences should be minimized rather than stressed is evident in the equipment and procedures we have developed to modify our bodies—diets, exercises, girdles, bras, make-up, braces, hair straighteners or curlers, elevator shoes, and shoulder pads.

But the willingness to conform could also be a reflection of human needs as represented in Maslow's hierarchy. Conformity helps us to achieve a sense of belonging. Having satisfied this need, we can begin to develop a sense of self-esteem. To some extent this sense of self-esteem would reflect self-differentiation, *but* it would also require a large measure of conformity since esteem needs can be met only by having other people give you positive evaluation. That is most apt to occur when we are more like the other people, although perhaps a bit superior. Thus, "specialness" is safely proclaimed only by being just a *little* different.

Integration

Integration is usually achieved by identifying social norms and behavioral standards and conforming to them. Dress is one area of these behavioral standards. It is a particularly important one because it is constant and unavoidable. Conformity helps to fill a social need by maintaining order through uniformity and tradition.[2] The tendency to conform is promoted by certain conditions of the modern world: (1) tensions between the East and the West, which have strengthened our national allegiance and ideological orthodoxy, (2) mass communication, which promotes more homogeneity, (3) the complexity and volume of information with which the individual is bombarded, (4) the rapidity and constancy of change, and (5) "the development of far-reaching new psychological methods for behavior control . . . [which] implies *thought* control" (Crutchfield 1963, p. 209). Societies enforce conformity explicitly through laws with specific punitive measures or overt threats, or implicitly through the individual's fear of social ridicule, social rejection, or being wrong.

But most individuals also seem to need to conform. The degree of conformity or our need to conform is not a constant but varies throughout our lives. For example, during a peak experience conformity may be less needed. Motivations for conformity may also differ. Some conformity is motivated primarily by group loyalty, solidarity, and identification, while some is motivated more by monotony, totalitarianism, and rigidity (Mandelbaum 1963). By conforming we decrease the possibility and probability of social criticism and/or rejection and increase our sense of belonging and being integrated. This feeling will enhance our ability to communicate effectively with the group, our sense of security, our confidence, and our self-esteem and reduce our sense of anxiety. Thus, it should not be surprising that research has found conformity to be the most important factor in determining what clothing women purchase and when they purchase it (Barr 1934).

Individuals belong to many groups, each of which has its own unique combination of purposes, patterns, and norms. The groups vary in their importance to the individual, with reference groups having the greatest importance. A reference group may be a group to which the individual belongs or aspires to belong. For most other-directed people the peer group is such a group.[3] Each individual may have several reference groups, which are usually mutually sustaining. If they are not, their differences are often easy to ignore since we "tend to lead compartmentalized lives, shifting from one [often unrelated] perspective to another as [we] participate in a succession of transactions. . . ." (Shibutani 1962, p. 139). When conflicts cannot be ignored, selective and distorted perception may make them more consistent. But if that is not

---

[2] More-conforming societies with a high value of tradition are more resistant to change and thus more stable.

[3] Other-directed people give higher priority to the wishes and values of others than to their own, whereas inner-directed individuals are motivated more by their own wishes and values (Reisman et al. 1950).

Figure 14.5 These women belong to the same peer group. They are remarkably similar in their dress, from their fur neckpieces to the height of their heels. (Library of Congress)

effective, the individual will accede to the group to which he has the greatest affinity or attraction. That group will usually be the one with which he most frequently interacts and to which he is most committed. It is the group whose values and norms of behavior he is most apt to conform to or adopt. In return, the group will give the individual its approval and acceptance. It is this power that gives groups social control. Rarely does a group need to coerce; rather the individual determines his behavior by taking "into account the expectations that he imputes to other people" (ibid. p. 129).

Some groups impose or have imposed upon them a condition of uniformity in dress. This is most common among groups that are opposed to some aspect of society. Adolescent peer groups, for example, are often opposed to the established authority. By preventing individual variance within the group while promoting it between the group and the rest of society, the group strengthens the bonds of member loyalty and limits involvements between its members and the greater society. A few groups, such as those organized to achieve a specific goal, may desire greater diversity between their members in order to enhance their potential for achieving that goal. However, it is unlikely that that diversity includes dress, and they, like most groups, will discover that most of their members will dress in a way to conform with the other group members.

The desire for integration is particularly powerful during the years of middle childhood and adolescence, and conformity in dress is one of the most significant ways to ensure such integration (Kelly and Eicher 1962; Smucker and Creekmore 1972). It is during these years that the individual separates himself from his family and integrates himself more fully into the greater society. This difficult task is ameliorated or even enabled by the support of the peer group. However, the peer group can exercise so much power over its members that it prevents them from becoming independent and actually causes greater dependence and more conformity. School dress codes can have a positive effect on feelings of security, especially for the more insecure adolescent. However, they also reduce the freedom to explore, which could be detrimental to the secure teen. Integration through dress conformity is a life-stage issue that explains the frequency of the question, "What should I wear?" Adults ask this because they continue to want to know the dress expectations associated with various social situations.

Differentiation

Differentiation is accomplished when an individual asserts or expresses her uniqueness. She may consciously assert her individuality by being aware of the norms and choosing not to adhere to them. This individual is more apt to be counter society, and her behavior might be evaluated as delinquent or abnormal. But she may express herself simply because she is so inner-directed that it is natural for her to behave in ways consistent with her inner state. This may be

Figure 14.6 This "bloomered" woman's notation, "yours in bloomers," indicates her awareness of her differentiating dress. (Library of Congress)

unconscious behavior, although it would be grounded in conscious ideas. She may even be somewhat unaware of the "differentness" of her behavior as she may assume that everyone else is acting on the basis of his or her inner self. She is an independent thinker. In reality, each of us is unique; there is no one like us, and we are therefore very special. Yet many modern Americans, for example, seem to have lost any awareness of their uniqueness. They would find it extremely difficult to identify just five ways in which they are different. This situation may not improve in the foreseeable future, since the privacy needed for independent thinking and inner-directedness is becoming ever more difficult to achieve (Crutchfield 1963).

Being different, however, may result in rejection. Thus, the fashion dissenter, whether consciously or unconsciously so, often experiences a degree of social rejection. This is obvious in the pejorative terms we use to denote differentiating behavior: deviant, aberrant, abnormal, unnatural, peculiar, odd. We use these labels when we feel in some way threatened by the specific behavior. When we feel supported rather than threatened, we use a different kind of label: independent, individualistic, eccentric, self-expressive. However, it is difficult to be different *and* nonthreatening. To do so seems to require previous association in which the individual has made manifest contributions to the group. Through her contributions, the individual builds idiosyncrasy credit: "an accumulation of positively disposed impressions residing in the perceptions of relevant others; it is defined operationally in terms of the degree to which an

Figure 14.7 Dame Edith Sitwell was an individualist both in her dress and her writing. (Loomis Dean, *Life* Magazine © 1963 Time Inc.)

individual may deviate from the common expectancies of the group" (Hollander 1958, p. 120). The more the individual helps the group, the more latitude for idiosyncratic behavior the group will give him.

Samuel Clemens had a large idiosyncrasy credit with most people who had read and enjoyed his humor. Thus, he was not a threat when he wore a white suit regardless of the season or the event. Of course, he further defused his aberrant behavior so that it became eccentric and self-expressive, by wryly noting his "impudence." He wrote:

> I talked in a snow-white fulldress, swallow-tail and all, and dined in the same. It's a delightful impudence. I think I will call it my dontcareadam suit. But in the case of the private dinner I will always ask permission to wear it first, saying: "Dear Madam, may I come in my dontcareadams?" (C. Clemens 1931, p. 153)

When Twain spoke at a dinner of the Savage Club in London in July 1907, he apologized for his white clothes, which his family had ordered him not to wear in England. For several weeks he refrained from white in order to obey their wishes, but not being "in the habit of obeying instructions," he found himself unable to "invent a new process in life right away." Thus, he was indebted to the club for permitting him to dress in white since he was quite tired of gray and black.

> I wear white clothes in the depth of winter in my home, but I don't go out in the streets in them. I don't go out to attract too much attention. I like to attract some, and always I would like to be dressed so that I may be more conspicuous than anybody else.
> If I had been an ancient Briton, I would not have contented myself with blue paint, but I would have bankrupted the rainbow. I so enjoy gay clothes in which women clothe themselves that it always grieves me when I go to the opera to see that, while women look like a flower-bed, the men are a few gray stumps among them in their black evening dress. These are . . . reasons why I wish to wear white clothes. When I find myself in assemblies like this, with everybody in black clothes, I know I possess something that is superior to everybody else's. Clothes are never clean. You don't know whether they are clean or not, because you can't see.
> Here or anywhere you must scour your head every two or three days or it is full of grit. Your clothes must collect just as much dirt as your hair. If you wear white clothes you are clean, and your cleaning bills get so heavy that you have to take care. I am proud to say that I can wear a white suit of clothes without a blemish for three days. If you need any further instruction in the matter of clothes I shall be glad to give it to you. I hope I have convinced some of you that it is just as well to wear white clothes as any other kind. I do not want to boast. I only want to make you understand that you are not clean. (Clemens 1923, p. 354)

Clemens's warm humor allowed him to dress uniquely without threatening his "dirtier" peers, who could, therefore, comfortably tolerate his eccentricity.

However, differentiating behavior, including dress, is more often found among members of marginal groups, such as ethnic minorities, teenagers, and the economically impoverished, who lack the traditional vehicles for gaining social approval from the greater society. Thus, they assert their "deviance" from society, which has already pejoratively labeled them. They may wear attention-getting dress to do so (Reeder and Drake 1980). But this assertion often has an antisocial character because the individual frequently feels hostile to the greater society and defensive about his own subgroup. In some cases the individual closely adheres to his subgroup's rigid dress standards. For example, in the early days of the women's liberation movement, so many women activists wore blue jeans and T-shirts or jerseys that it became a uniform associated with the movement. However, once women's rights and blue jeans became accepted by the greater society, the activists could change their dress. Gloria Steinem, for instance, has put aside her turtleneck jersey and jeans for blouses and skirts or classic slacks. In other cases, individuals strive to use dress to attest to their uniqueness. Field slaves, for example, used their clothing to "express their identity and gain the respect and admiration of their fellows" (Tandberg and Durand 1981, p. 40).

Even when dress behavior is a defiantly antisocial assertion of a marginal group's position out of the social mainstream, it may be motivated more from a desire to belong to their reference group(s) than to differentiate themselves from society. However, sometimes belonging does not appear to be the prime motive for a group's dress behavior. There is some evidence to suggest that the hippies of the late 1960s and early 1970s were dressing more for differentiation and self-assertion than for peer-group integration (Gurel et al. 1972).

Differentiation in dress is an excellent way to express our uniqueness, our separateness from others. In our society, we are more apt to find dress for this purpose among our more mature members. A greater range of deviation in

Figure 14.8 Even individuals in cultures with simple dress can express their uniqueness, as these Zulu men do in their hairstyles and other adornments. (Library of Congress)

dress is allowed the elderly and the young child. But when dress standards have been conventionalized, as they are for funerals or weddings in our society, deviation from the norm is not tolerated. Such a ban on deviation is more acceptable than a ban on conformity would be, even though differentiation has been found to be a moderately important motive in dress selection (Barr 1934). After all, a ban on conformity would essentially prevent us from having fashionable dress.

FASHIONABLE DRESS. Fashionable dress allows us to conform comfortably and feel integrated while *safely* differentiating ourselves. We gain control over situations through wearing fashionable dress. There is a wide-enough range of fashionable dress that we can all select styles to effectively express ourselves, especially since our choice will inexorably reflect our society and culture. Thus, the dress we select because we like it is often liked because it fits in—is fashionable—with our era and group. Differentiation is possible in the way we put an outfit together, as in our selection of textures and colors, the angle we wear our hat, whether we turn our collar up or let it lie flat. Yet even these attempts will be somewhat limited by the available choices. For example, one year, the predominant colors are greys and blues and it may be impossible to find a dark brown skirt. The next year it may be the grey skirt that cannot be found. Thus, fashion enhances our freedom to differentiate by choosing clothes that express our "individual moods, tastes, and esthetic propensities" while also limiting it by forcing us to stay within the limits of the alternatives of fashionable dress (Ellis 1962, p. 58).

Freedom in Dress

Freedom is a psychological concept pertaining to one's ability to make choices *and* to act on them. The relationship of freedom with dress has only recently begun to be investigated. One of the research findings pertaining to this area is that freedom is not the opposite of conformity but a different factor altogether (Lowe and Buckley 1982). Of course, absolute freedom is nonexistent. The moment we make a choice we limit our potential choices, our alternatives. Thus, freedom in dress is a relative term and actually refers to the individual's perception of her ability to make her own dress choices. Lowe and Anspach (1973) proposed four criteria for freedom in dress: (1) economic purchasing power, (2) personal control over purchasing choices, (3) a variety of alternatives available, and (4) the ability to experience satisfaction from one's choices. They also suggested that freedom in dress is restricted by (1) economic limits, (2) limited market access, (3) limited knowledge of alternatives, (4) social restrictions and group norms, and (5) lack of confidence in one's clothing selections (Lowe and Anspach, 1978). The relativity of freedom makes these criteria and restrictions guidelines for evaluation or understanding rather than absolutes. For example, the poor person living in an impoverished community may lack purchasing power and have limited alternatives available to him. His consumer needs may be aimed solely toward physical survival, and his consumer wants may be extremely few. However, because he has few wants and those that he has are directed just to physical survival, he may feel free to choose independently from a satisfactory number of alternatives and to enjoy his choices. He has freedom in dress. In the same way, the proposed limits are only limits to freedom if they are so perceived by the individual. One other note of caution seems to be required: freedom is not necessarily positive. It can be a burden that produces anxiety and, therefore, avoidance. This is most apt to occur when the individual has been dissatisfied by his choices.

Conformity-Proneness versus Individuality-Proneness

Crutchfield (1963) suggested that an individual's way of attempting to reduce the dissonance from inconsistency between his beliefs or behaviors and those of his group(s) (cognitive dissonance) relates to his proneness to conform or to differentiate. For example, the person who blames herself by saying something like "I misunderstood" is most apt to conform to the group's perception. The person who instead says "they misunderstood" is most apt to differentiate in a countersociety method. The person who tries to reduce the dissonance in a way that lets "him accommodate both his judgment and that of the group" (p. 218) is most apt to differentiate in an inner-directed way, although he may conform if he decides that the group's decision is more accurate. The self-actualized person will be comfortable with the dissonance and will accept it and continue to differentiate out of his inner directedness.

There are two basic determinants of an individual's proneness either to conform or to differentiate. The first is one's past experience. It is past experience that determines our habits, our usual responsive/reactive behavioral style. It also determines our perception and performance of our roles; for example, women tend to be more conforming than men because our society rewards conformity in females more than in males. However, in matters of dress, research has shown that males tend to conform more than females and to dress in a more defined style and one that is consistent with their preferred appearance. Females have had a greater variety of style alternatives, more often dress to be conspicuous, and are less likely to prefer the appearance to which they are conforming (Creekmore 1980; Hambleton et al. 1972). Several possible and plausible causes for this difference have been suggested. Since clothing interest has been classified as feminine behavior in our culture, the male who expresses or evidences such an interest is often considered effeminate (Young 1956). For this reason men may be afraid to pay attention to fashion or appear to do so, and therefore they wear "tried and true" styles or copy what most men are wearing. The "tried and true" in menswear changes very little, so that a man wearing last year's suit would not look as dated as a woman would wearing last year's dress style. Changes in men's fashions have tended to be in details, such as style of cuff, collar, or pocket or length of sleeve or pants or width of tie, rather than overall style. Traditionally, men have had a variety of avenues, such as occupation, to express or demonstrate their uniqueness so that they did not need to differentiate in dress. In fact, since men have been more involved in the competition of the "rat race," their dress has often been used to demonstrate their success, which means that it has conformed to the most universally accepted style. Some research suggests that adolescent males have a greater fear of social rejection than their female counterparts have. If that is true for adults, this fear could also be involved with the higher incidence of male conformity in dress.

The second determinant is the individual's personality. Table 14.3 lists the personality characteristics associated with conformity proneness and with differentiation proneness as determined through objective measures of personality. Many of these tendencies "are mutually reinforcing, operating together to increase even further the individual's vulnerability to group pressure" (Crutchfield 1963, p. 226) or ability to be independent. These groupings of characteristics also seem to reflect value development, self-concept, and placement on Maslow's hierarchy of needs. Since the individualistic individual is more aware of his values, it should be easier for him to act on them. Having a more positive self-concept will give the individualist more security in his inner self and will reduce the threat of being different, thereby reducing his anxiety. The characteristics also suggest that it is the individualist who is most apt to be involved with the being needs on Maslow's hierarchy rather than the becoming.

Table 14-3
Traits Associated with Conformity-Proneness and Differentiation Proneness*

CONFORMITY PRONENESS	DIFFERENTIATION PRONENESS
Anxiety prone	
Fear of anxiety	
Feelings of *inadequacy* or incompetency	**Feelings of competency**
Panic reaction to stress	**Effective in dealing with stress**
Feelings of inferiority	*More positive self-esteem*(Humphrey et al. 1971)
Outer-directed	Inner directed
Less trusting of others	More trusting of others
Less able to accurately evaluate others	More able to accurately evaluate others
Passive	Less passive
Suggestible	Less suggestible
Dependable	Less dependable
Less self-aware	Self-aware
Emotionally constricted	**Emotionally expressive and free**
Less spontaneous	**Spontaneous**
Indirect in expressing hostility	Direct in expressing hostility
Conventional in behavior and values	High **aesthetic** and theoretic values and more *aware of own values*
Moralistic	Nonjudgmental
Less tolerance for ambiguity	More tolerance for ambiguity
Dogmatic (closed belief system)	Less dogmatic
Authoritarian	**Independent**
More dependent on frame of reference in visual perception	Less dependent on frame of reference

Table 14-3 continued
Traits Associated with Conformity-Proneness and Differentiation Proneness*

CONFORMITY PRONENESS	DIFFERENTIATION PRONENESS
Deficient cognitive processes including:	Efficient cognitive processes
lower IQ scores	higher IQ scores
more thought and perceptual rigidity	**flexibility in cognitive restructuring**
fewer ideas	more ideas
Uncreative	*Creative*
More submissive	*Ascendant in interpersonal relations, leader*
More compliant	*Persuasive*
Narrower range of interests	*More informed*
Inhibited	
Needlessly delays or denies gratification	
Difficulty in decision making	*Efficient and competent*
	More ego strength
Need for social acceptance (Taylor and Compton 1968)	
Fear of conspicuousness(Dearborn 1918; Flaccus 1906)	*Active and vigorous*

*Italics indicate data only from clinical observation, and boldface indicates data from clinical observation and objective measures of personality. Boldface italics indicate data from research into conformity in dress specifically and is taken from Gurel et al. (1972), Aiken (1963), Taylor and Compton (1968), Drake and Ford (1979), and Dittes (1959).

How do these personality traits specifically relate to dress other than in the variables of conformity and differentiation? Motivation for dress would also seem to be involved. For example, since the differentiating-prone individual is confident, self-aware, and self-expressive, she would probably be more likely to select dress specifically to express herself. Being creative and having high aesthetic and theoretic values would lead her to be more creative and exploratory in her dress behavior. For someone who is efficient, active, and vigorous, comfort would be a more important factor in dress selection. One who is persuasive and on the social ascendancy would find dressing for leadership and conspicuousness of greater importance. The conforming individual, on the other hand, would be more likely to dress to be inconspicuous because of his fear of conspicuousness and of anxiety, his need for social acceptance, and his feelings of inferiority. His dress would be more conventionally modest because of his lack of trust in others, his moralistic attitudes, his conventionality, his dogmatism, and his cognitive deficiency. He would probably not be creative or emotionally expressive in his dress, which would be carefully planned to fit in with each particular situation because of his lack of spontaneity and his authoritarianism. Thus, the dress needs, interests, and motives of the conformity prone and the differentiating prone individuals will be quite different.

SUMMARY

Values are one's basic beliefs about what things are important and desirable. All people seem to ascribe, although in varying degrees, to six basic types of values: theoretic, aesthetic, economic, political, social, and religious. Just as each individual has a unique value hierarchy, so does each culture. These mass values are compatible with the value hierarchies of most of that society's members.

Attitudes and interests are behavioral manifestations of values. Interests are the areas we are motivated to explore and act upon while attitudes are our affective judgements and positions. All humans appear to have some interest in and attitudes about dress. These interests and attitudes, as well as choices of dress, reflect our individual values and also the mass values we have incorporated. For a fashion to be successful for us as individuals, it must be congruent with our individual values, just as it must be compatible with the mass values of the era in order to become the fashion.

One of the major human dilemmas is our desire to belong or to be integrated while concomitantly wanting to be unique or differentiated. We usually fulfill our desire to integrate by identifying in groups important to us social norms and behavior standards, such as those pertaining to dress, and by conforming to them. Differentiation is accomplished when an individual asserts or expresses his unique self. He may do this because he is inner-directed or because he is hostile in some way—usually because he feels unaccepted by the group. Modern American society seems to be promoting conformity more than differentiation, and the majority of us conform in our dress behavior(s).

Fashionable dress allows us to comfortably conform and feel integrated while *safely* differentiating ourselves. We identify with fashionable dress so that in choosing it we are selecting what we like. Yet we can differentiate ourselves through the way we put our costume together. Such differentiation cannot involve absolute and complete freedom in dress. Freedom is a relative concept, which can only be defined by the individual in relation to herself.

When our choices, interests, attitudes, or values are different from those expressed by the group, we will attempt to find a way to reduce this cognitive dissonance. How we do this is related to our own proclivity to conform or to differentiate, and that is determined by our past experiences and certain of our personality traits. It also relates to our dress needs, interests, and motives. Thus, dress is ultimately a pass key to the "doors" of the individual; it reveals our essential beliefs; our interests and attitudes; our personality characteristics including self-concept, emotionality, degree of dogmatism, cognitive processes, and creativity; our interpersonal functioning, including degree of ascendancy, level of outer- or inner-directedness, and need for social acceptance. It is also a pass key to the "doors" of society; it reveals the essential beliefs or values of a society—the degree to which that society requires conformity—as well as an enormous quantity of data about its institutions and technology. Dress is truly a key to the individual and his or her society.

Bibliography

ABBIE, A. A. *The Original Australians.* New York: American Elsevier Publishing Co., 1970.

ADAMS, J. D. *Naked We Came: A More or Less Lighthearted Look at the Past, Present, and Future of Clothes.* New York: Holt, Rinehart & Winston, 1967.

AIKEN, L. R. The Relationship of Dress to Selected Measures of Personality in Undergraduate Women. *Journal of Social Psychology,* 59 (1963), 119–28.

ALLEN, F. L. *The Big Change,* New York: Harper & Brothers, 1952, 192–93.

ALLPORT, G. W. *The Person in Psychology.* Boston: Beacon Press, 1968.

ANGELOGLOU, M. *A History of Make-up.* London: Macmillan, 1970.

ANSPACH, K. *The Why of Fashion.* Ames, Iowa: Iowa University Press, 1969.

AVEBURY, J. L. *The Origin of Civilization and the Primitive Condition of Man.* Freeport, N.Y. Books for Libraries Press, 1972.

BAKER, H. The Psychology of Clothes as a Treatment Aid. *Mental Hygiene,* 39 (1955), 94–98.

BALDWIN, F. E. *Sumptuary Legislation and Personal Regulation in England.* Baltimore: Johns Hopkins Press, 1926.

BARBER, B., and L. S. Lobel. "Fashion," In Women's Clothes and the American Social System. *Social Forces.* 31 (December 1952), 124–31.

BARON, R. A. Olfaction and Human Social Behavior: Effects of a Pleasant Scent on Attraction and Social Perception. *Personality and Social Psychology Bulletin* 7 (December 1981), 611–16.

BARR, E. D. Y. A Psychological Analysis of Fashion Motivation. *Archives of Psychology,* no. 171 (June 1934), 1–100.

BARRETT, D. M., and E. B. Eaton. Preference for Color or Tint and Some Related Personality Data. *Journal of Personality,* 15 (1947), 222–32.

BATES, M. *Where Winter Never Comes.* New York: Charles Scribner's Sons, 1952, ch. 7.

BEAUMONT, R. A. and B. J. James. The Sukhomlinov Effect. *Horizons* 13 (Winter 1971), 66–69.

BEEBE, L. *The Big Spenders.* New York: Doubleday & Co., 1966.

BEHLING, D. The Russian Influence on Fashion, 1909–1925. *Dress,* 5 (1979), 1–13.

BEHLING, D. A., and L. E. Dickey. Haute Couture: A 25-Year Perspective of Fashion Influences,

1900 to 1925. *Home Economics Research Journal* 8 (July 1980), 428–36.

BELDING, H. S. The Beneficient Influence of the Workman's Silk Shirt. *Literary Digest,* 62, May 15, 1920, 65.

BENEDICT, H. A History of Men's Underwear. *American Fabrics and Fashions* 124, 125 (Winter 1982), 88–94.

BENNETT-ENGLAND, R. *Dress Optional.* Chester Springs, Pa.: Dufour Editions 1968.

BERGLER, E. *Fashion and the Unconscious.* New York: Robert Brunner, 1953.

BERGSON, A., AND S. KUZNETS, eds. *Economic Trends in the Soviet Union.* Cambridge, Mass.: Harvard University Press, 1963.

BERKOWITZ, L., AND A. FRODI. Reactions to a Child's Mistakes as Affected by His/Her Looks and Speech. *Social Psychology Quarterly* 42 (1979), 420–25.

BERLANDIER, J. L. *The Indians of Texas in 1830.* Washington, D.C.: Smithsonian Institution Press, 1969.

BERNIER, O. *The Eighteenth-Century Woman.* New York: Doubleday & Co., 1981.

BERSCHEID, E., Walster, E., and G. Bohrnstedt. Body Images. *Psychology Today,* 7, November 1973, 119–23, 126, 128–31.

BETTENSON, A. Industrial Protective Clothing and Equipment. *Costume* 8 (1974), 46–50.

BINDER, P. *The Magic Symbols of the World.* New York: Hamlyn, 1972.

———. *Muffs and Morals.* London: G. G. Harrap, 1953.

BIRKET-SMITH, K. *The Eskimos.* London: Methuen and Co., 1971.

BJERSTEDT, A. Warm-Cool Color Preferences as Potential Personality Indicators: Preliminary Note. *Perceptual and Motor Skills* 10 (February 1960), 31–34.

BLAKER, M. Fashions in 1943. *Journal of Home Economics* 35 (February 1943), 73–76.

BLUMBERG, P. The Decline and Fall of the Status Symbol: Some Thoughts on Status in a Post-Industrial Society. *Social Problems* 21 (April 1974), 480–98.

BLUMER, H. Fashion: From Class Differentiation to Collective Selection. *Sociological Quarterly* 10 (Summer 1969), 275–91.

BOAS, F. *The Mind of Primitive Man.* New York: Macmillan Co., 1922.

BOGATYREV, P. *The Functions of Folk Costume in Moravian Slovakia.* Paris: Mouton, 1971.

BOONE, J. B. *On Fashions.* Baltimore: Murphy & Co., 1853.

BORSODI, R. *This Ugly Civilization.* New York: Simon & Schuster, 1929.

BRIARD, J. *The Bronze Age in Barbarian Europe from the Megaliths to the Celts.* Boston: Routledge & Kegan Paul, 1979.

BROBY-JOHANSEN, R. *Body and Clothes.* New York: Reinhold Book Corp., 1968.

BROOKER, G. The Self-Actualizing Socially Conscious Consumer. *Journal of Consumer Research* 3 (September 1976), 107–12.

BROWN, N. Playwright Remembered in Key West. *Miami Herald,* February 26, 1983, 11A.

BRUBACH, H. The Height of Fashion. *Atlantic,* 251, February 1983, 88–93.

BRYANT, A. T. *The Zulu People as They Were before the White Man Came.* New York: Negro Universities Press, 1970.

BUCKLEY, H. M. Attraction Toward a Stranger as a Linear Function of Similarity in Dress. *Home Economics Research Journal* 12 (September 1983), 25–34.

———, AND M. E. ROACH. Attraction as a Function of Attitudes and Dress. *Home Economics Research Journal* 1 (September 1981), 89–97.

———. Clothing as a Nonverbal Communicator of Social and Political Attitudes. *Home Economics Research Journal* 3 (December 1974), 94–102.

BURGER, G. D. Self-Esteem and Body Satisfaction as They Relate to Clothing Attitudes: A Comparison of Freshman and Junior College Women. Master's thesis, University of Tennessee, 1976.

BUSH, G., and P. London. On the Disappearance of Knickers: Hypothesis for the Functional Analysis of the Psychology of Clothing. *Journal of Social Psychology* 51 (1960), 359–66.

BYRDE, P. *The Male Image.* London: B. T. Batsford, Ltd., 1979.

CAMMANN, S. Costume in China, 1644 to 1912. *Bulletin of the Philadelphia Museum of Art,* 75, Fall 1979, 2–19.

CANNON, M. L. Relationship of Clothing and Social Activities of Physically Handicapped and Non-Handicapped Children of Junior High School Age. Master's thesis, University of Iowa, 1969.

CANTRIL, H. The Individual's Demand on Society. In *Man and Civilization: Conflict and Creativity, A Symposium,* S. M. Farber and R. H. L. Wilson, eds. New York: McGraw-Hill Book Co., 1963, 185–98.

CARTER, A. Year of the Punk. *New Society*, December 22/29, 1977, xiv–xvi.

CATLIN, G. *Letters and Notes on the Manners, Customs, and Condition of the North American Indians, vol. I.* Minneapolis: Ross & Haines, 1965.

CAWTHON, F. Erté Is Still in the Pink at 86. *Atlanta Journal and Constitution*, March 4, 1979, 1F.

CHILDERS, F. L. A Study of the Costumes of Ten Indian Tribes at the Time of Their Removal to Oklahoma. Master's thesis, Oklahoma Agriculture and Mechanical College, 1938.

CHRISTIANSEN, K., AND A. KERNALEGUEN. Orthodoxy And Conservatism—Modesty in Clothing Selection. *Journal of Home Economics* 63 (April 1971), 251–55.

CIBA Review 4 (1965).

CLARK, J. E. R. *Aspects of Hawaii as Inspiration for Modern Day Apparel for Women.* Masters thesis, Colorado State University, 1963.

CLEMENS, C. *My Father Mark Twain.* New York: Harper & Row, 1931.

CLEMENS, S. The Czar's Soliloquy. *North American Review*, 580, March 1905, 321–23.

CLEMENS, S. *Mark Twain's Speeches.* New York: Harper & Row, 1923 (originally published 1910).

COMBS, A. W., AND D. SYNGG. *Individual Behavior.* New York: Harper & Row, 1959.

COMPTON, N. H. Body-Image Boundaries in Relation to Clothing Fabric and Design Preferences of a Group of Hospitalized Psychotic Women. *Journal of Home Economics* 56 (January 1964), 40–45.

COON, C. S. *The Hunting Peoples.* Boston: Little, Brown & Co., 1971.

———. There Are Neanderthals Among Us. In *Human Variations: Readings in Physical Anthropology*, H. K. Bleibtreu, and J. F. Downs, eds. Beverly Hills: Glencoe Press, 1971, 114–18.

———, GARN, S. M., AND J. B. BIRDSELL. Adaptive Changes in the Human Body. In *Readings in Anthropology*, J. D. Jennings and E. A. Hoebel, eds. New York: McGraw-Hill, 1972, 88–92.

COOPER, W. *Hair: Sex, Society, Symbolism.* London: Aldus Books, 1971.

COTLOW, L. *In Search of the Primitive.* Boston: Little, Brown & Co., 1966.

CRAWFORD, M. D. C. *Philosophy in Clothing.* New York: Brooklyn Museum, 1940.

CRAWLEY, A. E. *The Mystic Rose.* New York: Meridan Books, 1960.

CRAWLEY, E. *Dress, Drinks, and Drums, Further Studies of Savages and Sex.* London: Methuen and Co., 1931.

CREEKMORE, A. M. Clothing and Personal Attractiveness of Adolescents Related to Conformity, to Clothing Mode, Peer Acceptance, and Leadership Potential. *Home Economics Research Journal* 8 (January 1980), 203–15.

———. Clothing Behaviors and Their Relationship to General Values and the Striving for Basic Needs. Ph.D. diss., Pennsylvania State University, 1963.

CRUTCHFIELD, R. S. Independent Thought in a Conformist World. In *Conflict and Creativity*, S. M. Farber and R. H. L. Wilson, eds. New York: McGraw-Hill, 1963, 208–28.

CUNNINGTON, C. W. *Why Women Wear Clothes.* London: Faber and Faber, 1941.

CURRAN, M. *Collecting Jewelry.* London: Arco Publications, 1963.

DARDIS, R., F. DERRICK AND A. LEHFELD. Clothing Demand in the United States: A Cross-Sectional Analysis. *Home Economics Research Journal* 10 (December 1981), 212–21.

DAVIES, M. Corsets and Conception: Fashion and Demographic Trends in the Nineteenth Century. *Comparative Studies in Society and History* 24 (October 1982), 611–41.

DAVIS, L. Shoes ə Embroidery. *Embroidery* 31 (Summer 1980), 48–50.

DEAN, B. *Helmets and Body Armor in Modern Warfare.* New Haven Conn.: Yale University Press, 1920.

DEARBORN, G. V. N. The Psychology of Clothing. *The Psychological Monographs* 26 (1918).

DITTES, J. E. Attractiveness of Group as Function of Self-Esteem and Acceptance Group. *Journal of Abnormal and Social Psychology* 59 (1959), 77–82.

DOWNS, D. British Influences on Creek and Seminole Men's Clothing 1733–1858. *Florida Anthropologist* 33 (June 1980), 46–65.

———. Patchwork Clothing of the Florida Indians. *American Indian Art* 4 (Summer 1979), 1–41.

DRAKE, M. F. AND I. M. FORD. Adolescent Clothing and Adjustment. *Home Economics Research Journal* 7 (May 1979) 283–91.

DRIVER, H. E. *Indians of North America.* Chicago: University of Chicago Press, 1970.

DUNLAP, K. The Development and Function of Clothing. *Journal of Genetic Psychology* 1 (1928), 64–78.

DUPREE, N. H. Behind the Veil in Afghanistan. *ASIA* 1 (July–August 1978) 10–15.

EHRLICH, P. Pakistan Says Mills Need $1.28B Funding. *Daily News Record* 13, May 20, 1983, 5.

ELKINS, A. P. *The Australian Aborigines.* New York: Doubleday & Co., 1964.

ELLIS, A. *The American Sexual Tragedy.* New York: Grove Press, 1962.

ELLIS, H. *Studies in the Psychology of Sex*, Vol. I. Philadelphia: F. A. Davis, 1918.

EVANS, S. E. Motivations Underlying Clothing Selection and Wearing. *Journal of Home Economics* 56 (December 1964) 739–43.

EVELYN, J. *Tyrannus or the Mode in a Discourse of Sumptuary Lawes.* London: G. Bedel and T. Collins, 1661.

EWERS, J. C. Notes on the Weasel in Historic Plaines Indian Culture. *Plains Anthropologist* 22 (November 1977) 253–62.

FAIRSERVIS, W. A., JR. Costumes of the East. *Natural History* 80, November 1971, 28–37.

FARIS, J. C. *Nuba Personal Art.* London: Duckworth, 1972.

FAST, J. *The Body Language of Sex, Power and Aggression.* New York: M. Evans and Co., 1979.

FEATHER, B. L., B. B. MARTIN, AND W. R. MILLER. Attitudes toward Clothing and Self-Concept of Physically Handicapped and Able-Bodied University Men and Women. *Home Economics Research Journal* 7 (March 1979), 234–40.

FEIGHTNER, M. M. Clothing and Accessories Available to Pioneers of Southern Indiana 1816–1830. Master's thesis, Iowa State University, 1977.

FELKER, D. W. *Building Positive Self-Concepts.* Minneapolis: Burgess Publishing Co., 1974.

FERTILE-BISHOP, S., AND M. GILLIAM. In View of the Veil: Psychology of Clothing in Saudi Arabia. *Journal of Home Economics* 73(Winter 1981), 24–26.

FIELD, H. *Body-Marking of Southwestern Asia.* Cambridge, Mass.: Peabody Museum, 1958.

FISHER, S. *Body Consciousness.* Englewood Cliffs, N.J.: Prentice-Hall, 1973.

———. Experiencing Your Body: You Are What You Feel. *Saturday Review* 55, July 8, 1972, 27–32.

———, AND S. E. CLEVELAND. *Body Image and Personality.* Princeton, N.J.: D. Van Nostrand, 1958.

FLACCUS, L. W. Remarks on the Psychology of Clothes. *The Journal of Genetic Psychology* 13 (1906), 61–83.

FLORKEY, L. A. Clothing Attractiveness and Personal Attractiveness Related to Social Acceptance of Adolescent Boys and Girls. Master's thesis, Michigan State University, 1976.

FLOWER, W. H. Fashions in Deformity. *Humboldt Library of Popular Science,* 2 January 1882, 158–77.

FLUGEL, J. *The Psychology of Clothes.* London: Hogarth Press, 1930.

FORD, I. M., AND M. S. DRAKE. Attitude Toward Clothing, Body and Self: A comparison of two groups. *Home Economics Research Journal* 11 (Dec. 1982), 189–96.

FORM, W. H., AND G. P. STONE. Urbanism, Anonymity, and Symbolism. *American Journal of Sociology* 62 March 1957, 504–14.

FORMAN, M. Tutmania. *Dress* 4 (1978), 7–13.

FOUQUIER, E. On the Interpretation of Other People's Dress. *diogenes,* no. 113 (1981), 177–93.

FOWLES, J. Why We Wear Clothes. *ETC.: A Review of General Semantics* 31 (December 1974), 343–52.

FRASER, K. *The Fashionable Mind: Essays on Fashion, 1970–1981,* New York: Alfred A. Knopf, 1981, 250–54.

FRAZER, J. G. *The New Golden Bough.* New York: Criterion Books, 1959.

FRAZER, J. S. *Totemism and Exogamy,* vol. 1. New York: Edward Macmillan, 1935.

FREEDMAN, D. G. The Survival Value of the Beard. *Psychology Today,* 3 October 1969, 36–39.

FREUDENBERGER, H. Fashion, Sumptuary Laws, and Business. *Business History Review* 37 (1963), 37–48.

GARLAND, M. *The Changing Form of Fashion.* New York: Praeger, 1971.

GERNET, J. *Daily Life in China on the Eve of the Mongol Invasion, 1250–1276.* New York: Macmillan, 1967.

GERNSHEIM, A. *Fashion and Reality.* London: Faber & Faber, 1963.

GIBBINS, K. Communication Aspects of Women's Clothes and Their Relation to Fashionability. *British Journal of Social and Clinical Psychology* 8 (1969), 301–12.

GILL, E. *Clothing without Cloth: An Essay on the Nude.* Waltham Saint Lawrence Berkshire: Golden Cockerel Press, 1931.

———. *Trousers and the Most Precious Ornament.* London: Faber & Faber, 1937.

GOFFMAN, E. *Behavior in Public Places.* New York: Free Press of Glencoe, 1963.

GOLDMAN, M. I. *Soviet Marketing.* New York: Free Press, 1966.

GORDON, L. J., AND S. M. LEE. *Economics for Consumers.* New York: D. Van Nostrand, 1977.

GOURHAN, L. Adornment: For Gods, for Love, for War. *Vogue* 159, December 1970, 151–56, 206.

GREEN, P. Psychology Gives Meaning to Fashion. *Apparel South,* January 1981, 56–57.

GREEN, W. P., AND H. GILES. Reactions to a Stranger as a Function of Dress Style: The Tie. *Perceptual and Motor Skills* 37, (1973), 676.

GREENFIELD, K. R. *Sumptuary Laws in Nurnberg: A Study in Paternal Government.* Baltimore: Johns Hopkins Press, 1918, chs. 8–9.

GRINDERENG, M. P. Fashion Diffusion. *Journal of Home Economics* 59 (March 1967), 171–74.

GUBSER, N. J. *The Nunamiut Eskimos, Hunters of Caribou.* New Haven, Conn.: Yale University Press, 1965.

GUNTHER, E. *Indian Life on the Northwest Coast of North America as Seen by the Early Explorers and Fur Traders during the Last Decades of the Eighteenth Century.* Chicago: University of Chicago Press, 1972.

GUREL, L. M., J. C. WILBUR AND L. GUREL. Personality Correlates of Adolescent Clothing Styles. *Journal of Home Economics* 64 (March 1972) 42–47.

GUTHRIE, R. D. *Body Hot Spots: The Anatomy of Human Social Organs and Behavior.* New York: Van Nostrand Reinhold Co., 1976.

HALL, C. S., AND G. LINDZEY. *Theories of Personality.* New York: John Wiley & Sons, 1967.

HALL, L. Fashion and Style in the Twenties: The Change. *Historian* 34 (May 1972), 485–97.

HALLOWELL, A. I. The Backwash of the Frontier: The Impact of the Indian on American Culture. In *Readings in Anthropology,* J. D. Jennings and E. A. Hoebel, eds. New York: McGraw-Hill Book Co., 1972, 353–67.

HALLPIKE, C. R. Social Hair. *Man* 4 (June 1969), 256–64.

HAMBLETON, K. B., M. E. ROACH, AND K. EHLE. Teenage Appearance: Conformity, Preferences, and Self-Concepts. *Journal of Home Economics* 64 (February 1972), 29–33.

HAMID, P. N. Changes in Person Perception as a Function of Dress. *Perceptual and Motor Skills* 29 (1969), 191–94.

——. Style of Dress as a Perceptual Cue in Impression Formulation. *Perceptual and Motor Skills* 26 (1968), 904–6.

HARRINGTON, M. *The Other America.* New York: Macmillan Co., 1962.

HARTMANN, G. W. Clothing: Personal Problem and Social Issues. *Journal of Home Economics* 41 (June 1949), 295–98.

HEARD, G. *Narcissus an Anatomy of Clothes.* New York: E. P. Dutton & Co., 1924.

HEMLINE OF BATTLE. *Business Week,* April 18, 1942, 32–34.

HERALD WIRE SERVICES. Nancy Reagan Rejects "Polyester" Likeness. *Miami Herald.* September 20, 1982, p. 4A.

HILER, H. *From Nudity to Raiment.* New York: Educational Press, 1930.

HOEBEL, E. A. *Man in the Primitive World.* New York: McGraw-Hill, 1958.

HOFFMAN, A. M. *Clothing for the Handicapped, the Aged, and Other People with Special Needs.* Springfield, Ill.: Charles C. Thomas, 1979.

HOLLANDER, E. P. Conformity, Status, and Idiosyncrasy Credit. *Psychological Review* 5 (1958), 117–27.

HOLTZCLAW, K. Costume and Culture. *Journal of Home Economics* 48 (June 1956), 401–4.

HORNBACK, B. The Influences upon and Identifying Criteria of Women's Fashion in the U.S. from 1939–1948. Master's thesis, Indiana University, 1967.

HOULT, T. F. Experimental Measurement of Clothing as a Factor in Some Social Ratings of Selected American Men. *American Sociological Review* 19 (1954), 324–28.

HOWE, K. R. *The Loyalty Islands: a History of Culture Contacts 1840–1900.* Honolulu: University of Hawaii Press, 1977.

HOWES, M. *Amulets.* New York: St. Martin's Press, 1976.

HUGHES, C. C. *An Eskimo Village in the Modern World.* Ithaca, N.Y.: Cornell University Press, 1960.

HUMPHREY, C., M. KLAASEN, AND A. M. CREEKMORE. Clothing and Self-Concept of Adolescents. *Journal of Home Economics* 63 (April 1971), 246–50.

HURLOCK, E. B. *Psychology of Dress.* New York: Arno Press, 1976.

Inuit Amautik. Winnipeg, Ontario: Winnipeg Art Gallery, 1980.

JOHNSON, B. H., R. H. NAGASAWA, AND K. PETERS. Clothing Style Differences: Their Effect on the Impression of Sociability. *Home Economics Research Journal* 6 (September 1977), 58–63.

JOURARD, S. M., AND P. F. SECORD. Body-Cathexis and Personality. *British Journal of Psychology* 46 (May 1955), 130–37.

JOYCE, T. A. *South American Archaeology.* New York: Hacker Art Books, 1969.

JUNOD, H. A. *The Life of a South African Tribe.* New York: University Books, 1966.

KATZ, E., AND P. F. LAZARSFELD. *Personal Influences.* New York: Free Press, 1964.

KEENAN, J. H. The Tuareg Veil. *Middle Eastern Studies* 13 (January 1977), 3–13.

KEESING, F. M. *Cultural Anthropology.* New York: Holt, Rinehart & Winston, 1958, 202–4.

KEFGEN, M., AND P. TOUCHIE-SPECHT. *Individuality in Clothing Selection and Personal Appearance.* New York: Macmillan Co., 1976.

KELLEY, E. A., C. W. DAIGLE, R. S., LaFLEUR, AND L. J. WILSON. Adolescent Dress and Social Participation. *Home Economics Research Journal* 2 (March 1974), 167–75.

KELLEY, E. A., AND J. B. EICHER. A Longitudinal Analysis of Popularity, Group Membership, and Dress. *Journal of Home Economics* 62 (1970), 240–50.

KEMPER, R. H. *Costume.* New York: Newsweek Books, 1977.

KESHISHIAN, J. M. Anatomy of a Burmese Beauty Secret. *National Geographic* 155, June 1979, 798–801.

KHRUSHCHEV, N. S. Central Committee Report. *Current Soviet Policies IV.* New York: Columbia University Press, 1962, 42–77.

KIDWELL, C. B. Women's Bathing and Swimming Costume in the United States. *Contributions From the Museum of History and Technology.* Bulletin paper 64. Washington, D.C.: Smithsonian Institution Press, 1968, 3.

KITAMURA, S. On the Feelings of Satisfaction and Dissatisfaction with One's Own Appearance and Disposition. *Tohoku Psychologica Folia* 12 (1954), 67–81.

KÖNIG, R. *A La Mode.* New York: Seabury Press, 1973.

KORDA, M. *Power!* New York: Random House, 1975.

KRIDER, M. A. Comparative Studies of the Self-Concept of Crippled and Noncrippled Children. *Dissertation Abstracts* 19 (1959), 2143–44.

KRIEGER, H. W. American Indian Costumes in the United States National Museum. *Annual Report, Smithsonian Institution,* 1928, 623–61.

KUPER, H. Costume and Identity. *Comparative Studies in Society and History* 15 (June 1973), 348–67.

LAFFERTY, H. K., AND L. E. DICKEY. Clothing, Symbolism and the Changing Role of Nurses. *Home Economics Research Journal* 8 (March 1980), 294–301.

LANDERS, M. How Do They Get Their Ideas? *Miami Herald,* July 18, 1984, 6E.

LANE, E. W. *Manners and Customs of the Egyptians.* New York: E. P. Dutton & Co., 1966.

LANGNER, L. *The Importance of Wearing Clothes.* New York: Hastings House, 1959.

LAPITSKY, M. *Clothing Values and Their Relation to General Values and to Social Security and Insecurity.* Ph.D. diss., Pennsylvania State University, 1961.

LAWRENCE, T. E. *Seven Pillars of Wisdom.* New York: Doubleday Book Co., 1938.

LAVER, J. *Clothes.* London: Burke, 1952.

———. *Dress.* London: John Murray, 1957.

———. *Modesty in Dress.* New York: Houghton Mifflin, 1969.

———. War and Fashion. *Living Age* 359 (December 1940) 361–64.

LEE, D. Are Basic Needs Ultimate? *Journal of Abnormal and Social Psychology* 43(1948), 391–95.

LEWIS, O. *La Vida.* New York: Random House, 1965.

LINTON, R. *Acculturation in Seven American Indian Tribes.* Gloucester, Mass.: Peter Smith, 1963.

———. Marquesan Culture. In *The Individual and His Society,* T. Kardiner ed. Westport, Conn.: Greenwood Press, 1974.

———. *The Study of Man.* New York: Appleton-Century-Crofts, 1964.

———. *Tree of Culture.* New York: Alfred A. Knopf, 1969.

LOTZE, H. *Microcosmus: An Essay Concerning Man and His Relation to the World.* Edinburgh: T. & T. Clark, 1885.

LOWE, E. D., AND K. A. ANSPACH. Freedom in Dress: A Search for Related Factors. *Home Economics Research Journal* 7 (November 1978), 121–27.

———. Toward a Definition of Freedom in Dress. *Home Economics Research Journal* 1 (June 1973), 246–50.

LOWE, E. D., AND H. M. BUCKLEY. Freedom and Conformity in Dress: A Two-Dimensional Approach. *Home Economics Research Journal* 11 (December 1982), 197–204.

LOWIE, R. H. *Are We Civilized? Human Culture in Perspective.* New York: Harcourt, Brace & Co., 1929.

LUCAS, C. Postmen and Postwomen in Rural Areas. *Costume* 13 (1979), 52–53.

LUCAS, SISTER K. Religious Habit: Past and Present. Master's thesis, Colorado State University, 1971.

LUNDBERG, F., AND M. F. FARNHAM. *Modern Woman.* New York: Grosset & Dunlap, 1947.

LUTWINIAK, P. M. The Relationship of Selected Clothing Behaviors to Self Esteem. Master's thesis, University of Tennessee, 1972.

LYND, R. S. AND H. M. LYND. *Middletown: A Study in American Culture.* New York: Harcourt, Brace & World, 1956.

————. *Middletown in Transition a Study in Cultural Conflicts.* New York: Harcourt, Brace & World, 1937.

LYNES, R. *A Surfeit of Honey.* New York: Harper & Brothers, 1957.

MACK, J. Bakuba Embroidery Patterns: A Commentary on Their Social and Political Implications. *Textile History* 11 (1980), 163–74.

MAEDER, J. Sugar and Spice and Everything Nice. *Miami Herald,* January 18, 1984, 2A.

MANDELBAUM, D. G. The Interplay of Conformity and Diversity. In *Conflict and Creativity,* S. M. Farber and R. H. L. Wilson, eds. New York: McGraw-Hill, 1963, 241–52.

MANSEL, P. Monarchy, Uniform and the Rise of the Frac 1760–1830. *Past and Present,* no. 96 (August 1982), 103–32.

MARDEN, L. Ama, Sea Nymphs of Japan. *National Geographic* 140, July 1971, 122.

MASLOW, A. H. *Toward a Psychology of Being.* Princeton, N.J.: D. Van Nostrand, 1962.

MASSOLA, A. *The Aborigines of South Eastern Australia as They Were.* Melbourne: William Heinemann Australia PTY, 1971.

MATHES, E. W., AND S. B. KEMPER. Clothing as a Nonverbal Communicator of Sexual Attitudes and Behavior. *Perceptual and Motor Skills* 43 (1976), 495–98.

MAXWELL, J. A., ED. *America's Fascinating Indian History.* Pleasantville, N.Y.: Reader's Digest Association, 1978.

MAZRUI, A. A. The Robes of Rebellion Sex, Dress, and Politics in Africa. *Encounter* 34 (February 1970), 19–30.

MCINTYRE, L. The Amazon. *National Geographic* 142, October 1972, 445–95.

MCLAUGHEN. Beauty Businesses Fix Their Economic Make-up. *Miami Herald,* October 3, 1983, Business 8–9.

MEISSNER, A. L., R. W. THORESON, AND A. J. BUTLER. Relation of Self-Concept to Impact and Obviousness of Disability among Male and Female Adolescents. *Perceptual and Motor Skills* 24 (June 1967), 1099–1105.

MEURISSE, D. D. Dress Design Inspired by Early Ireland. Master's thesis, Colorado State University, 1970.

MOORE, B. J. The Relationship of Clothing Values to Behavior of Junior High School Girls in a Selected School. Master's thesis, Texas Woman's University, 1972.

MORGANOSKY, M., AND A. M. CREEKMORE. Clothing Influence in Adolescent Leadership Roles. *Home Economics Research Journal* 9 (June 1981), 356–62.

MORRIS, D. *The Human Zoo.* New York: McGraw-Hill, 1969.

————. *Manwatching: A Field Guide to Human Behavior.* New York: Harry N. Abrams, 1977.

MULREADY, P. M., J. M. LAMB, AND R. G. WALSH. Cosmetics Therapy for Female Chemo-Therapy Patients. *Research Report Summary.* American Home Economics Association, 1982.

MURPHY, R. W. *Status and Conformity.* New York: Time-Life Books, 1976.

NANSEN, F. *Eskimo Life.* New York: Longmans, Green, and Co., 1893.

NASA FACTS. *A Wardrobe for Space.* Houston: National Aeronautics and Space Administration, 1978.

NAKAGAWA, K., AND H. ROSOVSKY. The Case of the Dying Kimono: The Influence of Changing Fashions on the Development of the Japanese Woolen Industry. *Business History Review* 37 (Spring/Summer 1963), 59–68.

NIBLACK, A. P. The Coast Indians of Southern Alaska and Northern British Columbia. *Report of National Museum,* 1888, 225–387.

NIELSEN, J. P., AND A. KERNALEGUEN. Influence of Clothing and Physical Attractiveness in Person Perception. *Perceptual and Motor Skills* 42 (1976), 775–80.

NOESJIRWAN, J. A., AND J. M. CRAWFORD. Variations in Perception of Clothing as a Function of Dress Form and Viewer's Social Community. *Perceptual and Motor Skills* 54 (1982), 155–63.

NYSTROM, P. *Economics of Fashion.* New York: Ronald Press Co., 1928.

OGIBENIN, B. L. Petr Bogatyrev and Structural Ethnography. In *The Functions of Folk Costume in Moravian Slovakia,* P. Bogatyrev. Paris: Mouton, 1971.

OLFERS, J. A. The Influence of Clothing on Advertising Effectiveness. Master's thesis, Texas Tech University, 1975.

O'REILLY, R. New Diving Equipment May Open Ocean's Secrets. *Miami Herald,* November 3, 1982, 1E-2E.

OSGOOD, C. *The Koreans and Their Culture.* Tokyo: Charles E. Tuttle, 1966.

PAIGE, K. E. The Ritual of Circumcision. *Human Nature* 1 (May 1978), 40–46.

"A PAPIST." *A Just and Seasonable Reprehension of Naked Breasts and Shoulders.* London: Jonathan Edwin, 1678.

PARRY, A. *Tattoo Secrets of a Strange Art as Practiced among the Natives of the United States.* New York: Simon & Schuster, 1933.

PASNAK, M. F. D., AND R. W. AYRES. Fashion Innovators. *Journal of Home Economics* 61 (November 1969), 698–701.

PENDLETON, W. N. Philosophy of Dress. *Blackwoods Magazine* 53 (February 1843), 230–234.

PERROT, P. Suggestions for a Different Approach to the History of Dress. *diogenes,* nos. 113/114 (Spring/Summer 1981), 157–76.

PERRY, M. O., H. G. SCHUTZ, AND M. H. RUCKER. Clothing Interest, Self-Actualization and Demographic Variables. *Home Economics Research Journal* 11 (March 1983), 280–88.

PHILLIPS, J. W., AND H. K. STALEY. Sumptuary Legislation in Four Centuries. *Journal of Home Economics* 53 (October 1961), 673–77.

PLOGSTERTH, A. The Modernization of Roman Catholic Sisters' Habits in the United States in the 1950's and 1960's. *Dress* 1 (1975), 7–13.

POLHEMUS, T. Fashion, Anti-Fashion and the Body Image. *New Society* 26 (October 11, 1973), 73–76.

———. Social Bodies. In *The Body as a Medium of Expression,* J. Benthall and T. Polehemus, eds. New York: E. P. Dutton & Co., 1975.

———, AND L. PROCTER. *Fashion & Anti-Fashion: An Anthropology of Clothing & Adornment.* London: Thames & Hudson, 1978.

POLL, S. *The Hasidic Community of Williamsburg.* New York: Free Press of Glencoe, 1962.

THE PURE PHYSICIAN. *Human Behavior* 8 (May 1979), 49.

REEDER, E. N., AND M. F. DRAKE. Clothing Preferences of Male Athletes: Actual and Perceived. *Home Economics Research Journal* 8 (May 1980), 339–43.

REISMAN, D., N. GLAZER, AND R. DENNEY. *The Lonely Crowd.* New Haven, Conn: Yale University Press, 1950.

RENBOURN, E. T. *Materials and Clothing in Health and Disease.* London: H. K. Lewis & Company, 1972.

RICHARDS, E. A., AND R. E. HAWTHORNE. Values, Body Cathexis, and Clothing of Male University Students. *Journal of Home Economics* 63 (March 1971), 190–94.

RILEY, L. D. America's Best Dressed Women. *Ladies' Home Journal* 75 (March 1958), 64–65, 118, 120, 122–25.

ROACH, M. E., AND J. B. EICHER. *The Visible Self: Perspectives in Dress.* Englewood Cliffs, N.J.: Prentice-Hall, 1973.

ROBINSON, D. E. The Importance of Fashions in Taste to Business History: An Introductory Essay. *Business History Review* 37 (1963), 5–36.

ROSE, A. M. Race and Ethnic Relations. In *Contemporary Social Problems,* R. K. Merton and R. A. Nisbet, eds. New York: Harcourt, Brace & World, 1961, 324–89.

ROSENCRANZ, M. L. *Clothing Concepts.* New York: Macmillan, 1972.

ROSSI, W. A. *The Sex Life of the Foot and Shoe.* New York: Saturday Review Press, 1976.

ROTH, H. L. *The Aborigines of Tasmania.* Halifax, England: F. King & Sons, 1899.

ROTH, J. M. Ritual and Magic in the Control of Contagion. *American Sociological Review* 22 (June 1957), 310–14.

RUBENS, A. *A History of Jewish Costume.* New York: Funk & Wagnalls, 1967.

RUDOFSKY, B. *The Unfashionable Human Body.* New York: Anchor Books, 1974.

RYAN, M. S. *Clothing: A Study in Human Behavior.* New York: Holt, Rinehart & Winston, 1966.

SABOL, B., AND L. TRUSCOTT IV. The Politics of Costume. *Esquire* 75, May 1971, 123–34.

SAKATA, F. Y. Factors That Have Affected the Survival of the Japanese Kimono as a Style of Dress. Master's thesis, California State University, Fresno, 1973.

SCHICK, I. T., ED. *Battledress: the Uniforms of the World's Great Armies, 1700 to the Present.* Boston: Little, Brown & Co., 1978.

SCHRANK, H. L. Correlates of Fashion Leadership: Implications for Fashion Process Theory. *Sociological Quarterly* 14 (Autumn 1973), 534–43.

SCHREIDER, H., AND F. SCHREIDER. Taiwan: The Watchful Dragon. *National Geographic* 135 (January 1969), 1–45.

SCHROEDER, F. E. W. Feminine Hygiene, Fashion and the Emancipation of American Women. *American Studies* 17 (Fall 1976), 101–110.

SCHULTZ, H. Blue-eyed Indian. *National Geographic* 120 July 1961, 64–89.

SCHWARTZ, J. Men's Clothing and the Negro. *Phylon* 24 (Fall 1963) 224–331.

SCUTT, R. W. B., AND C. GOTCH. *Art, Sex and Symbol: The Mystery of Tattooing.* New York: A. S. Barnes and Co., 1974.

SECORD, P. F., AND S. M. JOURARD, The Appraisal of Body-Cathexis: Body-Cathexis and the Self. *Journal of Consulting Psychology* 17 (1953), 343–47.

SHALLECK, J. *Masks.* New York: Viking Press, 1973.

SHIBUTANI, T. Reference Groups and Social Control. In *Human Behavior and Social Processes*, A. M. Rose, ed. Boston: Houghton Mifflin Co., 1962.

SIEBER, R. *African Textiles and Decorative Arts.* New York: Museum of Modern Art, 1972.

SIMMONS, R. G., D. A. BLYTH, E. F. VAN CLEAVE, AND D. M. BUSH. Entry into Adolescence: The Impact of School Structure, Puberty, and Early Dating on Self-Esteem. *American Sociological Review* 44 (1979), 948–62.

SIPLE, P. A. Clothing and Climate. In *Physiology of Heat Regulation and the Science of Clothing*, L. H. Newburgh, ed. Philadelphia: W. B. Saunders Co., 1949.

SMITH, B. G. *Ladies of the Leisure Class.* Princeton, N.J.: Princeton University Press, 1981.

SMITH, G. E. *The Evolution of the Dragon.* New York: Longmans, Green and Co., 1919.

SMUCKER, B., AND A. M. CREEKMORE. Adolescents' Clothing Conformity, Awareness, and Peer Acceptance. *Home Economics Research Journal* 1 (December 1972), 92–97.

SNYDER, A. E. *Sensuous Clothing in Relation to Self-Esteem and Body Satisfaction.* Masters thesis, University of Tennessee, 1975.

SONTAG, M. S., AND J. D. SCHLATER. Proximity of Clothing to Self: Evolution of a Concept. *Clothing and Textiles Research Journal* 1 (1982), 1–8.

SPENCER, B., AND F. J. GILLEN. *The Native Tribes of Central Australia.* New York: Humanities Press, 1969.

SPIEGEL, L. A. The Child's Concept of Beauty: A Study of Concept Formation. *Journal of Genetic Psychology* 77 (1950), 11–23.

STONE, G. P. Appearance and the Self. In *Human Behavior and Social Processes: Interactionist Approach*, A. M. Rose, ed. New York: Houghton Mifflin Co., 1962, 86–118.

————. The Circumstance and Situation of Social Status. In *Social Psychology Through Symbolic Interaction*, G. P. Stone and H. A. Faberman, eds. New York: John Wiley & Sons, 1970, 250–59.

————. Sex and Age as Universes of Appearance. In *Social Psychology Through Symbolic Interaction*, G. P. Stone and H. A. Faberman, eds. New York: John Wiley & Sons, 1970, 227–37.

STRATHERN, A. *Man As Art New Guinea.* New York: Viking Press, 1981.

————, AND M. STRATHERN. *Self-Decoration in Mount Hagen.* London: Gerald Duckworth & Co., 1971.

SUEDFELD, P., S. BOCHNER, AND C. MATAS. Petitioner's Attire and Petition Signing by Peace Demonstrators. *Journal of Applied Social Psychology* 1 (1971), 284–91.

————, AND D. WNEK. Helper-Sufferer Similarity and a Specific Request for Help: Bystander Intervention during a Peace Demonstration. *Journal of Applied Social Psychology* 2 (1972), 17–23.

SUMNER, W. G. *Folkways: A Study of the Sociological Importance of Usages, Manners, Customs, Mores, and Morals.* New York: Blaisdell Publishers, 1965.

SWAN, S. B. The Pocket Lucy Locket Lost. *Early American Life* 10 (April 1979), 40–43.

SWANTON, J. R. *The Indians of the Southeastern United States.* Washington, D.C.: U.S. Government Printing Office, 1969.

SYBERS, R., AND M. E. ROACH. Clothing and Human Behavior. *Journal of Home Economics* 54 (March 1962), 184–87.

TAGUIRI, R., AND L. PETRULLO. *Person Perception and Interpersonal Behavior.* Stanford: Stanford University Press, 1958.

TANDBERG, G. G., AND S. G. DURAND. Dress-up Clothes for Field Slaves of Ante-Bellum Louisiana and Mississippi. *Costume*, no. 15 (1981), 40–48.

TATE, M., AND O. GLISSON. *Family Clothing.* New York: John Wiley & Sons, 1961.

TAYLOR, E. S., AND W. J. WALLACE. *Mohave Tattooing and Face-Painting.* Los Angeles: Southwest Museum, no. 20, 1947.

TAYLOR, G. R. *Sex in History.* New York: Vanguard Press, 1954.

TAYLOR, L. C., AND N. H. COMPTON. Personality Correlates of Dress Conformity. *Journal of Home Economics* 60 (1968), 653–56.

TEIT, J. A. *Tattooing and Face and Body Painting of the Thompson Indians, British Columbia.* Seattle: Shorey Book Store, 1927–1928.

THOMAS, L. E. Clothing and Counterculture: An Empirical Study. *Adolescence* 8 (Spring 1973), 93–112.

THOMPSON, T. Fashion Therapy. *Journal of Home Economics* 54 (December 1962), 835-36.

Tinling, T. *The Story of Women's Tennis Fashions.* London: Wimbledon Lawn Tennis Museum, 1977.

Toffler, A. *Future Shock.* New York: Random House, 1970.

Turner, T. S. Tchikrin. *Natural History,* 78 October 1969, 50–59, 70.

Twala, R. G. Beads as Regulating the Social Life of the Zulu and Swazi. *African Studies* 10 (September 1951), 113–23.

Tyrrell, A. M. The Relationship of Certain Cultural Factors to Women's Costume in Boston, Massachusetts from 1720–1740. Master's thesis, Virginia Polytechnic Institute and State University, 1975, 51–59.

Tyrrell, B. *Tribal Peoples of Southern Africa.* Cape Town: Books of Africa, 1968.

Van Syckle, C. The Clothing Situation, 1943. *Journal of Home Economics* 35 (February 1943), 80–83.

Vasilyeva, E. Fashions. *Soviet Life,* September 1981, 52–55.

Veblen, T. *The Theory of the Leisure Class: An Economic Study of Institutions.* New York: Random House, 1934.

Vener, A. M., and C. R. Hoffer. Adolescent Orientations to Clothing. In *Dress, Adornment, and the Social Order,* M. E. Roach and J. B. Eicher, Eds. New York: John Wiley & Sons, 1965.

Vincent, J. M. *Costume and Conduct in the Laws of Basel, Bern, and Zurich 1370 -1800.* Baltimore: Johns Hopkins Press, 1935.

Viola, H. J. *Diplomats in Buckskins: A History of Indian Delegations in Washington City.* Washington, D.C.: Smithsonian Institution Press, 1981.

Virel, A. *Decorated Man.* New York: Harry N. Abrams, 1980.

Vlahos, O. *Body: The Ultimate Symbol.* New York: J. B. Lippincott Co., 1979.

Vogler, J. Third World Finds Gold in Waste. *Miami Herald,* April 1, 1982, 31A.

Vollmer, J. E. *Five Colors of the Universe: Symbolism in Clothes and Fabrics of the Ch'ing Dynasty.* Edmonton, Alberta: Edmonton Art Gallery, 1980.

Warnick, S. Costumes of the Hutzels: An Ethnographic Group in Western Ukraine. Master's thesis, University of Washington, 1974.

Warning: Beards may be hazardous. *Miami Herald,* January 29, 1984, 2A.

Warren, V. *The Wimbledon Lawn Tennis Museum.* London: Wimbledon Lawn Tennis Museum, 1982.

Wax, M. Themes in Cosmetics and Grooming. *American Journal of Sociology* 62 (May 1957) 588–93.

Webb, W. M. *The Heritage of Dress Being Notes on the History and Evolution of Clothes.* London: Times Book Club, 1912.

Wilbur, D. N. *Afghanistan: Its People, Its Society, Its Culture.* New Haven, Conn.: HRAF Press, 1962.

Wildeblood, J., and P. Brinson. *The Polite World.* London: Oxford University Press, 1965.

Wilkinson, F. *Battle Dress.* New York: Doubleday & Co., 1970.

Williams, M. C., and J. B. Eicher. Teen-Agers' Appearance and Social Acceptance. *Journal of Home Economics* 58 (June 1966), 457–61.

Winter, C. Looks Can Get Under Your Skin. *Miami Herald,* May 15, 1983, 5G.

Woodforde, J. *The Strange Story of False Hair.* London: Routledge & Kegan Paul, 1971.

Wulsin, F. R. Adaptations to Climate among Non-European Peoples. In *Physiology of Heat Regulation and the Science of Clothing,* L. H. Newburgh, ed. Philadelphia: W. B. Saunders Co., 1949.

Young, K. *Social Psychology.* New York: Appleton-Century-Crofts, 1956, 310–29.

Zahan, D. *diogenes* no. 90 (Spring 1975), 100–119.

Zweig, F. *The British Worker.* Harmondsworth, Middlesex: Penguin Books, 1952.

Text Acknowledgments

Index

Mohammedanism, dress of, 247
Mohave Indians, 12, 167
Moi of Indonesia, 28
Monarchies, 211
Mongolian women, dress symbols of, 115
Monroe, Marilyn, 118
Mood, dress and, 113, 314
Moore, B.J., 315
Morale boosting, 312–14
Morality, 250–56
  body exposure and, 250–52
  conformity to, 253–56
  norms of, 252–53
  sumptuary laws regulating, 227–29
Moravian Slovakia, traditional dress in, 118
Morganosky, M., 276
Morris, D., 7, 16, 116, 119, 147–48, 157, 159, 176, 252, 302, 314
Mosaic law, 8, 10
Moslem dress of sanctity, 243–44
Moslem sumptuary legislation, 248–49
Mother-in-law, relationship between husband and, 167
Motivation, 270–76
  for conformity, 325, 334
  developmental needs, age groups and, 273–76
  hierarchy of needs and, 270–73, 322, 325, 333
  spending, 183–86
Mount Hageners, 2, 192–93
Mourning dress, 142–44
Move intensives, 306–9
Movies, influence of, 294–95
Mulready, P.M., 313
Multidimensionality of self-concept, 262
Murphy, R.W., 324
Museum exhibits, 296
Mustaches, 46
Mutilations, 2–3

Nagasawa, R.H., 110
Namba, 167
Nansen, F., 66
Napoleon, 77, 78
National costumes, 117–18, 230–31
Natural resources, 3–5
Navahos, 40, 167
Nazi dress, 217, 224
Neck elongation, 16, 17
Necklet, calendar, 50
Needs:
  aesthetic, 322
  becoming, 270–72
  "being," 276, 333
  developmental, age groups and, 273–76
  esteem, 271–72, 273, 274, 322
  hierarchy of, 270–73, 322, 325, 333
  love and belonging, 270, 271, 273, 274, 322

physiological, 270–71, 322
psychological, 7
safety and security, 271, 322
transcendence, 322
Nekbwe, 40–41
New Guinea, mourning dress in, 142
New Look, 225
New Zealand, sartorial adornment in, 38
Niblack, A.P., 307
Nielsen, J.P., 112
Nijinsky, W., 95
Noesjirwan, J.A., 110
Norms, social, 94–95, 146, 252–53. See also Role(s)
North American Indians. See American Indians
Nose ornaments, 27
Nouveau riche, 175, 184
Nubas, 9, 10, 52
Nubians, 27
Nudity, 94, 98–100, 152, 250–51
Nystrom, P., 150, 200

Occupation, 135–38, 180. See also Work clothes
Oceania, 88, 189
Ogibenin, B.L., 112, 266
Old age, status of, 164–65
Olfers, J.A., 109
One kind barrier signals, 314
Open class systems, 172–73
Opinion leader, 299
Ordering of environment, 50–54
O'Reilly, R., 62
Ornamental dress. See Adornment
Orthodox Judaism, signs of sanctity among, 242–43
Ovambi tribe, 57

Pacific Northwest American Indians, 25, 69, 70, 152
Padaung women of Burma, elongation practices of, 16–18
Padded derriere, 40–41
Paige, K.E., 23, 24
Pain, 7, 23
Paint, 29–31, 72. See also Make-up
Paiutes, 66
Panares, 70, 71
Panic of 1907, 200
Papuan Pygmies, 88
Parasols, 72
Parry, A., 14
Participation, social, 315–16
Pasnak, M.F.D., 269, 298, 300
Past fashion, 147
Payaguans, 289
Peak experiences, 272n
Peer groups, 326, 327
Pendleton, W.N., 179–80
Penis:
  circumcision of, 22–23, 149
  covers, 87–90, 159

See also Genitals; Sexuality, dress and
Penitential garments, 254
Perception, 105–12
  defined, 105
  person, 108–12
  selective, 105–6, 111
  self-concept and, 258
  variables in, 106–8
Perfume, 33
Peripheral self, 258
Permanent Care Labeling Act (1972), 234
Perrot, P., 92
Perry, M.O., 273, 276
Personal dress expenditures, 204–7
Personality:
  characteristics, conformity-proneness and, 333–34
  development, effect of roles on, 124
  fashion interest and, 322–23
Person perception, 108–12
Peters, K., 110
Pettrullo, L., 108
Phallic symbolism, 114
Phenomenal self, 258–59, 269
Philip, John, 119
Phillips, J.W., 226
Physical body, perception and, 107
Physical fitness as prestige symbol, 156
Physical functioning, body image development and, 265–66
Physically enabling dress, 58–63
Physical protection, use of dress for, 63–82
  against animals, 73–78
  against climate and weather, 63–73
  against disease, 80–82
  against vegetation and terrain, 79–80
Physical setting, 107, 110
Physiological factors, 270–71, 303–4. See also Body
Picasso, Pablo, 292
Piercing, 24–28, 57
Pilgrimage, dress for, 241–42
Place as modesty variable, 93–94
Plastic body, 14–20
Plastic surgery, 24
Plate armor, 76–77
Plogsterth, A., 239
Pockets, evolution of, 61
Poiret, Paul, 292, 293
Polhemus, T., 11, 12, 110, 185, 217, 219
Political leaders, role in fashion of, 214–15
Political nudity, 99–100
Political rebellion, 217–19
Political symbols, 215–17
Pompadour, Marquise de, 214
Pondo, the, 9
"Poor boy" look, 176
Population growth, sumptuary